D1126669

2012
The Supreme Court Review

2012
The

"Judges as persons, or courts as institutions, are entitled to no greater
immunity from criticism than other persons or institutions . . .
[J]udges must be kept mindful of their limitations and
of their ultimate public responsibility by a vigorous
stream of criticism expressed with candor however blunt."
—*Felix Frankfurter*

". . . while it is proper that people should find fault when
their judges fail, it is only reasonable that they should recognize the
difficulties. . . . Let them be severely brought to book,
when they go wrong, but by those who will take the trouble
to understand them."
—*Learned Hand*

THE LAW SCHOOL

THE UNIVERSITY OF CHICAGO

Supreme Court Review

EDITED BY

DENNIS J. HUTCHINSON

DAVID A. STRAUSS

AND GEOFFREY R. STONE

THE UNIVERSITY OF CHICAGO PRESS

CHICAGO AND LONDON

INTERNATIONAL STANDARD BOOK NUMBER: 978-0-226-05201-4

LIBRARY OF CONGRESS CATALOG CARD NUMBER: 60-14353

THE UNIVERSITY OF CHICAGO PRESS, CHICAGO 60637

THE UNIVERSITY OF CHICAGO PRESS, LTD., LONDON

The paper used in this publication meets the minimum requirements of American National Standard for Information Sciences–Permanence of Paper for Printed Library Materials, ANSI Z39.48-1984. ∞

CONTENTS

COMMERCE CLAUSE REVISIONISM AND THE AFFORDABLE
  CARE ACT   1
  David A. Strauss

ENFORCEMENT REDUNDANCY AND THE FUTURE OF
  IMMIGRATION LAW   31
  Adam B. Cox

THE CURIOUS HISTORY OF FOURTH AMENDMENT SEARCHES   67
  Orin S. Kerr

CONFRONTING SCIENCE: EXPERT EVIDENCE AND THE
  CONFRONTATION CLAUSE   99
  Jennifer Mnookin and David Kaye

LIES AND THE CONSTITUTION   161
  Helen Norton

BANKRUPTCY STEP ZERO   203
  Douglas G. Baird and Anthony J. Casey

ONE VOICE OR MANY? THE POLITICAL QUESTION DOCTRINE
  AND ACOUSTIC DISSONANCE IN FOREIGN AFFAIRS   233
  Daniel Abebe

"TO REGULATE," NOT "TO PROHIBIT": LIMITING THE
  COMMERCE POWER   255
  Barry Friedman and Genevieve Lakier

CAROLENE PRODUCTS AND CONSTITUTIONAL STRUCTURE   321
  Barry Cushman

DAVID A. STRAUSS

COMMERCE CLAUSE REVISIONISM AND THE AFFORDABLE CARE ACT

"The path of our Commerce Clause decisions," the Chief Justice said last Term, "has not always run smooth."[1] For most of the twentieth century, though, the path was very smooth. Between 1937 and 1995, the Court upheld every statute that was challenged as exceeding Congress's power under the Commerce Clause. That included such controversial and far-reaching laws as the National Labor Relations Act[2] and the Civil Rights Act of 1964.[3] And, as is usually true, the litigated cases were only a small part of the story. Many extensive federal regulatory programs that were based on Congress's Commerce Clause power—much of federal criminal law and the regulation of, for example, financial markets, the environment, and the workplace—were not even challenged in the Supreme Court, because their constitutionality was so clear.

During this period, the Court recited that there were limits to Congress's power, but the operating premise of the Court's deci-

David A. Strauss is Gerald Ratner Distinguished Service Professor of Law, the University of Chicago.

AUTHOR'S NOTE: I am grateful to Aziz Huq and Alison LaCroix for their comments on an earlier draft, and to the Burton and Adrienne Glazov Faculty Fund at the University of Chicago Law School for its support.

[1] *NFIB v Sebelius*, 132 S Ct 2566, 2585 (2012), citing *United States v Lopez*, 514 US 549, 552–59 (1995).

[2] *NLRB v Jones & Laughlin Steel Corp.*, 301 US 1 (1937).

[3] *Heart of Atlanta Motel, Inc. v United States*, 379 US 241 (1964); *Katzenbach v McClung*, 379 US 294 (1964).

sions was that there was no judicially enforceable limiting principle. That premise was plausible because, in a highly integrated economy, anything important enough to attract Congress's attention is likely to be connected, in a meaningful way, to interstate commerce. And, the Court's defenders reasoned, the Court was justified in standing aside because Congress, which is responsive to the interests of state governments, could be trusted not to go too far.[4]

Before 1937, though, and again beginning in 1995, the Court did try to enforce a limiting principle. And that path was not smooth. Before 1937, the Court tried out a series of limits, frequently invalidating major pieces of federal legislation. It tried to differentiate between commerce and other activities, such as manufacturing, agriculture, and mining. It tried to distinguish between "direct" and "indirect" effects on commerce. It invalidated some regulations of commerce on the ground that Congress's intent was not to regulate commerce but to do something else.[5] All of these attempts at limiting Congress's power collapsed. The doctrinal categories proved to be incoherent. The Court was attacked by a popular president, Franklin Roosevelt.[6] And the Court changed course sharply, beginning in 1937.

In 1995, the Court started trying to define enforceable limits on the Commerce Clause again. For the most part, it has not been especially aggressive.[7] But the case last Term in which the Chief Justice wrote his words, *NFIB v Sebelius*,[8] was a challenge to the

---

[4] This idea is associated with Herbert Wechsler, *The Political Safeguards of Federalism: The Role of the States in the Composition and Selection of the National Government*, 54 Colum L Rev 543 (1954). It can be traced to Chief Justice Marshall's opinion in *Gibbons v Ogden*, 22 US 1, 197 (1824). See also Larry Kramer, *Putting the Politics Back Into the Political Safeguards of Federalism*, 100 Colum L Rev 215 (2000), and John D. Nugent, *Safeguarding Federalism: How States Protect Their Interests in National Policymaking* (Oklahoma, 2009).

[5] See, for example, *United States v E. C. Knight Co.*, 156 US 1 (1895) (Sherman Antitrust Act construed not to apply to manufacturing); *The Employers' Liability Cases*, 207 US 463, 495–96 (1908) (invalidating law regulating interstate common carriers because the effects on commerce were "indirect"); *Hammer v Dagenhart*, 247 US 251, 271–72 (1918) (invalidating law prohibiting interstate shipment of goods manufactured by child labor because "[t]he act, in its effect, does not regulate transportation among the States, but aims to standardize the ages at which children may be employed in mining and manufacturing within the States."). See also *United States v Morrison*, 529 US 598, 642 (2000) (Souter, J, dissenting) (citing cases).

[6] See, for example, Jeff Shesol, *Supreme Power* 149–52 (Norton, 2010); Gregory Caldeira, *Public Opinion and the U.S. Supreme Court: FDR's Court-Packing Plan*, 81 Am Pol Sci Rev 1139 (1987).

[7] See text at notes 64–71.

[8] 132 S Ct 2566 (2012).

constitutionality of one of the most significant federal statutes in decades, the Patient Protection and Affordable Care Act. A central issue in the litigation was whether the Commerce Clause authorized Congress to enact the so-called individual mandate—a provision of the ACA requiring that individuals have health insurance. A majority of the Court, by a vote of 5–4, concluded that the mandate exceeded Congress's power under the Commerce Clause, although a different 5–4 majority sustained the mandate as an exercise of Congress's power to tax under the General Welfare Clause.[9]

On any conventional analysis, the Commerce Clause, coupled with the Necessary and Proper Clause, obviously gave Congress the power to enact the mandate. That was true not just under the post-1937 cases, but under any plausible reading of the Court's post-1995 decisions taking a narrower view of Congress's power. The Court's contrary conclusion demonstrates, in a backhanded way, the wisdom of the approach the Court took between 1937 and 1995. If there really is no coherent limiting principle that courts can enforce, then the search for a limiting principle is an invitation to judicial overreaching. It empowers judges to seize on a feature of a law that strikes them as vaguely problematic and to invalidate it, intoning that if Congress can do *that*, it can do anything. The danger is particularly acute in a time of overheated politics, when a judge's intuition that Congress has "gone too far" may be unconsciously influenced by the political controversy.

The Court in *NFIB*—in fact, the Court since 1995—has simply taken it as axiomatic that there must be a judicially enforceable limit on Congress's power under the Commerce Clause. The Court has recited the undisputed point that the Constitution establishes a federal government of limited powers and has assumed, from there, that it is the Court's job to enforce the limits on the Commerce Clause. The Court has not tried to explain why the approach taken throughout most of the twentieth century was wrong—except for the bare fact that it did not supply any limiting principle—or why the Court will have more success this time than it did before 1937.[10]

---

[9] "The Congress shall have Power To lay and Collect Taxes, Duties, Imposts and Excises, to pay the Debts and provide for the common Defense and general Welfare of the United States . . . ." US Const, Art I, § 8, cl 1.

[10] Justice Robert Jackson commented in a 1942 letter to then-judge, later Justice, Sherman Minton: "I suspect . . . that in any case where Congress thinks there is an effect on interstate commerce, the Court will accept that judgment. All of the efforts to set up formulae to confine the commerce power have failed." John Q. Barrett, *Wickard v Filburn*

One of the great features of the common law tradition is that judges can learn from other judges' experience. They do not have to start with a blank slate. If previous efforts to limit Congress's power collapsed into incoherence, and two generations of Supreme Court Justices thought that judicially enforceable limits were neither necessary nor workable, perhaps there is a lesson there.

Even more remarkably, the Court in *NFIB* paid scant attention to the more recent, post-1995 decisions. Those cases have not articulated a very clear limiting principle, but it is possible to discern a plausible principle under the surface. The *NFIB* Court, though, did not seem interested in working out the implications of the relatively modest post-1995 limits. Instead it imposed a new categorical limit. It seems fair to say that, in its treatment of the Commerce Clause, the Court in *NFIB* engaged in a dramatic act of Constitutional revisionism: it returned to the days before 1937 to hold, on the basis of arguments that do not withstand analysis, that the Commerce Clause did not authorize a major piece of federal legislation.

I. The Individual Mandate and the ACA Litigation

A. THE MANDATE

The Patient Protection and Affordable Care Act was designed to reform the way health care is provided in the United States and to make health care more readily available to more people. One central problem addressed by the ACA concerns people with preexisting conditions. Before the ACA, insurance companies were, in some circumstances, free to take an individual's medical history into account in deciding whether to insure the person. If a person seeking insurance already had a medical condition that made him or her a worse risk for the insurance company, the insurer would charge more in premiums or refuse to insure the applicant.[11] The ACA dealt with this problem by imposing two regulatory requirements on health insurers. The "guaranteed issue" provision prohibits insurers from denying insurance coverage

---

(1942), *The Jackson List* (June 26, 2012), http://stjohns.edu/academics/graduate/law/faculty/Profiles/Barrett/JacksonList.stj, quoted in Pamela S. Karlan, *The Supreme Court, 2011 Term—Foreword: Democracy and Disdain*, 126 Harv L Rev 1, 43 (2012).

[11] See, for example, *NFIB*, 132 S Ct at 2613 (Ginsburg, J, concurring and dissenting), citing Dept. of Health and Human Services, *Coverage Denied: How the Current Health Insurance System Leaves Millions Behind* 1 (2009).

on account of an individual's medical history or preexisting condition.[12] The "community rating" provision limits the extent to which insurers may charge higher premiums because of a preexisting condition.[13]

These provisions, by themselves, would have threatened to cause the health insurance market to collapse. Insurance companies are effectively required to charge people with preexisting conditions less than what is actuarially required. Therefore that group of people will, on net and in the aggregate, cause insurers to lose money. In order to make up for those losses, the insurance companies will have to charge healthy individuals more than the actuarially determined amount. But that means that, in many cases, insurers will charge healthy individuals more than the insurance is worth to those individuals. That would cause some healthy people to refrain from buying insurance. The problem is exacerbated because the guaranteed issue and community rating provisions enable healthy people to acquire insurance at the last minute if they become sick. When healthy people forgo insurance, insurers must raise their premiums further; that makes insurance a bad bargain for a slightly less healthy set of individuals. If that group leaves the market, the overall pool of insureds will again become less healthy, on average, and the insurance company will have to raise premiums again—thus causing another group to depart. In this way, the market can unravel and insurers will be driven from business.[14] This was, in fact, the experience of some states that had adopted the equivalent of community rating and guaranteed issue requirements.[15]

The individual mandate is a response to this problem. It requires all "applicable individual[s]" to maintain "minimum essential coverage."[16] An "applicable individual" is anyone except for certain religious conscientious objectors, people who are incarcerated, and

---

[12] 42 USC §§ 300gg-1(a), 300gg-3, 300gg-4(a).

[13] 42 USC § 300gg(a).

[14] "[I]mposition of community-rated premiums and guaranteed issue on a market of competing health insurers will inexorably drive that market into extinction, unless these two features are coupled with . . . a mandate on individual[s] to be insured." *NFIB*, 123 S Ct at 2613–14 (Ginsburg, J, concurring and dissenting), quoting *Hearings before the House Ways and Means Committee*, 111th Cong, 1st Sess, 10, 13 (2009) (testimony of Uwe Reinhardt) (brackets and ellipsis in original; emphasis omitted).

[15] See *NFIB*, 132 S Ct at 2614 (Ginsburg, J, concurring and dissenting).

[16] 26 USC § 5000A (a).

people not lawfully present in the United States.[17] "Minimum essential coverage" can be secured in a variety of ways—through Medicare or Medicaid, or by employer-supplied insurance, for example.[18] But an individual who does not have insurance from those or other sources must buy it from a private insurer.

The ACA provided that a person who does not maintain "minimum essential coverage" must make a "shared responsibility payment."[19] This payment is made on a person's tax return. The amount is calculated, in part, by reference to the person's income;[20] some individuals are exempt.[21] The ACA also provides subsidies to certain individuals to enable them to buy health insurance.

By requiring nearly all individuals to have health insurance, the individual mandate, if it works as planned, will prevent the unraveling threatened by the guaranteed issue and community rating provisions. Healthy individuals will have to obtain insurance even if they believe (correctly) that it is not economically rational for them to do so. The effect is a cross-subsidy: the premiums charged to healthy individuals offset the below-cost premiums charged to individuals with preexisting conditions. This cross-subsidy, and the mandate, are needed to make the guaranteed issue and community rating provisions workable.

There was another principal justification for the individual mandate. Under federal and state law, as well as codes of medical ethics, individuals cannot be denied certain forms of medical care because they are unable to pay for it.[22] In effect, therefore, everyone already has a limited form of health insurance: if people need care that they cannot afford, it will be provided to them for free, or below cost, in certain circumstances. The unpaid costs of that care are borne initially by health care providers, who then pass them on to people who do pay—almost entirely, people who do have insurance. The mandate prevents uninsured individuals from shifting the costs of their care in this way, that is, from free-riding on others' health insurance. Put another way, the mandate requires uninsured indi-

---

[17] 26 USC § 5000A (d).
[18] 26 USC § 5000A (f).
[19] 26 USC § 5000A (b).
[20] 26 USC § 5000A (c).
[21] 26 USC § 5000A (e).
[22] See, for example, 42 USC § 1395dd; *NFIB*, 132 S Ct at 2611 (Ginsburg, J, concurring and dissenting).

viduals to pay for the health insurance that, de facto, they have anyway.

B. THE LITIGATION

In the litigation challenging the individual mandate, there was no dispute about the constitutionality of the guaranteed issue and community rating provisions. The parties challenging the constitutionality of the mandate conceded that those regulations of the insurance market were within Congress's power under the Commerce Clause. But they asserted that the mandate exceeded Congress's power under Article I of the Constitution.

The federal government's defense of the individual mandate relied both on the Commerce and Necessary and Proper Clauses and on Congress's power to tax and spend under the General Welfare Clause. The argument under the General Welfare Clause, which ultimately succeeded, was that the "shared responsibility payment" was a tax levied on the condition of not having insurance. That is, the General Welfare Clause argument was that the mandate does not prohibit or punish the failure to obtain insurance; instead, the argument was, the mandate gives individuals an option. They may obtain insurance and not pay a tax, or forgo insurance and make the payment. The Court accepted this argument by a 5–4 vote. The government's argument on this point was certainly not airtight, but the Court's resolution of the issue was not nearly as remarkable as its decision on the Commerce Clause question.

The Commerce Clause argument did proceed on the assumptions that the mandate requires people to obtain insurance and that the shared responsibility payment is a penalty. The government's specific Commerce Clause arguments paralleled the two purposes that the mandate served. The government asserted that the individual mandate is "necessary to make effective the Act's core reforms of the insurance market, i.e., the guaranteed-issue and community-rating provisions."[23] Without the individual mandate, or something that served essentially the same function, those provisions would not accomplish their objectives. "Ample evidence before Congress," the government argued, "supported [Con-

---

[23] Brief for the Petitioners (Minimum Coverage Provision), *Dept. of Health and Human Services v Florida*, No 11-398, decided with *NFIB v Sebelius*, 132 S Ct 2566 (2012) at 24.

gress's] conclusion that the minimum coverage provision is indispensable to the viability of the Act's guaranteed-issue and community-rating reforms, which were unquestionably within
Congress's commerce power to enact."[24] Under the Necessary and
Proper Clause, therefore, the individual mandate is constitutional
because it is a means of carrying out measures that the Commerce
Clause authorized Congress to enact.

The government also argued that the mandate is itself a regulation of commerce, so that the Commerce Clause alone, without
any aid from the Necessary and Proper Clause, is enough to sustain
it. The argument was that the health insurance and health care
markets are interstate markets, and the mandate—by preventing
cost-shifting—regulates the way in which individuals participate
in those markets.[25] The mandate "creates a financial incentive (by
means of a tax penalty) for uninsured participants in the health
care market to internalize their own risks and costs, rather than
externalizing them to others."[26]

A majority of the Court rejected the Commerce Clause argument in all its forms. The Chief Justice wrote for himself; four
justices (Justices Scalia, Kennedy, Thomas, and Alito—a plurality
on this issue) joined a separate opinion that reached the same
conclusion. Justice Ginsburg, for herself and Justices Breyer, Sotomayor, and Kagan, dissented from the Commerce Clause holding but joined the parts of the Chief Justice's opinion that concluded that the mandate was constitutional under the General
Welfare Clause. The Court also ruled that a different aspect of
the ACA—provisions that required states to expand Medicaid coverage as a condition of continuing to participate in the Medicaid
program—was unconstitutional.

C. THE MANDATE AND THE NECESSARY AND PROPER CLAUSE

The most straightforward defense of the mandate was based on
the Necessary and Proper Clause: that the mandate was, at the
least, a reasonable way to make the guaranteed issue and community rating provisions workable. *McCulloch v Maryland*, and
many cases since then, have held that the Necessary and Proper

---

[24] Id at 29–30.

[25] Id at 33–37.

[26] Id at 34.

Clause of the Constitution permits Congress to enact measures that are "plainly adapted" to achieve Congress's legitimate objectives.[27] The mandate, without question, satisfies this test. The mandate was not the only way to make the guaranteed issue and community rating provisions work. The government might, for example, accomplish its objectives by subsidizing the purchase of health insurance, rather than penalizing the failure to purchase it. But *McCulloch* is clear on precisely this point: the means chosen by Congress need not be indispensable but only reasonably well adapted to Congress's objectives.[28]

The *NFIB* majority did not seriously dispute any step in this argument, and there is no way it could have. The constitutionality of the guaranteed issue and community rating provisions was conceded by the parties challenging the ACA. The connection between the mandate and those provisions was obvious, and the Court did not deny that connection. Under *McCulloch* and many cases since then, a statute is constitutional when it is reasonably well adapted to accomplishing a legitimate objective. Justice Scalia—who nevertheless joined the majority in rejecting the Commerce Clause argument in *NFIB*—put the point plainly just a few years earlier: "[W]here Congress has the authority to enact a regulation of interstate commerce, 'it possesses every power needed to make that regulation effective.'"[29] The mandate easily met that test.[30]

In fact, when the mandate is compared to many other well-accepted things that the federal government does, what stands out is that the justification for the mandate is exceptionally strong. Innumerable things that the federal government does—and that are unquestionably constitutional—are justified by the Commerce

---

[27] *McCulloch v Maryland*, 17 US 316, 421 (1819).

[28] Id at 413–14.

[29] *Gonzales v Raich*, 545 US 1, 36 (2005) (Scalia, J, concurring), quoting *United States v Wrightwood Dairy Co.*, 315 US 110, 118–19 (1942).

[30] Many commentators made arguments along these lines. For comprehensive treatments, see, for example, Andrew Koppelman, *The Tough Luck Constitution and the Assault on Health Care Reform* 38–90, 109–22 (Oxford, 2013), Einer Elhauge, *Obamacare on Trial* (2012), and Mark A. Hall, *Commerce Clause Challenges to Health Care Reform*, 159 U Pa L Rev 1825 (2011). More far-reaching arguments might also be advanced in support of the individual mandate. See, for example, Robert Cooter and Neil S. Siegel, *Collective Action Federalism: A General Theory of Article I, Section 8*, 63 Stan L Rev 115 (2010); Jack Balkin, *Commerce*, 109 Mich L Rev 1 (2010). But no novel or far-reaching argument was required to sustain the mandate.

Clause and the Necessary and Proper Clause even though they have a much weaker connection to interstate commerce than the individual mandate.

United States v Comstock,[31] decided just two years before *NFIB*, makes the point. A federal statute, 18 USC § 4248, allows a federal district judge to order the civil commitment of a federal prisoner who has completed his prison sentence, if the judge finds the prisoner to be mentally ill and sexually dangerous. Section 4248 was challenged on the ground that it exceeded Congress's powers under Article I of the Constitution. Congress has no general power to confine dangerous or mentally ill individuals; that is ordinarily the responsibility of state governments. The only difference between the inmates in *Comstock* and other people subject to civil commitment was that the inmates had been in federal prison. But they were no longer federal inmates; they had completed their federal sentences. They accordingly claimed that only a state, not the federal government, could subject them to civil commitment proceedings.

The Court rejected the challenge. The basis for the decision was the Commerce Clause (and some other enumerated powers) and the Necessary and Proper Clause. But the connection between Section 4248 and the enumerated powers was orders of magnitude more remote than the connection between the ACA mandate and interstate commerce. For example, three of the inmates involved in *Comstock* had been convicted of possession of child pornography that had moved in interstate commerce.[32] The Commerce Clause was the only enumerated power the Court relied on in holding that the Constitution authorized those inmates' continued detention. The Court's reasoning, in effect—not all the steps were spelled out in the opinion—was as follows. Because Congress has the power to regulate interstate commerce, it has the power to forbid interstate shipments of things it considers harmful, like child pornography. It is useful—not indispensable, but useful—to enforce that prohibition not just against those who ship child pornography in interstate commerce, but against those who possess pornography that has been illegally shipped.

If Congress can forbid those actions, it also has the power, under

---

[31] 130 S Ct 1949 (2010).

[32] *United States v Comstock*, 507 F Supp 2d 522, 526 & n 2 (ED NC 2010).

the Necessary and Proper Clause, to make it a crime to violate that prohibition.[33] This is so even though the Constitution explicitly authorizes Congress to create only certain crimes—counterfeiting, treason, piracy and felonies committed on the high seas, and offenses against the law of nations[34]—which, under the principle of *expressio unius est exclusio alterius*, suggests that Congress may create no other crimes. But it has been established since *McCulloch* that the federal government "may, legitimately, punish any violation of its laws."[35]

If Congress has the power to create crimes, it also, again under the Necessary and Proper Clause, has the power to establish prisons.[36] If Congress can establish a prison system, then it can "enact laws that seek to ensure that system's safe and responsible administration," by, for example, forbidding escapes.[37] And Congress's "power to act as a responsible federal custodian" includes the "power to act in order to protect nearby (and other) communities from the danger federal prisoners may pose."[38] In this highly indirect way, Section 4248 was authorized by the Commerce Clause (and the enumerated powers that were the basis of other criminal convictions), supplemented by the Necessary and Proper Clause.

Comstock was a relatively difficult case; it reached the Supreme Court, and two Justices dissented. But absolutely routine operations of the federal government rest on chains of inference that are only slightly less attenuated. For example, the federal government has elaborate enforcement powers, civil and criminal, that are connected to the enumerated powers in the same kind of indirect way that *Comstock* highlighted. The government may require businesses to keep records; it may issue subpoenas and compel testimony under oath; it may punish conspiracy and aiding and abetting. Many of these powers are used to enforce laws—wire and securities fraud statutes, environmental statutes, narcotics statutes—that are based on the Commerce Clause. Those elaborate enforcement powers are not essential to the regulation of interstate

---

[33] 130 S Ct at 1957–58.

[34] See US Const, Art I, § 8, cls 6, 10; Art III, § 3.

[35] 17 US at 416; see also *United States v Fox*, 96 US 670, 672 (1878).

[36] *Comstock*, 130 S Ct at 1958, citing *Ex parte Karstendick*, 93 US 396 (1876).

[37] *Comstock*, 130 S Ct at 1958.

[38] Id at 1961.

commerce. Congress could do a satisfactory job of keeping narcotics or pollutants out of interstate channels without punishing
aiding and abetting or conspiracies, without having systems of
parole and probation with all of their attendant personnel and
institutions, without the ability to compel testimony, and so on.
But the constitutionality of those aspects of the federal government's power is beyond question. When compared to them, the
most notable thing about the individual mandate is how closely
connected it is to a conceded congressional power.

II. "This Unprecedented Individual Mandate" and the Regulation of Inaction

The Court's response to the Necessary and Proper Clause
argument was, as I said, not to deny the closeness of that connection; instead, the Court insisted that the mandate was such an
unusual requirement that it posed special dangers and could not
be upheld. This was the revisionist aspect of *NFIB*. Before 1937,
the Court limited Congress's power not by finding that the legislation regulated conduct that had too slight an effect on interstate
commerce, but by asserting that it was the wrong kind of legislation. In fact the pre-1937 Court was sometimes explicit in saying
that the effect of a regulated activity on interstate commerce was
irrelevant if the activity were of a kind that could not be regulated,
or if the regulation took the wrong form.[39]

In *NFIB* the Court was not quite as explicit, but it proceeded
in the same way—indeed, as I will explain, in perhaps an even less
defensible way. The *NFIB* Court emphasized four related claims
about the mandate: that it was unprecedented—the plurality opinion referred to "this unprecedented Individual Mandate"; that it
regulated individuals who had not entered into any commercial
market; that it regulated inaction, not action; and that upholding
it would mean that there was no limit on Congress's power under
the Commerce Clause.

---

[39] See, for example, *Carter v Carter Coal Co.*, 298 US 238, 308 (1936):

> The distinction between a direct and an indirect effect turns, not upon the
> magnitude of either the cause or the effect, but entirely upon the manner in
> which the effect has been brought about. . . . [T]he matter of degree has no
> bearing upon the question here, since that question is not—What is . . . the
> *extent* of the effect produced upon interstate commerce? but—What is the *re-
> lation* between the activity or condition and the effect?

A. THE "UNPRECEDENTED" MANDATE

Seen from one point of view, the mandate is about as far from being unprecedented as it is possible for something to be. The mandate requires citizens to pay money; in return they will receive services. This is what governments always do, and always have done. They require people to relinquish something of value—today, usually, money—in return for services. The most basic service is protection against violence, from home and abroad; of course governments now provide more than that. But the essential nature of any transaction between a government and its citizens is the same as the transaction required by the mandate. If you are within the territory, you have to contribute, but you will get something in return. That kind of "individual mandate" is as old as government itself. There were suggestions by the parties challenging the mandate, and even by the Justices,[40] that the mandate was truly extraordinary—that it represented a far-reaching innovation in the relationship between the government and its citizens. That claim overlooks something fundamental about the nature of government.

Of course, when the government demands contributions from citizens, it usually does so by taxing them. The Court may have meant that the individual mandate was an unprecedented use of the Commerce Clause, as opposed to the taxing power. And, in the usual case, the government collects the contributions and supplies the services itself. So the Court may have meant that the mandate is unprecedented because it requires individuals to pay money not to the government but to a private firm, in exchange for services.

On the latter point, though, the Court did not explicitly say that the private nature of the transaction was problematic, and the tenor of both the Chief Justice's opinion and the plurality opinion suggests the opposite: that the majority saw the mandate as threatening because it gave too much power to the government, not because of the role it assigned to private insurance companies. So

---

[40] See Transcript of Oral Argument, No 11-398, *Dept. of HHS v Florida*, decided with *NFIB v Sebelius*, 132 S Ct 2566 (2012), March 27, 2012, at 12 (Justice Kennedy): "I understand that we must presume laws are constitutional, but, even so, when you are changing the relation of the individual to the government in this, what we can stipulate is, I think, a unique way, do you not have a heavy burden of justification to show authorization under the Constitution?"

apparently what was troubling about the supposedly unprecedented nature of the mandate was that, in funneling an exchange through the private sector, it used the Commerce Clause, rather than the power to tax. But the Commerce Clause seems like a more natural basis than the taxing power for mandating a relationship between private parties. And the use of the Commerce power to require the payment of money is not unusual: the government imposes fees on various activities that implicate interstate commerce.

Even if the individual mandate was unprecedented in some significant respect, it is hard to see why that should matter very much. As Justice Ginsburg's opinion noted, the argument that a law is novel and unprecedented, and therefore suspect, has been advanced over and over in cases seeking to limit Congress's power under the Commerce Clause, whenever Congress has tackled a new national problem.[41] The ACA was a major piece of federal legislation that attempted, for the first time, a comprehensive reform of the nation's health care system. It would not be surprising if it did some unprecedented things. The unprecedented features of the statute should be judged in the way innovative legislation has been judged since Chief Justice Marshall upheld the Bank of the United States in *McCulloch*: the question is whether it is reasonably adapted to carry into effect one of Congress's enumerated powers.

In any event, the claim that the mandate was an unprecedented use of the Commerce Clause does not hold up. There are well-established uses of the Commerce Clause power that mandate commercial transactions and that ought to be, by the *NFIB* Court's own lights, more troubling than the individual mandate. The clearest example is the Civil Rights Act of 1964, which the Court upheld as a proper use of Congress's power under the Commerce Clause.[42] Title II of the Civil Rights Act made it illegal for the operators of public accommodations, such as restaurants and hotels, to discriminate on the basis of race. Title II was a mandate:

---

[41] 132 S Ct at 2625, citing *Hoke v United States*, 227 US 308, 320 (1913) (brackets in original) ("[I]n almost every instance of the exercise of the [commerce] power differences are asserted from previous exercises of it and made a ground of attack."); *Perez v United States*, 402 US 146 (1971); *Katzenbach v McClung*, 379 US 294 (1964); and *Wickard v Filburn*, 317 US 111 (1942).

[42] *Heart of Atlanta Motel, Inc. v United States*, 379 US 241 (1964); *Katzenbach v McClung*, 379 US 294 (1964).

like the ACA provision, Title II mandated a commercial transaction between private parties. The owner of a restaurant had to serve racial minorities, whether he wanted to or not. Many antidiscrimination laws share this feature. They require employers, schools, public facilities, and the owners of residential property to do business with people whom they would rather turn away.

Today the constitutionality of Title II and similar antidiscrimination laws is, in general, beyond question. But if the concern is simply that Congress has mandated a commercial transaction, then, on any plausible scale of values, the ACA's individual mandate is much less troubling than the Civil Rights Act. The ACA requires, at most, that an individual send a check to an insurance company of his or her own choosing; in return the individual will get health insurance. Title II requires that the proprietor of a restaurant personally serve a customer, not just engage in a financial transaction. And Title II, unlike the ACA, does not allow the individual who is subject to the mandate to choose the counterparty. The proprietor has to serve any member of a minority group who wants to come to his restaurant.

Finally, the proprietor—unlike a person who does not want health insurance—cannot buy his way out of the obligation. A person who does not want to comply with the ACA's mandate need only make a "shared responsibility payment," which is calibrated so as not to be too financially burdensome, to the Internal Revenue Service. People who do not want to serve racial minorities do not have that option. Their only choice is to relinquish their business. If the claim is that the ACA, by requiring people to engage in a commercial transaction, imposes an unprecedented burden, then that claim is simply false. There is a precedent—an unchallengeable one, at that—in the Civil Rights Act. And the burdens the Civil Rights Act imposes on the refusal to engage in commerce are unquestionably greater.

B. THE REGULATION OF NONMARKET PARTICIPANTS

The Court did not specifically address the Civil Rights Act, but it is clear from the opinions what its response would be: the proprietors of public accommodations have entered into commerce and thereby subjected themselves to Congress's regulatory power. By contrast, people have to comply with the individual mandate even if they have in no way engaged in a commercial activity.

There are many things wrong with this argument, however.

To begin with, while the people subject to the Civil Rights Act willingly entered one market—they willingly became suppliers of public accommodations to whites—they emphatically did not enter the market that the act was concerned with, the market in which accommodations are provided to racial minorities. That was the whole point of Title II of the Civil Rights Act. It was designed precisely to force restaurant and hotel owners into a market they were determined to stay out of.

Of course it might be argued that the markets were not distinct, or, if they were, that entering one market is enough to make a person legitimately subject to Congress's Commerce Clause power over a related market. But markets are not self-defining. If Congress's power under the Commerce and Necessary and Proper Clauses is limited to people who are participating in a market—there is no reason for it to be so limited, but on the assumption that it is—the question is how much latitude Congress has in defining the relevant market and in determining who is a participant in it. If Congress can, in effect, declare that restaurant proprietors who have strenuously avoided entering the market for serving minorities are, nonetheless, participants in that market, then Congress should have similar latitude in defining the market for purposes of the ACA.

A central part of the justification for the individual mandate was precisely that virtually everyone has been, or will be, at one time or another, a participant in the market for health care. If Congress can define the market for public accommodations in a way that included buyers whom the sellers wanted to exclude, it should also be able to define the market for health care in a way that included all people who had in the past, or would in the future, consume health care services. The mandate requires that participants in that market—that is to say, everyone—participate in a certain way, by buying health insurance. If participation in a related market is enough to make it constitutional to require unwilling proprietors to do business with minorities, then participation in the same market at a different time should be enough to require unwilling individuals to do business with health insurers. No discernible principle related to the Commerce Clause distinguishes those cases.

In any event, the premise that only market participants can be regulated under the Commerce and Necessary and Proper Clauses is itself unfounded. To give a simple example, Congress has the power to punish, as an accessory, an individual who harbors an escapee from a federal prison; no one would deny that. If the inmate's prison sentence is for an offense that is based on the Commerce Clause—most drug offenses are in that category—then the source of the power to punish the accessory is the Commerce and Necessary and Proper Clauses, on logic like *Comstock*'s. But the accessory is not participating in a market, or engaging in interstate commerce, in any recognizable sense.

Beyond that, though, in two well-known cases, the Court allowed Congress to regulate conduct by people who had specifically refused to enter *any* relevant market. In *Wickard v Filburn*,[43] a farmer who grew wheat and consumed it on his own farm planted more acres of wheat than were allowed under a regulatory regime established by the Agricultural Adjustment Act.[44] The purpose of that regime was to support the price of wheat in the interstate and international markets.[45] The farmer had no intention of marketing his wheat. The Court nonetheless upheld the application of the regulation: "[E]ven if appellee's activity be local, and though it may not be regarded as commerce, it may still, whatever its nature, be reached by Congress if it exerts a substantial economic effect on interstate commerce."[46]

The Court in *Wickard* commented that wheat initially grown for consumption rather than trade could nonetheless "overhang[] the market" and be sold if market prices rose, thus affecting the price of wheat shipped in interstate commerce. But the Court emphasized that even wheat "that . . . is never marketed" would affect interstate commerce because it would "suppl[y] a need of the man who grew it which would otherwise be reflected by purchases in the open market."[47] That is, a person who grows wheat for himself will buy less wheat, and that affects interstate commerce. The parallel to the ACA mandate is obvious. The basis for the mandate was that, because of the way the guaranteed issue and community rating provisions worked, and because of the risk of

---

[43] 317 US 111 (1942).

[44] Id at 114–15.

[45] Id at 115.

[46] Id at 125.

[47] Id at 128.

cost-shifting, a decision to self-insure instead of entering the market for health insurance might affect interstate commerce—just as a decision to grow one's own wheat instead of entering the market can affect interstate commerce in that product. Under *Wickard*, those kinds of market effects justify regulation under the Commerce Clause.

In support of the notion that the Commerce Clause permits the regulation only of market participants, the majority in *NFIB* asserted that the Commerce Clause authorizes Congress only to "regulate" commerce and does not "include[] the power to create it."[48] But this form of the argument was foreclosed by *Wickard*, too: "The stimulation of commerce is a use of the regulatory function quite as definitely as prohibitions or restrictions thereon."[49] The Court in *Wickard* also endorsed the use of regulation to work a cross-subsidy, as the individual mandate did: "It is of the essence of regulation that it lays a restraining hand on the self-interest of the regulated and that advantages from the regulation commonly fall to others."[50]

Gonzales v Raich[51] presented, arguably, facts that were even more stark than those in *Wickard*. Two individuals, Raich and Monson, grew marijuana on their own property (or had caregivers grow it for them) and used it for medicinal purposes, to relieve pain that would not respond to any other treatment. The law of California, where they lived, purported to authorize them to grow and use marijuana in this way, but the federal Controlled Substances Act forbade it.[52] The Court held that applying the federal law to Raich and Monson was consistent with the Commerce Clause. The Court reasoned that Congress had established a regulatory scheme to prevent the interstate movement of marijuana, and that the prohibition even on growing it for one's own medicinal use was closely enough connected to that regulatory scheme. "Prohibiting the intrastate possession or manufacture of an article of commerce

---

[48] 132 S Ct at 2586 (Roberts, CJ); see id at 2646 (Scalia et al, JJ) (referring to "[t]he mandating of economic activity").

[49] 317 US at 128.

[50] Id at 129.

[51] 545 US 1 (2005).

[52] Id at 6–7, 14–15.

is a rational (and commonly utilized) means of regulating commerce in that product."[53]

Wickard and *Raich* are flatly inconsistent with the suggestion—implausible in any event—that Congress's power under the Commerce and Necessary and Proper Clauses is limited to individuals who have in some way entered a market. In *Wickard*, the farmer's failure to enter the market was, in Congress's view, precisely the problem. As for Raich and Monson, not only did they not enter any market; they were prohibited by law from entering the interstate market for marijuana. In fact, in both *Wickard* and *Raich*, individuals were engaged in an ancient form of quintessential nonmarket activity: growing crops for one's own consumption. Everyone, sooner or later, will enter the market for health care, but there was no inevitability that the parties in *Wickard* or *Raich* would ever enter the relevant markets. *Wickard* and *Raich*, both of which were left undisturbed by *NFIB*, demonstrate that the Commerce Clause extends to individuals who are even further removed from market activity than the individuals subject to the individual mandate.

C. THE REGULATION OF INACTION

A central theme of the majority's opinions in *NFIB* was that the mandate was unconstitutional because it regulated inactivity, rather than activity.[54] Of course, the restaurant proprietor who refused to serve minorities could have said that he engaged in no activity. He literally did nothing; he just ignored the person sitting at the lunch counter. But presumably the *NFIB* majority would regard the decision to offer public accommodations as action in the relevant sense. The statutes upheld in *Wickard* and *Raich* regulated people who had not entered a market; but those cases involved the activity of raising crops. Only the ACA mandate, on the Court's reasoning, regulated pure inactivity. The Court saw the distinction between action and inaction as the key to maintaining a limiting principle. The individual mandate, the plurality said, "threatens [the constitutional] order because it gives such an expansive meaning to the Commerce Clause that *all* private con-

---

[53] Id at 26.

[54] See, for example, 132 S Ct at 2587 (Roberts, CJ); id at 2588 ("The farmer in *Wickard* was at least actively engaged in the production of wheat"); id at 2649 (Scalia et al, JJ).

duct (including failure to act) becomes subject to federal control, effectively destroying the Constitution's vision of governmental powers."[55]

The problem with the distinction between action and inaction—a problem thoroughly canvassed in lower court opinions upholding the individual mandate, as well as in Justice Ginsburg's opinion—is that the distinction is arbitrary. Even "inaction" involves a choice and, in that sense, is an action. It is easy to proliferate examples. If a person has a health insurance policy, but cancels it, is that an action, or is it just inaction? What if an employer offers health insurance as the default option, but the employee chooses to remain uninsured? Or if an employee leaves a job that provides insurance because she prefers one that provides no insurance but higher wages? Or if the employee chooses the higher-wage, no-insurance job in the first place?

The government argued in *NFIB* that the decision not to have insurance should be characterized as self-insurance and, therefore, a form of activity subject to regulation under the Commerce Clause. Self-insurance has identifiable economic consequences: a self-insured individual who does not have enough capital or liquidity will be unable to cover certain risks, should they materialize. And self-insurance withdraws an individual from a larger pool, creating the risks that caused Congress, in the ACA, to conjoin the individual mandate with the community rating and guaranteed issue provisions. The Chief Justice rejected arguments like these in what seems to be almost a self-refuting passage: "To an economist, perhaps, there is no difference between activity and inactivity; both have measurable economic effects on commerce. But the distinction between doing something and doing nothing would not have been lost on the Framers, who were 'practical statesmen,' not metaphysical philosophers."[56]

Surely, for purposes of the Commerce Clause—and to carry out the project of "'practical statesmen'"—it should be the "measurable economic effects on commerce," and the perspective of the economist, that govern. As the Chief Justice all but admitted, it is the distinction between action and inaction that falls into the realm of supposed "metaphysical philosoph[y]." Or at least if that

[55] 132 S Ct at 2649.

[56] Id at 2589, quoting *Industrial Union Dept., AFL-CIO v American Petroleum Institute*, 448 US 607, 673 (Rehnquist, J, concurring).

distinction is going to be drawn for purposes of the Commerce Clause, it makes no sense to draw it in a way that ignores the economic significance of the behavior. If self-insurance has recognizable economic effects on interstate commerce—which it undoubtedly does—then it should be subject to regulation under the Commerce Clause.

The fundamental problem with the claim that the Commerce Clause can extend only to "action" is that this claim—as the District of Columbia Circuit commented, in an opinion upholding the mandate[57]—presupposes a constitutional right. The premise of the distinction is that there has to be some way, some safe harbor, that people can use to escape regulation under the Commerce Clause. People who do nothing should be assured that Congress cannot reach them under the Commerce Clause. But that is the same thing as asserting that in certain circumstances, individuals have a right to be free from regulation. The logic of the distinction between action and inaction is that if—but only if—individuals engage in certain kinds of conduct, such as entering a market, then they have effectively given up the right to be free from regulation. But in *NFIB*, the parties attacking the mandate explicitly renounced any claim that there was such a right, and it is easy to see why. The idea that there is a constitutional right to avoid economic regulation was the defining feature of the repudiated era associated with *Lochner v New York*.[58]

Unless there is such a right, though, there is no basis for insisting that people must have a safe harbor from regulation. To the extent the Court insisted on some form of commercial activity as a precondition for the exercise of Congress's Commerce Clause power, the Court was treating the Commerce Clause as if it gave Congress only the power "to regulate individuals engaged in commerce among the states." The Clause, of course, is not written that way.[59]

---

[57] *Seven-Sky v Holder*, 661 F3d 1, 19 (DC Cir 2011) ("[The] view that an individual cannot be subject to Commerce Clause regulation absent voluntary, affirmative acts that enter him or her into, or affect, the interstate market expresses a concern for individual liberty that seems more redolent of Due Process Clause arguments. But it has no foundation in the Commerce Clause.").

[58] 198 US 45 (1905).

[59] See Martha Minow, *The Supreme Court, 2011 Term—Comment: Affordable Convergence: "Reasonable Interpretation" and the Affordable Care Act*, 126 Harv L Rev 117, 130 (2012) ("Rather than adhering to a strict textual reading, the [plurality]'s concern about individual liberty read into the Commerce Clause—or the Necessary and Proper Clause—extra protectiveness that was not specified in the text.").

But the more fundamental point is that even if the Commerce Clause were written that way, the Necessary and Proper Clause would allow Congress to regulate people not engaged in commerce. Congress could undoubtedly regulate people who aided or obstructed individuals engaged in commerce, for example.

In this respect, the *NFIB* majority committed an error that even the pre-1937 Court avoided. That Court designed its limits on the Commerce Clause to protect federalism. It recoiled when it thought Congress was regulating subjects—manufacturing, mining, employee benefits, labor relations, child labor—that were properly the business of the states. While the specific limits that the pre-1937 Court adopted were misguided, and ultimately failed, the underlying idea—that the Commerce Clause power should be limited in order to preserve state autonomy—was plausible. The enumeration of powers in Article I is, of course, designed to protect state prerogatives. The error of the pre-1937 Court was in the way it tried to protect states' interests from federal incursions or, perhaps, in not simply deferring to Congress's decisions about how much protection states should be given.

The principles adopted by the *NFIB* Court are of a different character. The emphasis on whether an individual has acted, by entering a market or otherwise, does not correspond to a concern with federalism. It reflects a concern with individual rights—with preserving some way for individuals to escape federal regulation. But that is not the purpose of the enumeration of powers in Article I. The ultimate goal of federalism may be to protect individual liberty, but the definition of Congress's powers under Article I is a matter not of identifying individual rights but of adjudicating between the interests of the United States and the interests of the states. Chief Justice Marshall made this point in *McCulloch v Maryland*: when the question is the scope of Congress's Article I authority, "the great principles of liberty are not concerned, but the respective powers of those who are equally the representatives of the people, are to be adjusted."[60] The *NFIB* Court imported limits that have to do with preserving the autonomy not of states but of individuals, and that was bound to produce incoherent results, such as the arbitrary distinction between action and inaction, and the

---

[60] 17 US at 401.

implicit treatment of *Wickard* and *Raich* as cases involving participation in a market.

D. NO LIMITING PRINCIPLE?

The *NFIB* majority repeatedly invoked the specter of no limiting
principle: that if the Commerce Clause authorized Congress to
enact the individual mandate, then Congress could do anything.[61]
This aspect of the majority's reasoning is doubly mistaken. The
approach that the majority took does not actually provide an effective limiting principle. And a potential limiting principle—one
that, arguably, better reflected the values the majority purported
to protect—might have been derived, although with some difficulty, from the Court's earlier decisions. That principle, however,
would not have led to the invalidation of the individual mandate.

The problem with the majority's approach is that distinctions
like those that the majority adopted—between action and inaction,
for example—simply do not confine Congress very much. The
power to forbid actions, even if it were limited to market transactions, would give a maleficent Congress everything it needed to
enact all manner of oppressive regimes. Justice Ginsburg made
the point: under well-established precedents that *NFIB* did not
begin to question, "[t]he commerce power . . . would enable Congress to prohibit the purchase and home production of all meat,
fish, and dairy goods, effectively compelling Americans to eat only
vegetables. . . ."[62]

One could make the same point even if the Commerce Clause
power were given the narrowest limit that is even remotely plausible—if it were confined, for example, to the regulation of the
actual interstate movements of goods and services, and could be
exercised only in connection with a clearly defined set of interstate
movements.[63] For a court to impose such a limit today would be
an extremely aggressive act: it would effectively nullify the Necessary and Proper Clause in this context, and it would overrule

---

[61] See, for example, 132 S Ct at 2587 (Roberts, CJ); id at 2589; id at 2592; id at 2646
(Scalia et al, JJ) ("If Congress can reach out and command even those furthest removed
from an interstate market to participate in the market, then the Commerce Clause becomes
a font of unlimited power . . . .")

[62] 132 S Ct at 2625 (citations omitted).

[63] This resembles Justice Thomas's position, although he might permit Congress more
power. See *Lopez*, 514 US at 586–89 (Thomas, J, concurring); *Raich*, 545 US at 58–59
(Thomas, J, dissenting).

many cases and invalidate many laws that are now considered beyond question—laws forbidding the simple possession of narcotics, for example.

But even this unrealistically severe limit would still leave Congress with immense power. To state the obvious, consumers buy all manner of goods and services that have moved in interstate commerce, and producers depend on interstate markets for inputs and sales. As long as Congress can restrict the interstate movements of goods and services, it can, if it wishes, have an extraordinary effect on the economy and the society. The ability to regulate interstate commerce—even if defined in the narrowest possible way—is, unavoidably, the ability to regulate much of modern life.

This is, in a way, a vindication of the post-1937 vision of the Commerce Clause: interstate commerce is woven so deeply into the fabric of the modern economy and society that it is pointless to try to draw a boundary around it. Perhaps this wasn't always true. In a dispersed and mostly agrarian society, where many local communities are self-sufficient, the power to regulate interstate commerce is more interstitial, and it might make sense to try to limit that power in the way the Court has in mind. But that is not our society. In a highly interdependent economy, in which people have become accustomed to a nationwide market, the power to regulate interstate commerce will necessarily be a very extensive power. The effort to define a limiting principle is likely to be arbitrary or, worse, to reflect judicial second-guessing of Congress's policy decisions.

Still, if the Court were intent on providing some limiting principle, it could have derived one from the two post-1995 decisions, before *NFIB*, that invalidated federal statutes on the ground that they were not authorized by the Commerce Clause. *United States v Lopez*[64] struck down the Gun-Free Schools Zone Act, which made it a federal crime to possess a firearm near a school. *United States v Morrison*[65] declared unconstitutional a provision of the Violence Against Women Act that gave victims of gender-motivated violence a federal civil remedy.

It is far from clear that either of these decisions is correct.

---

[64] 514 US 549 (1995).

[65] 529 US 598 (2000).

Congress more or less reversed the result in *Lopez* by modifying the Gun-Free Schools Zone Act to limit it to firearms "that ha[ve] moved in or otherwise affect[ed]" interstate commerce.[66] As modified, the act seems to be squarely within Congress's power, and every court of appeals that has considered the issue has so held.[67] But most firearms satisfy the criterion that Congress added to the statute, and the Necessary and Proper Clause could have been interpreted to make the amendment unnecessary: to allow Congress to generalize—and apply the prohibition to all weapons—thus avoiding the danger of errors, and the administrative costs, that result from requiring proof in each case. In *Morrison*, Congress justified the civil remedy as a measure to enforce the Fourteenth Amendment, as well as a regulation of interstate commerce; the record of state underenforcement of laws protecting victims of gender-based violence should have been enough to sustain that remedy. Beyond that, Congress assembled an extensive record supporting the argument that gender-based violence had an effect on interstate commerce.[68]

Taking *Lopez* and *Morrison* as established, however, it may be possible to discern a limiting principle in the Court's reasoning in the two cases. In both cases, Congress had enacted a freestanding prohibition on traditionally wrongful conduct—freestanding in the sense that, unlike the prohibition in *Raich*, it was not part of a regulatory scheme that included a provision explicitly regulating interstate commerce.[69] In both *Lopez* and *Morrison*, the government's principal argument under the Commerce Clause was that the wrongful acts would, in the aggregate, have a harmful effect on economic activity and therefore on interstate commerce. The Court's reaction was that this would justify too much: "Congress could regulate any activity that it found was related to the economic productivity of individual citizens: family law (including marriage, divorce, and child custody), for example."[70] So *Lopez* and

---

[66] 18 USC § 922(q)(2)(A).

[67] See, for example, *United States v Dorsey*, 418 F3d 1038, 1046 (9th Cir 2005); *United States v Danks*, 221 F3d 1037, 1039 (8th Cir 1999). See also *Thomas More Law Center v Obama*, 651 F3d 529, 555 (6th Cir 2010) (Sutton concurring in part).

[68] See *Morrison*, 529 US 619–20; id at 629–36 (Souter, J, dissenting).

[69] See *Lopez*, 514 US at 561 (asserting that the Act "is not an essential part of a larger regulation of economic activity, in which the regulatory scheme could be undercut unless the intrastate activity were regulated.").

[70] *Lopez*, 514 US at 564; see *Morrison*, 529 US at 613.

Morrison may stand for the principle that Congress cannot invoke its power under the Commerce Clause when the only justification for a statute is that it will promote aggregate economic activity and thereby increase interstate commerce.

It is not clear that that principle can be applied in a coherent way. Among other things, the decision whether a provision is part of a larger regulatory scheme risks being arbitrary; regulatory schemes, like markets, are not self-defining.[71] Congress regulates firearms and devotes resources to education, and the statute struck down in *Lopez* could have been characterized as part of either of those legislative programs. The provision invalidated in *Morrison* might be seen as part of comprehensive efforts to protect women against discrimination in employment and education. But, in any event, this kind of limiting principle derived from *Lopez* and *Morrison* at least reflects the concern that underlies the enumeration of powers in Article I: that Congress should not have a general power to regulate in the national interest. The Court in *NFIB* did not explain why such a principle, derived from the post-1995 cases, was inadequate to deal with the threat of unlimited federal power that the Court perceived.

III. After NFIB

NFIB was a remarkable decision, and not in a good way. Five Justices were willing to conclude that an important Act of Congress exceeded Congress's power under the Commerce Clause, and to reach that conclusion on the basis of reasoning that, if I am right, was very weak. In both of these respects—the Court's willingness to invalidate major federal legislation, and its use of a deeply flawed approach to the Commerce Clause—the Court seemed to be engaged in a troubling form of revisionism, a reprise of the pre-1937 Commerce Clause cases.

Nonetheless, it is not clear how much significance *NFIB* will have in the future.[72] Obviously *NFIB* signals that the Court has no inclination to return to the post-1937 pattern of deference to congressional uses of the Commerce Clause. The approach that

---

[71] See *Morrison*, 529 US at 657 (Breyer, J, dissenting).

[72] See, for example, Gillian E. Metzger, *The Supreme Court, 2011 Term—Comment: To Tax, to Spend, to Regulate*, 126 Harv L Rev 83, 87 (2012) ("*NFIB* may carry the seeds of its own irrelevance."); id at 112 ("If the institutionalism concern ultimately prevails, it will be difficult for the Court to impose meaningful limits on Congress.").

the Court took in *Lopez* and *Morrison* is likely to continue; that is, the Court will find occasions to invalidate laws that seem to it to be remote from the regulation of interstate commerce and to rely on attenuated aggregate effects. But it seems unlikely that the Court will attempt a full-fledged revival of the pre-1937 regime. The instability of that regime is no secret. And *Comstock* and *Raich* suggest that the Court is not inclined to challenge even relatively peripheral exercises of federal power, at least in areas related to criminal law enforcement. That would further complicate the task of reestablishing something resembling the pre-1937 system, even if the Court were inclined to do so.

NFIB seems likely to be of limited practical importance for another reason: it will be relatively easy for Congress to work around it. Congress can, for example, do exactly what the mandate did in a way that was untouched by the *NFIB* Court's ruling—in fact, that seems to have been implicitly endorsed by the plurality opinion.[73] Specifically, Congress could have increased income taxes for everyone and then provided an equivalent tax credit to individuals who have health insurance. The effect would be that people who lack health insurance, but only people who lack health insurance, would pay more to the Internal Revenue Service. That is exactly what the mandate did. In the future, if Congress wants to implement a program like the mandate, it could do so in this way.

Several provisions of the tax code operate in a similar way. A taxpayer can reduce her taxes, in certain circumstances, if she has paid college tuition, for example, or bought an energy efficient vehicle, or made certain home improvements.[74] In each of these cases, the government gives an individual a choice between buying something from a private vendor—such as higher education or a hybrid car—or paying more in taxes. This is, in substance, the same choice that the individual mandate gave: buy health insurance from a private vendor, or pay more to the Internal Revenue Service.

In fact, this is, essentially, how the government encourages the

---

[73] See 132 S Ct at 2647: "[T]hose who did not purchase insurance . . . could be denied a full income tax credit given to those who do purchase insurance."

[74] See, for example, Sean M. Stegmaier, *Tax Incentives for Higher Education in the Internal Revenue Code: Education Tax Expenditure Reform and the Inclusion of Refundable Tax Credits*, 37 Sw U L Rev 135, 137 n 4 (2008) (citing provisions).

purchase of employer-provided health insurance. The value of health insurance provided by employers is not included in income for purposes of the income tax.[75] That means that an employee has, in principle, a choice between obtaining health insurance in exchange for a lower wage—effectively, buying health insurance— or forgoing health insurance, collecting more of her compensation in wages, and paying more in taxes. That is the choice that the mandate gives: buy health insurance or pay more to the IRS. In these ways, requirements that are functionally indistinguishable from the mandate can be found in many places, and no one doubts that they are constitutional. That further calls into question the alarmist tone of the *NFIB* opinions, quite apart from the flaws in the analysis of the Commerce Clause issues.

There is, though, one kind of federal legislation that *NFIB* might preclude. The *NFIB* majority that rejected the Commerce Clause argument evinced a deep skepticism about the government, notably in its overriding concern about a limiting principle. But the more the government is involved in a program, the less *NFIB* will affect it; *NFIB* will come into play, if at all, when the government increases the role of the private sector. That is because government-run programs will be funded out of tax revenues. They will rely on the General Welfare Clause, not the Commerce Clause. *NFIB* becomes important only when the government tries to involve private parties, and therefore may have to resort to the Commerce Clause. In those circumstances, *NFIB* may make it difficult for the government to establish privatized social welfare programs.[76]

For reasons comparable to those that underlay the ACA's individual mandate, contributions to social welfare programs often must be compulsory: otherwise only the people who have the greatest needs will enroll, and the programs can collapse. If the government wants private firms to operate the programs—with compulsory universal contributions—the program will resemble

---

[75] See 26 USC §§ 105, 106.

[76] See *Seven-Sky v Holder*, 661 F3d 1, 53 (DC Cir 2011) (Kavanaugh dissenting):

> Privatized social services combined with mandatory-purchase requirements of the kind employed in the individual mandate provision of the Affordable Care Act might become a blueprint used by the Federal Government over the next generation to partially privatize the social safety net and government assistance programs and move, at least to some degree, away from the tax-and-government-benefit model that is common now.

the ACA mandate. Individuals will have to be given some incentive to contribute. If the government is content to use increased taxes to encourage people to contribute, it may be able to rely on the tax code, just as the equivalent of the ACA mandate could have been implemented through the tax code. But if the government wants to ensure compulsory contributions to a privatized social welfare program by using a different kind of incentive—a fine, for example—then it will have to invoke its power under the Commerce Clause, and *NFIB* will become an issue. If *NFIB* has the result of consolidating more power in the government, and diminishing the attractiveness of involving the private sector, that will be ironic testimony to the perils of Commerce Clause revisionism.

ADAM B. COX

ENFORCEMENT REDUNDANCY AND
THE FUTURE OF IMMIGRATION LAW

It is commonplace for states to help enforce federal law. Local police regularly arrest people for violating federal criminal law, and state actors frequently alert federal prosecutors and agencies when they discover violations of federal law. Similarly, states criminalize wide swaths of conduct, like dealing drugs, that are also federal offenses. They also often attach civil penalties to conduct, such as workplace discrimination, already proscribed by federal law. Enforcement redundancy, as we might call it, is the norm.

Typically, this aspect of American federalism is treated as unremarkable. In recent years, however, it has spawned divisive debates and extensive litigation in one context: immigration law. Amid growing disagreement over immigration policy, a number of states recently passed laws that provide for redundant enforcement of immigration law. These laws authorize state officials to arrest noncitizens for violating federal immigration law. They also impose penalties under state law for violations of the federal immigration code. As soon as they were enacted, the laws triggered a wave of lawsuits. The most prominent suits were brought, quite unusually, by the United States itself. Suing six states, the United States argued

Adam B. Cox is Professor of Law, New York University School of Law.

AUTHOR'S NOTE: Many thanks to Ahilan Arulanantham, Ryan Goodman, Alison LaCroix, Adam Samaha, and David Strauss for invaluable comments. Thanks also to Charity Lee, Madalyn Wasilczuk, and Allison Wilkinson for impeccable research assistance.

that their redundant enforcement measures conflicted with federal law and were therefore preempted.

Given how common enforcement redundancy is in American law, one might have thought that the federal government was sure to lose. But it did not. In *Arizona v United States*,[1] the Supreme Court struck down the core provisions of Arizona's law. The law, SB 1070, had done four things: criminalized violations of the federal alien registration statute; criminalized violations of federal law's prohibition on unauthorized employment; authorized local officials to arrest (some) deportable noncitizens; and required local officials to check the immigration status of noncitizens detained or arrested on criminal charges. Every provision but the last was invalidated by the Court. And underlying the Court's discussion of each provision was an implicit rejection of the idea of enforcement redundancy.

This article explores the significance of the Court's rejection of enforcement redundancy in *Arizona* despite its pedigree in the practice and jurisprudence of American federalism. Some might think that the Court's departure from conventional practice requires no explanation beyond the subject matter of the suit—immigration law. The long (though sometimes mistaken) intellectual tradition of "immigration exceptionalism" among legal scholars has led many to conclude that the Court's approach in *United States v Arizona* is simply the result of the fact that, when it comes to immigration law, everything is exceptional. But while that approach can provide a label for a phenomenon, it does not itself explain it. What we need is an explanation of *why* the Court might deviate so dramatically from the ordinary acceptance of enforcement redundancy and of the implications of that departure. To generate such an explanation, we need to focus on the roots of that principle.

My central claim is that the *Arizona* Court rejected redundant enforcement by conceptualizing law as a set of prices rather than a series of obligations. This Holmesian view is foreign to the Court's typical thinking about redundant enforcement, and it has two dramatic consequences. First, this approach leads inevitably to the conclusion that *any* action by state officials to assist in the enforcement of federal law is impermissible: conceptualized as a price, law is nothing more than the expected sanction associated with particular

---

[1] 132 S Ct 2492 (2012).

conduct, and anything a state actor does to enforce federal law will alter either the chance of getting caught or the severity of punishment. Second, the approach elevates every act of prosecutorial discretion by an executive branch official to the status of supreme federal law for purposes of preemption analysis. This is a radical departure from conventional approaches to preemption, and it makes clear why the Court cannot plausibly embrace the law-as-price conception as a general way of analyzing intergovernmental conflicts. Doing so would dramatically restrict the regulatory authority of states and radically reshape federalism doctrine.

The Court's approach makes *Arizona* as much a case about separation of powers as about federalism. It consolidates tremendous immigration policymaking power in the executive branch, endorsing the idea that immigration law is centrally the product of executive "lawmaking" that bears little relation to immigration law on the books. This view is consistent with recent developments in immigration law. Formal immigration law has become less and less important in a world where roughly one-third of all immigrants are formally deportable. Moreover, executive branch actions demonstrate that the failure to deport all of these noncitizens is a deliberate choice—not simply the result of resource constraints or enforcement failures. In other words, the president has made clear that a perfect world is not a world of perfect compliance with existing immigration statutes. The Court need not have endorsed that view, but Justice Kennedy's majority opinion in effect does so.

The Court's decision to ratify this sort of presidential control over migration policy has important implications for the future of immigration law. Presidents tend to be more open to immigration than Congress. Perhaps this institutional predisposition of the president flows from her distinctively national electoral mandate, or perhaps from her more direct engagement in foreign affairs. Whatever the source, the historical pattern is remarkable: since the 1880s, presidents from Woodrow Wilson, to Harry Truman, to George W. Bush have all promoted immigration policies more generous and less discriminatory than those that emerged from Congress.

This fact is centrally important today, as the nation again turns its attention to once-in-a-generation immigration reform. Right now public debate is focused largely on flashpoint issues like legalizing the more than 10 million immigrants living without status in the United States. But lurking in the background are reform's potentially sweeping consequences for the president's power over immigration policy. Congress could further extend the trajectory advanced in *Arizona*—perhaps by formally delegating to the president the power to set visa quotas. Or Congress could roll *Arizona*'s reasoning back, attempting to claw back authority that has slowly accreted to the executive over the last three or four decades. Which path is taken could profoundly affect the long-term success of comprehensive immigration reform.

This article fleshes out these arguments in four parts. Part I describes the concept of enforcement redundancy. Part II highlights the widespread acceptance of the redundant enforcement of federal law, despite the federalism and separation-of-powers arguments that might plausibly be raised against it. Part III argues that the Court's decision in *United States v Arizona* is best understood as nothing less than a rejection of enforcement redundancy in the context of immigration law. Part IV evaluates this rejection and explores its implications for the future of immigration law.

I. What Is Redundant Enforcement?

Legal rules typically need to be enforced by someone. In most classic treatments of law, that someone is a monolithic state. But this stylized understanding is far from reality. The state is a they, not an it, with myriad officials who could be involved in the enforcement of legal rules. In federal systems, the number of states is multiplied. Beyond the state itself, private parties are also available as agents of enforcement.

The proliferation of available agents raises an important question of institutional design: which agent or agents should do the enforcing? A public agent might be chosen, or instead a private one. In federal systems, there is a choice between state and federal officials. And, of course, more than just one agent could be chosen: rather than giving an enforcement monopoly to a single agent, many agents might be involved, either jointly or independently, in the task of enforcing a legal rule. This can facilitate either a cooperative or a competitive environment of enforcement.

Several large literatures are concerned, either directly or indirectly, with the question of which institutional arrangements are optimal in which settings. These include scholarship on private attorneys general,[2] federalism,[3] and administrative law,[4] as well as more general scholarship like that prompted by Gary Becker and George Stigler's classic piece on the private enforcement of law.[5] This work confirms the wide array of potential advantages and disadvantages of different arrangements: for example, private enforcement can lead to higher (and more efficient) levels of enforcement, or it can lead to insufficient enforcement because of free-riding problems; it can put enforcement power in the hands of those with superior information about the existence of legal violations, or it can empower those more likely to make mistakes in meting out punishments; it can reduce agency slack within government and thus help perfect democracy, or it can undermine the responsiveness and accountability of enforcement efforts and thus distort democracy.[6]

Whatever theoretical case might be made for one approach or another in any particular context, in practice monopolistic enforcement is much less common than one might expect. To be sure, there are parts of the criminal law where a single state actor—like a local district attorney—has a meaningful monopoly on enforcement within a particular jurisdiction.[7] Relatedly, some legal rules are typically enforced only by the injured private party. Classic tort and

---

[2] See, for example, Jerry L. Mashaw, *Private Enforcement of Public Regulatory Provisions: The "Citizen Suit,"* 4 Class Action Reports 29 (1975); Jeremy A. Rabkin, *The Secret Life of the Private Attorney General*, 61 L & Contemp Probs 179 (1998).

[3] See, for example, Roderick M. Hills, *The Political Economy of Cooperative Federalism: Why State Autonomy Makes Sense and "Dual Sovereignty" Doesn't*, 96 Mich L Rev 813 (1998); Heather K. Gerken and Jessica Bulman-Pozen, *Uncooperative Federalism*, 118 Yale L J 1256 (2009).

[4] See, for example, Jacob E. Gersen, *Overlapping and Underlapping Jurisdiction in Administrative Law*, 2006 Supreme Court Review 201; Jonathan R. Macey, *Organizational Design and Political Control of Administrative Agencies*, 8 J Law Econ & Org 93 (1992).

[5] See Gary Becker and George Stigler, *Law Enforcement, Malfeasance, and Compensation of Enforcers*, 3 J Legal Stud 1 (1974). For critical responses and extensions of the basic idea, see William M. Landes and Richard A. Posner, *The Private Enforcement of Law*, 4 J Legal Stud 1 (1975); A. Mitchell Polinsky, *Private versus Public Enforcement of Fines*, 9 J Legal Stud 105 (1980).

[6] For a summary of these arguments, see Matthew C. Stephenson, *Public Regulation of Private Enforcement: The Case for Expanding the Role of Administrative Agencies*, 91 Va L Rev 94 (2005); Polinksy, 9 J Legal Stud 105 (cited in note 5).

[7] Of course, even here things are more complicated than they might initially seem. Criminal law involves at least three partially distinct institutions—the police, the prosecutors, and the courts—that each play roles in enforcing criminal law. See, for example, Daniel Richman, *Prosecutors and Their Agents, Agents and Their Prosecutors*, 103 Colum L Rev 749 (2003). In an important sense, then, there are essentially no situations in modern legal systems where a legal rule is truly enforced by a single actor.

contract claims of the sort taught to first-year law students are a good example. But many, many legal rules are enforced simultaneously by more than one enforcement agent. Simultaneous enforcement by both public and private parties, for example, is common in environmental law, securities law, antitrust, and many other arenas.[8]

For present purposes, I want to emphasize the prevalence of a different sort of simultaneous enforcement—where both state and federal actors participate in enforcement. In our federal system, enforcement redundancy is the norm. States and the federal government often participate in enforcing the same legal norms.

Enforcement redundancy is most widely noticed and discussed when the federal government tries to encourage or coerce states to enforce federal law. Compelling states to serve as enforcement agents is now prohibited by the anticommandeering rule. So, for example, Congress cannot force state officials to do things like perform federal background checks for gun purchasers, and it probably cannot force local law enforcement officials to hold immigration violators who otherwise would be released from county jails.[9] But the anticommandeering rule does not prevent Congress from inviting state officials to serve as enforcement agents, and Congress often does so. The enforcement role states are asked to play varies widely. Sometimes states are integrated deeply into a regulatory regime created by the federal government. For example, the Affordable Care Act authorizes states to set up health care exchanges to enforce the insurance carriage provisions of the new federal health care law.[10] In other cases state actors play the same role that might be played by private parties. This is the case for many federal consumer protection laws, which deputize state officials as enforcement agents by creating private rights of actions that permit those officials to sue (typically, though not always, in federal court) to

---

[8] See Margaret H. Lemos, *State Enforcement of Federal Law*, 86 NYU L Rev 698, 700 (2011).

[9] See *Printz v United States*, 529 US 898, 933 (1997); *ACLU Files Lawsuit Against Los Angeles County Sheriff's Department*, ACLU (Oct 19, 2012), online at http://www.aclu.org/immigrants-rights/aclu-files-lawsuit-against-los-angeles-county-sheriffs-department; Mary E. O'Leary, *Yale Law School Immigration Clinic Files Class Action Lawsuit Challenging Secure Communities Detainers*, New Haven Register, Feb 22, 2012, online at http://www.nhregister.com/articles/2012/02/22/news/doc4f45623a99923180233858.txt.

[10] See Abbe R. Gluck, *Intrastatutory Federalism and Statutory Interpretation: State Implementation of Federal Law in Health Reform and Beyond*, 121 Yale L J 534, 581 (2011) (describing health insurance exchanges created by the Affordable Care Act).

enforce federal law.[11] Interestingly, a fair amount of this sort of redundant enforcement is authorized even in situations where the federal government has explicitly preempted state lawmaking authority.[12]

While enforcement redundancy is most widely noticed when explicitly authorized, most redundant enforcement by states is never expressly authorized by Congress. One type occurs when a state penalizes conduct that also violates federal law. This is very common in our federal system, in both the criminal and civil arenas. Consider, for example, drug offenses. Every state prohibits possession of cocaine with intent to distribute it.[13] So does the federal government.[14] Thus, two different sets of agents—one set state and one set federal—enforce the same formal legal norm. To be sure, these enforcement agents may have different priorities and resources, and there is no reason to think that they will enforce the ban on cocaine distribution in the same fashion or contexts. That is, of course, precisely the point of the large literature on picking enforcement agents—that different ways of institutionalizing the enforcement of *the same legal norm* will produce different patterns of enforcement. But it is, nonetheless, redundant enforcement as I have defined it: a situation in which the same legal rule is enforced by both states and the federal government. And while drug enforcement is one of the most obvious criminal law examples, there are many others, including gun laws, prohibitions against the possession of child pornography, and so on.[15]

Outside the criminal context, state law often also makes illegal, and subject to civil sanction, conduct identical to that prohibited by federal law. Consider state antidiscrimination laws. Most states prohibit discrimination on the basis of race and sex in the employment context, just as the federal government does under Title

---

[11] Lemos, 86 NYU L Rev at 760–61 (cited in note 8); Harold J. Krent, *Fragmenting the Unitary Executive: Congressional Delegations of Administrative Authority Outside the Federal Government*, 85 Nw U L Rev 62, 80–84 (1990).

[12] Lemos, 86 NYU L Rev at 703 (cited in note 8).

[13] See, for example, Cal Health & Safety Code §§ 11055, 11351 (West 2012); NY Penal Law § 220.06 (McKinney 2003); NY Pub Health Law § 3306 (McKinney 2013).

[14] See 21 USC § 841.

[15] Compare 18 USC § 2252A with Va Code Ann § 18.2-374.1:1 (West 2012) and Ala Code § 13A-12-192 (2013) (criminalizing possession of child pornography); compare 18 USC § 922(d)(1) with NC Gen Stat § 14-415.1(a) (2013) and Or Rev Stat § 166.270(1) (2012) (criminalizing possession of a firearm by a felon).

VII of the 1964 Civil Rights Act.[16] Some state antidiscrimination laws sweep more broadly, defining discrimination in a more expansive fashion,[17] or permitting larger damage awards for the same misconduct.[18] But large parts of many state laws seek to enforce the same legal norm—the same primary rules of conduct—as does federal law.[19] States even sometimes directly incorporate the federal antidiscrimination rules by reference: state courts enforcing state antidiscrimination law frequently conclude that the law tracks Title VII, and therefore rely on federal case law interpreting Title VII in order to resolve state-law employment discrimination suits.[20]

---

[16] See, for example, Cal Govt Code § 12940 (Deering 1980); Mich Comp Laws Ann § 37.2204(a) (Supp 1982); NY Exec Law § 296 (McKinney 1982). See also Andrea Cantania, *State Employment Discrimination Remedies and Pendent Jurisdiction Under Title VII: Access to Federal Courts*, 32 Am U L Rev 777, 784 (1983).

[17] State law may do this either by adding additional protected classifications, such as sexual orientation, or by defining discrimination on the basis of race or sex to include behavior that would not be prohibited by Title VII. On the former, see, for example, DC Code Ann § 1-2512(a) (1981) (sexual preference); Mass Gen Laws Ann ch 151B, § 4(9A) (West 1976) (history of treatment for mental disorder); Mich Stat Ann § 3.548(202) (Callaghan Supp 1981) (weight); Cantania, 32 Am U L Rev at 784 n 27 (cited in note 16). On the latter, see, for example, *Goodyear Tire & Rubber Co. v Dept. of Indus. Labor & Human Relations*, 87 Wisc 2d 56, 273 NW2d 786 (Ct App 1978) (holding that the exclusion of pregnancy from disability benefits plan violates the Wisconsin fair employment practices act even though it does not violate federal law). In addition to having broader substantive provisions, state antidiscrimination laws also sometimes have broader scope, reaching small employers not covered by federal law. See, for example, Alaska Stat § 18.80.300 (1999); Ark Code Ann § 16-123-102 (1993); Del Code Ann title 19, § 710 (1998); Iowa Code § 216.6 (2009).

[18] Some state antidiscrimination laws permit compensatory and punitive damages, while Title VII authorizes only equitable relief. See Cantania, 32 Am U L Rev at 784 (cited in note 16). Compare 42 USC § 2000e-5(g) with Fla Stat § 725.07 (1981); Mich Comp Laws Ann § 37.2801 (West Supp 1981); NY Exec Law § 297(4)(c)(iii) (McKinney 1982).

[19] Of course, the ability (and often obligation) of state courts to adjudicate many federal causes of action—including those that arise under Title VII—means that state courts will sometimes act identically regardless of whether state law includes antidiscrimination provisions that track Title VII. See *Testa v Katt*, 330 US 386 (1947) (obligating state courts in many cases to enforce federal law); *Yellow Freight System v Donnelly*, 494 US 820 (1990) (holding that state courts have concurrent jurisdiction over Title VII causes of action). But this simply shows another way in which redundant enforcement of federal legal norms is even more pervasive than we often notice. State courts operate pervasively to enforce federal law that is also enforced by federal courts.

[20] See, for example, *Valenzuela v Globe Ground North America*, 18 So 3d 17 (Fla 3d DCA 2009) (concluding that, because the Florida state law is patterned after Title VII, federal case law is authoritative—right down to federal case law's *McDonnell Douglas* burden-shifting framework of proof in employment discrimination cases); *Williams v Wal-Mart Stores*, 184 SW3d 492, 495 (Ky 2005) (stating that Kentucky courts have "consistently interpreted the civil rights provisions of [Kentucky state law] consistent with the applicable federal antidiscrimination laws"); *Kings v Phelps Dunar*, 743 So 2d 181, 187 (La 1999) (stating that "Louisiana courts have looked to federal jurisprudence to interpret Louisiana discrimination laws" because they are "similar in scope"); *Schroeder v Texas Iron Works*, 813 SW2d 483 (Tex 1991) (stating that the Texas state employment discrimination statute

Nor is antidiscrimination law an outlier. Across many regulatory areas—from antitrust to education law—state and federal law frequently prohibit identical conduct.[21] This overlap even extends to constitutional law. Many states incorporate federal constitutional norms by reference, interpreting the individual rights guarantees in their state constitutions to be coextensive with the federal guarantees.[22] In Ohio, for example, courts have held that the state constitution's protection of free speech should be interpreted to be identical to the First Amendment of the U.S. Constitution.[23]

Another type of redundant enforcement occurs when state officials participate in the enforcement of federal law even though the state *does not* formally prohibit the same conduct as does federal law. This occurs most commonly when state and local law enforcement officials make arrests for violations of federal law. When federal law criminalizes certain conduct—and authorizes federal officials to arrest people who engage in that conduct—state law also often authorizes state and local officials to make arrests for those very same violations of federal criminal law. In many instances arrests by state or local law enforcement are triggered by the existence

---

was patterned after Title VII), overruled on other grounds by *In re United Services Automobile Assn.*, 307 SW3d 299 (Tex 2010).

[21] See, for example, Barry E. Hawk and James D. Veltrop, *Dual Antitrust Enforcement in the United States: Positive or Negative Lessons for the European Community*, in Slot and McDonnell, eds, *Proceedings of the Leiden Europa Instituut Seminar on User-Friendly Competition Law* 21, 28 (1993) ("Many state [antitrust] statutes provide that they are to be interpreted consistently with federal precedent and most are generally so interpreted."); Minn HR Research Dept, Information Brief on *Federal and State Laws Governing Access to Student Records* (2000), online at http://www.house.leg.state.mn.us/hrd/pubs/studrec.pdf (discussing how the Minnesota statutes "largely parallel [Family Educational Rights and Privacy Act] FERPA provisions" and noting that "a number of subdivisions specifically incorporate FERPA provisions by referring to federal statutory citations in the state law").

[22] See, for example, *Love v Borough of Stroudsburg*, 597 A2d 1137 (Pa 1991) (equal protection provision); *State v Robinette*, 685 NE2d 762 (Ohio 1997) (searches and seizures). See generally Robert F. Williams, *State Courts Adopting Federal Constitutional Doctrine: Case-by-Case Adoptionism or Prospective Lockstepping*, 47 Wm & Mary L Rev 1499, 1502 (2005); James A. Gardner, *The Positivist Revolution That Wasn't: Constitutional Universalism in the States*, 4 Roger Williams U L Rev 109 (1998) (arguing that the convergence of state and federal constitutional doctrines is in part the "natural continuation of a long, powerful tradition on the state level of constitutional universalism"); James A. Gardner and Jim Rossi, *Foreword* to *New Frontiers of State Constitutional Law* (Oxford, 2009); *Developments in the Law—The Interpretation of State Constitutional Rights*, 95 Harv L Rev 1324, 1348 (1982) ("More often, the [state] court legitimates its holding either by matching the state law result with a corresponding result under federal law or by incorporating federal law doctrine into state constitutional analysis.").

[23] See, for example, *Eastwood Mall, Inc. v Slanco*, 626 NE2d 59 (Ohio 1994) (holding that the "free speech guarantees accorded by the Ohio Constitution are no broader than the First Amendment, and that the First Amendment is the proper basis of interpretation.").

of a federal warrant for the person apprehended.[24] This often happens in traffic stops: a local police officer stops a person for speeding, discovers that the person has an outstanding federal arrest warrant, and arrests the person.[25] Moreover, state and local arrest authority is often much broader. Even in the absence of an outstanding warrant, many states authorize arrests for violations of federal criminal law.[26]

In any of the above examples of redundant enforcement, some might quibble about what, exactly, counts as state enforcement rather than federal. When state officials make an arrest for a violation of federal law, it is ultimately federal prosecutors who decide whether to proceed with the case, and it is a federal court which ultimately will resolve the guilt or innocence of the accused. Similarly, when state attorneys general file civil actions to enforce consumer protection laws, those suits are often litigated (and sometimes are required by federal statute to be litigated) in federal court. Thus, state agents are not enforcing the federal legal norm all by themselves.

---

[24] Where a federal warrant has issued, courts historically have interpreted Federal Rule of Criminal Procedure 4, along with 18 USC § 3041, as authorizing state and local law enforcement officers to execute federal warrants. See *United States v Bowdach*, 561 F2d 1160, 1167–68 (1977); *Gill v United States*, 421 F2d 1353, 1355 (1970); Fed R Crim P 4 ("only a marshal *or other authorized officer* may execute a warrant"); 18 USC § 3041 (authorizing many different officials, including local judges and mayors, to authorize the arrest of an offender for "any offense against the United States"). These officers must also, of course, be authorized by state law to make an arrest under the circumstances. See *People v LaFontaine*, 92 NY2d 470 (1998).

[25] Local officers regularly use the FBI's National Crime Information Center database to check for outstanding warrants and many other sorts of information indicating that a person is wanted by law enforcement. See National Crime Information Center, online at http://www.fbi.gov/about-us/cjis/ncic.

[26] See, for example, Conn Gen Stat §§ 53a-24(a), 54 (2013) (authorizing arrest for violation of any criminal offense within the state, regardless of whether the offense is a violation of the law of that state, the law of another state, or federal law). In a series of cases, federal courts upheld the authority of state officers to make warrantless arrests for federal crimes under similar provisions of state law. See *Marsh v United States*, 29 F2d 172 (2d Cir 1928); *United States v Di Re*, 332 US 581 (1948); *Johnson v United States*, 333 US 10, 15 (1948). In those cases, decided around the time that *Erie R.R. v Tompkins* was handed down, the Court struggled with the question of what law authorized and regulated these arrest practices: were they regulated by uniform federal common law, there being no general federal statute governing warrantless arrests for federal offenses? Or were the officers regulated by state laws relating to arrest authority? Over time, the Court came to conclude that in the absence of a federal statute, state law governed—perhaps an unsurprising conclusion given *Erie*'s impact on constitutional law in this period. See *Di Ri*, 332 US at 581, 589–90 (rejecting the idea that there is "any general federal law of arrest"). Thus, if a state officer makes a warrantless arrest for a federal offense, it will be upheld so long as it accords with state law and, of course, whatever requirements the Constitution imposes. See *Marsh*, 29 F2d at 714; *Di Re*, 332 US at 589–91; *Miller v United States*, 357 US 301, 305–06 (1958).

But the same thing could be said about the private enforcement of the law. What others mean when they talk about choosing private agents to enforce the law—as in debates about "private attorneys general"—is never that a private party will enforce a legal rule *without any state intervention.* The most commonly discussed form of private enforcement is a civil suit by an injured private party in a court system run by the state. Another form of "private enforcement," qui tam litigation, often involves even more participation by government officials, as they are frequently permitted to intervene in or otherwise control the lawsuit after it is filed.[27] Thus, in most modern states it will seldom be the case that the choice of enforcement agents includes the option of having a single human agent—private or public—hold a literal monopoly on enforcement; enforcement almost inevitably involves the participation of more than one agent. But that does not mean that there is no meaningful distinction between different combinations of enforcement agents, or that it is incoherent to talk about the choice between public and private enforcement. And for that reason, the involvement of federal officials in some of my examples above does not lessen the sense in which they constitute instances of redundant enforcement by states.

II. THE CONSTITUTIONAL STATUS OF ENFORCEMENT REDUNDANCY

There are two obvious questions we might ask about redundant enforcement of federal law by states. First, is it desirable? Second, is it constitutional? The first question is a hugely important one, but one that I want to bracket here. As I mentioned above, there is already a large, and largely inconclusive, theoretical literature on the choice of enforcement agents. Which actors have the best incentives and information, whether an enforcement monopoly produces under- or overdeterrence, whether nonfederal enforcement can improve the political functioning of the federal government (by reducing agency slack, shaping the federal agenda, and so on) are all important and difficult questions—questions for which pure theory is unlikely to provide conclusive answers.

Instead, I want to note here that, whatever the optimal structure

---

[27] See *False Claims Act Cases: Government Intervention in Qui Tam (Whistleblower) Suits,* US Dept of Justice, online at http://www.justice.gov/usao/pae/Civil_Division/Internet Whistleblower%20update.pdf; 31 USC §§ 3730(b)(4)(A), (c), 3731(c) (laying out the statutory framework for the intervention of the DOJ in False Claims Act litigation).

of enforcement, redundant enforcement by states is widely accepted as constitutional. That is not to say, of course, that it is universally accepted. There are two obvious constitutional concerns that enforcement redundancy might trigger: that it violates principles of federalism on the one hand, and principles of separation of powers on the other.

Consider constitutional norms of federalism first. Most everyone believes that Congress has the authority to explicitly authorize states to enforce federal law (even though it cannot compel them to do so). Moreover, even in the absence of any congressional authorization or delegation, few question the constitutionality of state measures that provide for redundant enforcement. The authority of state and local officials to make arrests for federal offenses is uniformly accepted.[28] No one thinks that the creation of federal drug laws rendered unconstitutional state laws criminalizing the same conduct, or that state employment discrimination statutes are ousted by federal statutes covering the same ground. In other words, enforcement redundancy is the conventional default position in most regulatory arenas.

This does not mean Congress cannot alter the default. Were Congress prohibited from depriving states of their power of redundant enforcement, enforcement redundancy would be a constitutional entitlement of states. Such an enforcement entitlement is conceivable. It would operate as a kind of compliment to the anticommandeering doctrine in modern federalism jurisprudence: the anticommandeering doctrine prohibits Congress from *conscripting* states as enforcement agents;[29] a state entitlement to engage in redundant enforcement would prohibit the national government from *excluding* states from participating in the enforcement of federal law. That said, there is little or no support in modern federalism jurisprudence for such a rule. Instead, the Supremacy Clause is conventionally understood to empower the federal government in many regulatory arenas to oust states entirely and monopolize enforcement for itself.

Ordinarily, of course, Congress is silent about redundant enforcement. In those cases, as I have said, constitutional law typically

---

[28] See notes 24–26 and accompanying text above.

[29] See *Printz v United States*, 521 US 898 (1997); *New York v United States*, 505 US 144 (1992); see also Evan H. Caminker, *State Sovereignty and Subordinacy: May Congress Commandeer State Officers to Implement Federal Law?*, 95 Colum L Rev 1001 (1995).

treats enforcement redundancy as the norm. But why this is the accepted convention in our federal system is far from obvious. Most modern accounts of the Supremacy Clause—in preemption doctrine and elsewhere—emphasize that the permissibility of state law turns on whether that law creates a "conflict" with federal law. Where a conflict arises, state law must give way to superior federal law. Seen through this lens, there are two polar opposite perspectives one might take toward enforcement redundancy:

- On the one hand, one might say that state enforcement of federal law could not possibly create a conflict between state and federal law. State law literally duplicates federal law, enforcing precisely the same legal rule. On this account, redundant enforcement presents the clearest case against preemption one can imagine, because there is no conceptual space between state and federal law.
- On the other hand, one might say that state enforcement of federal law inevitably creates a conflict between state and federal law. State law piles on an additional sanction when it prohibits conduct already prohibited by federal law. And states ratchet up the likelihood of imposing a sanction when they authorize state officials to enforce federal law, by making arrests for federal crimes, by suing in court to enforce federal rules, or by engaging in any other enforcement-related behavior. Altering either the sanction or the probability of sanction, one might conclude, amounts to changing federal law.

Which of these accounts is more persuasive? Notice that what separates them is their conception of law. The first account conceptualizes law—for purposes of thinking about intergovernmental conflict and preemption—as centrally about the formal obligations imposed by legal rules. The content of the legal rule is marked by the scope of obligation, irrespective of the particular sanction that may or may not follow from failing to obey the legal rule. On that understanding, if a state imposes a legal obligation that is identical to the legal obligation imposed by the federal government, there can be no conflict between the state and federal law.[30] Thus, instances of redundant enforcement are preserved from preemption.

[30] A slightly different way to conceptualize this is to say that the law-as-obligation idea assumes that the world would be best if there were perfect compliance with legal rules. I rely a bit on this related idea below.

In contrast, the second account conceptualizes law in a way that is typical within the law-and-economics tradition: as a "price" for engaging in particular conduct.[31] This view, associated most famously with Oliver Wendell Holmes, treats the state's sanction as nothing more than the price for doing what would otherwise be prohibited.[32] More precisely, the price for engaging in particular conduct is the expected sanction, which is equal to the sanction for doing what is prohibited multiplied by the likelihood that the sanction will be applied. On this account, *anything* a state does that alters the total sanction or the probability of sanction for particular conduct alters the content of the law. Thus, when a state criminalizes conduct that is also criminalized under federal law, or when it authorizes arrests for violations of federal law, the state's actions always conflict with federal law: those actions change the content of federal law by altering either the sanction or the likelihood of punishment.

Seen in this light, it is easy to see why courts have not (and cannot plausibly) embrace the law-as-price approach when thinking about federalism and preemption. Consider what would happen if they did unequivocally embrace this view: across sweeping domains, there would be literally *no* space for state regulation. Once the federal government adopted a particular legal prohibition, such as a prohibition on the possession of cocaine, anything a state did to enforce that prohibition would change the expected sanction. The adoption of federal drug laws would thus necessitate the preemption of state drug laws, and even prohibit efforts by state officials to arrest persons in violation of federal drug laws. In short, states would be neutered in any arena into which the federal government stepped. Such a rule would replicate the vision of dual sovereignty imagined by *Gibbons v Ogden*,[33] in which states and the federal government operated in mutually exclusive regulatory spheres. The implausibility of this vision, which even in the *Gibbons* era did not accurately describe the practice of American federalism, explains why it has little purchase on the way courts typically think about enforcement redundancy.

Before proceeding, recall that federalism concerns were not the only constitutional concern one might have about enforcement re-

---

[31] See, for example, Robert Cooter, *Prices and Sanctions*, 84 Colum L Rev 1523 (1984).

[32] See Oliver Wendell Holmes, *The Path of the Law*, 10 Harv L Rev 457 (1897).

[33] 22 US 1 (1824).

dundancy. One might also worry that it is inconsistent with important separation-of-powers principles. Article II vests the "executive power" exclusively in the president of the United States and directs that the president "shall take care that the laws be faithfully executed."[34] Over the past few decades, some have argued that this language makes clear that the Constitution establishes a "unitary executive." While belief in a unitary executive might mean many things, a number of prominent scholars and judges have contended that it means that the Constitution makes the president of the United States a single human agent to whom all control over (and responsibility for) the execution of federal law must ultimately be traced.[35] While this understanding is controversial, if taken seriously it precludes anyone other than the president or his subordinates from enforcing federal law.

Interestingly, those who subscribe to the unitary executive hypothesis frequently overlook the pervasiveness of redundant enforcement within our federal system. Some of this can be chalked up to their formalist priors. They likely would not consider some forms of enforcement redundancy, such as a state's prohibiting conduct identical to that prohibited by federal law, to implicate Article II at all, on the ground that the states are enforcing a state rather than a federal legal rule—albeit legal rules with content identical to federal law, and sometimes drawn specifically from federal law.[36] But other redundant enforcement practices, such as qui tam suits filed by state officials, are harder to ignore.[37] In such cases, unitary executive theorists have sometimes tried to explain how such practices remain subject to presidential control, though there is also the

---

[34] US Const, Art II, § 1, 3.

[35] See, for example, Steven G. Calabresi and Christopher S. Yoo, *The Unitary Executive: Presidential Power from Washington to Bush* 51–52 (2008); Steven G. Calabresi and Saikrishna B. Prakash, *The President's Power to Execute the Laws*, 104 Yale L J 541 (1995); Harold J. Krent, *Separating the Strands in Separation of Powers Controversies*, 74 Va L Rev 1253 (1988); *Morrison v Olsen*, 487 US 654, 705 (1989) (Scalia, J, dissenting). For an argument that the idea of a unitary executive does not entail the requirement that the president control all the implementation of the laws, see Cass Sunstein, *Article II Revisionism*, 92 Mich L Rev 132, 135 (1993).

[36] See Evan Caminker, *The Unitary Executive and State Administration of Federal Law*, 45 U Ka L Rev 1075, 1102–03 (1997).

[37] See id; Calabresi and Prakash, 104 Yale L J at 661 (cited in note 35) ("Without going into great detail, suffice it to say that *qui tam* actions are rather problematic."); Harold J. Krent and Ethan G. Shenkman, *Of Citizen Suits and Citizen Sunstein*, 91 Mich L Rev 1793, 1820–21 (1993) (suggesting qui tam suits raise Article II problems—though perhaps not fatal ones given the existing level of executive control over such suits).

frequent suggestion that such practices are at worst an "extremely limited exception to the rule of presidential control of all aspects of" federal law enforcement.[38]

Far from being an extremely limited exception, the practice of redundant enforcement creates a deep and pervasive conflict with the rule of absolute presidential control. Consider the enforcement of federal criminal law. As Justice Scalia, the theory's leading proponent on the bench, argued in his famous dissent in *Morrison v Olsen*: "the conduct of a criminal prosecution (and of an investigation to decide whether to prosecute) [is] the exercise of purely executive power" and that, as a consequence, the president must have "exclusive control over the exercise of that power."[39] This categorical view that the president must have absolute control over criminal investigations would preclude state officials from participating in the enforcement of federal criminal law, since these officials are not within what Justice Scalia would understand to be the "exclusive control" of the president. To be sure, this theory of absolute control appears to contradict widespread historical practice, as state officials and even private citizens have participated in the enforcement of federal criminal law from the founding period forward.[40] And perhaps the theory itself is not perfectly pure: after all, Justice Scalia argued in his *Arizona* dissent that state officers should be able to investigate violations of federal immigration law

---

[38] See Calabresi and Prakash, 104 Yale L J at 661 (cited in note 35) ("At most, English practice suggests that *qui tam* actions can be understood as but an extremely limited exception to the rule of presidential control of all aspects of prosecution. This exception is hardly fatal to the rule of presidential superintendence of federal and state prosecutors."); Calabresi and Yoo, *The Unitary Executive* at 51–52 (cited in note 35) (arguing that "there is no reason to think [President] Washington could not have extinguished any privately brought qui tam actions during his tenure as president had he chosen to do so.").

[39] *Morrison v Olsen*, 487 US 654, 705 (1989) (Scalia, J, dissenting). Justice Scalia went on to say that "the President's constitutionally assigned duties include *complete control* over investigation and prosecution of violations of the law, and that the inexorable command of Article II is clear and definite: the executive power must be vested in the President of the United States." Id at 710 (emphasis added).

[40] See Harold J. Krent, *Executive Control Over Criminal Law Enforcement: Some Lessons from History*, 38 Am U L Rev 275, 278 (1988) (discussing founding era participation in criminal enforcement by private parties and state officials, and concluding that the delegation of some criminal law enforcement powers to nonexecutive actors does not violate separation-of-powers principles because "at least from a historical perspective, criminal law enforcement cannot be considered a core or exclusive power of the executive branch."); but see Calabresi and Yoo, *The Unitary Executive* at 50 (cited in note 35) (disagreeing with Krent about whether the president in the founding period exercised control over state prosecutors and federal district attorneys who enforced federal law). See also notes 23–26 above (discussing widespread practice of arrests by state officers for federal offenses); Sunstein, 92 Mich L Rev at 134–35 (cited in note 35).

and make arrests for suspected violations. Nonetheless, for those who take the theory seriously, this understanding of the unitary executive is in deep tension with Arizona's efforts to participate in the enforcement of federal immigration law.

For theorists who subscribe to such a strong version of the unitary executive, there are only two solutions to this Article II problem: prohibit states across the board from engaging in redundant enforcement, or bring state actors under the direct supervision of the president. Either solution would require a radical change in existing constitutional norms. The first would wipe out widespread state practices and move our pervasively cooperative federalism sharply in the direction of *Gibbons v Ogden*'s mythical world of completely separate spheres of action for states and the federal government. The second is no less dramatic: it would empower the president to directly control state officials. As Evan Caminker has persuasively argued, meaningful supervisory power over state officials would, for those who subscribe to the unitary executive theory, almost surely require the power to fire these officials for insubordination.[41] (The power to fire is precisely the power these theorists argue the president must have in order to control the federal bureaucracy, and it is the absence of this authority that grounds their claim that independent agencies are unconstitutional.) But giving the president the power to remove state officials is unfathomable in a doctrinal landscape that includes a prohibition on the federal government "commandeering" state officials. This conclusion makes it all the more remarkable that Justice Scalia supports the power of Arizonian officials to enforce federal immigration law.[42]

In short, therefore, there are available theories on which redundant enforcement by states might violate either federalism or separation-of-powers principles. Yet accepting these theories would have radical implications for the structure of federal-state relations.

---

[41] See Caminker, 45 U Ka L Rev at 1088–91 (cited in note 36); *Morrison v Olsen*, 487 US at 715 (Scalia, J, dissenting) (concluding that the independent counsel statute was unconstitutional in part because it restricted the president's power to remove the independent counsel).

[42] To be sure, Justice Scalia believes that Arizona has the authority to craft its own immigration law as well—and likely sees this as an important (if formalistic) distinction that avoids certain Article II issues. See *Arizona*, 132 S Ct at 2511–13. But even when he puts aside this possibility and considers directly the possibility that state officials will enforce federal law, he is surprisingly unconcerned about the Article II obstacles that figure so prominently in the rest of his jurisprudence.

It is unsurprising, therefore, that our existing constitutional norms generally accept enforcement redundancy.

III. Arizona's Rejection of Enforcement Redundancy

The preceding discussion makes the federal government's position in the Arizona litigation look pretty anemic.

Arizona's SB 1070 looks like a classic example of enforcement redundancy. Sections 3 and 5 of the act track the first form of redundancy I focused on above: these provisions prohibit conduct already proscribed by federal law. Section 3 prohibits the "willful failure to complete or carry an alien registration document . . . in violation of 8 United States Code section 1304(e) or 1306(a)."[43] The provision literally incorporates the federal prohibition by reference. As the Supreme Court itself described, this provision "adds a state-law penalty for conduct proscribed by federal law."[44] Similarly, Section 5(C) prohibits noncitizens without work authorization from working in Arizona, conduct already barred by federal immigration law.[45] Sections 2 and 6 track the second form of redundant enforcement I emphasized earlier: rather than prohibit any conduct directly, these provisions authorize law enforcement officials to participate in the enforcement of federal law by investigating and making arrests for suspected violations. Section 2(B) requires that state law enforcement officers check the immigration status of some non-

---

[43] Ariz Rev Stat Ann § 11-1509(A) (West Supp 2011).

[44] *Arizona*, 132 S Ct 2501.

[45] See Ariz Rev Stat Ann § 13-2928(C) (forbidding "an unauthorized alien to knowingly apply for work, solicit work in a public place or perform work as an employee or independent contractor"). The INA forbids noncitizens without work authorization from working in the United States through a complex combination of statutory provisions. Lawful permanent residents ("LPRs") are in effect given permanent and unlimited work authorization as a matter of federal law. Lawful *nonimmigrants*—that is, those who enter the country on temporary visas—are eligible to work only in accordance with the terms of their visas, and become deportable if they violate the terms of those visas. See INA § 237(a)(1)(C). Those who enter the country without any authorization or fall out of status after entering may also obtain work authorization, even before they receive a visa that regularizes their immigration status, but that authorization must be affirmatively granted by the government. Such authorizations are most frequently provided to noncitizens working their way through the asylum process, or waiting to adjust their status to that of an LPR on the basis of marriage to an American citizen. See, for example, INA §§ 208, 245; 8 CFR 208.7. Recently, however, such authorizations have also been provided to noncitizens who are eligible for new Obama administration programs such as Deferred Action for Childhood Arrivals. See Memorandum from Janet Napolitano, *Exercising Prosecutorial Discretion with Respect to Individuals Who Came to the United States as Children* (June 15, 2012), online at http://www.dhs.gov/xlibrary/assets/s1-exercising-prosecutorial-discretion-individuals-who-came-to-us-as-children.pdf.

citizens they encounter in their ordinary law enforcement duties.[46] Section 6 authorizes the arrest of a noncitizen on probable cause that she is deportable for being in violation of the criminal deportability grounds of immigration law.[47] Suspected deportability is also an arrestable offense under the Immigration and Nationality Act.[48]

In short, Arizona's SB 1070 sought to use state officials to enforce the same legal prohibitions that are already a part of federal immigration law. This is part of what made the Arizona litigation so different from the canonical cases of immigration federalism. These cases—lawsuits like *Chy Lung v Freeman*[49] and *Hines v Davidowitz*[50]—did not involve redundant enforcement. Instead they involved state laws imposing legal obligations different, or entirely absent, from federal law. Consider *Chy Lung*. That case concerned a California law authorizing state immigration inspectors to deny admission to several classes of immigrants—among them certain criminals and "lewd and debauched women"—unless the master of the ship transporting those immigrants paid a bond to indemnify the state.[51] At the time California passed the law, there was no federal statute requiring such bonds, and in fact no federal exclusion law of any kind.[52] So there was no sense in which California was enforcing legal norms also imposed by the federal government.[53]

---

[46] See Ariz Rev Stat Ann § 11-1051(B) (West 2012) (requiring officers to make a "reasonable attempt . . . to determine the immigration status" of any person they stop, detain, or arrest on some other legitimate basis if "reasonable suspicion exists that the person is an alien and is unlawfully present in the United States."). See also id ("Any person who is arrested shall have the person's immigration status determined before the person is released.").

[47] Section 6 provides that a state officer "without a warrant, may arrest a person if the officer has probable cause to believe . . . [the person] has committed any public offense that makes [her] removable from the United States." Ariz Rev Stat Ann § 13-3883(A)(5).

[48] See INA § 236(a).

[49] 92 US 275 (1876).

[50] 312 US 52 (1941).

[51] See *Chy Lung*, 92 US at 277.

[52] California enacted the provisions at issue in 1873. See id (citing "c. 1, art. 7, of the Political Code of California, as modified by sec. 70 of the amendments of 1873, 1874"). The first federal exclusion law, the Page Act, was adopted in March of 1875. See An Act Supplementary to the Acts in Relation to Immigration, 43d Cong, 2d Sess, c. 141, 18 Stat 477.

[53] One interesting wrinkle is that the Page Act, which among other things made inadmissible women "imported for the purposes of prostitution," was passed by Congress while *Chy Lung* was pending before the Supreme Court. See *Ex Parte Ah Fook*, 49 Cal 402 (Ca 1874) (noting that the steamer *Japan*, whose passengers filed *Ah Fook* and appealed

Moreover, when the federal government started enacting restrictive immigration laws just a few years later, some of those laws were initially enforced by state officials. The Immigration Act of 1882, for example, "authorized the secretary of the Treasury to 'enter into contracts with such State commission, board, or officers as may be designated for that purpose by the governor of any State' to administer federal immigration policy."[54] The federal government lacked a standing enforcement bureaucracy up to the task, so it relied on state officials. This reinforces the notion that the concern in *Chy Lung* was not about state officials participating in the enforcement of federal law.

Hines was similar. In that case, Pennsylvania set up a mandatory system of alien registration when no such requirement existed under federal law. Among other things, the scheme required every adult noncitizen to register with the state each year, carry an alien registration card at all times, and show the card whenever demanded by any police officer.[55] *Hines*'s posture is complicated a bit by the fact that Congress did pass a registration statute—the Alien Registration Act of 1940—while the litigation was pending.[56] But the federal scheme contained different requirements, and it pointedly did not require that noncitizens carry registration papers on them at all times and show them on demand. This requirement—backed by a criminal penalty in Pennsylvania—was rejected by Congress for being "at war with the fundamental principles of our free government."[57] Even after the enactment of the federal Alien Registration Act, therefore, the concern was that Pennsylvania, far from enforcing federal obligations, was imposing obligations quite deliberately rejected by Congress.

Given the different posture of these earlier cases, as well as the

---

the case to the Supreme Court as *Chy Lung*, arrived in San Francisco in August 1874); Page Act, 18 Stat 477 (enacted March 3, 1875); *Chy Lung*, 92 US 275 (decided during the fall of 1875). But the Court in *Chy Lung* took no notice of the Page Act.

[54] See Hidetaka Hirota, *The Moment of Transition: State Officials, the Federal Government, and the Formation of American Immigration Policy*, J Am Hist 1092, 1099 (2013). See also Lucy Salyer, *Laws Harsh as Tigers: Chinese Immigrants and the Shaping of Modern Immigration Law* 5–6 (1995).

[55] See *Hines*, 312 US at 56.

[56] Alien Registration Act of 1940, Public Act No 670, 76th Cong, 3d Sess, c. 439, 54 Stat 670, 8 USCA s 451 et seq. Unlike in *Chy Lung*, where the Court ignored congressional action that took place while the case was pending, in *Hines* Justice Black took the position that the Court "must therefore pass upon the state Act in the light of the Congressional Act." 312 US at 60.

[57] *Hines*, 312 US at 71.

widespread acceptance of redundant enforcement in American federalism, one might have expected the United States to lose when it sued Arizona. So what happened? Why did the Court side with the federal government and strike down the core provisions of SB 1070? The short answer is that the Court's opinion in *United States v Arizona* rejects the logic of enforcement redundancy.

Consider, for example, the Court's discussion of the provision of SB 1070 that penalizes violations of the federal alien registration law. As I noted above, the Court acknowledges that the provision simply "adds a state-law penalty for conduct proscribed by federal law." Its legal obligations are identical to those imposed by federal law. Nonetheless, the Court finds the provision problematic because it empowers state officials to sanction noncitizens for violating federal immigration law in situations where federal officials have decided (or hypothetically might decide) not to punish the violation on the ground that enforcing the letter of the law would frustrate federal policies: "Were § 3 to come into force, the State would have the power to bring criminal charges against individuals for violating a federal law even in circumstances where federal officials in charge of the comprehensive scheme determine that prosecution would frustrate federal policies."[58] In other words, the problem is that a state official may choose to punish a person for violating the immigration code when a federal official might choose not to do so. But this is, by definition, true in every single instance where more than one agent is empowered to enforce the law. It is the conceptual foundation of the large literature on the choice of enforcement agents. Only by rejecting enforcement redundancy entirely can this "problematic" possibility be avoided.

This line of reasoning is not limited just to an isolated passage; nor is it limited just to the evaluation of Section 3. It is the analytic thread that ties together the entire opinion. Identifying the problem with Section 6, which authorizes state officers to arrest deportable noncitizens, the Court writes in the same vein: "This state authority could be exercised without any input from the Federal Government about whether an arrest is warranted in a particular case," undermining the federal government's ability to make discretionary determinations about whether to arrest a particular noncitizen who

---

[58] *Arizona*, 132 S Ct at 2503.

is in violation of immigration law.[59] The Court is absolutely correct, of course. But the same is also true anytime a state officer arrests a person for a suspected federal criminal violation—authority no one doubts state officers possess even though it may interfere with the discretionary decisions of federal officials.[60]

Implicitly, this reasoning is a rejection of the view that law should be conceptualized as a series of obligations. The majority rejects redundant enforcement in *Arizona* precisely by conceptualizing federal immigration law as a set of prices. On that understanding, even if Arizona mimics perfectly the obligations contained in federal immigration law, that is not enough to save it from preemption. Instead, the "law" against which state action must be compared is every hypothetical action that might influence the "expected sanction" for violating the INA—that is, everything that could conceivably influence either the severity of the sanction or the probability that the sanction is actually imposed for a particular violation.

In other words, every time the Court emphasizes that Arizona's efforts interfere with a careful federal "balance" about immigration law, it is not saying that the state has disrupted the balance by creating legal obligations that the federal government declined to create as part of its carefully crafted scheme. Arizona quite deliberately mimicked the INA's legal obligations precisely to avoid this complaint.[61] Instead, the Court is saying that Arizona has interfered with the balance by attaching an additional sanction to an *identical* legal obligation, or by raising the likelihood that a person will be sanctioned for violating that federal legal obligation. Certainly no court would accept the legal argument that a state prosecution for

[59] Id at 2506; see also id ("§ 6 violates the principle that the removal process is entrusted to the discretion of the Federal Government.").

[60] Note that there are two ways of thinking about this concern—as about preserving policy control on the one hand, and preventing enforcement mistakes on the other. The Court focuses on the former, but the latter is also important. As the literature on the selection of enforcement agents emphasizes, a monopoly on enforcement is sometimes justified by the risk of enforcement mistakes that might arise if other actors (like private parties, or states) are allowed into the enforcement game. See sources cited in notes 2–8 above. The concern that state officials will make mistakes when they try to enforce immigration law is not a trivial one, especially in light of the complexity of immigration law. But this risk is not unique to immigration law; it is present in many of the areas where enforcement redundancy is our constitutional norm. More importantly, the Court's approach makes clear that it would not be comfortable with redundant immigration enforcement even were there no mistakes by states.

[61] Moreover, were misfit of legal obligation the real problem, Arizona could eliminate the concern by being more careful about tracking perfectly federal obligations. Justice Kennedy most definitely does not think this is the case.

cocaine possession should be impermissible whenever federal officials have decided (or hypothetically would decide) to decline to prosecute the possession offense under federal drug laws criminalizing the same conduct. Yet that is the result of the Court's decision in *Arizona*.

If the Court had conceptualized immigration law as a set of obligations rather than prices, then under conventional preemption logic it would have accepted Arizona's efforts for the same reasons that redundant enforcement is typically thought to be fine. It is hard to see how there is a conflict between federal and state law in this traditional sense, because state law proscribes exactly the same conduct as federal law. State action simply serves to increase compliance with federal law—something that should further federal interests to the extent that the letter of federal immigration law embodies a series of obligations that, in the best of worlds, would be followed perfectly.

Moreover, it is hard to argue that state sanctions, arrests, or information sharing would interfere with federal officials, consume federal resources, or change federal priorities. The imposition of state sanctions would use state, not federal resources, and leave the federal officials free to pursue whatever priorities they like. The same is true for arrests. State officials consume their own resources, not federal ones, when they arrest suspected immigration violators. And if federal officials conclude that it is not worth initiating removal proceedings against the person, they can simply decline. State involvement may, of course, change the political economy of federal enforcement, leading federal officials to behave differently. But as I explained above, that is true of all instances of redundant enforcement. (In fact, some scholars see this as the most powerful argument *in favor* of redundant enforcement.[62]) And even in Arizona it is equally true of SB 1070's information-sharing provision, the only one the Court *did* uphold. That provision, Section 2(B), requires state officers to make a status "inquiry even in cases where

---

[62] See Roderick M. Hills Jr., *Against Preemption: How Federalism Can Improve the National Legislative Process*, 82 NYU L Rev 1 (2007). For the argument that state arrest authority will fundamentally change federal behavior in the immigration context, see Hiroshi Motomura, *The Discretion That Matters: Federal Immigration Enforcement, State and Local Arrests, and the Civil-Criminal Line*, 58 UCLA L Rev 1819 (2011). For some skepticism about this claim, see Adam B. Cox and Eric A. Posner, *Delegation and Immigration Law*, 79 U Chi L Rev 1286 (2012). As part of a large-scale empirical project on immigration enforcement, Tom Miles and I are currently exploring the hypothesis that state arrest authority will dramatically reshape federal enforcement priorities.

it seems unlikely that the Attorney General would have the alien removed."[63] Yet the fact that "§2(B) does not allow state officers to consider federal enforcement priorities" does not trouble the Court, because the federal government is formally free to do nothing with the information about immigration violators that it receives from the state.[64]

In short, the Court's treatment of law as a price rather than an obligation leads it to reject redundant enforcement. But this reasoning comes with a radical consequence: it gives executive branch officials near complete control over the content of immigration law. Federal immigration law on the books becomes mostly a sideshow. In the Court's Holmesian world, the content of the code is no longer the central determinant of "immigration law." Instead, immigration law is determined by the actual or hypothetical decisions of executive branch officials. These actions set the official "price" for particular conduct, and hence control the shape of immigration law understood as a price.

Thus, the practical consequence of the Court's approach in *Arizona* is to elevate prosecutorial decisions by executive branch officials to the status of law for purposes of preemption analysis. This is a possibility the Court has explicitly rejected before—in *Gonzales v Oregon* and other cases—and it is part of what makes the Court's approach in *Arizona* so unusual.[65] Moreover, the reason for the Court's prior rejection should be clear from the preceding discussion: were every enforcement decision by an executive branch official "law" for purposes of preemption analysis, *no* state regulation would be permissible in any regulatory arena into which the federal government had stepped. Anything the state did would conflict with either an action or an inaction of some federal official. To return to the drug possession analogy: the number of federal possession

---

[63] *Arizona*, 132 S Ct at 2508.

[64] Id.

[65] 546 US 243 (2006). In *Gonzales v Oregon*, the Court refused to allow the attorney general to use his exercise of prosecutorial discretion under the federal drug laws to preempt Oregon state law that permitted physicians to prescribe drugs to facilitate assisted suicide by terminally ill patients. This did not mean that the attorney general was prohibited, in a federal prosecution, from arguing that such prescriptions do in fact violate criminal law. Rather, the Court's point was that the attorney general's exercise of prosecutorial discretion, like any other run-of-the-mill exercise of charging discretion, could not properly be conferred with the force of law necessary to preempt state law affirmatively permitting physicians to prescribe Schedule II drugs in order to facilitate assisted suicide. See id at 255–56, 274; see also *Crandon v United States*, 494 US 152, 177 (1990) (Scalia, J, concurring in judgment).

prosecutions would itself define the "law" against which potential
state conflicts would be judged. Since any state prosecutions would
alter that number, they would lead inexorably to conflict preemption. In this fashion, applying the *Arizona* Court's approach broadly
would collapse conflict preemption into field preemption and destroy broad swaths of state regulatory authority.

IV. Federalism as Separation of Powers

United States v Arizona is thus as much a case about separation
of powers as it is a case about federalism. Note how far the Court's
approach takes us away from traditional ideas about separation-of-
powers problems. This is not a context in which Congress has failed
to speak—certainly not in any conventional sense. Nor is the executive interpreting ambiguous statutory language. The immigration code makes crystal clear that the noncitizens targeted by Arizona's law are in violation of federal statutes. But even in this
context, the Court has authorized the executive, through the ordinary exercise of prosecutorial discretion, to make immigration
law that preempts state laws that appear perfectly consistent with
(and in some cases literally incorporate by reference) the black-
letter commands that Congress wrote into the Immigration and
Nationality Act. *Youngstown* this is not.[66]

How should we evaluate the Court's approach? As the earlier
discussion makes clear, the Court's approach is deeply inconsistent
with a convention that ordinarily operates in federalism jurisprudence—a convention whose widespread rejection would have radical
implications for the role of states in our federal system. Thus, we
might just stop there and criticize the Court for ignoring this convention and giving the executive the radical power to preempt state
law through the use of ordinary prosecutorial discretion. Instead,
I want to suggest that the Court's approach may be defensible—
but only if one holds a particular view about the structure of modern
immigration law. Thus, the Court's approach in *United States v
Arizona* may reveal its thinking about this structure.

To see this, consider the legal conclusion that flows from the
underlying logic of the Court's opinion—that the discretionary decisions of executive branch officials are elevated to the status of law
for purposes of preemption analysis. While this conclusion may

---

[66] See *Youngstown Sheet and Tube v Sawyer*, 343 US 579 (1952).

seem untenable in many contexts, for the Court it seems to comport with the structure of modern immigration law. Even in the modern regulatory state, where the executive holds broad lawmaking power, immigration law stands out. Immigration law can be seen today to be rooted principally in unilateral executive action. It is easy to miss this fact, because the prolix immigration code appears to describe in painstaking detail, over hundreds of pages, the legal rules that regulate the details of noncitizens' lives. As I have explained elsewhere, however, in work with Eric Posner and Cristina Rodriguez, this perspective is misleading.[67] The reason is that the central features of modern immigration law—including exceptionally broad grounds of deportability and long-standing acceptance of high levels of unauthorized migration—have left huge numbers of noncitizens formally deportable. Today there are almost certainly more than 10 million such people—roughly one out of every three noncitizens living in the United States. In addition, other recent changes to the immigration code have consolidated executive branch authority to decide whether formally deportable noncitizens get to stay.[68] In such a world the formal rules of deportability are irrelevant across a huge swath of cases. All that matters is whom the president decides to deport.

This singular, defining feature of modern immigration law is not just the product of a lack of resources. The executive is not declining to pursue so many deportable noncitizens solely because it lacks the information or personnel it needs to locate, apprehend, and deport immigration law violators. To be sure, the administration does often say publicly that immigration enforcement looks the way it does because of resource constraints: prosecutorial discretion is the only option, the government says, in a world where the Department of Homeland Security has finite time and money. These resource constraints are real, and they can explain some aspects of underenforcement in immigration law. Nonetheless, these public explanations are inconsistent with what the government is actually doing.

---

[67] See Adam B. Cox and Eric A. Posner, *The Second-Order Structure of Immigration Law*, 59 Stan L Rev 809 (2007); Adam B. Cox and Cristina M. Rodriguez, *The President and Immigration Law*, 119 Yale L J 458 (2009).

[68] See Cox and Rodriguez, 119 Yale L J at 510–19 (cited in note 67). For a discussion of the executive's large-scale project to systematize and centralize the exercise of this vast discretion, see Adam B. Cox and Thomas J. Miles, *Policing Immigration*, 80 U Chi L Rev 87 (2013).

Instead, the executive's actions drive home the fact that, for immigration law today, a perfect world is not a world of perfect compliance. Many people who are formally deportable are not thought to be deserving of deportation, and in fact the executive branch affirmatively does not want to deport many of these noncitizens. We might describe this as a gap between *formal* deportability and *normative* deportability—a gap that is similar, perhaps, to the gap that Bill Stuntz and others believe exists in some parts of criminal law.[69] This gap is a pervasive part of our "illegal immigration" system, which operates in the United States as a shadow guest-worker program in which millions of migrant workers enter and live in the country without formal permission. The executive screens out a tiny fraction of these workers on the back end of the system, most prominently by removing those who are arrested on or convicted of state criminal charges.[70] The gap is also prominent in many recent decisions by the Obama administration. The most salient was President Obama's announcement in June 2012 that the administration would grant "deferred action"—a two-year promise not to deport—to as many at 1.5 million young immigrants.[71] The president did not say that his decision was driven by a lack of enforcement resources. To the contrary: he defended deferred action for childhood arrivals as "the right thing to do," because "it makes no sense to expel talented young people who, for all intents and purposes, are Americans."[72] This is not the language of limited resources.

Even the government's position in the Arizona litigation itself highlights the gap between formal and normative deportability. After all, if the nature of legal obligation in the immigration arena were understood by the executive in a way that made perfect compliance with immigration law optimal, then it would be very hard to explain why state efforts that increase compliance at no cost to

---

[69] See William Stuntz, *The Collapse of American Criminal Justice* (2011); Josh Bowers, *Legal Guilt, Normative Innocence, and the Equitable Decision Not to Prosecute*, 110 Colum L Rev 1655 (2010); Richard McAdams, *Bill Stuntz and the Principal-Agent Problem in Criminal Law*, in M. Klarman, D. Skeel, and C. Steiker, eds, *The Political Heart of Criminal Procedure: Essays on Themes of William J. Stuntz* (2012).

[70] See Cox and Posner, 59 Stan L Rev at 844–49 (cited in note 67); Cox and Rodriguez, 119 Yale L J at 511–14 (cited in note 67).

[71] See Napolitano Memo (cited in note 45). See also Julia Preston and John H. Cushman Jr., *Obama to Permit Young Migrants to Remain in U.S.*, NY Times A1 (June 16, 2012).

[72] See the White House, Office of the Press Secretary, *Remarks by the President on Immigration* (June 15, 2012), online at http://www.whitehouse.gov/the-press-office/2012/06/15/remarks-president-immigration.

the federal government would be spurned by the Justice Department. The rejection of these efforts is tacit acknowledgment that, in the executive's view, perfect compliance with the immigration rules on the books is not desirable.

There is, then, a tremendous gap between immigration law on the books and immigration law in practice. Why immigration law came to look like this is a complicated question. It is easy to imagine why a large number of actors in the political system might favor such a structure: it secures a cheap workforce for employers, preserves flexibility for the government, and provides opportunities for many more migrants than the country has been willing thus far to accept within the formal allotment of labor visas. Nonetheless, it is far from clear how much of the status quo reflects the deliberate choices of some set of political actors or instead is the product of happenstance and path dependency. Whatever the root causes, the important point is that a large number of actors within the system accept the idea that this gap exists.

United States v Arizona, in my view, shows that the Supreme Court now also accepts and endorses the existence of this gap. Justice Kennedy's majority opinion implicitly rejects the idea that the underenforcement of immigration law's formal obligations is simply the result of insufficient resources or a lack of information that would allow the government to locate immigration law violators. Had the Court thought that, it would have been much more likely to embrace Arizona's efforts—efforts designed to use redundant enforcement to improve compliance with federal law. Instead, the Court treats the deliberate decisions by federal officials to underenforce the INA as reflecting the contours of immigration law more accurately than the formal rules laid down in the immigration code.

At bottom, this is a big part of what separates the majority from the dissent. Many have criticized Justice Scalia's dissent for its anachronistic account of the power states have to close their own borders,[73] as well as for the strident tone of the dissent's concluding

---

[73] Justice Scalia takes the position that "[a]s a sovereign, Arizona has the inherent power to exclude persons from its territory, subject only to those limitations expressed in the Constitution or constitutionally imposed by Congress." *Arizona*, 132 S Ct at 2511 (Scalia, J, dissenting). The possibility that states might wield significant authority over the exclusion and expulsion of noncitizens was a real one during the nineteenth century. See Gerald L. Neuman, *The Lost Century of American Immigration Law (1776–1875)*, 93 Colum L Rev 1833 (1993). But there was never the clear consensus that Justice Scalia attempts to extract from the founding period.

remarks, which some have taken as little more than a screed against the Obama administration's recent immigration policies.[74] But these features of the dissent have distracted attention from the fact that Justice Scalia's central argument is that black-letter immigration law describes a series of obligations that demand perfect compliance—by immigrants and, it seems, by the federal enforcement bureaucracy. This is clear in Justice Scalia's scathing critique of the Obama administration's announcement of deferred action for young immigrants:

> It has become clear that federal enforcement priorities—in the sense of priorities based on the need to allocate "scarce enforcement resources"— is not the problem here. . . . The President said at a news conference that the new program is "the right thing to do" in light of Congress's failure to pass the Administration's proposed revision of the Immigration Act. Perhaps it is, though Arizona may not think so. But to say, as the Court does, that Arizona contradicts federal law by enforcing applications of the Immigration Act that the President declines to enforce boggles the mind.[75]

Thus, rather than accepting the actions of the executive as evidence of a gap between formal and normative deportability, Justice Scalia sees them as evidence of "[a] Federal Government that does not want to enforce the immigration laws as written,"[76] of an executive whose "priorities include willful blindness or deliberate inattention to the presence of removable aliens in Arizona."[77]

One might chalk up Justice Scalia's position to his self-professed commitment to a positivist vision of the nature of legal rules. Whether or not it is possible to show that Justice Kennedy's price conception of law is in some way inconsistent with positivism, it is interesting to note that Justice Scalia's dissenting views are in deep

---

[74] See Richard A. Posner, *Supreme Court Year in Review*, Slate, June 27, 2013, online at http://www.slate.com/articles/news_and_politics/the_breakfast_table/features/2012/_supreme_court_year_in_review/supreme_court_year_in_review_justice_scalia_offers_no_evidence_to_back_up_his_claims_about_illegal_immigration_.html.

[75] *Arizona*, 132 S Ct at 2521. Note that this is why Justice Scalia correctly understands that the real disagreement with the majority is not over whether immigration law is field preemptive in any ordinary sense. The majority's claim is not as a general matter that federal regulation of immigration is so comprehensive that it leaves no room for state involvement. Instead, it rests on the premise that there is a gap between formal deportability and normative deportability. Justice Scalia simply believes that there is no such gap.

[76] Id. See also id ("Are the sovereign States at the mercy of the Federal Executive's refusal to enforce the Nation's immigration laws?").

[77] Id at 2517.

tension with positions he has taken elsewhere. In the above passage, for example, he sees something legally objectionable about the executive's failure to fully enforce federal immigration law. But such concern is hard to square with his view about the Constitution's commitment to a unitary executive. Elsewhere Justice Scalia has heralded the idea that the executive is free to underenforce laws with which he disagrees—and that Congress should be prohibited from empowering private citizens to sue to ensure that the executive strictly enforces the law.[78] If so, then what business do states have "enforcing applications of the Immigration Act that the President declines to enforce"?

In addition to illuminating the root of the disagreement between the majority and dissent, this account can also help explain why the Supreme Court upheld one provision of SB 1070—Section 2(B). That information-sharing section, which has been referred to widely as the "show your papers" provision, requires that state and local law enforcement officials check the immigration status of people they encounter in the ordinary course of their law enforcement duties, wherever there is reasonable suspicion that the person might be in violation of immigration law.[79] At first glance, the majority's decision to sustain this provision appears puzzling. On the majority's reasoning, any action that increases the "expected sanction" for violating the immigration code—either by increasing the total sanction or by increasing the likelihood of sanction—interferes with federal prosecutorial discretion and alters the content of immigration law. That logic explains the invalidation of the arrest provision in SB 1070: even though the federal government could decline to pick up and charge a person arrested by state officers, the arrest plausibly might change the expected sanction. But that logic seems

---

[78] As he has written:

> Does what I have said mean that, "important legislative purposes, heralded in the halls of Congress, [can be] lost or misdirected in the vast hallways of the federal bureaucracy"? Of course it does—and a good thing, too. . . . [L]ots of once-heralded programs ought to get lost or misdirected, in vast hallways or elsewhere. . . . The ability [of the executive] to lose or misdirect laws can be said to be one of the prime engines of social change. . . . Sunday blue laws, for example, were widely unenforced long before they were widely repealed—and had the first not been possible the second might never have occurred.

Antonin Scalia, *The Doctrine of Standing as an Essential Element of the Separation of Powers*, 17 Suffolk L Rev 881, 897 (1983). This view is also implicit in Justice Scalia's majority opinion in *Lujan v Defenders of Wildlife*, 504 US 555 (1992).

[79] See Ariz Rev Stat Ann § 11-1051(B).

like it should lead to the same conclusion about the information-sharing provision. Identifying a suspected immigration violator to the federal government certainly might raise the likelihood that that person is ultimately removed. Moreover, asking for papers might even itself be seen as a "sanction"—a form of harassment that imposes costs on those suspected by state officers of being in violation of immigration law. Certainly some Arizona officials appear to have hoped that the provision would have this effect, instilling fear in out-of-status immigrants and thereby driving them out of the state.

While there may be little functional difference between the arrest and information-sharing provisions,[80] the Court's decision to uphold the latter might reflect the fact that this provision is the one that most clearly facilitates the consolidation of authority in the hands of the federal executive. It is, in some ways, critical to the rationalization of immigration law's application in a world where a tremendous gap exists between formal and normative deportability. In such a world, the biggest challenge for the executive is informational: how does it acquire information about where all the formally deportable noncitizens are, and what they are up to, in order for the executive to make systematic rather than arbitrary decisions about whom to deport?[81] How can it identify and locate the migrants

---

[80] In fact, there might be literally no distinction in a world where local law enforcement officials have very broad discretion to make arrests, even for minor offenses like traffic infractions. For this reason, the Court is probably mistaken when it suggests in dicta that the Fourth Amendment may operate as a significant constraint on the implementation of Section 2(B) by prohibiting officers from extending an otherwise permissible encounter solely to check immigration status. The Fourth Amendment might well do so, but an officer can obviate any potential Fourth Amendment concern by simply arresting the person for the infraction that led to the encounter in the first place. Thus, the possibility of pretextual arrest might trivialize the formal availability of a Fourth Amendment constraint. In other words, given the breadth of arrest authority, there may be very little practical difference between (1) a provision that authorizes local officials to arrest noncitizens who are in violation of immigration law (authorized by Section 6 of SB 1070), (2) a provision that permits local officials to check the status of a person who is stopped on some other basis (authorized by Section 2(B) of SB 1070), and (3) a provision that permits local officials to check the status of a person arrested on some other basis (authorized by the Secure Communities program discussed below).

[81] This is the sort of challenge that by and large did not exist in the late nineteenth century, when immigration law screened people only at the borders (there were no deportation laws) and most migrants passed through points of entry. See Salyer, *Laws Harsh as Tigers* (cited in note 54); Mae Ngai, *Impossible Subjects: Illegal Aliens and the Making of Modern America* (2005). The government still faced an informational problem in those days, but it had much less to do with identifying immigrants for purposes of screening and much more to do with the fact that it was often difficult to get information about identifiable immigrants—except in instances where the immigration rules screened migrants on the basis of visible characteristics like race or ethnicity.

it wants to put through this screening process? Without comprehensive information it is much harder for the executive to implement a fine-grained system of ex post screening; the screening system becomes progressively more arbitrary, reflecting chance more than the president's priorities.

Arizona's information-sharing provision helps overcome this informational deficit. States have many, many more contacts with noncitizens than the federal government can ever hope to have—even in a world like today's, where the immigration enforcement budget is bigger than the combined budgets of all of the criminal federal law enforcement agencies.[82] Thus, preserving the information-sharing role of states is consistent with the consolidation of immigration power in the executive branch. In fact, that is precisely why the government recently rolled out a federal program quite similar to Arizona's section 2(B), even while it was litigating against section 2(B) in the Supreme Court. The new federal program is designed to ensure that *every single person* arrested anywhere in the country by a state or local law enforcement official will have her immigration status checked upon arrest. Called Secure Communities, the program is basically a giant information-sharing regime designed to leverage the contacts people have with state and local law enforcement in order to provide the federal government with much more information about the identities of those in violation of the immigration code.[83] That information, provided by state officials, could of course change the expected sanctions faced by immigrants for violations of immigration law. Yet that possibility appears less important to the executive than the fact that this information sharing helps promote the possibility that federal discretion can be wielded in a comprehensive fashion. It therefore serves more as a precondition than an obstacle to executive branch control over immigration policy.

V. Conclusion

Ultimately, the Supreme Court's decision in *United States v*

---

[82] See Doris Meissner et al, *Immigration Enforcement in the United States: The Rise of a Formidable Machinery*, Migration Policy Institute (January 2013), online at http://www.migrationpolicy.org/pubs/enforcementpillars.pdf ("[T]he US government spends more on its immigration enforcement agencies than on all its other principal criminal federal law enforcement agencies combined.").

[83] For a comprehensive description of Secure Communities, see Cox and Miles, 80 U Chi L Rev at 90–102 (cited in note 68).

Arizona may be less significant for its impact on state immigration initiatives than for ratifying and furthering the consolidation of immigration authority in the executive branch. Evaluating this shift is well beyond the scope of this article (though I have written about certain aspects elsewhere).[84] One result is, however, fairly clear: systematic policy consequences are likely to flow from jurisprudential developments that shift the locus of immigration policymaking power toward the president and away from Congress.

Historically, presidents have generally been more open to immigration than Congress. Chester A. Arthur vetoed the first Chinese Exclusion bill passed in 1882 on the ground that its twenty-year ban on migration was excessively restrictionist and that the act's registration requirements were "undemocratic and hostile to the spirit of our institutions."[85] Woodrow Wilson and his predecessors repeatedly vetoed efforts in the early twentieth century to require literacy tests for immigrants.[86] Congress eventually overrode Wilson's veto. Harry Truman fought with Congress over the Displaced Persons Act of 1948 on the ground that it was discriminatory and unfair to refugees,[87] and he later vetoed the McCarran-Walter Act of 1952 because it retained the restrictive national origins quota system.[88] Again Congress overrode the veto, and the national origins quota system continued until its abolition was pushed for by John F. Kennedy and secured in part by the efforts of Lyndon Johnson.[89]

[84] See id at 131–35; Cox and Posner, 59 Stan L Rev at 844–52 (cited in note 67); Cox and Rodriguez, 119 Yale L J at 528–46 (cited in note 67).

[85] See Chester A. Arthur, *Chinese Immigration—Veto Message*, 13 Cong Rec 2551 (1882). President Arthur also argued that the bill breached treaty amendments that had recently been negotiated with China. See id. Those amendments to the Burlingame Treaty of 1868 permitted only a reasonable suspension of immigration. See Kitty Calavita, *Chinese Exclusion and the Open Door with China: Structural Contradictions and the "Chaos" of Law, 1882–1910*, 10 Social and Legal Stud 204, 207 (2001). Moreover, before those amendments were agreed to, President Hayes had vetoed earlier congressional attempts to restrict Chinese migration. See E. P. Hutchinson, *Legislative History of American Immigration Policy 1798–1965*, at 73 (1981).

[86] See Hiroshi Motomura, *Americans in Waiting: The Lost Story of Immigration and Citizenship in the United States* 125 (2006); Hans P. Vought, *The Bully Pulpit and the Melting Pot* (2004).

[87] See Roger Daniels, ed, *Immigration and the Legacy of Harry S. Truman* (2010).

[88] Truman argued that the act was discriminatory, violating "the great political doctrine of the Declaration of Independence that 'all men are created equal.'" See *Message from the President of the United States to the House of Representatives*, 82d Cong, 98 Cong Rec 8082 (1952). For more on Truman's seeming openness to higher levels of immigration, see Cox and Rodriguez, 119 Yale L J at 485–91 & n 271 (cited in note 67).

[89] See Motomura, *Americans in Waiting* at 131–32 (cited in note 86); see also John F. Kennedy, *A Nation of Immigrants* (1958).

I certainly do not mean to suggest that presidents have been immune to restrictionist sentiment. After all, President Arthur did go on to sign the Chinese Exclusion Act of 1882 after it was amended by Congress to reduce the period of exclusion.[90] Nor do I mean to suggest that presidents are inevitably less restrictionist than Congress. Counterexamples certainly occur, and perhaps they are ever more likely in an era in which political parties have become more polarized and staked out sharply divergent positions on immigration policy.[91] Nonetheless, presidents are plausibly more predisposed than Congress to pursue open immigration policies. The president's more nationalistic electoral mandate, as well as his more direct engagement in foreign affairs, both suggest as much.[92]

The fact that presidents are likely to have different preferences about immigration policy than Congress is critical for understanding the consequences of *United States v Arizona*. It is also crucial to the ongoing discussions about comprehensive immigration reform. Immigration reform is a top priority for President Obama as his second term gets under way. Congressional Democrats are also renewing their reform push. To this point, public reform discussions have focused principally on flashpoint issues like legalizing the more than 10 million immigrants living without status in the United States. But lurking behind these discussions are reform's potentially sweeping consequences for the president's power over immigration policy. A large legalization program, combined with a substantial temporary worker program for low-skilled workers, could as a func-

---

[90] Act of May 6, 1882 (Chinese Exclusion Act), ch 126, 22 Stat 58.

[91] See, for example, Alan I. Abramowitz, *The Disappearing Center* (2010); Nolan McCarty et al, *Polarized America: The Dance of Ideology and Unequal Riches* (2006).

[92] On the president's national constituency, see, for example, Sharyn O'Halloran, *Politics, Process, and American Trade Policy* 11 (1994); Lawrence Lessig and Cass R. Sunstein, *The President and the Administration*, 94 Colum L Rev 1 (1994); Michael Novak, *President of All the People*, in Vanessa B. Beasley, ed, *Who Belongs in America?* 19 (2006). For some skepticism, see Jide Nzelibe, *The Fable of the Nationalistic President and the Parochial Congress*, 53 UCLA L Rev 1217 (2006). On the role of the president's engagement with foreign affairs, see, for example, Shirley Hune, *Politics of Chinese Exclusion: Legislative-Executive Conflict 1876–1882*, 9 Amerasia 5 (1982); Lawrence H. Chamberlain, *The President, Congress, and Legislation* 352 (1946); J. Donald Kingsley, *Immigration and Our Foreign Policy Objectives*, 21 L & Contemp Probs 301 (1956); Marc R. Rosenblum, *Congress, the President, and the INS: Who's in Charge of U.S. Immigration Policy?* (working paper on file with author). Chester A. Arthur might present an early example of the role of foreign engagement. When he addressed the opening of the 47th Congress—the Congress that would go on to enact the Chinese Exclusion Act of 1882—Arthur apparently recommended that Congress "be considerate of the interests and susceptibilities of the Chinese government in any modification of the immigration laws." Hutchinson, *Legislative History of American Immigration Policy* at 77 (cited in note 85).

tional matter dramatically reduce the president's power by shrinking the gap between formal and normative deportability. On the other hand, Congress could choose to extend and formalize the president's power—for example by delegating to the president the authority to set annual admissions quotas for many categories of labor migrants. This power would help solve the pervasive problem that the legislative process is simply too sclerotic to respond in a timely way to changes in domestic labor market conditions. But it would also solidify the president's role as immigration-law-maker-in-chief.

In short, immigration separation of powers—the allocation of lawmaking authority *within* the federal government—is among the most pressing questions of institutional design facing immigration law today. Immigration federalism has gotten all of the attention, but it should be treated as the sideshow that it often is. *United States v Arizona* implicitly acknowledges this reality. Members of Congress contemplating once-in-a-generation changes to immigration law should do the same.

ORIN S. KERR

THE CURIOUS HISTORY OF FOURTH
AMENDMENT SEARCHES

In *United States v Jones*,[1] the Supreme Court announced the return
of the trespass test for what is a Fourth Amendment "search."[2] The
standard account in Fourth Amendment scholarship teaches that
the Supreme Court equated searches with trespasses until the
1960s.[3] The Court then abandoned the trespass test in favor of a
two-part inquiry into expectations of privacy introduced in Justice

Orin S. Kerr is Fred C. Stevenson Research Professor, George Washington University
Law School.

AUTHOR'S NOTE: The author thanks Thomas Y. Davies, William J. Cuddihy, David
Strauss, George Thomas, Wesley Oliver, Chip Lupu, Renee Lerner, Tom Colby, Richard
Pierce, Alan Morrison, and participants in the George Washington faculty workshop for
comments and helpful feedback. Thanks to Ken Rodriguez and David Bender for valuable
research assistance.

[1] 132 S Ct 945 (2012).

[2] The Fourth Amendment states that "[t]he right of the people to be secure in their
persons, houses, papers, and effects, against unreasonable searches and seizures, shall not
be violated." US Const, Amend IV.

[3] As Morgan Cloud has noted, "[h]istories of the Supreme Court's interpretive theories
of the Fourth Amendment inevitably include some version" of this narrative. Morgan
Cloud, *A Liberal House Divided: How the Warren Court Dismantled the Fourth Amendment*,
3 Ohio St J Crim L 33, 33 (2005). For just a few recent examples among many from
prominent scholars, see Carol S. Steiker, *Brandeis in Olmstead: "Our Government Is the
Potent, the Omnipresent Teacher,"* 79 Miss L J 149, 162 (2009); David Sklansky, *"One Train
May Hide Another": Katz, Stonewall, and the Secret Subtext of Criminal Procedure*, 41 UC
Davis L Rev 875, 882 (2008); Christopher Slobogin, *Surveillance and the Constitution*, 55
Wayne L Rev 1105, 1111 (2009); Jed Rubenfeld, *The End of Privacy*, 61 Stan L Rev 101,
105–06 (2008); Daniel J. Solove, *Digital Dossiers and the Dissipation of Fourth Amendment
Privacy*, 75 S Cal L Rev 1083, 1086 (2002).

Harlan's concurring opinion in *Katz v United States*.[4] In *Jones*, the
Court revived what it saw as the pre-*Katz* test for searches: According to Justice Scalia's majority opinion, *Katz* had supplemented
the pre-*Katz* trespass test but not replaced it.[5] The Court then
applied the trespass test to the government's installation of a GPS
device on the underbody of the car Jones drove to monitor his
location. According to the Court, the government had "searched"
Jones's car because installing the GPS device was a trespass.

The apparent restoration of a pre-*Katz* trespass test in *Jones* reflects the widely shared assumption that pre-*Katz* search doctrine
was in fact based on trespass law. Like many Fourth Amendment
scholars, I have previously echoed the common wisdom that this is
true.[6] But because the point was only of historical interest, I had
not looked closely at pre-*Katz* law to assess its accuracy. *Jones* makes
the history of Fourth Amendment law doctrinally significant, however, meriting a more careful look at the early understandings of
"searches." This essay explores the history of the Fourth Amendment and reaches the surprising conclusion that no trespass test
was used in the pre-*Katz* era. Neither the original understanding
nor Supreme Court doctrine equated searches with trespass. *Jones*
purports to revive a test that did not actually exist.

In short, the common wisdom is false. Before *Katz*, the Court
did not use a specific formulation to identify what counted as a
Fourth Amendment search. Supreme Court cases on the meaning
of "searches" generally reasoned by analogy to the canonical ex-

---

[4] 389 US 347 (1967). The precise moment when the Court adopted Justice Harlan's
framework is not entirely clear. It seems to have guided the Court in *Rakas v Illinois*, 439
US 128 (1978). By the next year, in *Smith v Maryland*, 442 US 735 (1979), the Court
referred to the Harlan framework as the Court's "lodestar" and applied it as the exclusive
test. See id at 739.

[5] See Jones, 132 S Ct at 952 ("the *Katz* reasonable-expectation-of-privacy test has been
added to, not *substituted for*, the common-law trespassory test") (emphasis in original). This
came as a surprise to every student and scholar of the Fourth Amendment. Cf. John P.
Elwood and Eric A. White, *What Were They Thinking: The Supreme Court in Revue, October
Term 2011*, 15 Green Bag 2d 405, 409 (2012) (humorously noting the trespass test's
unexpected return by noting, "[i]t turns out that approach was not dead, just taking a
really long nap."). In this article, I focus exclusively on the reasoning of the majority
opinion by Justice Scalia. In a separate article, I have analyzed the even more surprising
reasoning of the concurring opinions by Justices Alito and Sotomayor. See Orin S. Kerr,
The Mosaic Theory of the Fourth Amendment, 111 Mich L Rev 31 (2012).

[6] Orin S. Kerr, *The Fourth Amendment and New Technologies: Constitutional Myths and the
Case for Caution*, 102 Mich L Rev 801, 816 (2004) (cited in *Jones*, 132 S Ct at 949–50)
(stating that "early courts interpreted the Fourth Amendment as a claim against government interference with property rights, and in particular, rights against trespass.").

ample of home invasion. But the decisions used no particular methodology to guide the analogy, and opinions sometimes focused on privacy or the perceived invasiveness of the government's conduct. The Court began to focus on physical intrusion as a guide starting in the 1920s. But even decisions focused on physical intrusion eschewed reliance on the technicalities of trespass law. No historical trespass era existed. Surprisingly, the first Supreme Court case applying a trespass test to identify Fourth Amendment searches appears to be *United States v Jones*.

An obvious question is how the common wisdom came to deviate from the history. The source of the error appears to be two cases from 1967, *Warden v Hayden*[7] and *Katz* itself. Both cases wrongly claimed that prior law had adopted a trespass standard. Later commentators assumed these claims to be true, cementing the trespass narrative for pre-*Katz* search doctrine. But a closer look at the history reveals a different picture and an accompanying irony. To the extent the early cases reveal any consistent methodology, they suggest a mix of property, privacy, and policy concerns not entirely dissimilar to those that have influenced the *Katz* test. Labels have changed. But there is much less of a difference in how the Supreme Court has interpreted searches before and after *Katz* than has been realized.

This history has both practical and theoretical implications. The practical implication is that there is no trespass test to restore. As a result, implementing the *Jones* trespass test will require courts to resolve its scope. Both today and when the Fourth Amendment was adopted, trespass has been a protean concept that can be construed broadly or narrowly. Trespass law today may be different in some ways from trespass law then, raising questions of which era of trespass doctrine counts. Because the trespass test did not exist before *Jones*, pre-*Katz* law does not directly answer these questions. Courts called on to interpret the trespass test must do so with little in the way of history or precedent to guide them.

The theoretical implication is that *Jones* may be more important for its form than for its substance. Precedents interpreting the meaning of searches must distinguish government practices that the Fourth Amendment restricts from those that it leaves unregulated. Labels may offer little guidance in drawing this line. And labels can

[7] 387 US 294 (1967).

be deceiving: In the *Katz* era before *Jones*, an expectation of privacy was very likely to be reasonable when backed by a property right.[8] As a result, the shift from an exclusive *Katz* test to a bifurcated *Katz* and trespass test may move around the doctrinal boxes without changing outcomes.

I will develop the argument as follows. I begin with the history of Fourth Amendment search doctrine divided into three parts: first, the original understanding; second, the cases before the *Olmstead* decision in 1928; and third, the cases from *Olmstead* to the period immediately before *Katz*. I then offer three lessons drawn from this history. The lessons start with a possible explanation of why the pre-*Katz* doctrine has been misunderstood, turn to the uncertainties of the new trespass test, and conclude with implications for the future of Fourth Amendment search doctrine.

I. The Original Understanding of "Searches"

The word "search" has several possible meanings. On one hand, a search might refer merely to looking for an item. In that sense, you might gaze up at the night sky and search for the Big Dipper. On the other hand, a search might mean the act of observing an item closely. For example, you might search a page to find a particular word. Finally, a search might refer to the physical act of looking through a space in ways that expose its contents to plain view. In that sense, you might search a bedroom closet by rifling through the clothes it contains. The ambiguity of the word ensures that a wide range of concepts might plausibly define the meaning of searches. To understand which meanings have been associated with the Fourth Amendment, we need to start at the beginning and trace the understandings over time.

In the second half of the eighteenth century, a series of widely publicized abuses by King George III and his officials led the colonists in the New World to consider a right against unreasonable searches and seizures to be one of the important rights held against government.[9] That right was articulated in several state constitu-

---

[8] See *Rakas v Illinois*, 439 US 128, 144 n 12 (1978) ("One of the main rights attaching to property is the right to exclude others, see W. Blackstone, *Commentaries*, book 2, ch. 1, and one who owns or lawfully possesses or controls property will in all likelihood have a legitimate expectation of privacy by virtue of this right to exclude.").

[9] See generally Nelson B. Lasson, *The History and Development of the Fourth Amendment to the United States Constitution* 43–84 (Johns Hopkins, 1937); William J. Cuddihy, *The Fourth Amendment: Origins and Original Meaning* 537–75 (2008).

tions after the Declaration of Independence. In 1780, for example, the Constitution of Massachusetts drafted by John Adams announced that every individual has "a right to be secure from all unreasonable searches and seizures of his person, his house, his papers, and all his possessions."[10] The text of the Fourth Amendment ratified in 1791 closely resembled state provisions by asserting a "right of the people to be secure in their persons, houses, papers, and effects, against unreasonable searches and seizures."[11]

What did the Framing generation understand "searches" to mean? The question is difficult to answer with precision in part because the question rarely arose. That is true for several reasons,[12] perhaps the most important being the remedial context in which search and seizure questions were litigated. Under the modern exclusionary rule, the precise bounds of searches and seizures are critical because a criminal defendant must first identify a search or seizure to succeed on a motion to suppress.[13] But the search and seizure principles of the eighteenth century mostly arose when asserted as defenses to civil tort actions. The plaintiff would sue the officer, and the officer would claim that a warrant or common law search and seizure principles provided an affirmative defense. The meaning of "searches" was neither an element of the tort nor part of the affirmative defense. Attention primarily focused elsewhere, such as on whether a warrant was valid and therefore established a defense.[14]

---

[10] Mass. Declaration of Rights of 1780, Art XIV, reprinted in Lasson, *The History and Development of the Fourth Amendment* at 82 n 15 (cited in note 9). See generally Thomas K. Clancy, *The Framers' Intent: John Adams, His Era, and the Fourth Amendment*, 86 Ind L J 979 (2011).

[11] US Const, Amend IV.

[12] Another likely reason is that most crimes in the eighteenth century were investigated by their victims rather than by government officials. See Wesley MacNeil Oliver, *The Neglected History of Criminal Procedure, 1850–1940*, 62 Rutgers L Rev 447, 449–57 (2010). The modern concept of police officers employed by government to investigate crimes was not yet common. See David A. Sklansky, *The Private Police*, 46 UCLA L Rev 1165, 1202–08 (1999). In that period, part-time constables could play a supporting role aiding victims by obtaining warrants on their behalf, see Oliver, 62 Rutgers L Rev at 449–52, but warrants could be obtained only in relatively narrow circumstances. Id. Because the modern notion of a police force restrained by the legal limitations on the scope of searches was largely unknown, the need to interpret the term did not arise with the frequency that it does today.

[13] Defendants carry the burden of proof of establishing that they were the subject of a search. See *Rakas v Illinois*, 439 US 128, 130 n 1 (1978); *United States v Symonevich*, 688 F3d 12, 21 n 6 (1st Cir 2012) ("The burden to establish a reasonable expectation of privacy protected under the Fourth Amendment lies squarely on the movant.").

[14] See Thomas Y. Davies, *Recovering the Original Fourth Amendment*, 98 Mich L Rev 547, 619–68 (1999).

The little evidence of what searches meant in the late eighteenth century is mostly by way of example. The enactment of the Fourth Amendment responded to a series of specific abuses. We can examine those facts, and expressions of concern about similar scenarios, to see what kinds of actions by government officials were understood to have been the kinds of acts that the Fourth Amendment was enacted to avoid.[15] Famous search and seizure cases leading up to the Fourth Amendment involved physical entries into homes, violent rummaging for incriminating items once inside, and then arrests and the taking away of evidence found. These examples, and some contemporaneous statements during the ratification debates, suggest that home entries and rummaging around inside were understood as the paradigmatic examples of "searches."

Consider *Wilkes v Wood*,[16] a famous case involving a search under a general warrant targeting those involved in a pamphlet harshly critical of the King. Following the search, the plaintiff brought suit "for entering the plaintiff's house, breaking his locks, and seizing his papers."[17] When the Solicitor General argued that the general warrant provided a defense, Lord Chief Justice Pratt characterized the Solicitor General's position as "claim[ing] a right, under precedents, to force persons' houses,"[18] and "break open escrutores"[19] under the general warrant and then to "seize their papers"[20] and remove them. This passage seems to suggest an understanding of search and seizure by way of example: Forcing open a house and breaking open desks was a search, while grabbing the papers and removing them was a seizure.

The same judge (then Lord Camden) made a similar characterization two years later in *Entick v Carrington*.[21] Like *Wilkes*, *Entick* involved a trespass action following the destructive search of a home pursuant to a general warrant seeking evidence of libel against the King. When the searching officials responded that the general warrant authorized the trespass, the Court explained that to rule for

---

[15] See William J. Stuntz, *Privacy's Problem and the Law of Criminal Procedure*, 93 Mich L Rev 1016, 1060–61 (1995).

[16] 98 Eng 489 (CP 1763).

[17] Id at 489.

[18] Id at 498.

[19] Id. Escrutores are writing desks.

[20] Id.

[21] (1765) 95 Eng Rep 807 (KB), 19 Howell's State Trials 1029.

the officials would mean that "the secret cabinets and bureaus of every subject in this kingdom will be thrown open to the search and inspection of a messenger."[22] Under the warrant as written, the Court wrote, the suspect's house would be "rifled,"[23] and "the lock and doors of every room, box, or trunk must be broken open."[24] These passages from *Entick* suggest a general understanding of what "searches" might be that is consistent with *Wilkes*. Searches referred to the forcing open of persons' houses and the breaking open of their desks and cabinets in an effort to find the evidence inside.

That general understanding is reflected in the occasional discussions of search and seizure powers in the ratification debates. During Virginia's convention to vote on the ratification of the Constitution, Patrick Henry spoke against ratification in part on the ground that the Constitution contained no protections against unreasonable searches and seizures. Henry gave examples of the scenarios that could arise without such protections: "Suppose an exciseman will demand leave to enter your cellar or house, by virtue of his office; perhaps he may call on the militia to enable him to go. If Congress be informed of it, will they give you redress?"[25] Without the protections of a bill of rights, Henry argued, federal officials seeking to enforce excise taxes could "go into your cellars and rooms, and search, ransack and measure, everything you eat, drink and wear."[26] Once again, the need for protections against search and seizure was articulated in the context of physical entry into the home.

Although illustrative, these examples do not establish a doctrinal test to define "searches" in Fourth Amendment law. Devising a test from a set of examples raises a level-of-generality problem: Examples alone cannot identify how far beyond their facts the principle should extend. Clearly, physical entry of individuals inside the home to find evidence counts as a search. At the narrowest level, then, a search might be only a physical entry by government officials. A broader approach could focus on whether the officials interfered

---

[22] *Entick v Carrington*, 19 Howell's State Trials 1029, 1063 (1765).

[23] Id at 1064.

[24] Id.

[25] Patrick Henry, Debates, the Virginia Convention (June 16, 1788), in 10 *The Documentary History of the Ratification of the Constitution* 1301 (State Historical Society of Wisconsin, 1993) (John P. Kaminski and Gaspare J. Saladino, eds).

[26] Id at 1331. See also Cuddihy, *The Fourth Amendment* at 683 (cited in note 9).

with property interests, such as whether a trespass occurred. Or perhaps the test should be whether the government interfered with privacy, with physical intrusion being just one example of government acts that violate privacy interests. Examples alone cannot identify which principle to use.

The Supreme Court's opinion in *Jones* articulates one specific approach among the various possibilities: It suggests that searches were originally understood as coextensive with trespasses. I use the word "suggests" deliberately, as Justice Scalia repeatedly hints at the position without directly adopting it. *Jones* rules that conduct amounting to a trespass must be a search to ensure that the Fourth Amendment maintains the "degree of protection it afforded when it was adopted,"[27] which implies that all trespasses were searches at that time. Justice Scalia further states that Supreme Court precedents equating searches with trespasses are "[c]onsistent" with the original understanding.[28]

At the same time, Justice Scalia's evidence linking trespasses with the original understanding of searches is more modest. First, Scalia argues that property rights were "significan[t]"[29] to the original understanding of the Fourth Amendment. This is clear, he says, from the following famous passage in *Entick v Carrington*:

> [O]ur law holds the property of every man so sacred, that no man can set his foot upon his neighbour's close without his leave; if he does he is a trespasser, though he does no damage at all; if he will tread upon his neighbour's ground, he must justify it by law.[30]

Justice Scalia contends that the text of the Fourth Amendment also "reflects its close connection to property, since otherwise it would have referred simply to 'the right of the people to be secure against unreasonable searches and seizures'; the phrase 'in their persons, houses, papers, and effects' would have been superfluous."[31]

To the extent *Jones* is read as claiming that all trespasses were originally understood as searches, however, there turns out to be little specific historical support for it. Justice Scalia is surely correct that principles of property law provided important influences on

---

[27] Id at 953.

[28] Id.

[29] *United States v Jones*, 132 S Ct 945, 950 (2012).

[30] *Entick v Carrington*, (1765) 95 Eng Rep 807, 817 (KB).

[31] *Jones*, 132 S Ct at 949.

eighteenth-century understandings of search and seizure law. Infamous abuses that inspired the passage of the Fourth Amendment involved trespasses. At the same time, the evidence does not clearly indicate that property law generally or the scope of trespass specifically was understood to define the scope of searches.

Consider the famous passage from *Entick*. Although this passage could be read as linking property law to search and seizure protections, it could also be read as merely placing the legal and rhetorical burden on government officials to justify their actions in the context of a high-profile dispute.[32] Lord Camden's opinion declared a practice illegal that may have been quite widespread,[33] and his decision was a controversial and widely noted political statement as much as it was a legal opinion.[34] Stressing the sanctity of property placed the legal and rhetorical burden on the officials to justify their conduct based on the validity of the warrant.[35] It did not purport to shed light on the word "searches" generally or to equate it with the common law definition of trespass more specifically.

Similarly, Justice Scalia's textual point provides only modest grounds to tie search doctrine to trespass law. It is true that the Fourth Amendment protects the right of security in "persons, houses, papers and effects," all of which are items over which an individual would enjoy property rights. James Madison's initial draft of what became the Fourth Amendment would have made the connection even clearer. When Madison proposed his draft in the House of Representatives in June 1789, it referred to a right of the people "in their persons, their houses, and their other property."[36]

---

[32] Cf. *Warden v Hayden*, 387 US 294, 303 (1967) (noting Lord Camden's claim in *Entick* that "great end, for which men entered into society, was to secure their property," and remarking that it "derived no doubt from the political thought of his time").

[33] There is some historical disagreement on how common general warrants may have been during this general period. See Davies, 98 Mich L Rev at 655–57 n 299 (cited in note 14) (contrasting his views on this point with those of William Cuddihy).

[34] James M. Beck, *Nullification by Indirection*, 23 Harv L Rev 441, 441 (1910) (stating that "Lord Camden's great decision on general warrants" was a "political topic[] of foremost interest" to the Framers of the US Constitution).

[35] This reading is suggested by the longer version of *Entick* published in the State Trials reporter, although it is not clear if this version of *Entick* was widely read in the colonies leading up to the time of the Fourth Amendment's ratification. See Davies, 98 Mich L Rev at 566 n 25 (cited in note 14). In this version of *Entick*, Lord Camden is reported as following up this passage by explaining that the defendant was "bound to sh[o]w by way of justification, that some positive law has empowered or excused him." *Entick v Carrington*, 19 Howell's State Trials 1029, 1066 (1765). The fact of the trespass made it "incumbent upon the defendants to sh[o]w the law, by which this seizure is warranted." Id.

[36] Cuddihy, *The Fourth Amendment* at 692 (cited in note 9).

Even so, it does not follow that all trespasses are searches. The relevant text of the Fourth Amendment indicates two separate concepts: first, the general right to be secure against unreasonable searches and seizures; and second, the limitation of that right to persons, houses, papers, and effects. It is unclear why the nature of the latter requires equating the former with the particular elements of trespass law.

To be clear, I am not arguing that trespass law is necessarily an improper standard for originalists to use in interpreting the Fourth Amendment. Trespass provides a plausible standard that a court might use to fashion a deductive test that is consistent with the recognized examples of searches from the late eighteenth century. In the language advocated by Randy Barnett and Larry Solum, adopting a trespass test for searches is a plausible act of originalist construction.[37] My point here is narrower. Because searches were understood mostly by way of example, there is little evidence that searches were originally understood as coextensive with trespasses.

II. The Meaning of "Searches" from Ratification to Olmstead

Jones makes the additional claim that until the latter half of the twentieth century, "Fourth Amendment jurisprudence was tied to common-law trespass."[38] For this point, Justice Scalia relies largely on the Court's 1928 decision in *Olmstead v United States*,[39] which held that wiretapping a telephone line from a public street was not a search. According to Justice Scalia, *Olmstead* reflected a simple trespass rationale: Wiretapping could not be a search because

[37] See Randy E. Barnett, *Interpretation and Construction*, 34 Harv J L & Pub Pol 65, 66 (2011); Lawrence B. Solum, *The Interpretation-Construction Distinction*, 27 Const Comment 95, 101–08 (2010).

[38] *United States v Jones*, 132 S Ct 945, 949 (2012).

[39] 277 US 438 (1928). Justice Scalia also cites an article of mine for this point, and in particular a page at which I state that "early courts interpreted the Fourth Amendment as a claim against government interference with property rights, and in particular, rights against trespass." Orin S. Kerr, *The Fourth Amendment and New Technologies: Constitutional Myths and the Case for Caution*, 102 Mich L Rev 801, 816 (2004) (cited in *Jones*, 132 S Ct at 949–50). In retrospect, I was guilty of reciting the common wisdom without pausing to consider its accuracy. My focus in that article was the role of property in the post-*Katz* cases, and I relied on the common wisdom for the pre-*Katz* history. After studying the pre-*Katz* cases more closely, my conclusion is that the pre-*Katz* cases and post-*Katz* cases offered surprisingly similar kinds of protection. In neither era did search doctrine precisely track property law, and in neither era did results deviate extensively from property law.

"there was no entry of the houses or offices of the defendants."[40]

A close look at the cases reveals a different picture. The Supreme Court never tied the definition of a "search" to trespass law. From the period of the Fourth Amendment's ratification until *Olmstead*, the Supreme Court classified government conduct as searches or nonsearches by analogy: The Court construed the government's act either as analogous or disanalogous to physical intrusion into private spaces. But no particular framework guided the analogy, and the Court often referred to privacy as much as property. During the subsequent period, from *Olmstead* to *Katz*, the Court came to rely on physical penetration into a protected space as the guide to what counted as a search. But even in this period, the Court expressly distanced its inquiry from the specifics of common law trespass. The Court dismissed trespass as a common law technicality and focused instead on whether physical penetration had occurred.

The starting point is *Boyd v United States*,[41] in 1886, which was arguably the first Supreme Court decision to focus on the meaning of searches.[42] *Boyd* involved a constitutional challenge to an 1874 federal civil forfeiture law. Investigators had obtained an order requiring Boyd to provide the government with the invoice for items he had recently imported to determine if he had paid the required customs taxes on them. Boyd objected that forcing him to provide the invoice was an unreasonable search and seizure in violation of the Fourth Amendment. Importantly, however, investigators had not entered Boyd's home. They had only obtained a court order requiring him to turn over his property. As the Supreme Court noted, the typical scenario of "forcible entry into a man's house and searching among his papers"[43] was "wanting."[44] Had any search occurred?

The Court held that complying with the government's order counted as a Fourth Amendment search and seizure. "Though the proceeding in question is divested of many of the aggravating in-

---

[40] *Jones*, 132 S Ct at 950 (quoting *Olmstead*, 277 US at 464).

[41] 116 US 616 (1886). The fact that many years passed before the Court addressed the meaning of searches partly reflects the limited nature of federal law enforcement in that period. The Fourth Amendment only applied to the federal government, and federal law enforcement was minimal by modern standards.

[42] The possible exception is the extensive dicta on Fourth Amendment protection for postal mail in *Ex Parte Jackson*, 96 US 727, 732–36 (1877).

[43] *Boyd*, 116 US at 622.

[44] Id.

cidents of actual search and seizure,"[45] the Court explained, "it contains their substance and essence, and effects their substantial purpose."[46] By construing the Fourth Amendment "liberally" rather than in "literal" fashion, the Court concluded that complying with the order was the "equivalent" of an "actual" search and seizure and thus equally condemned.[47] The leading case of *Entick v Carrington* reflected the spirit of the Fourth Amendment, *Boyd* reasoned, but it had not meant merely to condemn physical entries: "It is not the breaking of [a man's] doors, and the rummaging of his drawers, that constitutes the essence of the offense."[48] Rather, the principles of *Entick*, and therefore the Fourth Amendment, "apply to all invasions on the part of the government and its employees of the sanctity of a man's home and the privacies of life."[49] That included attempting to compel a man's private papers. How trespass doctrine might apply never arose.

Trespass law was similarly ignored when the Supreme Court considered the constitutionality of government subpoenas to compel documents in an investigation into violations of the Sherman Act in *Hale v Henkel*[50] in 1906. The Court noted that "a search ordinarily implies a quest by an officer of the law,"[51] which did not occur when government officials issued a subpoena. Nonetheless, compelled compliance with a government subpoena was a search under *Boyd*.[52] The only mention of trespass appeared in a concurrence by Justice McKenna. In explaining why subpoenas raised only slight dangers of abuse, McKenna noted that complying with subpoenas, unlike executing search warrants, contained "no element of trespass or force . . . [and] does not disturb the possession of property."[53] Importantly, however, Justice McKenna did not suggest a link between searches and trespass. The absence of trespass was

---

[45] Id at 635.

[46] Id.

[47] Id.

[48] Id at 630.

[49] Id.

[50] 201 US 43 (1906).

[51] Id at 76.

[52] Id.

[53] Id at 80 (McKenna, J, concurring).

invoked as grounds for thinking that compliance with subpoenas was not unreasonable rather than not a search.[54]

Trespass law failed to surface in subsequent search cases as well. Consider the now-forgotten case of *Perlman v United States*[55] from 1918, which involved an effort by the government to secure exhibits from previous litigation in a subsequent perjury prosecution. Perlman had submitted property he owned as exhibits for trial in a patent litigation suit. Prosecutors later decided that Perlman had committed perjury, and they obtained the exhibits from the prior court and sought to use the exhibits against Perlman in the criminal prosecution. Perlman objected that taking control of his property was an unreasonable search and seizure akin to breaking into his home and retrieving evidence inside. The Court disagreed. Physical entry into the home involved "an invasion of the defendant's privacy, a taking from his immediate and personal possession."[56] In Perlman's case, by contrast, there was no invasion of privacy: Perlman had voluntarily exposed the articles for evidence in court in the infringement case.[57]

Also consider *United States v Lee*,[58] which asked whether use of a searchlight constituted a Fourth Amendment search.[59] Government officials pursuing a boat at night shone a searchlight onto it to reveal cases of liquor on deck.[60] The Court held that using the searchlight was not a "search."[61] If trespass formed the primary understanding of what constituted a search, one might expect that the Court would simply have noted that shining a flashlight was not a trespass. Instead, the Court reasoned by analogy: Using a searchlight was not a search because it was "comparable to the use of a marine glass or a field glass"[62]—what today we would call binoculars.

Cases like *Boyd*, *Hale*, *Perlman*, and *Lee* suggest that early Supreme Court search doctrine was not tied to property law. Physical invasion

---

[54] Id at 81 ("[W]e are surely not prepared to say that such uses are unreasonable.").

[55] 247 US 7 (1918).

[56] Id at 14.

[57] Id at 15.

[58] 274 US 559 (1927).

[59] Id at 563.

[60] Id at 561.

[61] Id at 563.

[62] Id.

of a home clearly counted as a search. But the cases do not draw
the equivalence between searches and trespass or suggest a doctrinal
linkage, and they often suggest something broader. *Boyd* reasons
that the Fourth Amendment applies to "all invasions" of "the privacies of life."[63] *Hale* notes that a search is normally understood as
"a quest" and finds a search where no trespass occurred.[64] *Perlman*
focuses on whether the government's act was "an invasion of the
defendant's privacy."[65] And these were not the only statements tying
the Fourth Amendment to privacy rather than property in an age
when the Fourth Amendment is thought to have been mired in
property concepts. In 1932, the Court announced without dissent
that the Fourth Amendment must be "construed liberally to safeguard the right of privacy."[66] Whatever the Fourth Amendment
meant to the Justices of this period, it was more than just common
law trespass.

Indeed, the Fourth Amendment cases of this period occasionally
suggested hostility to common law property principles. An intrigu-
ing example is *McGuire v United States*,[67] which involved a search
of a home for illegal liquors during Prohibition. Agents lawfully
entered McGuire's home with a warrant to seize liquor. Once inside,
however, the agents decided to destroy most of the liquor rather
than seize it pursuant to the warrant. McGuire sought suppression
based on the common law doctrine of trespass *ab initio*, by which
improper conduct after a person has been admitted to a private
place is deemed to have made the initial entry an unlawful trespass.[68]
The Supreme Court rejected the effort to invoke common law
trespass. Even if the officers had become civilly liable by exceeding
the scope of the warrant, the doctrine of trespass *ab initio* was merely
"a fiction whose origin, history, and purpose do not justify its application where the right of the government to make use of evidence
is involved."[69] To modern eyes, *McGuire* reads in part as a case
about Fourth Amendment remedies rather than rights. Nonetheless,
the Court's dismissive attitude toward common law property prin-

---

[63] *Boyd v United States*, 116 US 616, 630 (1886).

[64] *Hale v Henkel*, 201 US 43, 76 (1906).

[65] *Perlman v United States*, 247 US 7, 14 (1918).

[66] *United States v Lefkowitz*, 285 US 452, 464 (1932).

[67] 273 US 95 (1927).

[68] Id at 97–98.

[69] Id at 100.

ciples seems hard to square with the widely held view that pre-*Katz* cases embraced common law trespass.

III. The Meaning of "Searches" from Olmstead to Katz

The second period of pre-*Katz* caselaw on searches starts with *Olmstead* and ends just before *Katz*. During this period, the Court developed the notion of physical penetration of a protected area as a guide to identifying searches. Importantly, however, the Court distinguished physical penetration from the technical doctrine of trespass. When parties tried to harness trespass as a standard, the Court generally dismissed trespass as of questionable help in construing constitutional protections.

In *Olmstead*, federal prohibition agents wiretapped Olmstead's telephone lines outside his home and office in order to gather evidence of his directing a massive bootlegging conspiracy. The Supreme Court ruled that tapping Olmstead's phone from the public street was not a search. *Olmstead* is often viewed as the paradigmatic case equating trespass with searches. In *Jones*, Justice Scalia relied on the case as an example of how pre-*Katz* cases based the definition of a "search" in trespass.[70] But a closer look at the reasoning of *Olmstead* suggests that trespass law played little role in the Court's decision.

Chief Justice Taft's majority opinion relied primarily on a textualist claim. The Fourth Amendment protects rights in persons, houses, papers, and effects. But accessing telephone lines from a public street accessed none of these specifically enumerated places. "There was no entry of the houses or offices of the defendants,"[71] so the wiretapping implicated no rights in houses. And conversations over telephone lines, unlike postal letters, were neither papers nor effects.[72] Even recognizing *Boyd*'s rule of liberal construction, the text of the Fourth Amendment was clear. The rule of liberal interpretation could not "justify enlargement of the language employed beyond the possible practical meaning of houses, persons, papers, and effects, or so to apply the words search and seizure as to forbid hearing or sight."[73]

---

[70] *United States v Jones*, 132 S Ct 945, 949–50 (2012).

[71] 277 US at 464.

[72] Id.

[73] Id at 465.

Trespass is mentioned only twice in the *Olmstead* opinion. The first mention appears in the fact section, where the opinion states that the wires were installed "without trespass upon any property of the defendants."[74] The second mention appears in a brief paragraph distinguishing *Hester v United States*,[75] the first case on the open-fields doctrine. In *Hester*, the officers had trespassed on the defendant's land and observed him from 100 yards away from his house.[76] According to the opinion in *Olmstead*, the officers' acts in *Hester* did not violate the Fourth Amendment for the same reason that there was no Fourth Amendment violation in *Olmstead*. "While there was a trespass" in *Hester*, no Fourth Amendment violation occurred because "there was no search of person, house, papers, or effects."[77]

The phrase acknowledging a trespass in *Hester* is the closest *Olmstead* comes to suggesting that trespass might control the scope of searches. But such a reading is implausible for two reasons. First, the most significant precedent on the meaning of searches was *Boyd*, which had linked searches to invasions of "the privacies of life"[78] instead of trespass. If the Court meant to equate trespasses with searches in *Olmstead*, in conflict with *Boyd*, the majority presumably would have said so more directly than an oblique and unexplained reference to trespass in the course of distinguishing *Hester*. Second, Justice Brandeis's famous dissent in *Olmstead* did not even mention trespass. Justice Brandeis criticized the majority for adopting an "unduly literal"[79] interpretation of the Fourth Amendment instead of following the liberal approach taken in *Boyd*.[80] If the *Olmstead* majority had adopted a trespass test, surely Justice Brandeis would have said something about it.

Search decisions after *Olmstead* also failed to embrace a trespass rationale. In *Goldman v United States*,[81] agents listened in on con-

---

[74] Id at 457.

[75] 265 US 57 (1924).

[76] Id at 58.

[77] 277 US at 465. Chief Justice Taft also cited the searchlight case, *United States v Lee*, for this position. Id.

[78] *Boyd*, 116 US at 630.

[79] Olmstead, 277 US at 476 (Brandeis, J, dissenting).

[80] Id at 474–79 (Brandeis, J, dissenting).

[81] 316 US 129 (1942).

versations inside a lawyer's office.[82] Agents first broke into the lawyer's office with the help of the superintendent and installed a microphone in the partition wall.[83] The microphone didn't work,
however, so agents instead obtained access to the adjoining office
and pressed a sensitive microphone to the wall to hear the conversations.[84] The defendant made two arguments. First, the defendant argued that the initial trespass had tainted the subsequent use
of the microphone, turning all of the government's conduct into a
trespass.[85] At first blush, this seems like support for a linkage between trespass and search doctrine. But the Court did not accept
this argument. The factual findings below indicated that the trespass
had not aided use of the microphone through the wall, so the Court
simply reasoned that the two were separate events and provided no
further analysis.[86]

The defendant's second argument in *Goldman* was that pressing
the microphone against the wall was a search.[87] This claim provided
a natural opportunity to discuss trespass law. If the Court understood trespass to be coextensive with the definition of a "search,"
the Court could have analyzed the search question by applying
trespass doctrine. Instead, the Court decided this issue without even
mentioning trespass. Justice Roberts concluded that pressing the
microphone to the wall did not constitute a search because the facts
were too close to *Olmstead* to justify a different result.[88] The defendant sought to distinguish *Olmstead* on the ground that a person
in a room intended to keep his conversation inside the four walls
of the room, unlike the person on a phone call who intentionally
sent the call out into the public street.[89] Justice Roberts rejected
this effort out of hand as not a "reasonable or logical distinction"
that appeared "too nice for practical application of the Constitutional guarantee."[90]

Perhaps the most extended discussion of the connection between

---

[82] Id at 131–32.
[83] Id.
[84] Id.
[85] Id at 133.
[86] Id at 134.
[87] Id.
[88] Id at 135.
[89] Id.
[90] Id.

trespass and search doctrine before *Katz* occurred in *On Lee v United States*.[91] An undercover informant entered the defendant's laundry store wearing a recording device.[92] The defendant, On Lee, made incriminating statements to the informant that were recorded and transmitted to a federal agent outside the store.[93] The defendant argued that the informant had committed a trespass by recording the conversation.[94] The informant had consent to enter generally, but using the recording device had exceeded the consent and there-fore rendered the entry a trespass under the common law doctrine of trespass *ab initio*.[95] The trespass thus constituted a search, the defendant argued, relying on the Court's apparent assumption in *Goldman* that the initial entry was a trespass.[96]

In rejecting On Lee's claim, the majority opinion by Justice Jack-son began by denying that a trespass was necessarily a search. Ac-cording to Justice Jackson, *Goldman* had "expressly reserved decision as to the effect on the search-and-seizure question of a trespass in that situation."[97] The Court had not ruled on that issue because there was no causal relationship between the initial trespass and the subsequent conduct that yielded evidence; thus the Court had left "undecided"[98] the Fourth Amendment implications of the initial trespass.[99] Justice Jackson then reasoned that even if the undercover agent had committed a trespass *ab initio*, no search had occurred. Putting aside precedent, it was "doubtful that the niceties of tort law initiated almost two and a half centuries ago" were "of much aid in determining rights under the Fourth Amendment."[100] And the *McGuire* case had rejected the reliance on the trespass *ab initio* theory decades earlier. Under *McGuire*, whether the conduct tech-nically was "a trespass under orthodox tort law" was a "fine-spun doctrine[]"[101] that had no place in determining whether the evidence could be used in court.

---

[91] 343 US 747 (1952).

[92] Id at 749.

[93] Id.

[94] Id at 750.

[95] Id at 752.

[96] Id.

[97] Id at 751.

[98] Id.

[99] Id.

[100] Id at 752.

[101] Id.

The final pre-*Katz* case is *Silverman v United States*,[102] decided just a few years before *Katz*. Agents investigating a gambling ring operating from a rowhouse obtained permission from the owner of the adjoining rowhouse to enter and conduct surveillance from inside.[103] Agents found a large crack in the wall between the two houses, and they inserted a "spike mike" consisting of a foot-long spike connected to a microphone.[104] By trial and error, the agents were able to position the spike so that it touched a heating duct inside the neighboring house. That allowed the microphone to pick up conversations throughout the neighboring home.[105]

The *Silverman* Court unanimously ruled that this constituted a search because it was "accomplished by means of an unauthorized physical penetration into the premises occupied by the petitioners."[106] The act of physical penetration "usurp[ed] part of the petitioners' house or office,"[107] distinguishing the case from *Goldman* if only by a few inches. Importantly, however, *Silverman* expressly distanced its inquiry from trespass law. "[W]e need not pause to consider whether or not there was a technical trespass under the local property law relating to party walls,"[108] the Court cautioned. Citing precedents such as *On Lee* and *Hester*, the Court explained that "[i]nherent Fourth Amendment rights are not inevitably measurable in terms of ancient niceties of tort or real property law."[109]

The path from *Olmstead* to *Silverman* shows the Court eventually focusing on physical penetration into a protected space as the primary test for a Fourth Amendment search. This plainly shares a connection to property law: Physical penetration into a private space often will constitute a trespass. At the same time, the Court did not equate searches with trespasses. In *On Lee* and *Silverman*, the Court expressly distanced its analysis from trespass doctrine. And in *Olmstead* and *Goldman*, the Court did not invoke trespass to analyze search questions even though it could have easily done so. The

---

[102] 365 US 505 (1961).

[103] Id at 506.

[104] Id.

[105] Id at 506–07.

[106] Id at 509.

[107] Id at 511.

[108] Id.

[109] Id.

widespread belief that pre-*Katz* decisions adopted a trespass test appears to be incorrect.

IV. The Creation of the Trespass Myth

We are left with a puzzle. Although courts and scholars claim that pre-*Katz* cases' definition of Fourth Amendment "searches" was based on trespass, a close look at the cases reveals a different picture. What happened? As best I can tell, subsequent Supreme Court cases introduced the trespass myth. Two decisions in 1967, *Warden v Hayden*[110] and *Katz* itself, reconceptualized the pre-*Katz* search cases as trespass rulings. Today's judges and scholars have looked to those cases to understand pre-*Katz* law, and they have assumed the accuracy of its description of prior law. In short, the reason so many people think that pre-*Katz* cases adopted a trespass test is that *Katz* says so.

The first of these two cases, *Warden v Hayden*, overturned the common law "mere evidence" rule. The mere evidence rule imposed a limit on the purposes of warrants: The government could not obtain a warrant to search for and seize mere evidence of crime.[111] Justice Brennan's opinion in *Hayden* reasoned that the mere evidence rule was no longer proper because Fourth Amendment law was undergoing a transformation from protecting property to protecting privacy.[112] The mere evidence rule was premised on a property notion: The government could obtain warrants to search for and seize evidence only if the possessor had no right to it (as would be the case with contraband or stolen goods).[113]

According to Justice Brennan in *Hayden*, however, "[t]he premise that property interests control the right of the Government to search and seize has been discredited."[114] Citing *Silverman*, Justice Brennan argued that Fourth Amendment law had begun to depart from property: "the principal object of the Fourth Amendment is the protection of privacy rather than property, and [we] have increasingly discarded fictional and procedural barriers rested on

---

[110] 387 US 294 (1967).

[111] *Gouled v United States*, 255 US 298, 311–12 (1921).

[112] 387 US at 301–02.

[113] Id.

[114] Id at 304.

property concepts."[115] The mere evidence rule could be abolished because the property-obsessed era of Fourth Amendment interpretation was over.

Whatever the merits of *Hayden*'s rule as a matter of policy, its recounting of Fourth Amendment history does not ring true. Contrary to Justice Brennan's claim in *Hayden*, the Court had never held that "property interests control" Fourth Amendment law. Property traditionally had played a role in Fourth Amendment law, just as it continues to play a role today.[116] But it was never the exclusive test. Further, *Silverman*'s embrace of physical entry instead of technical trespass had not departed from prior doctrine. *Silverman*'s emphasis on physical entry was consistent with both early history and subsequent cases such as *Olmstead* and *Goldman*.

The Court further cemented the property-to-privacy myth when it handed down *Katz v United States* a few months later. According to the *Katz* opinion, *Olmstead* and *Goldman* created a "trespass doctrine"[117] by which "surveillance without any trespass and without the seizure of any material object fell outside the ambit of the Constitution."[118] Echoing *Hayden*, *Katz* used *Silverman* as the alleged turning point. According to *Katz*, the *Silverman* decision had departed from the narrow trespass rationale by finding a search without a "technical trespass under . . . local property law."[119] With such a recent departure from trespass doctrine, it was only a small step to say that the definition of a "search" was no longer linked to physical penetration. *Katz* took that extra step by holding that use of a microphone taped to the top of a public phone booth to listen to a caller's conversation in the booth was a Fourth Amendment search.[120] Although the microphone did not physically penetrate the phone booth, and the phone booth was not the caller's property, the caller reasonably relied on the privacy the phone booth provided.[121]

The source of *Katz*'s claim of a prior trespass test remains unclear. One explanation may be that some litigants before the Court had

---

[115] Id.

[116] See Kerr, 102 Mich L Rev at 815–27 (cited in note 39).

[117] *Katz v United States*, 389 US 347, 352–53 (1967).

[118] Id at 353.

[119] Id.

[120] Id.

[121] Id at 352.

described *Olmstead* and *Goldman* as trespass cases. In 1964, for example, the Supreme Court had decided the now-forgotten case of *Clinton v Virginia*,[122] which had facts similar to those of *Silverman* except the microphone was in the wall rather than through the wall. At oral argument, counsel for the defendant argued that *Olmstead* and *Goldman* had enacted a physical trespass test that *Silverman* had later rejected.[123] Under *Silverman*, counsel argued, the precise location of the microphone no longer mattered. It's hard to say how the Justices evaluated those claims in *Clinton*. The Supreme Court ruled for the defendant in four words—"The judgment is reversed"—followed by a citation to *Silverman*. Justice Clark added a one-sentence concurrence in the judgment: "Since the Court finds that the 'spiked' mike used by the police officers penetrated petitioner's premises sufficiently to be an actual trespass thereof, I join in the judgment."[124] Such sparse sources cannot support a confident conclusion about the Justices' conception of searches during the period. But, at the very least, the Justices had been exposed to the characterization of *Olmstead* and *Goldman* as trespass cases.[125]

The notion that *Olmstead* and *Goldman* had adopted a trespass test resurfaced in the briefing in *Katz*. During the period after *Silverman*, a handful of circuit courts had linked Supreme Court search decisions with trespass.[126] The Ninth Circuit had described search

---

[122] 377 US 158 (1964).

[123] *Clinton v Virginia* Oral Argument Transcript, Apr 27, 1964, online at http://www.oyez.org/cases/1960-1969/1963/1963_294. Interestingly, counsel recognized that pre-*Olmstead* cases such as *Boyd* had not adopted a trespass test. See id.

[124] *Clinton*, 377 US at 158 (Clark, J, concurring in the judgment).

[125] Exposure does not mean acceptance. At oral argument in *Clinton*, Justice Stewart pushed back on counsel's claim that the Court had previously adopted a trespass test.

> Counsel. [*Silverman*] deviated from the previous test of the necessity of a physical trespass.
>
> Justice Harlan. That's correct. I see.
>
> Justice Stewart. Well, there was a case called *Hester* where there was a physical trespass, an actual trespass on somebody's land where they said it was not a violation of the Fourth Amendment. So I'm not sure that trespass of the—or its absence has ever been the—the only test. In other words, even prior to *Silverman*, that's all I'm suggesting.

Clinton v Virginia Oral Argument Transcript, Apr 27, 1964.

[126] See *Smayda v United States*, 352 F2d 251, 256 (9th Cir 1965) (describing Supreme Court doctrine by noting that "[i]n each such case" that a search has been identified, "there has been an actual physical invasion—a trespass."); *Todisco v United States*, 298 F2d 208, 209–10 (9th Cir 1961) (stating that whether government eavesdropping constitutes a search or seizure is "largely dependent upon whether entry upon the premises amounted

doctrine as "largely dependent" on trespass.[127] The Second Circuit had gone further, stating without analysis that *Goldman* made "technical trespass" an "essential" requirement of a search.[128] In *Katz*, the United States relied on those cases to cast *Goldman* as a trespass case. Citing the circuit decisions, the government's brief claimed that *Goldman* "has been deemed to stand for the proposition that a trespass, either of an eavesdropper or an eavesdropping device, is necessary to constitute a violation of the Fourth Amendment."[129] This was an inaccurate summary of *Goldman*. But it provided the United States a simple argument in *Katz*: Because taping the microphone to the phone booth was not a trespass, no search had occurred.[130]

It is possible that *Katz* described prior law as based on trespass simply because litigants and some lower courts had done so. Or perhaps that characterization provided a straw man useful to justify departing from precedent. Whatever the reason, *Katz* misportrayed the history of Fourth Amendment searches. The law had never adopted a trespass test. *Silverman* had not departed from either *Olmstead* or *Goldman*, while *Katz* broke sharply from *Silverman*. But the property-to-privacy narrative allowed the Court to present *Katz*'s fresh start as a logical consequence of past cases. Nearly a

to trespass"); *Anspach v United States*, 305 F2d 48, 50 (10th Cir 1962) ("Traditionally the concept of an invasion upon the right of privacy was premised within the theories of the law of trespass.").

[127] *Todisco*, 298 F2d at 209.

[128] *United States v Pardo-Bolland*, 348 F2d 316, 321 (2d Cir 1965) (Smith, J). Agents had bugged the defendants' hotel rooms to listen to conversations inside. One bug was placed on the outside of the keyhole of a door, and another was placed immediately outside a common door to the two rooms. The Second Circuit's analysis was remarkably sparse. First, Judge Smith noted that the trial court had denied the defendants' motion to suppress because "there had been no technical trespass into either of the hotel rooms of the defendants, which is still essential to a violation of federal law under United States v. Goldman." Id. Judge Smith then stated a conclusion: "There is substantial evidence in the record to support those findings." Id.

[129] Brief of Respondent at 13, *Katz v United States*, 389 US 347 (1967).

[130] See id at 14. Katz's main brief shared a somewhat similar characterization of *Goldman*. See Brief for Petitioner at 8, *Katz v United States*, 389 US 347 (1967) ("The basis of [*Goldman*] was that the action by the agents did not constitute a physical trespass into the area occupied by the defendant."). At the same time, it is unclear whether Katz's brief used the phrase "physical trespass" merely as a shorthand for the "unauthorized physical penetration" that was the focus in *Silverman*, 465 US at 509, or, alternatively, as a reference to the doctrines of trespass law. Katz's brief also expressed caution as to whether *Goldman* had actually adopted a physical trespass test. See id at 12 ("[T]he inquiry as to whether or not a physical trespass has occurred is no longer relevant in discussing a search and seizure issue and, to the extent that *Goldman v. United States, supra*, stands for such a proposition, it must be overruled.").

half-century later, the myth lives on. To today's lawyers and scholars, *Katz* is the Fourth Amendment's north star. *Katz* claims to supplant a search doctrine based on trespass, and subsequent scholars—and the Supreme Court in *Jones*—have assumed this to be true.

V. What Trespass Test Did Jones Introduce?

The history of the Fourth Amendment search doctrine brings us to a surprising conclusion: *Jones* purports to restore a trespass test that never previously existed. This poses a potential challenge for future courts because there is little precedent to guide courts in interpreting the protean concept of trespass. Trespass has taken many forms and changed over time, rendering it a tricky doctrine to pin down. In this section, I want to explore two ambiguities in the *Jones* trespass test. First, post-*Jones*, which of the various eighteenth-century understandings of trespass does the definition of a Fourth Amendment search incorporate? And second, do changes in the law of trespass since the late eighteenth century change the scope of the *Jones* trespass test and, therefore, the scope of the Fourth Amendment?

The first challenge is identifying which version of trespass the Fourth Amendment search doctrine incorporates. The word "trespass" signifies a constellation of related ideas.[131] Blackstone emphasized the accordion-like quality of trespass in his *Commentaries*. "[I]n its largest and most extensive sense," Blackstone explained, trespass "signifies any transgression or offence against the law of nature, of society, or of the country in which we live, whether it relates to a man's person or his property."[132] "[A]ny misfeasance or act of one man whereby another is injuriously treated or damnified is a transgression or trespass in its largest sense"—a definition that included everything from a failure to perform a promise to beating another person.[133] On the other hand, trespass could be understood in a "limited and confined sense" as only trespass to land: that is, "no more than an entry on another man's ground without a lawful authority, and doing some damage, however inconsiderable, to his

---

[131] 1 Dan B. Dobbs, Paul T. Hayden, and Ellen M. Bublick, *The Law of Torts*, §§ 17, 49 (2d ed 2011).

[132] 2 William Blackstone, *Commentaries on the Laws of England* *208 (1765).

[133] Id.

real property."[134] The term "trespass" could be understood as embracing a wide range of ideas.

The Supreme Court's failure to explain how the trespass test applied in *Jones* hints at the problem. Investigators installed a GPS device on the undercarriage of the target's car.[135] This is not an obvious case for trespass. A trespass usually implies some sort of invasion into property, whereas the agents placed the device on or under the property rather than inside it. The Court's opinion breezes by why a trespass occurred. The Court describes the act as "trespassory"[136] and announces a conclusion: "We have no doubt that such a physical intrusion would have been considered a 'search' within the meaning of the Fourth Amendment when it was adopted."[137] No explanation is offered. Justice Scalia's expression of confidence substitutes for analysis, hinting that the conclusion may be harder to explain than Justice Scalia lets on.[138]

Given the possible options, which version of trespass does the Fourth Amendment now recognize? In light of *Jones*, it must be something beyond trespass to land. Justice Alito suggests in his concurrence that the majority is referring to a trespass to chattels.[139] The majority did not contradict Alito's claim; given Scalia's many volleys with Alito in *Jones*, this may suggest tacit agreement. If so, perhaps the trespass standard tracks the common law doctrine most directly suited to each of the four constitutionally protected areas, "persons, houses, papers, and effects." Perhaps the standard adopts traditional principles of trespass to land for acts concerning houses, trespass to chattels for acts concerning papers and effects, and trespass to the person for acts concerning persons.

This is a possibility but hardly a certainty. As Blackstone emphasized, trespass can be understood "in its largest and most extensive sense" or only in a "limited and confined" one. It might conceivably include the full range of common law trespass doctrines, or it might include only a few. It might merely mean attachment

---

[134] Id at *209.

[135] *United States v Jones*, 132 S Ct 945, 948 (2012).

[136] Id at 954.

[137] Id at 959.

[138] Cf. Peter A. Winn, *Trespass and the Fourth Amendment: Some Reflections on Jones*, http://usvjones.com/2012/06/04/trespass-and-the-fourth-amendment-some-reflections-on-jones/ (arguing that the Court's trespass analysis is "utterly disconnected from the historical reality of eighteen century common law.").

[139] *Jones*, 132 S Ct at 957–58 (Alito, J, concurring).

to or penetration of personal property, or it might suggest broader types of interference with property interests. *Jones* sets up the question, but neither *Jones* nor the relevant history provides much in the way of answers.

A second question is whether the definition of "search" in the Fourth Amendment was fixed by late eighteenth-century trespass law or adapts to later developments. Trespass law can change over time. According to Justice Alito, for example, the common law test for trespass to chattels did not require actual damage to the chattel, while the modern test does.[140] If trespass law evolves over time, does the scope of the Fourth Amendment change as well?

At first blush, it might appear that *Jones* answered the question by adopting the eighteenth-century standard. The *Jones* majority emphasized that the officers' conduct "would have been considered a 'search' within the meaning of the Fourth Amendment when it was adopted."[141] The same conduct must be a search today, Justice Scalia reasoned, because the Fourth Amendment "must provide *at a minimum* the degree of protection it afforded when it was adopted."[142] These passages suggest that the scope of Fourth Amendment protection remains fixed despite intervening changes in trespass law.

Matters may not be so simple, however. Indeed, Justice Scalia's dissent in *Georgia v Randolph*[143] suggests the opposite answer. *Randolph* considered whether the police could lawfully search a home when the co-owning husband and wife were both present and yet only one consented.[144] Justice Stevens penned a brief concurrence that used the facts of *Randolph* to criticize originalism.[145] According to Justice Stevens, an originalist would have to conclude that a husband's consent was all that mattered in *Randolph* because he was the primary property owner at common law.[146] Justice Stevens used this ground to claim that originalism could not keep up with the

---

[140] Id at 957 n 2 (citing W. Keeton, D. Dobbs, R. Keeton, and D. Owen, *Prosser & Keeton on Law of Torts* 87 (5th ed 1984)). Peter Winn contends that this claim is incorrect, but the broader point of changing doctrine remains. See Winn, *Trespass and the Fourth Amendment* (cited in note 138).

[141] *Jones*, 132 S Ct at 949.

[142] Id at 953 (emphasis in original).

[143] 547 US 103 (2006).

[144] Id at 106.

[145] Id at 123–24 (Stevens, J, concurring).

[146] Id at 124.

times: Modern property law and modern social norms justified a new rule that originalism could not accommodate.[147]

Justice Scalia took the bait and filed a dissent that rejected Justice Stevens's understanding of originalism. According to Justice Scalia, originalist readings of the Fourth Amendment properly adapt to changing property rules.[148] "[C]hangeable law presents no problem for the originalist,"[149] Justice Scalia insisted. Although the Fourth Amendment historically was tied to trespass law, "our unchanging Constitution refers to other bodies of law that might themselves change."[150] Changes in trespass law could be recognized as changing the scope of protections without truly changing the Fourth Amendment: "As property law developed," the scope of rights may change, but "changes in the law of property to which the Fourth Amendment referred would not alter the Amendment's meaning."[151]

The tension seems clear. Although Justice Scalia's originalism in *Jones* suggests that the trespass test follows eighteenth-century trespass law, his originalism in *Randolph* suggests that the test follows trespass law today. And we might add to the mix Justice Scalia's originalist opinion in *Kyllo v United States*,[152] in which the Court held that the government had conducted a Fourth Amendment search when it used a new technology to obtain, from inside a home, information that previously could not have been gathered without a trespass. *Kyllo* suggests a third approach, by which the trespass test is based on what information would have been known in the eighteenth century absent a trespass rather than what can be known without a trespass today. To the extent these standards differ in practice, future courts will have to determine which version of the trespass standard controls.

VI. The Surprisingly Stable Search Inquiry—and the Normative Question of Search Doctrine

The history of the Fourth Amendment also suggests deeper lessons about the surprising consistency of the definition of a

---

[147] Id at 124–25.

[148] Id at 144 (Scalia, J, dissenting).

[149] Id.

[150] Id.

[151] Id at 143.

[152] 533 US 27 (2001).

"search." It turns out that the kinds of inquiries that the Supreme Court used to identify searches before *Katz* are not much different from the kind of inquiries used in the *Katz* era. Post-*Katz* decisions use the language of *Katz*, of course. But the nature of the inquiry, and the results reached, are more similar than the formal shift in doctrine would suggest. This stability suggests that something beyond formal blackletter doctrine is guiding what the Supreme Court labels a "search."

The most likely explanation is a functional one. Because the scope of the term "search" usually defines what the police can and can't do either without a warrant or at least some suspicion, the Supreme Court will inevitably interpret the scope of searches with an eye to the policy question of how much power to give government agents. Given the wide range of investigative techniques, no one principle will answer this question. Instead, factors such as the degree of infringement on privacy, the intrusiveness of the act, and the government's need to successfully investigate crimes can all influence the Court's decision. *Katz* or no *Katz*, Fourth Amendment doctrine grapples with many of the same basic questions. And from that perspective, *Jones* may merely rearrange doctrinal boxes more than fundamentally alter the nature of the search inquiry.

To appreciate the stability of the search inquiry, consider how the Supreme Court has applied the "reasonable expectation of privacy" test. The Supreme Court's cases have treated the phrase "reasonable expectation of privacy" as a term of art. In interpreting this phrase, the cases have looked to four different arguments (or "models") to determine when an expectation of privacy is reasonable.[153] In some cases, the Court has used what I call the probabilistic model: An expectation of privacy becomes reasonable as the likelihood decreases that others would invade that privacy.[154] In other cases, the Court has used what I call the private facts model, by which a reasonable expectation of privacy is violated when the government's act reveals particularly private information.[155] In still other cases, the Court has used what I call the positive law model.[156] Under the positive law model, the government violates a reasonable expecta-

---

[153] Orin S. Kerr, *Four Models of Fourth Amendment Protection*, 60 Stan L Rev 503, 503 (2007).

[154] Id at 508–09.

[155] Id at 512–13.

[156] Id at 516.

tion of privacy when it violates the suspect's rights under some source of nonconstitutional law such as property law.[157] And finally, in some cases the Court uses a policy model, by which the reasonableness of an expectation of privacy hinges on whether it is normatively desirable to limit the government's power in a particular setting.[158]

The Court's decisions since *Katz* mix and match from these four models. To many commentators, the mix of arguments makes the *Katz* test incoherent. But the use of multiple models has a significant strength in that it enables a decentralized Fourth Amendment in which different models apply in different contexts depending on which model best identifies practices in need of constitutional regulation in that setting.[159] The open-ended nature of the *Katz* test allows the Court to pick models based on which best identifies the kinds of troublesome law enforcement practices that are in need of regulation.

The history of pre-*Katz* search doctrine suggests a surprising degree of similarity between the kinds of questions the Supreme Court considered when analyzing searches before *Katz* and the kinds of questions the Court has focused on in the *Katz* era. Comparisons are difficult because many of the pre-*Katz* cases were underreasoned by modern standards.[160] But pre-*Katz* cases sometimes considered whether the government conduct constituted an invasion of privacy, hinting at the private facts model.[161] Other cases emphasized the policy implications of the rule, hinting at the policy model.[162] The occasional mention of trespass law hints at the positive law model.[163] To be fair, no pre-*Katz* decisions relied on the probabilistic model. But on the whole, the pre-*Katz* search cases include much of the same kinds of reasoning that the Court's decisions have used applying the *Katz* reasonable expectation of privacy test.

The similarity likely explains why Supreme Court decisions ap-

---

[157] Id.

[158] Id at 519.

[159] Id at 507.

[160] For example, *Goldman v United States*, 316 US 129, 135 (1942), just a. ˚ounces the result.

[161] See, for example, *Perlman v United States*, 247 US 7, 14 (1918) (distinguishing entry into a home from access to disclosed record by noting that entry into a home amounted to "an invasion of the defendant's privacy").

[162] See, for example, *Boyd v United States*, 116 US 616, 635 (1886).

[163] See, for example, *Goldman*, 316 US at 135.

plying the *Katz* test often ended up reaffirming pre-*Katz* search precedents. *Texas v Brown*[164] reaffirmed the holding of *United States v Lee*[165] that use of a flashlight is not a search. *United States v White*[166] reaffirmed the rule from *On Lee v United States*[167] that no search occurs when agents go undercover wearing a wire. *Oliver v United States*[168] reaffirmed the open fields doctrine of *Hester v United States*.[169] *Rakas v Illinois*[170] reaffirmed the standing concepts of *Gouled v United States*.[171] To be sure, *Katz* did move the ball slightly, as it provided the analytical framework for undermining *Goldman* and *Olmstead*. But the surprise is how much search doctrine remained the same after *Katz*.

The likely explanation for this similarity is that before and after *Katz*, the search inquiry has distinguished government conduct that the Fourth Amendment leaves unregulated from government conduct that it regulates through the default of a warrant requirement. The word "search" is subject to a wide range of plausible interpretations. Clear doctrine can control outcomes. But murky doctrine creates an environment in which Justices can be drawn to holdings in specific cases that aim to limit more troublesome police practices while leaving less troublesome practices free from regulation. The textual ambiguity of "searches" has allowed judicial attention to focus on what police practices are sufficiently invasive to require regulation.

From that perspective, the introduction of the *Katz* test did not transform the search inquiry from property to privacy. Rather, Justice Harlan's formulation in *Katz* represented the first time that a Justice tried to articulate a top-down test for what constitutes a search. The Court's adoption of Harlan's formulation established an open-ended inquiry that replaced a vacuum in which no consistent inquiry prevailed. Announcing a new standard freed the Supreme Court to undermine a few precedents that no longer drew sensible lines for an increasingly technological age. But the new

---

[164] 460 US 730, 740 (1983).

[165] 274 US 559, 563 (1927).

[166] 401 US 745, 750 (1971).

[167] 343 US 747, 751 (1952).

[168] 466 US 170, 177 (1984).

[169] 265 US 57, 58–59 (1924).

[170] 439 US 128, 134 (1978).

[171] *Gouled v United States*, 255 US 298, 304 (1921).

standard left much of the prior law intact. Because the normative question remained the same, the scope of the Fourth Amendment remained surprisingly stable.

When viewed in this light, the impact of *Jones* may be a matter of form instead of substance. *Jones* bifurcates the search inquiry, but it may do so without changing results in many (or even any) cases. *Jones* allows courts to reclassify the positive law model cases under *Katz* as trespass cases. The remaining *Katz* precedents can continue on the books as before, with future applications of *Katz* drawing from three models instead of four. The uncertain scope of the trespass test will give courts the flexibility to interpret positive law cases just as it did in the *Katz* era. The four models of the *Katz* test known before *Jones* will become four models of search doctrine more broadly, with three models based on *Katz* and the last based on trespass. But the results will remain the same.

VII. Conclusion

Fifteen years ago, Justice Scalia dismissed the *Katz* framework as a "fuzzy standard"[172] and a "self-indulgent test"[173] that was based on a "catchy slogan"[174] but that had "no plausible foundation in the text of the Fourth Amendment."[175] For Justice Scalia, *Jones* represents a long-sought victory. Although *Jones* does not purport to finish off the *Katz* test, it did render *Katz* nonexclusive. But the history of pre-*Katz* search doctrine offered in this article suggests that Scalia's victory may prove more a matter of rhetoric than substance. The Fourth Amendment search doctrine has never precisely tracked trespass law, and the *Katz* test did not impose major changes on what the Fourth Amendment protected before *Katz*. Instead, cases both before and after *Katz* have struggled to identify the precise line when Fourth Amendment protection begins in light of its significance for police power. Whatever label courts use, the need to identify that line will remain.

---

[172] *Minnesota v Carter*, 525 US 83, 91 (1998) (Scalia, J, concurring).

[173] Id at 97.

[174] Id at 98 n 3.

[175] Id at 97.

JENNIFER MNOOKIN
AND DAVID KAYE

CONFRONTING SCIENCE: EXPERT EVIDENCE AND THE CONFRONTATION CLAUSE

For most of its history, the Supreme Court had little to say about expert and scientific evidence. Then tranquility turned to turmoil. In the closing decade of the twentieth century, a trilogy of cases, starting with *Daubert v Merrell Dow Pharmaceuticals*,[1] introduced and elaborated on a new standard for admitting scientific evidence under the Federal Rules of Evidence. This trilogy, on which much ink has been spilled over the past two decades, spelled out the need for judges to engage in preliminary gatekeeping to determine the admissibility of expert evidence. While the evaluative criteria by which courts were to assess scientific validity were purposefully flexible, and trial judges were to be given substantial discretion in these judgments, these cases both reflected and generated a sense

Jennifer Mnookin is Vice Dean and Professor of Law, UCLA School of Law. David Kaye is Distinguished Professor and Weiss Family Scholar, School of Law, and Graduate Faculty Member, Forensic Science Program, The Pennsylvania State University.

AUTHORS' NOTE: This article benefited from comments posted on the Evidence Professors Discussion List, from exchanges with Edward Imwinkelried and Jeffrey Fisher, and from an update to George Fisher's teacher's manual for *Evidence* (Foundation, 2d ed 2012). Portions of Section II.A.2 and II.B draw on material from David H. Kaye, David E. Bernstein, and Jennifer L. Mnookin, *The New Wigmore—A Treatise on Evidence: Expert Evidence* (Aspen, Supp 2012).

[1] 509 US 579 (1993).

that scientific evidence required special attention and careful scrutiny.[2]

Now, in the opening decades of a new millennium, another expert-evidence trilogy has appeared. This new trilogy arises not from a statute but from the Constitution: it relates to the intersection between the Confrontation Clause of the Sixth Amendment and the many varieties of forensic science evidence that often provide a mainstay of prosecutors' cases against criminal defendants. The origins of this new trilogy date to 2004, when, in *Crawford v Washington*,[3] the Supreme Court substantially changed its understanding of how the Confrontation Clause applies to hearsay evidence. *Crawford* was a seemingly mundane murder case that did not involve or address expert or scientific evidence. There were no fingerprints to compare, no drugs to identify, no DNA to analyze, and no fMRI tests to run. The sole disputed question was self-defense. But it was inevitable that *Crawford*'s doctrinal framework, with its focus on the newly emphasized category of the "testimonial," would be applied to expert evidence and that thorny doctrinal difficulties would emerge.

The basic questions seem, at first glance, straightforward enough. To satisfy the Confrontation Clause, must those forensic scientists or technicians who produce inculpatory evidence against a criminal defendant testify live, or will sworn affidavits and reports suffice? If live testimony *is* required, what, if anything, can the testifying witnesses say about procedures they did not conduct personally? If multiple analysts contribute to producing a forensic test result, which ones must appear in court? But these questions turn out not to be so easily answered. The Court has issued three expert-evidence-related Confrontation Clause decisions in the past four years, and each one has generated at least as many questions as answers. Moreover, each of these cases is marked by narrow majorities, fractious and fractured opinions, and unsatisfying doctrinal elisions. In the most recently decided case, *Williams v Illinois*,[4] the court issued a bewildering array of opinions in which majority support for admitting the evidence at issue was awkwardly knitted together out of several incompatible doctrinal bases. The result, at least for now,

[2] The trilogy consists of *Daubert*, 509 US at 579 (1993), *General Electric Co. v Joiner*, 522 US 136 (1997), and *Kumho Tire Co. v Carmichael*, 526 US 137 (1999).

[3] 541 US 36 (2004).

[4] 132 S Ct 2221 (2012).

is continued anxiety and confusion over the Confrontation Clause as it applies to forensic science evidence.

The Court's efforts to bring clarity to this area, especially in *Williams*, have been muddled by its struggle to determine precisely how to think about hearsay evidence in the context of expert evidence and the Confrontation Clause. As every student of evidence knows—though often imperfectly understands—evidence is considered to be hearsay only if it is introduced for the truth of the matter asserted. The phrase is more easily remembered than understood. What it means to introduce an item of evidence "for the truth of the matter asserted" has confused generations of law students, lawyers, and jurists.[5] In *Williams*, four Justices thought it clear that a laboratory report, which was fundamental to the testifying expert's conclusions, was mentioned by the expert for a purpose other than its truth. Five Justices thought it equally obvious that it was discussed solely for its truth—but because one of them agreed on other grounds with the other four Justices' conclusion regarding the scope of the Confrontation Clause, a majority of the Court deemed the testimony referencing the laboratory report to be admissible despite the absence of the opportunity to confront the report's author.

When it comes to understanding what "the truth of the matter asserted" means, we believe that neither group of Justices has it quite right. Understanding what it means for something to be offered for the "truth of the matter asserted" can be complicated enough in the general hearsay context. But in the expert-evidence setting, it is even more difficult, because courts have long been willing, sometimes to the point of absurdity, to say that information testifying experts detail to the jury in the guise of describing the basis for their conclusions is not introduced for its truth. On the particular facts of *Williams*, we maintain that notwithstanding several Justices' argument to the contrary, there were no plausible grounds for deeming the evidence introduced for a purpose other than its truth. But we do recognize that in other, relatively limited instances, expert basis evidence might legitimately be introduced

---

[5] See, for example, Peter Murphy and David N. Barnard, *Evidence and Advocacy* 19 (Blackstone, 1984) (To some "judges, practitioners and students (not to mention occasional law teachers) . . . the rule against hearsay has always been an awesome and terrifying mystery. Like its partner in terror, the rule against perpetuities, the rule against hearsay ranks as one of the law's most celebrated nightmares. To many practitioners, it is a dimly remembered vision, which conjures up confused images of complex exceptions and incomprehensible and antiquated cases.").

for a purpose other than its truth. Since this "not for the truth" rationale is the dominant argument offered by the *Williams* Court for justifying admissibility of the expert's articulation of the basis, ascertaining this argument's legitimate reach is important.

Yet precision on this doctrinal point is insufficient to provide adequate guidance and clarity. The ongoing anxiety about how to think about expert evidence and the Confrontation Clause exists in large part because the Court has yet to face directly a set of larger background concerns. This second expert-evidence trilogy reveals significant uncertainty about how, and to what extent, scientific evidence should be treated as special or distinct from other kinds of evidence. While the *Daubert* trilogy explicitly requires special scrutiny of expert evidence, other rules of evidence are structured to provide special privileges and deference to experts, generally letting them, for example, rely on hearsay and other inadmissible evidence in reaching their conclusions.[6] How do these privileges generated by other evidence rules—and, more generally, the sense that scientific evidence sometimes deserves special treatment—fit with the Confrontation Clause and its limits on testimonial hearsay? Is there any space for heightened deference to experts within the Confrontation Clause framework? For Confrontation Clause purposes, should scientific evidence be seen as just the same, structurally, as any other kind of evidence, or are there aspects related to its mode of creation and transmission that might warrant distinctive procedures? While we will not endeavor to answer this set of questions fully in this essay, we argue that the Court will not be able effectively or coherently to resolve the doctrinal issues surrounding forensic science evidence and the Confrontation Clause without tackling these questions head-on.

More specifically, we will suggest that scientific and expert evidence might warrant some limited special treatment, based on what we see as one of the most critical dimensions of scientific knowledge production—that it *is a collective, rather than an individual enterprise.* Scientific tests, research, and study, from high-energy physics to

---

[6] FRE 702 permits experts to give opinions. FRE 703 permits them to rely on inadmissible evidence "[i]f experts in the particular field would reasonably rely on those kinds of facts or data in forming an opinion on the subject." An amendment to this rule sought to partially close this backdoor use of hearsay. It added the proviso that "if the facts or data would otherwise be inadmissible, the proponent of the opinion may disclose them to the jury only if their probative value in helping the jury evaluate the opinion substantially outweighs their prejudicial effect."

medical research to forensic science procedures, are not carried out solo. This feature of science has two important consequences: first, it means that the scientific process typically depends on a certain degree of epistemic deference by scientists to their collaborators. Scientists and experts inevitably rely and build on facts, data, opinions, and test results of others; they do not merely defer to the authority of others, but they are, fundamentally, epistemically dependent on one another. It also means that scientists are engaged in what we might call "distributed cognition"—the knowledge that is produced is not entirely held by any one person, but stretches across a network. This reticulate reality creates significant tensions with the current Confrontation Clause framework. We suggest that recognizing these characteristics of science should invite courts to engage in a modest form of scientific exceptionalism within Confrontation Clause jurisprudence through efforts to create procedures that do respect the fundamental values of the Confrontation Clause, but also adapt, when necessary, to the epistemic structures and processes of science.

We first describe this new trilogy, focusing especially on the emerging tensions in these cases about whether scientific evidence warrants or deserves special treatment. We then look carefully at the "truth of the matter asserted" argument in the plurality opinion written by Justice Alito in *Williams*. We argue that the plurality's approach is ingenious but indefensible on the facts as given. In the final section, we offer thoughts on whether there ought to be a form of "science exceptionalism" within the Confrontation Clause—that is, to what extent, and why, a special or distinctive understanding of the Clause in the context of expert evidence might be warranted.

I. THE LABORATORY TRILOGY: MELENDEZ-DIAZ, BULLCOMING, AND WILLIAMS

In *Crawford*, the Supreme Court recast its approach to defendant's Sixth Amendment right to be "confronted with the witnesses against him."[7] For the previous several decades, the touchstone for assessing whether hearsay evidence implicated the Confrontation Clause was the hearsay evidence's reliability. If the evidence had adequate indicia of reliability—and all "firmly rooted"

---

[7] US Const, Amend VI.

hearsay exceptions were conclusively deemed to have such indicia—
then its introduction did not violate the Clause. If an item of hearsay
evidence did not fall into a "firmly rooted" hearsay safe harbor, then
it had to be excluded under the Confrontation Clause unless it had
particularized "indicia of reliability."[8] *Crawford* rejected this reli-
ability-plus-tradition framework both on functional and on histor-
ical-originalist grounds. Functionally, the Court deemed reliability
too murky to be useful—too subjective, amorphous, and unpredictable to provide significant operational guidance to courts or to
lead to consistent admissibility outcomes.[9] But still worse, in the
Court's view, the reliability approach did not comport with original
understandings of the boundaries of the Confrontation Clause.[10]
Justice Scalia's majority opinion declared that the right question to
be asked of hearsay statements by a nontestifying declarant that
potentially implicated the Confrontation Clause was whether they
were or were not *testimonial*. Were these statements, in other words,
akin to, or a substitute for, in-court testimony? If so, they generally
had to be excluded, for the Constitution, the Court held, barred
the prosecution from introducing "testimonial statements of a witness who [does] not appear at trial unless he [is] unavailable to
testify, and the defendant had . . . a prior opportunity for cross-
examination."[11]

This concept of the testimonial is, of course, not self-explicating.
At its narrowest, testimonial evidence might be limited to those
formalized materials most similar to in-court testimony (like affidavits, depositions, sworn confessions). At its broadest, it might
include any statements made in circumstances in which the speaker
or listener would reasonably understand its possible relevance to a
future criminal proceeding. The Court canvassed several formu-
lations, ranging from the narrow to the broad, but since the statements at issues in the case were, in the Court's view, testimonial
under any plausible definition of the term, it elected to "leave for
another day" any "comprehensive definition" of the pivotal term
that now marks the perimeter of the Confrontation Clause.[12] Six

---

[8] *Ohio v Roberts*, 448 US 56, 72 (1980).

[9] *Crawford*, 541 US at 63 ("Reliability is an amorphous, if not entirely subjective, concept.").

[10] Id at 43–50.

[11] Id at 53–54.

[12] Id.

Justices joined Justice Scalia's majority opinion, while Chief Justice Rehnquist wrote a concurrence (joined by Justice O'Connor) suggesting that there was actually no need, on either originalist or functionalist grounds, to overturn *Ohio v Roberts*, and that the Court's choice not to spell out more carefully the contours of its critical category of "testimonial evidence" was sure to generate myriad difficulties for courts and prosecutors.

As we noted at the outset, *Crawford* itself did not involve expert evidence. The statement at issue in the case was a recorded statement the defendant's wife had made to the police—she was unavailable to testify at trial because of the state's rules of marital privilege. But lower courts soon began wrestling with a lively set of issues relating to expert evidence and the Confrontation Clause, especially with regard to often-used forensic science evidence—matters like chemical drug testing, blood and urine analysis for alcohol or other substances, autopsy reports, and DNA profiling. In most states, some of these forms of forensic science evidence were often introduced via sworn certificate rather than live testimony. Did *Crawford* jeopardize this routine practice? What if many years passed between a forensic test and a trial, and the original analyst was unavailable? Could someone else then testify about those test results? More generally, could analysts regularly testify about one another's test results, as was frequently the practice prior to *Crawford*? Did it matter whether the testifying analyst was a supervisor or regularly conducted the kind of test at issue? And what if multiple analysts had all played some role in the tests that led to a specific conclusion—did each and every one of them really have to testify? If not, then whose testimony was required?

Lower courts began to work through the potential implications of *Crawford* in this variety of circumstances. For the most part, they were reluctant to read *Crawford* as requiring any significant changes to the preexisting methods for introducing forensic science testimony. In the first years following the *Crawford* decision, most (though certainly not all) trial courts instead endeavored to shoehorn the traditional methods for presenting forensic science testimony into this new framework without requiring modifications.[13] They argued, for example, that forensic science reports were exempt

---

[13] For a discussion of the lower courts' responses to forensic science evidence in the wake of *Crawford*, see Jennifer L. Mnookin, *Expert Evidence and the Confrontation Clause After Crawford v. Washington*, 15 Brooklyn J L & Policy 790, 847–50 (2007).

from the Confrontation Clause because they were business records, because they were factual, because they were neutral, or because it was just too impractical to require the state to produce the authors of these reports or the individuals who conducted the testing.[14]

In *Melendez-Diaz v Massachusetts*,[15] the first case in the laboratory trilogy, the Supreme Court weighed in on how the *Crawford* framework applied to expert testimony. In this case, the prosecution presented a state laboratory analyst's sworn certificates asserting that plastic bags found near the defendant contained cocaine of a certain weight. A state statute exempted such certificates from the rule against hearsay; indeed, the vast majority of states had similar statutes on their books.[16] The defendant objected that although Massachusetts was free to limit or abolish the hearsay rule, introducing these certificates without the testimony of the analyst violated the Confrontation Clause. The basic question, therefore, was whether these certificates of analysis were testimonial. Again writing for the majority, Justice Scalia did not find this question difficult in the least: "There is little doubt that the documents at issue in this case fall within the 'core class of testimonial statements.'"[17] They were, at essence, affidavits made precisely in order to substitute for testimony. Rejecting arguments that forensic scientists should be treated differently than other witnesses, *Melendez-Diaz* held that a signed, sworn piece of paper was no substitute for the actual testimony of the government chemists who conducted the tests.

From one perspective, this holding was unsurprising. It would be difficult to devise a coherent definition of "testimonial" that did not include sworn certificates like these. Indeed, Justice Scalia suggested that this holding is a simple extension of *Crawford*, signaling to reluctant lower courts that the Court meant for them to take its newly created category seriously even if it did require significant modification to the methods for adducing forensic evidence.

Justice Scalia's majority was fragile, however. Four Justices dissented, arguing that *Crawford* and its immediate progeny dealt with "ordinary witnesses," not scientific and expert evidence, and "the

---

[14] See generally id.

[15] 557 US 305 (2009).

[16] For a detailed discussion of the varieties of statutes permitting forensic ipse dixit testimony via certificate, see generally Pamela R. Metzger, *Cheating the Constitution*, 59 Vand L Rev 475 (2006).

[17] *Melendez-Diaz*, 557 US at 310.

Court should have done the sensible thing and limited its holding to witnesses as so defined."[18] The dissenters, led by Justice Kennedy, and joined by Chief Justice Rehnquist and Justices Breyer and Alito, emphasized that numerous analysts may all play a role in conducting a routine chemical test for drugs, and that it would be absurd to require every one of them to show up to testify in every case.[19]

The dissent also attempted to spell out several ways in which forensic analysts differ from "conventional" or "ordinary" witnesses. The opinion points out that at trial ordinary witnesses relate events they observed in the past, and often these events are singular or at least atypical, whereas forensic analysts have made, in accordance with their standard protocols, near-contemporaneous written observations of their routinely and regularly conducted tests. In addition, their in-court testimony more likely derives from these written observations than from any authentic memory of the specific test in question. Forensic analysts, the dissent suggested, are also more removed from the crime than many ordinary fact witnesses and are thereby unlikely to be as affected by the look-him-in-the-eye aspect of testifying in person.[20] Moreover, in making the statements that are presumed by the majority to be testimonial, experts are following scientific protocols rather than responding to interrogation, and they lack an overtly adversarial or accusatory relationship to the defendant.[21]

Justice Scalia's majority opinion flatly rejected these arguments, emphasizing that it is not obvious that "what respondent calls 'neutral scientific testing' is either as neutral or as reliable as respondent suggests," and that "Confrontation is designed to weed out not only the fraudulent analyst, but the incompetent one as well."[22] In this first case of the trilogy, then, we see the outlines of a critical divide over whether scientific evidence warrants special treatment under the Confrontation Clause. The thrust of the dissent's argument is less that these certificates are not testimonial, and more that these kinds of expert evidence should be excluded from the Confrontation Clause's strictures both for practical reasons and because of the distinctive qualities of science. Given the other available methods

---

[18] Id at 331 (Kennedy, J, dissenting).

[19] Id at 332–35.

[20] Id at 339–40.

[21] Id at 345–46.

[22] Id at 318–19 (Scalia, J).

of evidentiary regulation, coupled with the protections provided by scientific procedures themselves, "the Confrontation Clause is simply not needed for these matters."[23] To boil the dispute down to its basics, the dissent believes that the Confrontation Clause's provisos ought to apply differently to scientific evidence; by contrast, the majority wants to treat scientific evidence in precisely the same manner as any other kind of testimony.

While, doctrinally, *Melendez-Diaz* clarified that forensic science reports (at least if sufficiently formal)[24] were testimonial, it left many questions unresolved. Two years later, in *Bullcoming v New Mexico*,[25] the evidence at issue was a state laboratory report on the defendant's blood-alcohol concentration (BAC). This time, the prosecution had offered the live testimony of an analyst about the report. However, because the laboratory analyst who had actually conducted the test was on unpaid leave, the prosecution substituted another employee of the same laboratory. The testifying witness had no involvement in the specific test or in the preparation of the report, but he was familiar with the procedures used and had run this same test himself in other cases. This was enough to satisfy the New Mexico Supreme Court. Begrudgingly granting that the blood alcohol report was testimonial,[26] it deemed the absent analyst's role to be that of a "mere scrivener who simply transcribed the results generated by a gas chromatograph machine."[27] Moreover, the Court concluded that the testimony of a qualified alternative expert from the laboratory, who could, under the rules of evidence, rely upon this report to form his own opinion, who was knowledgeable about the testing procedure at issue, and who was available for cross-examination, provided the defendant with a constitutionally adequate opportunity for confrontation.

New Mexico's Rules of Evidence, like Federal Rule of Evidence 703 (and like nearly all state evidence rules), permit experts to rely on materials that have not been (and perhaps could not be) admitted into evidence, when forming their own expert opinions, so long as

---

[23] Id at 340 (Kennedy, J, dissenting).

[24] Justice Thomas filed a one-paragraph concurrence stating that the Confrontation Clause applies only to *formalized* testimonial materials, but deeming this report sufficiently formalized to fall within its purview.

[25] 131 S Ct 2705 (2011).

[26] Prior to *Melendez-Diaz*, the New Mexico Supreme Court had held that blood alcohol reports were not testimonial. *State v Dedman*, 102 P3d 628 (NM 2004).

[27] *State v Bullcoming*, 226 P3d 1, 4 (NM 2010).

the materials are of a type experts in the field would reasonably rely upon in forming their opinions.[28] This is, of course, one of the rules of evidence that treats experts as "special," giving them distinctive testimonial privileges that lay witnesses lack. Not only are experts expected to give opinions, whereas opinion testimony from lay witnesses is disfavored,[29] but these opinions can be based on a wide array of materials, even including inadmissible evidence. The underlying theory is that within their sphere of expertise, experts should be given significant leeway to determine what to rely upon and how much warrant it should have (just as they do when using their expertise outside of the courtroom). The New Mexico Supreme Court reasoned that under this rule, it was legitimate for the testifying expert to have relied upon the information contained in the report by the absent expert. The testifying expert might not have conducted the specific test, but he knew the procedure well, and under the evidence rules, could therefore rely on the data contained in the absent expert's report in shaping his conclusion.

The New Mexico court did not probe this argument very deeply. The difficulty is that it is well established that one expert cannot simply "parrot" or serve as the mouthpiece for another, absent expert.[30] So if the testifying expert were simply parroting the absent expert, gesturing to Rule 703 does not suffice.[31] Moreover, under New Mexico's rather idiosyncratic interpretation of its own evidence rules, its version of Rule 703 does not permit an expert to rely upon the "opinion" of another expert but extends only to "facts or data."[32] The court endeavored to finesse these issues by insisting

[28] New Mex Rule Evid 11-703 provides, "If of a type reasonably relied upon by experts in the particular field in forming opinions or inferences upon the subject, the facts or data need not be admissible in evidence in order for the opinion or inference to be admitted."

[29] See FRE 701 and FRE 702.

[30] To be sure, the line between legitimately relying on information provided by others and illegitimately serving as a mouthpiece for their conclusions is not always clear. For a case at the borderland, see *Dura Automotive Systems of Indiana Inc. v CTS Corp.*, 284 F3d 609 (7th Cir 2002).

[31] See David H. Kaye, David E. Bernstein, and Jennifer L. Mnookin, *The New Wigmore—A Treatise on Evidence: Expert Evidence* §§ 4.6.1(c), 4.7.1 (Aspen, 2d ed 2011).

[32] See *State v Aragon*, 225 P3d 1280 (NM 2010), cited in the state Supreme Court's opinion in *Bullcoming*. The cases cited in *Aragon* do not obviously support this idiosyncratic reading of Rule 703, but that is not our concern here. We simply note that the Advisory Committee to Rule 703 explicitly envisions the rule enabling experts to rely, at least in some circumstances, on the opinions and inferences of others if they otherwise meet the rule's requirements, such as doctors relying upon the opinions of specialists. See Advisory Committee Note, FRE 703.

that the results of the gas chromatograph machine reported by the absent witness "do not constitute expert opinion," but rather are simply facts and data upon which another expert could rely, since the absent expert was merely the "scrivener" for the machine data.[33]

The Supreme Court rejected the prosecutor's effort to substitute a surrogate witness unconnected to the specific test at issue for the actual forensic tester. Even if another laboratory employee was very familiar with the testing process, the Court determined that the surrogate could not provide the defendant with the same opportunity to probe the specifics of the test as performed in this instance based on firsthand knowledge. Although the Court granted that the analyst who did the testing might lack any recall of the specific test, it still thought this distinction mattered. Presumably, the distinction is that a surrogate could not *possibly* have any firsthand recall because he was not there, whereas the actual analyst could *in principle* have recall, even though in practice he might frequently (and understandably, given both the routine and frequent nature of such tests and the passage of time between test and trial) not remember. More generally, the Court emphasized that a surrogate cannot provide the defendant with the same opportunity to probe the actual analyst's competence, veracity, and work habits. The point was especially salient in *Bullcoming* given that the actual analyst was on administrative leave for unknown reasons. At bottom, even a surrogate witness capable of explaining the test, the results, and the general operation of the machine is not good enough for the Constitution: "the Clause does not tolerate dispensing with confrontation simply because the court believes that questioning one witness about another's testimonial statement provides a fair enough opportunity for cross-examination."[34] "Fair enough" is not fair enough for the Constitution.

Justice Ginsburg's majority opinion also brushed aside the New Mexico Supreme Court's "mere scrivener" argument. The majority noted that the report contained statements that went beyond simply reporting a machine result, including assertions (explicit or implicit) that a prescribed protocol had been followed and that no unusual test circumstances affecting validity were present.[35] The majority

---

[33] *Bullcoming*, 226 P3d at 10.

[34] *Bullcoming v New Mexico*, 131 S Ct 2705, 2716 (2011).

[35] Id at 2715.

opinion simply ignored without comment the state court's argument that the surrogate could legitimately rely upon the absent witness's report to inform his own expert opinion.

Like *Melendez-Diaz*, *Bullcoming* was a 5–4 decision, and this majority was both awkwardly cobbled together and tenuous. Only Justice Scalia joined Justice Ginsburg's opinion in full. Justices Kagan, Sotomayor, and Thomas joined only portions. Justice Kennedy dissented again, expressing continued irritation with *Melendez-Diaz*, exasperation at its extension in this case, and doubts about whether *Crawford* itself was an improvement over the *Ohio v Roberts* regime. Requiring testimony of the actual analyst in a case like this was, he said, a "hollow formality."[36]

In addition, Justice Sotomayor wrote a concurring opinion highlighting just how narrow the decision was. She succinctly laid out four still-open issues, one of which was the intersection of the Confrontation Clause and Rule 703.[37] Citing Rule 703—hers was the only opinion to do so—she wrote:

> This is not a case in which an expert witness was asked for his independent opinion about underlying testimonial reports that were not themselves admitted into evidence. . . . [T]he State does not assert that [the testifying expert] offered an independent, expert opinion about Bullcoming's blood alcohol concentration. . . . We would face a different question if asked to determine the constitutionality of allowing an expert witness to discuss others' testimonial statements if the testimonial statements were not themselves admitted as evidence.[38]

Soon enough, the Supreme Court faced that question. Last summer, in *Williams*, the prosecution finally found a winning combination of facts. Facing a backlog of DNA samples, the Illinois State Police laboratory (ISP) had shipped vaginal swabs and a sample of blood from a rape victim (L. J.) to Cellmark Diagnostics, a private laboratory in Maryland. Cellmark analysts performed a series of procedures to find certain distinctive features in semen in the swab. These included extracting DNA from the swabs and blood, making

[36] Id at 2724 (Kennedy, J, dissenting).

[37] The others were (1) when the evidence was produced not only for future use as testimony but also for some alternate purpose; (2) when the testifying witness was a supervisor or a reviewer who had some degree of firsthand connection to the actual test, even if he or she was not the primary analyst; and (3) when the state truly introduced only machine-generated results like a gas chromatograph. Id at 2722 (Sotomayor, J, concurring).

[38] *Bullcoming*, 131 S Ct at 2722.

millions of copies of identifying fragments of the DNA (called "STR alleles"), producing graphs that indicated the lengths of the fragments, and comparing the sets of length measurements from the blood and vaginal swabs to infer which one came from the rapist ("mixture deconvolution").[39] Cellmark then wrote up a report about what they had found, and sent it back to the ISP.

The state did not try to introduce the report submitted to the ISP into evidence. Nor did the state call anyone from Cellmark to testify about what that laboratory had done or what results it had found. Instead, the prosecution called a former ISP analyst named Sandra Lambatos who had studied the report, then checked the state's offender DNA database, and found one matching man. She opined, in effect, that this man—Sandy Williams—was a source of DNA on the vaginal swab that had been analyzed by Cellmark.[40]

The prosecution insisted that it was introducing this witness's references to Cellmark's testing only to show the basis for her own expert conclusions about the database match to Williams. "I'm not getting at what another lab did," the prosecutor assured the court.[41] The only reason for the ISP analyst's testimony, the prosecutor maintained, was to establish that she found a match in the database.[42]

---

[39] See David H. Kaye and George Sensabaugh, *Reference Guide on DNA Evidence*, in *Reference Manual on Scientific Evidence* 129 (National Academies, 3d ed 2011).

[40] See Joint Appendix, *Williams v People of the State of Illinois*, No 10-8505, *57–58 (filed Aug 31 2011) ("Joint Appendix") (available on Westlaw at 2011 WL 3873378):

> Q. In other words is the semen identified in the vaginal swabs of [L. J.] consistent with having originated from Sandy Williams?
>
> A. Yes.
>
> Q. What is the probability of this profile occurring in the general population?
>
> The Witness. This profile would be expected to occur in approximately 1 in 8.7 quadrillion black, 1 in 390 quadrillion white, or 1 in 109 quadrillion Hispanic unrelated individuals.
>
> Q. Do you know the approximate population of the world?
>
> A. Approximately 6 billion.
>
> Mr. Walsh. Objection.
>
> The Court. Overruled.
>
> Ms. Petrone. In your expert opinion, can you call this a match to Sandy Williams?
>
> A. Yes.

[41] Id at *56.

[42] "I was referring to a computer data base without saying any more about that but after

However, the prosecutor actually went one step further. Despite her representations to the court, she framed a question that referred, awkwardly, to Cellmark's conclusions: "Was there a computer match generated of the male DNA profile found in semen from the vaginal swabs of [L. J.] to a male DNA profile that had been identified as having originated from Sandy Williams?"[43] To which Lambatos answered, "Yes, there was."[44]

The appellate courts in Illinois saw no problem in this maneuver. Because the report was not formally offered for its truth, but only to provide a basis for the testifying expert's opinion about the source of the DNA on the swab, these courts thought the confrontation problem evaporated. After all, they explained, *Crawford* explicitly noted that its exclusionary rule does not apply when testimonial statements are introduced for some purpose other than establishing "the truth of the matter asserted" (TMA).[45] They saw the case as equivalent to a laboratory supervisor or director testifying to her own probability calculations based on the "bench work" of other employees even when those employees do not testify—a practice that the Illinois Supreme Court approved in 2006.[46]

The prosecution's fancy footwork in *Williams* stimulated four opinions—none of which commanded a majority. A majority did vote to affirm the conviction, but not on the Illinois courts' no-TMA theory. The strongest support for that theory came in an opinion written by Justice Alito. This opinion emphasized that "[i]t has long been accepted that an expert witness may voice an opinion based on facts concerning the events at issue in a particular case even if the expert lacks first-hand knowledge of those facts."[47] Justice Alito also pointed out that the prosecution could have asked the ISP analyst a hypothetical question with the content of the Cellmark report as its premise.[48] Then he explained that Federal and Illinois

she received that information for the data base she did her own testing based on that information." Id.

[43] Id. Before sending the samples to Cellmark, ISP staff had ascertained that semen was present in the vaginal swab. After sending it, it took and analyzed a DNA sample from Williams in an unrelated case. The two technicians who performed these actions testified at Williams's trial.

[44] Joint Appendix at *56.

[45] *People v Williams*, 939 NE2d 268, 277 (Ill 2010), citing *Crawford v Washington*, 541 US 36, 59 n 9 (2004), aff'd *Williams v Illinois*, 132 S Ct 2221 (2012).

[46] *Williams*, 939 NE2d at 275, citing *People v Sutherland*, 860 NE2d 178 (Ill 2006).

[47] *Williams*, 132 S Ct at 2233 (Alito, J) (plurality).

[48] Id at 2234.

Rule of Evidence 703 goes one step further: "an expert may base an opinion on facts that are 'made known to the expert at or before the hearing,' but such reliance does not constitute admissible evidence of this underlying information."[49] The underlying information is admissible, not for its truth, but only for "the legitimate nonhearsay purpose of *illuminating the expert's thought process.*"[50] Hence, it was fine for the analyst who had no connection to Cellmark to answer the prosecution's question about Cellmark's findings.

In addition to divining this supposedly "legitimate nonhearsay purpose," this opinion deemed dispositive the fact that the report was not "prepared for the primary purpose of accusing a targeted individual."[51] Because there was as yet no suspect in the case, "the primary purpose of the Cellmark report, viewed objectively, was not to accuse petitioner. . . ."[52] The opinion thus sought to confine the Confrontation Clause to statements made to accuse not just someone, but someone in particular. But Justice Alito made this argument largely in passing; it is the no-TMA argument that receives the most attention and care, and upon which we will focus.[53] Chief Justice Roberts and Justices Kennedy and Breyer signed on, although a separate opinion by Justice Breyer retreated slightly on the no-TMA reasoning.[54]

Another foursome, led by Justice Kagan, was incredulous. "Have we not already decided this case?" they asked.[55] As they saw it, the witness's testimony was "functionally identical to the 'surrogate tes-

---

[49] Id at 2235.

[50] Id at 2240 (emphasis added).

[51] *Williams*, 132 S Ct at 2243.

[52] Id.

[53] On the "no-accusation" theory, see Kaye et al, *Expert Evidence* § 4.12.8 (Supp, 2012) (cited in note 31) (concluding that "[w]hile a focus on whether evidence is accusatory might provide a valuable lens for exploring the . . . category of the "testimonial," the plurality opinion in *Williams* does not provide enough specificity to make the category workable, nor does it offer a satisfying defense of its definitions and categories."). See also note 67.

[54] Justice Breyer wrote that in permitting the putative nonhearsay use, the federal and Illinois rules of evidence are "artificial." Id at 2246 (Breyer, J, concurring). To ensure that the Confrontation Clause is not read to require the presence of every technician associated with a laboratory test, he would have preferred to rehear the case facing more directly and more broadly how the Confrontation Clause should apply to crime laboratory reports, perhaps with an eye to overturning or modifying *Bullcoming* and *Melendez-Diaz*. *Williams*, 132 S Ct at 2244, 2248 (Breyer, J, concurring).

[55] *Williams*, 132 S Ct at 2264, 2267 (Kagan, J, dissenting).

timony' that New Mexico proffered in *Bullcoming*, which did nothing to cure the problem identified in *Melendez-Diaz* (which, for its part, straightforwardly applied our decision in *Crawford*)."[56] These Justices scorned the theory of the Illinois courts that Cellmark's statements (whether or not true) were mentioned solely for the allegedly nonhearsay purpose of helping the factfinder understand the ISP expert's conclusions about a database match. Writing for herself and Justices Scalia, Ginsburg, and Sotomayor, Justice Kagan called "the idea that such 'basis evidence' comes in not for its truth, but only to help the factfinder evaluate an expert's opinion 'very weak,' 'factually implausible,' 'nonsense,' and 'sheer fiction.'"[57]

Justice Thomas agreed with these Justices that the no-TMA theory was implausible and the "targeted individual" requirement groundless. "There is," he wrote in a separate opinion, "no meaningful distinction between disclosing an out-of-court statement so that the factfinder may evaluate the expert's opinion and disclosing that statement for its truth."[58] Nevertheless, he added his vote to those of the Alito plurality "solely because Cellmark's statements lacked the requisite 'formality and solemnity' to be considered 'testimonial' for purposes of the Confrontation Clause."[59] So at the end of the day, there were three arguments in support of the holding: (1) that the statements were not offered for the truth of the matter asserted, (2) that the statements were insufficiently formalized to count as testimonial, and (3) that the statements were not accusatory. But not one of them mustered a majority; and they push in different directions in terms of what statements ought to be excluded as testimonial.

It is also worth noting that in *Williams*, it was Justice Breyer who was most explicitly arguing for a form of science exceptionalism under the Confrontation Clause, in terms similar to those offered by Justice Kennedy in *Melendez-Diaz*. Justice Breyer noted that "the need for cross-examination is considerably diminished when the out of court statement was made by an accredited laboratory employee

---

[56] Id.

[57] Id at 2269 (quoting Kaye et al, *Expert Evidence* § 4.10.1, at 196–97 (cited in note 31); id § 4.11.6, at 24 (Supp 2012)).

[58] Id at 2255, 2257 (Thomas, J, concurring). Justice Thomas added that "[t]o use the inadmissible information in evaluating the expert's testimony, the jury must make a preliminary judgment about whether this information is true." Id (quoting Kaye et al, *Expert Evidence* § 4.10.1, at 196 (cited in note 31)).

[59] Id at 2255 (Breyer, J, concurring).

operating at a remove from the investigation in the ordinary course of professional work," because "alternative features of such situations help to guarantee its accuracy," like professional guidelines, standards, and documentations norms.[60] Cross-examination of the actual expert is a less effective check on accuracy, in his view, than the structural mechanisms operating within science itself—though, to be sure, in *Crawford* and *Melendez-Diaz*, the majority opinions made clear that reliability was not to be understood as either the purpose or the lodestar of the Confrontation Clause.

This overview of the new trilogy has endeavored to describe the development of the Confrontation Clause as it affects laboratory reports and to show how the lurking question of science exceptionalism has made these cases difficult to resolve. One set of Justices has been prepared to apply the logic of *Crawford* across all kinds of witnesses equally, seeing no justification for carving out a different approach to forensic science. They emphasize that reliability is not a substitute for Confrontation—and, after all, a turn away from reliability was the key contribution of *Crawford*—and also point out that forensic science is far from foolproof and cannot simply be presumed reliable. Another group of Justices cannot fathom that a laboratory technician, doing his ordinary, routine job guided by standard operating procedures and protocols, who has probably never seen the defendant and, unless he testifies, in all likelihood never will, belongs in the same analytic box under the Confrontation Clause as someone making a statement to the police or undergoing interrogation.

From a certain point of view, Justice Alito's no-TMA argument is remarkably clever. A strong but plausible version of the no-TMA argument would provide a way for experts formally to remain subject to the Confrontation Clause's strictures just like any other witnesses, but practically speaking, it would permit prosecutors a good deal of flexibility. If a testifying expert can rely upon—and even disclose, albeit (allegedly) not for its truth—a testimonial report by a nontestifying expert, then the Court would be building a certain degree of scientific exceptionalism into the Confrontation Clause *through* Rule 703. Rather than exempting scientific experts wholesale, as the dissent in *Melendez-Diaz* seemed to desire, it would

---

[60] Id at 2250.

use the existing evidence rules to ensure that, practically speaking, the Confrontation Clause had little bite.[61]

It is therefore worth considering carefully the competing arguments regarding the no-TMA theory.[62] We show that in the setting of *Williams* the theory is ultimately implausible, but that in other settings it could have more traction. Rule 703, properly understood, should be neither the open ticket to admission that some state courts have been buying[63] nor the simple formalism depicted in the plurality opinion in *Williams*. We begin the next section by briefly asking why the Confrontation Clause only applies to statements introduced for their truth. We then consider two explanations for why the statements in *Williams* were offered for their truth. Both explanations appear in the opinions of Justices Thomas and Kagan in *Williams*, but they are intertwined. Untangling them helps show why the no-TMA theory fails in *Williams* but might succeed elsewhere. Finally, we briefly discuss the future of laboratory reports under the Confrontation Clause.

II. WILLIAMS, RULE 703, AND THE TRUTH OF THE MATTER ASSERTED

In *Williams*, the entire Court assumed that TMA is an essential element of the right to confrontation. But not a single opinion in *Williams*—or *Crawford*, in which the Court slipped the thought inside a single parenthetical sentence inside a footnote—explains why.[64] The most plausible answer stems from the perception of Justice Alito's plurality that an accuser is central to the Clause. As Justice Scalia wrote in *Coy v Iowa*,[65] the Clause encap-

---

[61] On the dangers of "stealth" testimonial hearsay under Rule 703, see generally Julie A. Seaman, *Triangulating Testimonial Hearsay: The Constitutional Boundaries of Expert Opinion Testimony*, 96 Georgetown L J 827 (2008).

[62] For a related, but broader treatment of the many theories in the case, see Kaye et al, *Expert Evidence* § 4.12 (Supp 2013) (cited in note 31).

[63] *Pendergrass v State*, 913 NE2d 703 (Ind 2009); *State v Crager*, 879 NE2d 745, 758 (Ohio 2007).

[64] *Crawford*, 541 US at 59 n 9.

[65] 487 US 1012 (1988). In *Coy* the trial court used a screen to block a man charged with sexually assaulting two thirteen-year-old girls from the sight of the girls as they testified. Justice Scalia wrote for the majority of the Court in holding that the barrier violated defendant's right to face-to-face confrontation. In *Maryland v Craig*, 497 US 836 (1990), the Court retreated from *Coy*'s seemingly per se rule requiring face-to-face confrontation. Justice O'Connor wrote for the majority, ruling that the Confrontation Clause merely embodies a "preference" for face-to-face, in-person confrontation, which may be limited to satisfy sufficiently important interests. Applying this balancing test, the Court

sulates the image painted by Shakespeare "when he had Richard the Second say: 'Then call them to our presence—face to face, and frowning brow to brow, ourselves will hear the accuser and the accused freely speak.'"[66] With this animating principle in mind, the domain of the Clause should be confined to statements that are not merely testimonial but also accusatorial.[67] A statement may have been intended to accuse someone of criminal misconduct, but if it is not being used that way at trial, then there is no accuser who needs to be confronted. More generally, if the prosecutor is not asking the factfinder to *credit* the out-of-court statement, to consider it to be true, then the veracity, the perceptual abilities, and the memory of the out-of-court speaker are irrelevant, or at least a good deal less important.[68] Therefore, whether the statement of the absent "accuser" is introduced for its truth should matter. Indeed, in *Williams*, while the Justices attacked each others' positions on whether the evidence was TMA with vehemence and vitriol,[69] that the Confrontation Clause applied only to evidence offered for its truth was simply taken for granted by all sides.

A. IF NOT TRUTH, THEN WHAT?

Before turning to the specific forms of argument Justice Alito's plurality opinion offers in defense of its no-TMA position, it is worth noting that there is nothing novel about the general argument that expert basis evidence is not offered for the truth of

---

held that the Confrontation Clause did not bar the use of one-way closed-circuit television to present testimony by an alleged child sex abuse victim when the trial court found that the child was reportedly unable to testify in the physical presence of the defendant due to severe emotional trauma.

[66] Id at 1016.

[67] Following *Crawford*, but prior to *Melendez-Diaz*, numerous courts attempted to bracket some or all forensic science evidence as nontestimonial with the notion that the Confrontation Clause applied only to accusatorial evidence. See Mnookin, 15 Brooklyn J L & Policy at 847–50 (cited in note 13); Robert P. Mosteller, *"Testimonial" and the Formalistic Definition—The Case for an "Accusatorial" Fix*, 20 Crim Just 14 (Summer 2005). The *Williams* plurality tried to revive this notion, but with an uncomfortably cramped conception of what makes a statement accusatorial.

[68] For the classic analysis of the "hearsay" dangers and an explanation for why hearsay is limited to TMA, see Lawrence H. Tribe, *Triangulating Hearsay*, 87 Harv L Rev 957 (1974).

[69] Justice Alito's plurality opinion condemns the reasoning of the dissent as "truly remarkable," 132 S Ct at 2237, and "a very clear error." Id at 2239 (Alito, J) (plurality). Justice Kagan's dissent derides the plurality's at exposition as "a simple abdication to state-law labels" and "a neat trick—but really, what a way to run a criminal justice system." Id at 2272 (Kagan, J, dissenting).

its contents. In fact, well before this set of *Crawford*-derived conundrums arose, many lower courts had taken an across-the-board
position that an expert's disclosure of such evidence to the factfinder is not for the truth of its contents, but rather for the limited,
nontruth purpose of helping the factfinder evaluate the adequacy
of the expert's basis evidence by illuminating the expert's thought
process.[70] According to this argument, the purpose of telling the
factfinder about the materials, data, or opinions upon which the
expert has relied is not to have the factfinder accept any of this
underlying material as true, but merely to assist the factfinder in
assessing the credibility of the expert. The theory is that the factfinder can assess whether the expert has an adequate basis for the
conclusions offered without substantively assessing whether this
basis is actually true.

The difficulty with this argument is that to evaluate meaningfully the adequacy of the expert's basis, the factfinder—let us assume a jury, but the point applies equally to bench trials—must
usually make a preliminary judgment about whether the information upon which the expert has relied is true. Much of the time,
if the jury believes the expert's basis is true, it will also believe
that the expert's reliance upon the basis is justified; conversely, if
it doubts the truth of the expert's basis, it will likely doubt the
legitimacy of the expert's reliance. But there are some situations
in which one might be able to use the expert's basis evidence for
credibility purposes without making a judgment about its truth.
If the jury believes that the expert's basis evidence, even if true,
is inadequate to support the expert's conclusions, then disclosure
can assist the jury without necessitating a preliminary determination of the truth of that basis evidence. Or if other evidence in
the record establishes the truth of the basis evidence, then the
jury need not rely on the expert's disclosure in order to evaluate
the adequacy of the basis evidence as grounds for the expert's
conclusion. (We will come back to this point below.) Most of the
time, however, it is simply not plausible to imagine that a factfinder, even a judge, can assess whether the expert's basis is adequate to support the expert's conclusion without also assessing—
or, perhaps more accurately, often simply assuming—that basis's
truth. Doing so would require reasoning like the following:

---

[70] For a detailed look at this issue, see Mnookin, 15 Brooklyn J L & Policy at 811–27
(cited in note 13).

I am being asked whether the expert's basis is adequate to support his conclusion. I believe that the basis evidence detailed by the expert does, in theory, provide enough good grounds to support his conclusion, if the basis is itself accurate. However, I cannot consider the disclosure by the expert as proof of the basis's accuracy, because I cannot consider the basis evidence to be offered for the truth of the matter asserted. So all I can do is say that if the basis evidence were true, it would provide an adequate basis for the expert. I also know that the expert himself has relied on this basis—that is why it is being disclosed to me. Hence, the expert himself believes that the basis evidence is worth relying upon, and, indeed, is true. But I cannot consider it to be true just because he does—that would still be taking its disclosure to me as helping to establish its truth, and I am prohibited from doing that. I am permitted, however, to defer to his conclusion, and the fact that he has relied upon a basis that would, if true, warrant his conclusion contributes to my willingness to believe his opinion is warranted. Still, I have no opinion—because I have no admissible evidence upon which to ground an opinion—about whether the basis evidence is actually true.

Granted, this inferential chain is logically possible. But it is incredibly formalistic and wildly implausible as a matter of human reasoning.[71] Even if jurors are given limiting instructions, it is hard to believe that they will not take the expert disclosure (and the fact of expert reliance) as providing some degree of evidentiary support for the basis itself. Nor is it plausible to believe that judges could altogether avoid doing so either. The notion that factfinders will not consider the truth of the basis evidence when assessing the credibility of the expert who has relied on this evidence is, quite simply, a legal fiction.

Prior to *Crawford*, the not-for-the-truth argument solved an otherwise awkward problem for the courts. Rule 703 permits both reliance and, to some extent, disclosure of otherwise inadmissible evidence—usually hearsay. But what was the status of this inadmissible evidence? Rule 703 does not present itself as an exception to the hearsay rule. Certainly, it is not one of the many exceptions enumerated in Rules 803 and 804.[72] Moreover, if experts' disclosures were permitted for the truth of their contents, it could lead to parties' funneling substantial quantities of otherwise inadmis-

---

[71] For more detailed versions of this argument, see generally id; Kaye et al, *Expert Evidence* §§ 4.7.2, 4.10.1 (cited in note 31).

[72] See generally FRE 803 and FRE 804.

sible evidence in through their experts.[73] By attributing a nontruth purpose to the basis evidence, courts reduced the incentive for such funneling, for the matters disclosed by experts, being substantively inadmissible, could not help establish the sufficiency of any element and could not be advanced as true in a closing argument.

In addition, then as now, a nontruth purpose avoided thorny Confrontation Clause issues. Since Rule 703 is not, formally, a hearsay exception at all and is of rather recent vintage, it could not be considered a firmly rooted hearsay exception. So if Rule 703 disclosures in the *Roberts* reliability era were made for their truth, then courts would have had to determine particularized indicia of reliability in every case. Given how little import the Confrontation Clause had in general in this period with respect to hearsay, for it to apply so strictly in the expert context seemed anomalous. Experts were only supposed to be able to rely upon materials "of a type reasonably relied upon by experts in the particular field,"[74] and at least arguably, this in conjunction with other rules regulating experts provided as much structural assurance for the reliability of an expert's basis as exists for many hearsay exceptions. In addition, much expert basis evidence could, in fact, be admissible with a little bit of rigmarole. Rule 703 therefore often operated as a shortcut to disclosure, rather than as a rule permitting disclosure of materials that were actually barred. Overall, then, prior to *Crawford*, the notion that such evidence was introduced for the allegedly nonhearsay purpose of helping the factfinder better understand and evaluate the expert's reasoning may have been a legal fiction, but it was a legal fiction that was largely of a piece with the broader approach to the Confrontation Clause.

Crawford and its progeny brought about three changes relevant to what we might term the Rule 703 compromise. First, reliability was no longer the critical conceptual category for determining the

---

[73] Some commentators viewed this as such a substantial risk that they advocated prohibiting experts from disclosing their basis evidence altogether unless it was otherwise admissible. See, for example, Ronald I. Carlson, *Policing the Bases of Modern Expert Testimony*, 39 Vand L Rev 577 (1986). By contrast, others advocated permitting basis evidence to be used substantively, in essence operating as a hearsay exception. See, for example, Paul R. Rice, *Inadmissible Evidence as a Basis of Expert Opinion Testimony: A Response to Professor Carlson*, 40 Vand L Rev 583, 587 (1987).

[74] FRE 703.

applicability of the Confrontation Clause—so if the Rule 703 compromise was implicitly predicated upon a sense that expert evidence had structural protections for reliability equivalent to firmly rooted hearsay exceptions, this theory of reliability no longer made a difference. Second, the *Crawford* line of cases substantially expanded the Confrontation Clause's power and reach. Hence, if the Rule 703 compromise stemmed from a reluctance to apply the Clause forcefully to expert basis evidence given how little wingspan it had elsewhere, well, its wingspan had significantly expanded. Third, prior to *Crawford*, the dominant reason for expert basis evidence inadmissibility was that it was hearsay. It was inadmissible because of a rule of evidence, not because of the Constitution.

It is certainly not obvious that Rule 703 should apply in the same way when the reason for the basis evidence's inadmissibility is a constitutional protection. As we have seen, using the information strictly for a purpose other than its truth usually demands a mental dexterity to which human factfinders can only aspire. The rules of evidence ask them to try their best. When jurors are involved, the judge must caution the jury against relying on the basis statements for their truth, but there is little reason to believe this will be effective. When a judge is the factfinder, we may hope that professional exposure to the nuances of hearsay law will permit the judge to compartmentalize his thinking, but even this may be unrealistic.[75] We hope for the best (and tolerate the worst) because expert opinions (even when based partly on hearsay) are thought to have enough value to justify their admission. Nevertheless, even though we tolerate the Rule 703 compromise when basis evidence is not testimonial, it is not clear we should rely on pious hopes to safeguard a constitutional right.

In the years following *Crawford*, a few courts began to recognize the fictional quality of the not-for-the truth argument and therefore began to disallow disclosure of expert basis evidence when it consisted of seemingly testimonial statements from declarants not produced for cross-examination.[76] But many courts chose instead to adhere mechanically to the Rule 703 compromise, and concluded, often with virtually no analysis, that experts can disclose

---

[75] See, for example, Andrew J. Wistrich et al, *Can Judges Ignore Inadmissible Information? The Difficulty of Deliberately Disregarding*, 153 U Pa L Rev 1252 (2005).

[76] See, for example, *People v Goldstein*, 843 NE2d 727 (NY 2005); *Vann v State*, 229 P3d 197 (Alaska Ct App 2010).

what otherwise would be testimonial statements as mere basis evidence so long as it meets the requirements of Rule 703 (and, for some courts, so long as the testifying expert is doing something beyond mere parroting of the absent expert's conclusions). These courts—including the Illinois courts in *Williams*—reasoned that this disclosure does not implicate the Confrontation Clause since the evidence technically was not being offered for its truth.[77]

1. *"Illumination" as a nontruth purpose in Williams.* This, then, was the lay of the land that the Supreme Court confronted in *Williams.* Justice Alito's plurality opinion accepts the broad pre-*Crawford* Rule 703 theory that basis evidence can be used for the nonsubstantive purpose of helping the judge or jury understand and evaluate the expert's opinions—while suspending all judgment on the truth of the basis evidence. Presuming that the trial judge followed the formal logic of Rule 703, the plurality maintained that the trial judge decided that Cellmark correctly characterized the DNA in the samples not because Cellmark prepared a report saying as much, but because of "circumstantial evidence."[78] This evidence included the ISP's repeated assurances that the Cellmark lab was accredited, the fact that the ISP often used the outside lab to cope with its backlog, and that the victim implicitly confirmed the DNA match by picking a man with the same DNA type from a lineup.[79]

The majority of the Justices—four of them in the dissent penned by Justice Kagan and one more in the concurring opinion of Justice Thomas—found this construction of the trial court's reasoning unpersuasive at best. Most human beings, we have suggested, do not reason in so well compartmentalized a manner, and the majority of the Court adopted the realist position that Rule 703 basis evidence is likely to be used for its truth regardless of the formal

---

[77] See, for example, *State v Lyles*, 615 SE2d 890 (NC Ct App 2005); *People v Thomas*, 130 Cal App 4th 1202 (2005); *United States v Mirabel*, 2010 US Dist LEXIS 91595 (D NM). For more thoughtful pre-*Williams* efforts to assess the relationship between expert basis evidence, hearsay, and expert disclosure under the Confrontation Clause, see, for example, *United States v Pablo*, 625 F3d 1285 (10th Cir 2010); *People v Hill*, 191 Cal App 4th 1104 (2011).

[78] 132 S Ct at 2237 n 7 ("[B]ecause there was substantial (albeit circumstantial) evidence on this matter, there is no reason to infer that the trier of fact must have taken [the ISP analyst's] statement as providing "the missing link.").

[79] Although the plurality opinion regarded that as a tremendous coincidence in the absence of guilt, the lineup was conducted more than a year after the attack, and it was no coincidence that a man—the defendant—with the incriminating DNA type was in the lineup.

logic that undergirds the rule. In response, the plurality indignantly dismissed the dissent's legal realism as constituting "a profound lack of respect for the acumen of the trial judge."[80]

However, speculation or presumptions about how the trial judge reasoned are immaterial to a narrower argument against the formal logic of Rule 703 in this setting. The argument is not necessarily that the psychology of Rule 703 is grossly unrealistic (though it may well be). It is that in this particular case, disclosure of Cellmark's role cannot be seen as serving "the legitimate nonhearsay purpose of illuminating the expert's thought process."[81] This, we believe, is the dominant, and stronger, strain of the Kagan-Thomas critique. It involves several subtleties that can be missed in the rapid-fire volleys back and forth in the *Williams* opinions. Consequently, we will explicate it in some detail. We begin with Justice Alito's description of the expert's testimony:

> She testified to the truth of the following matters: Cellmark was an accredited lab; the ISP occasionally sent forensic samples to Cellmark for DNA testing; according to shipping manifests admitted into evidence, the ISP lab sent vaginal swabs taken from the victim to Cellmark and later received those swabs back from Cellmark; and, finally, the Cellmark DNA profile matched a profile produced by the ISP lab from a sample of petitioner's blood. Lambatos had personal knowledge of all these matters, and therefore none of this testimony infringed petitioner's confrontation right.
>
> Lambatos did not testify to the truth of any other matter concerning Cellmark. She made no reference to the Cellmark report, which was not admitted into evidence and was not seen by the trier of fact. Nor did she testify to anything that was done at the Cellmark lab, and she did not vouch for the quality of Cellmark's work.[82]

In this inventory of statements, one critical piece is missing, or at least passed over too quickly. Cellmark did not simply send back *swabs* to the ISP. It also sent back *graphs and a table of DNA alleles* it claimed to have generated from the semen found on those swabs.[83] The ISP analyst testified that she relied on the graphs

---

[80] Id at 2237.

[81] Id at 2240.

[82] Id at 2235.

[83] In this case, the table of alleles did not correspond to only one possible DNA profile. See David H. Kaye, *Williams v. Illinois—Part II: More Facts, from Outside the Record, and a Question of Ethics, Forensic Science, Statistics and the Law Blog* (Blogspot, Dec 15, 2011), online at http://for-sci-law-now.blogspot.com/2011/12/williams-v-illinois-part-ii-more-facts.html. This ambiguity in the profile of the DNA in the semen affects the computation

and the table from Cellmark—what Justice Alito calls "the Cellmark DNA profile"—to reach her own conclusion that the samples sent to Cellmark and the one taken from Williams matched.[84] In addition, Ms. Lambatos implicitly but clearly offered a related opinion—that the information she received from Cellmark was trustworthy.

Although Justice Alito asserts that Lambatos did not vouch for the accuracy or quality of Cellmark's work, this depends on exactly what is meant by the word "vouch." She did not "vouch" for its accuracy based on personal involvement in the testing, for she acknowledged on cross-examination that she had nothing to do with that testing. But she clearly indicated that she trusted the outside laboratory to do reliable work, given its accredited status, its repeated work for the state, and, of course, her willingness to act on the information.[85] Her testimony made clear both that she had relied upon Cellmark's information, and that in her expert judgment, it was worthy of reliance.

Examined carefully, the record reveals not one, but three opinions offered by the expert about the DNA Cellmark provided to the ISP. Opinion 1 is that Cellmark's information attributing certain alleles to the semen found in L. J.'s vaginal swab is probably accurate. Opinion 2 is that those alleles match the defendant. Opinion 3 is that in all probability, they match no one else. Combining all these opinions produces a chain of reasoning culminating in the conclusion that Sandy Williams is the source of the semen. Only Opinion 1 poses a possible confrontation problem in the case because it is only here that the state's analyst relied on the work of another laboratory that was not presented by a witness who could be meaningfully cross-examined about that work.

Justice Alito endeavored to isolate and defang Opinion 1 by an analogy to a hypothetical question. According to the analogy, Cell-

---

of random-match probabilities slightly, but the oversimplification is of no importance on the confrontation issue.

[84] This much was implicit in her testimony on direct examination, and the cross-examination made her reliance on the Cellmark report explicit.

[85] For example, on cross-examination defense counsel asked, "You did not know if they observed or checked the calibration of their instruments—correct?" Lambatos replied: "Well, [Cellmark] Diagnostic is an accredited laboratory so they would have to meet certain guidelines to perform DNA analysis for the Illinois State police and so all those calibrations and internal proficiencies and controls would have had to have been in place for them to perform the DNA analysis." Joint Appendix at 59–60.

mark's statements are a mere premise to the analyst's testimony, to be established by other evidence. If other evidence persuasively suggests that Cellmark's analysis is reliable, then it would be perfectly permissible to ask an expert a hypothetical question that assumed this other evidence as true. In other words, Justice Alito treated the expert's testimony as if she had testified, "If I were to assume that the DNA profile of the semen is that given in Cellmark's report and then combine that assumed fact with my findings that this set of alleles is virtually unique and matches the alleles of Williams recorded in the database, then I would conclude that the semen came from Williams." This we may call "premise-only" testimony, for the only role that Opinion 1 plays is that of the premise in the reasoning that attributes the semen to Williams.[86]

Construing Lambatos's testimony as premise-only testimony is vital to the plurality's no-TMA theory because it makes it possible for the plurality at least to argue that the trial court did not rely on the analyst's beliefs about the quality of Cellmark's work. If other evidence supported a belief in the reliability of Cellmark's analysis, then crediting the judge with following Rule 703's strictures not to consider the truth of the basis evidence is at least plausible. However, the premise-only view of the testimony necessarily defeats the Rule 703 argument. Lambatos undertook what the prosecution called "her own testing"[87] and what the trial court called her "own independent testing of the data received"[88] only with regard to Opinions 2 and 3. Under the theory for which her testimony was offered, Rule 703 would allow her to disclose the origin of the alleles she input into the computer—but only insofar as this information could affect the soundness of those opinions, and the Opinion 1 premise had no effect on those independent opinions. That is, Cellmark's work neither enhanced nor dimin-

---

[86] However, this case does not fit comfortably into the premise-only mold. We give an example of true premise-only testimony in the final section.

[87] See note 42.

[88] The trial court admitted what it understood to be the ISP analyst's "own independent testing of the data received from [Cellmark]." Joint Appendix at 93–94. At most, this means that she not only input the Cellmark numbers and found a database match to Williams, but that she also inspected the graphs to verify that the numbers that Cellmark attributed to the male part of the DNA mixture were those for DNA fragments within the DNA profile of someone other than L. J. Her views on the deconvolution of the mixture might have been admissible, but the prosecution did not ask about her thought process for mixture interpretation. It asked for her opinion on a match in the database. See text accompanying notes 41–42.

ished the likely accuracy of her testimony that the computer found a match to the alleles she input and that this set of alleles was rare in the population (Opinions 2 and 3). Knowing that Cellmark fed her certain graphs and numbers explains *why* she typed those particular numbers, but this *why* sheds no light on the quality of the conclusion that Williams's database profile corresponds to the profile she input for her database query. It does nothing to illuminate how a computer makes a match, how the matching database record is linked to Sandy Williams, or how rare the matching features are in the population. And eliciting this latter set of explanations was the only ground the prosecution gave for calling the ISP analyst to the stand.[89] Recall that the prosecution insisted, "I'm not getting at what another lab did, but only asking the analyst about her own testing based on [DNA] information from Cellmark."[90] Under this quite delimited theory of what the testimony was provided for, disclosing her belief about the source of the DNA she analyzed simply does not illuminate her thought process vis-à-vis the methods of her own testing.

Under a less cramped theory of the purpose of the evidence, the ISP analyst's disclosure of Opinion 1 could indeed illuminate her thought process—but then, it would be running through a truth inference. As we have noted, Rule 703 permits experts to rely upon inadmissible evidence so long as it is of a kind that experts in the field would reasonably rely. It is probably reasonable for experts to rely on DNA analyses conducted by other accredited laboratories. So putting the Confrontation Clause to one side, under Rule 703, there would most likely be nothing impermissible about the ISP expert testifying to her ultimate conclusion that the DNA found in the vaginal swab matched the defendant, notwithstanding that this conclusion required reliance upon the accuracy of Cellmark's report.[91] But notice: to reach that ultimate conclusion, the ISP analyst had to accept the truth of Cellmark's report. There is nothing wrong with a scientist engaging in that kind of epistemic deference to the findings of other trusted experts. The point is simply that the inferential chain for that ultimate conclusion necessarily runs through the truth of Cellmark's report.

---

[89] See text accompanying notes 41–42.

[90] *Williams*, 132 S Ct at 2230.

[91] Indeed, this is an example of the kind of epistemic deference and distributed cognition that we discuss below in Part III.

We see, then, that disclosing Opinion 1 to the jury neither strengthens nor weakens the expert's testimony with regard to Opinions 2 and 3. So Opinion 1 illuminates her thought process only insofar as it reveals that she also believes Opinion 1, and that belief undergirds her opinion that Williams's DNA was found in the vaginal swabs from the victim.

It is also worth noting that although Cellmark's findings revealed nothing about the quality of the ISP analyst's admissible conclusion that the alleles used in her database query produced a match to a profile with a negligible random-match probability (Opinions 2 and 3), there was a valid reason for the state to disclose the fact that Cellmark attributed the alleles to semen from Williams. Without some explanation of why Lambatos input the numbers she did, her actions are barely intelligible and would lack relevance. Evidence of this sort certainly can be admissible to complete the prosecution's story.[92] But this source of illumination has no bearing on the hearsay issue in *Williams*. It pertains to relevance, and relevance does not provide a way around the argument that the evidence is testimonial unless the evidence is legitimately offered for a non-TMA purpose. Evidence of prior criminal conduct, for example, sometimes is required for narrative integrity. When this occurs, the evidence is relevant for a purpose other than indicating a propensity to commit crimes, which helps overcome an objection to character evidence.[93] Even in that situation, however, the background evidence is still introduced for its truth. If the proof of the missing part of the narrative is false, then the evidence has no probative value.[94]

The notion that an assertion that has no probative value when it is false supplies a heuristic with which to test any argument about TMA. We simply ask whether the factfinder would have

---

[92] See, for example, Kenneth Broun, ed, 1 *McCormick on Evidence* § 190 (West, 7th ed 2013); compare *Old Chief v United States*, 519 US 172, 189 (1997) (addressing the argument that evidence of an earlier crime should be admissible on the ground that "[p]eople who hear a story interrupted by gaps of abstraction may be puzzled at the missing chapters.").

[93] 1 *McCormick* § 190 (cited in note 92).

[94] In some situations, evidence that completes the story is not hearsay. This occurs when an out-of-court statement truly is introduced solely for its effect on the hearer. A police officer sued for an illegal arrest can defend by showing that the arrest came after learning from an apparently reliable source that a warrant for the plaintiff's arrest was outstanding—even though the warrant had been quashed. Compare *Arizona v Evans*, 514 US 1 (1995) (declining to apply the exclusionary rule for unconstitutionally seized evidence in this situation). The probative value of the report of the outstanding warrant does not depend on its truth. True or false, the report establishes a good-faith basis for the arrest.

any use for the out-of-court statements if their truth value were altered. Consider *Tennessee v Street*.[95] The *Crawford* Court cited *Street* as establishing that only statements introduced for their truth can offend the Confrontation Clause,[96] but the no-TMA majority in *Williams* easily distinguished the statements in *Street* from those in *Williams*. As Justice Thomas explained, in *Street*

> the defendant testified that he gave a false confession because police coerced him into parroting his accomplice's confession. On rebuttal, the prosecution introduced the accomplice's confession to demonstrate to the jury the ways in which the two confessions differed. Finding no Confrontation Clause problem, this Court held that the accomplice's out-of-court confession was not introduced for its truth, but only to impeach the defendant's version of events.[97]

This reasoning is correct because in *Street*, even if we flip the truth value of the accomplice's confession, it still proves the prosecution's point—that the defendant was not coerced into saying the same thing as the accomplice. If the two confessions are the same, it provides some element of support for the defendant's claim. If they are substantially different, it weakens his argument—and this is true whether the accomplice's confession is entirely true, entirely false, or somewhere in between.

This invariance under an inversion in the truth value exists in some expert opinion cases as well. Consider *Weber v BNSF Railway Co.*[98] A train engineer felt ill after he was stuck in a tunnel with fumes from other locomotives. The treating physician testified that the employee had brain damage from acute carbon monoxide poisoning. Not only was that his initial diagnosis, but he referred the patient to a neurologist who conducted a PET scan and reported to his primary physician that the scan indicated carbon monoxide poisoning. In *Weber*, one can at least argue that the physician's testimony that he had the neurologist do a PET scan is admissible independently of the truth of the neurologist's inferences—because it shows how thorough the physician was in making his diagnosis. Even if the PET scan had been inconclusive, the physician might have been able to defend his diagnosis (and show that he did everything he was supposed to do to make the

---

[95] 471 US 409 (1985).

[96] *Crawford*, 541 US 36, 59–60 n 9 (2004).

[97] *Williams*, 132 S Ct at 2256–57 (Thomas, J, concurring) (citations omitted).

[98] 261 P3d 984 (Mont 2011).

diagnosis, so that his opinion should be believed). The nonhearsay logic would be that his care and conscientiousness in bringing in a neurologist revealed his thoroughness in gathering information for his diagnosis and in using all the data, including information from his examination of the patient and other sources independent of the neurologist. In an alternative world in which the physician made his conclusion about carbon monoxide poisoning with an inconclusive PET scan, the conclusion would not be as strong as the one supported by the PET scan, but the disclosure of the inconclusive PET scan still would have relevance apart from its truth. Thus, changing the truth value of the neurologist's out-of-court statement about the PET scan affects only the weight the factfinder should accord the testifying physician's conclusion. If the physician's testimony with the weaker foundation is the only evidence of carbon monoxide poisoning, then a factfinder still might be able to credit it, and if so, the plaintiff's case should withstand a motion for a directed verdict. To be sure, in cases like this one, there might be a concern that the factfinder would take the corroborating PET scan as true, but at least there is a logical basis for arguing that the evidence would remain relevant even with a different conclusion, and hence it is not introduced solely for its truth.

The same nontruth reasoning does not work in *Williams*. If the prosecution wants the expert to give the limited opinion ostensibly desired in *Williams*—namely, that Williams is the only person whose DNA profile matches the alleles the analyst considered—then the prosecution has the previous problem of explaining how the expert's report that the alleles came from an unrelated laboratory that tested certain samples illuminates the thought process of going from those numbers to that conclusion. For that expert thought process, the Rule 703 rationale is inapposite. The analyst's reasoning that a set of numbers triggered a unique database match is neither stronger nor weaker depending on the source of the numbers. Had the numbers come to the analyst in a dream, or had she found them scrawled on her desk in an anonymous note, her reasoning from them to Sandy Williams would have been the same.

To make the situation analogous to *Weber* (and more like the hypothetical question envisioned in the plurality opinion), we must envision the analyst providing a different opinion. Suppose that the prosecutor in *Williams* had explained that her purpose in calling the ISP analyst was to have this expert opine not just that she found a database match to Williams, but also that *some of the DNA on the swab* came from Williams. Like the diagnosis of the physician in *Weber*, the DNA analyst's opinion then would rest on her own work (in the database matching and evaluation step) and on the preceding expert's information (in the prior step characterizing the rapist's DNA). Suppose that the court allows the expert to refer to Cellmark's testing solely to show the quality or nature of her reasoning from Cellmark's report to the revised conclusion that Williams is the source of the rapist's semen (what we designed as Opinions 2 and 3).

Now notice what happens when we change the truth content of Cellmark's report from "true" to "inconclusive." The prosecution can hardly argue that relying on the statements in that report to initiate a database search makes the final conclusion about Williams any more believable than if the expert used the dream sequence of numbers. This is unlike the consultation with the neurologist in *Weber*, which could have supported the diagnosis even if the neurologist had made a mistake. So the evaluation of the quality of the expert's new final conclusion does depend on the TMA in the report. If Cellmark made a mistake, the probative value of input from Cellmark is not just reduced, but nonexistent. Try as we might, the Rule 703 nonhearsay logic does not work in the context of *Williams*.[99]

---

[99] This difference between a valid use of Rule 703 and the one in *Williams* supports Justice Kagan's frustration with some of the plurality's analysis. She wrote that:

> In responding to this reasoning, the plurality confirms it. According to the plurality, basis evidence supports the "credibility of the expert's opinion" by showing that he has relied on, and drawn logical inferences from, sound "factual premises." Quite right. And that process involves assessing such premises' truth: If they are, as the majority puts it, "unsupported by other evidence in the record" or otherwise baseless, they will not "allay [a factfinder's] fears" about an "expert's reasoning." I could not have said it any better.

Williams, 132 S Ct at 2269 n 1 (Kagan, J, dissenting) (citations omitted). Tenacious to a fault, however, our prosecutor might not give up on Rule 703. Like the Alito plurality, she might say that the factfinder can rely on her expert's belief that Cellmark produces correct results because experts in the field reasonably rely on the fact that accredited laboratories always get things right. But even if the factfinder could possess such confidence in an outside laboratory, it does not change the hearsay nature of the statements from Cellmark. The surrogate expert's confidence, or the fact that Cellmark is accredited, just supplies a possible reason to believe the truth of the statements that, ostensibly, were not introduced for their truth. At best, this kind of circumstantial evidence could overcome a motion for a directed verdict if the ISP analyst's references to what Cellmark reported

What we see, then, is that it would be too hasty to reject absolutely the plurality's no-TMA theory for basis evidence. To conclude that the Rule 703 compromise is a legal fiction because, realistically, expert basis evidence is *always* disclosed for its truth goes too far. There are some limited instances like *Weber*, where if we modify the basis evidence, it still remains relevant to the expert's analysis. Such evidence is not hearsay and can be presented without violating the Confrontation Clause. But if the basis evidence is of no value to the prosecution unless it is true, as in the *Williams* case, then it cannot elude the Clause on the ground that it is not hearsay because it illuminates the expert's thought process.

2. *Hearsay and the improbability drive.* The plurality's discussion of TMA obliquely suggests another possible reason to treat the expert's reference to Cellmark's laboratory findings in *Williams* as nonhearsay and therefore beyond the reach of the Confrontation Clause. The plurality appears to find quite significant the fact that Cellmark returned a profile that happened to match someone in the database who then happened to be identified as the perpetrator by the victim in a lineup. Justice Alito wrote:

> [T]here is simply no plausible explanation for how Cellmark could have produced a DNA profile that matched Williams' if Cellmark had tested any sample other than the one taken from the victim. . . . Thus, the fact that the Cellmark profile matched Williams—the very man whom the victim identified in a lineup and at trial as her attacker—was itself striking confirmation that the sample that Cellmark tested was the sample taken from the victim's vaginal swabs.[100]

The factfinder can, Justice Alito suggests, believe in the accuracy of Cellmark's profile because of the eyewitness identification of the person said to match, rather than needing to rely on Lambatos's assertion of her own reliance and her own belief in its trustworthiness. (This is what, for Justice Alito, constitutes the other evidence of Cellmark's reliability that permits Opinion 1, discussed above, to be taken as "premise-only.")

This "striking" coincidence about the table of alleles in the Cellmark report calls to mind *Bridges v State*,[101] a well-known case about the limits of the definition of hearsay. In that case, a man

---

were introduced for their truth—which the Confrontation Clause prevents—or for some other purpose—which is not present here.

[100] Id at 2238 (Alito, J) (plurality).

[101] 19 NW2d 529 (Wis 1945).

was charged with sexually molesting a minor. Among the evidence presented were statements made by the victim to her mother and the police shortly after the incident, describing details of the perpetrator's house, furnishings, and location, including certain unusual details, such as a white, fenced playhouse set back from the street directly across from the house into which she was taken. Later, other admissible evidence established the accuracy of the girl's description, including the general accuracy of the unusual and specific details she had recalled. Additionally, in the circumstances of this case, there was absolutely no other conceivable explanation for the young girl having ever been in this room or this house on some other occasion, nor any other plausible way she would have known of its description. The court determined that in this unusual situation, the girl's out-of-court statements about where she was molested did not constitute hearsay. Her statements were admissible, the court said, not to prove the existence of the particular items or locations she described, but rather to prove, circumstantially, her knowledge of these things, which tended to prove that she had in fact been in the room, given that the room's description and location were unequivocally established by other, admissible evidence.[102]

Bridges has been controversial among evidence analysts. Some have argued that this evidence ought still to be viewed as hearsay and that this "circumstantial evidence of knowledge or state of mind" has no limits and could eviscerate the hearsay rule.[103] However, the argument that the statements are not hearsay is that, given these circumstances, including the existence of other evidence to support the accuracy of the girl's description, the young girl's statements do not need to be taken as true; rather, the very fact that she could describe such a room, proven to exist by other evidence, suggests that she was in fact in such a room—not because she says so, but because the chances of her being able to make up a description based on her imagination or other sources of knowledge is massively implausible and thus extraordinarily unlikely to be the result of mere coincidence or chicanery. So for her to be able to describe the room, with telling and specific detail that

---

[102] Id at 536.

[103] See, for example, Edmund Morgan, *Evidence 1941–1945*, 59 Harv L Rev 491, 544 (1945); G. Michael Fenner, *Law Professor Reveals Shocking Truth About Hearsay*, 62 UMKC L Rev 1 (1993).

3

turned out to correspond in every particular to an actual room, provides strong circumstantial evidence that she was, in fact, in that same room, separately and apart from her saying so. Indeed, if she had said, "Let me tell you about a room I have never seen," and went on to describe it in the same vivid detail, that too would provide circumstantial evidence that she had in fact seen it, her claim to the contrary notwithstanding.

Justice Alito did not cite *Bridges*, but his rationale is structurally quite similar. He suggests that the eyewitness identification by the victim of the person whose profile was returned by Cellmark circumstantially establishes the accuracy of Cellmark's analysis, and hence Cellmark's profile can meaningfully be mentioned by the expert for a purpose other than the truth of its contents. But there is a difficulty. That Cellmark reported the alleles of a man subsequently identified by the victim in a lineup does provide some independent evidence of the accuracy of its analysis, but not nearly so much as the plurality proposes. The fact of a database match shows us that the alleles that Cellmark returned to the ISP (1) in fact matched someone in the database (indeed, a man in the same geographical vicinity as L. J., notwithstanding that Cellmark handled samples from across the country); and (2) that when this man was included in a lineup, he was the very person identified by L.J. as the perpetrator. Had its table of alleles been plucked from the air, there most likely would not have been a match to anyone in the database. Had Cellmark fumbled the chain of custody and analyzed the wrong rape kit leading to a hit to the wrong man in the database, L. J. might not have identified this man in the lineup as her assailant. So Justice Alito is correct that this does provide some circumstantial support for the inference that Cellmark sent back the appropriate sample and engaged in an accurate analysis.

But how strong is this evidence? To answer this, we would need to understand both the probability of an incorrect set of alleles matching at least one person in the state database who would not be dismissed out of hand as the possible rapist, and the probability of L. J. making an erroneous eyewitness identification of this individual. With regard to the first issue, it should be clear that trawling large databases creates many opportunities for even an incorrectly generated DNA profile to match *somebody*.[104] Whatever

[104] See David H. Kaye, *Rounding Up the Usual Suspects: A Legal and Logical Analysis of DNA Database Trawls*, 87 NC L Rev 425 (2009).

that probability is, it is well above zero. Furthermore, one should not ignore the possibility of a sample switch in the course of the laboratory's processing of rape kits. What if Cellmark had somehow swapped this sample sent from the ISP containing L. J.'s vaginal swabs with another sample sent from a different Chicago-area case? It is far from obvious that a different potential rapist would not also be in the database. It may be fair to assume that both of these probabilities are small, but it is worth noting both that we do not know what they are, and that they do affect the strength of the circumstantial chain of inferences that runs from the fact of a match to the accuracy of the Cellmark report.

As for the second apparently surprising fact, it depends on the chances for an erroneous eyewitness identification. If we thought that L. J. was extremely unlikely to make a mistake in identifying the perpetrator, then her identification of Williams does provide substantial support for the premise that Cellmark returned the correct sample and that it analyzed the DNA correctly. But imagine, instead, that L. J. was not an especially careful observer, or suppose that some aspect of this specific identification procedure was psychologically suggestive and thereby raised the chances that any observer would pick the defendant from among the possibilities. The opinions do not tell us how many individuals were included in the lineup. We know nothing from the opinions about the specific procedures used. We do not know, for example, whether the person conducting the lineup knew which member was the actual suspect, or whether the police took other protections that have been shown to reduce the rate of erroneous identification. Some evidence in the case suggested that L. J. may have initially identified someone else as the perpetrator, shortly after the attack, strengthening an inference that L. J. could have been susceptible to making an erroneous identification.[105] The substantial length of time—fourteen months—that had passed between the attack and the lineup procedure that included Williams also decreases the probative value of her identification, since her memory could have faded over that period and the perpetrator's appearance could have changed. What if L. J. was likely to select *someone* from the identification, whether the actual perpetrator was present or not? In that case, if there were five people in the lineup,

---

[105] *People v Williams*, 385 Ill App 3d 359, 361 (2008).

there would be a 20 percent chance that Williams would be selected at random; if ten people in the lineup, a 10 percent chance.

Admittedly, we have no way to quantify the chances of either a
laboratory slipup or an erroneous identification. But we can be
confident that those odds, whatever they might be, are far higher
than the one-in-many-quadrillion random-match probabilities
presented for Williams's DNA. Note that the parallel to *Bridges*
is not precise. In *Bridges*, the argument was that the other evidence
established the description of the room and area; the girl's description was therefore not hearsay, but it was admissible to demonstrate her knowledge. Without her out-of-court statements the
prosecutor would have been missing a critical piece of the story.
By contrast, in *Williams*, the argument suggested by Justice Alito
is that the fact of the DNA match coupled with the eyewitness
identification provides strong circumstantial evidence of Cellmark's accuracy, both that they examined the correct sample and
that they performed their testing procedures correctly. Therefore,
the expert's references are not hearsay because they are, in a sense,
cumulative, or unnecessary. They need not be taken as true because
other evidence establishes the same thing; hence his argument that
they can be what we termed "premise-only."

This leaves us with the question whether the coincidence of an
eyewitness identification of Williams coming in the wake of Cellmark's report is so striking that it transforms the analyst's statements from hearsay into surplusage. We have our doubts. If there
had been a laboratory error in which samples were swapped, or
some other inaccuracy in Cellmark's process, there could nonetheless be a nonnegligible possibility of an erroneous eyewitness
identification. Thus, on the facts of *Williams*, the probative value
of the eyewitness identification as evidence of the laboratory report's accuracy is not as strong as the probative value of a young
girl being able to provide multiple, detailed, specific descriptions
of an unusual place, as evidence that she had been in that place
at some point. Moreover, the chain of inference from the expert's
testimony about Cellmark (taken as true) to her conclusion is far
more straightforward than the circumstantial chain the plurality
opinion posits as an alternative (and that was never directly argued
at trial). Still, Justice Alito is correct that these other items do
provide some quantum of evidence supporting the accuracy of
Cellmark's results, separate from the expert's say-so, if not quite

so overwhelming a quantum as he suggested. His argument, while perceptive, is not entirely persuasive.

At the same time, there may be cases in which this argument would be compelling. For instance, the circumstantial evidence would have been significantly stronger if the ISP laboratory and Lambatos had not only looked at the defendant profile, but independently compared the victim's profile as reported by Cellmark to an independently collected sample of L. J.'s profile. If those female samples matched, that could have provided an additional, probative, circumstantial piece of evidence suggesting the accuracy of the male DNA found in the same swab, and greatly decreasing the chances that the eyewitness identification was a mere coincidence. It would have made a sample swap significantly more unlikely, since it would show that the female portion of the samples clearly were not swapped; and the accuracy of the process as applied to L. J.'s DNA would provide circumstantial evidence of the accuracy of the process applied to the male portion as well. Then we would indeed have a story of remarkable coincidence comparable to *Bridges*. We would know that a sample was sent to Cellmark, and a sample was returned form Cellmark with the appropriate label, and, furthermore, that the female portion of that sample correctly matched the victim in the case and the male portion of the sample matched someone in the database who the victim subsequently identified as her perpetrator. While even this additional piece of evidence would not absolutely remove all possibility of some kind of laboratory inaccuracy, this body of circumstantial evidence would substantially reduce the possibility of a sample swap or some other error within Cellmark. On those facts, it would be easier to make the argument about the strength of the circumstantial proof no longer requiring or inviting the factfinder to take Lambatos's testimony as evidence of the reliability of Cellmark's analysis. Such facts would bring this case more in line with the approach taken in *Bridges*.

As in the previous section, we see that the argument that expert evidence can be offered for a purpose other than the truth is, on occasion, plausible. In some circumstances, Justice Alito's "premise-only" way of understanding some expert disclosure might be credible. But to be able to argue that expert disclosure does not also provide corroboration or bolstering of the other evidence, information that the factfinder—perhaps especially in jury trials but possibly in bench trials too—will be tempted to take as true, this other evidence would need to be extremely strong. We are doubtful that the circumstantial evidence of reliability on these facts is so overwhelmingly strong that the expert's assertions about it were taken by the factfinder as mere surplusage. Moreover, even if Justice Alito's argument holds some water here, in many cases, there will not be substantial independent evidence to support the expert's basis. We take that issue up in the next Section.

B. RULE 703 AND RELEVANCE

The plurality's dogged determination to cast the expert's testimony as strictly premise-only leads to a puzzling discussion of the need for independent evidence of the necessary facts preceding the short-chain reasoning that starts with the alleles specified by Cellmark and concludes with the expert's attribution of them to *Williams* (Opinions 2 and 3).[106] Suppose that L. J. had failed to make an identification of the defendant in the lineup. In that case, there would have been no independent evidence from which a factfinder could infer the accuracy of the alleles Cellmark reported as coming from the semen on L. J.'s swab. Would this require the information from Cellmark to be acknowledged as being introduced for the truth of its contents, and thus problematic under the Confrontation Clause? Justice Alito flatly denies this possibility, asserting that "even if the record did not contain any evidence that could rationally support a finding that Cellmark produced a scientifically reliable DNA profile based on L. J.'s vaginal swab, that would not establish a Confrontation Clause violation."[107] The absence of "proof that Cellmark produced an accurate profile based on that sample," he contends, would render "Lambatos' testimony regarding the match . . . irrelevant, but the Confrontation Clause . . . does not bar the admission of irrelevant evidence, only testimonial statements by declarants who are not subject to cross examination."[108] Confining his vision to premise-only testimony, he states that if there is not "independent admissible evidence to prove the foundational facts that are essential to

---

[106] See Part II.A.

[107] *Williams*, 132 S Ct at 2238 (Alito, J) (plurality).

[108] Id.

the relevance of the expert's testimony, then the expert's testimony cannot be given any weight by the trier of fact."[109]

This position would make sense if we truly viewed Lambatos's testimony as akin to a hypothetical question. Suppose she had testified, "While I cannot myself speak to the accuracy of Cellmark's report, nor can I confirm that they returned the correct sample, if they did in fact return the correct sample along with a correct analysis of it, then the DNA from the vaginal swab matches Sandy Williams." In that case, Justice Alito would have been correct. First, there would have been no Confrontation Clause problem. Second, without independent evidence of the premises necessary to her conclusion, her opinion would have been irrelevant and not entitled to any weight. But Lambatos did not answer a hypothetical question. Rather, she offered a conclusion that the samples sent to Cellmark and the one the ISP took from Williams in fact matched. In other words, she provided opinions about both the provenance and the nature of the samples based on the report that was not introduced into evidence.

Imagine that she gave her testimony in a case with the same facts but no eyewitness identification, either because L. J. was equivocal at the time of the lineup, or because for whatever reason, no lineup was ever conducted. Putting the Confrontation Clause issue to one side, Rule 703 probably would allow this testimony. Rule 703 explicitly permits an expert to rely upon inadmissible evidence to support a conclusion, so there would be nothing wrong with Lambatos relying upon Cellmark's report, presuming that it is indeed reasonable for DNA analysts to rely on profiles produced by other accredited laboratories (and it is difficult to argue that it is not). This kind of reliance—like one doctor relying on an X-ray produced by another—is precisely what Rule 703 permits. Under Rule 703 and most state equivalents, unlike the method for adducing expert testimony prior to the Federal Rules, the proffering party does not need to produce independent evidence of the foundational facts supporting the expert's conclusion as a precondition for admissibility of the conclusion.[110] Moreover, a fact-

[109] Id (footnote omitted).

[110] To be sure, under *Daubert v Merrell Dow Pharmaceuticals*, 509 US 579 (1993), a court may require information about these foundational facts in order to assess the validity of the testifying expert's conclusion, but the information supporting validity considered by the judge need not itself be admissible evidence. See FRE 702, FRE 104(a).

finder is permitted to give weight to that expert's conclusion even if the foundational facts are never disclosed. Indeed, Rule 703 disfavors such disclosure precisely because of the risk that if disclosed, the factfinder will take them as true.[111] So under the conventional understanding of Rule 703, if Lambatos's basis evidence did not create a Confrontation Clause problem, and if her reliance on Cellmark's report to establish both the provenance and nature of the samples was reasonable, her conclusions certainly would not be barred as irrelevant, even were there no other evidence to support the accuracy of Cellmark's DNA analysis. The whole thrust of Rule 703 is to dispense with the common-law requirement that experts must base their conclusions on otherwise admissible evidence—the rule creates no requirement that other evidence corroborate the data or facts upon which an expert relies.

If Justice Alito's intimations implying that admissible evidence supporting the expert's basis is a prerequisite for a factfinder to give any weight to expert opinions were applied to all expert evidence, expert witness practice would be radically altered. Applied literally and sweepingly, these dicta would unmake Rule 703's provision that expert conclusions can be admissible even when an expert's basis evidence is not itself admissible! Surely Justice Alito did not mean to state that, in all situations, relevance requires independent evidence proving the truth of the underlying facts essential to an expert's conclusions.[112]

---

[111] FRE 703. Rule 703 therefore partially enacts a deferential approach to a factfinder's assessment of expertise, in which a factfinder may credit a conclusion of an expert, even without knowing of the basis or the reasoning process that has produced it. On deference versus education in the assessment of expert evidence, see Ronald J. Allen and Joseph S. Miller, *The Common Law Theory of Experts: Deference or Education?* 87 Nw U L Rev 1131 (1993).

[112] Justice Alito wrote that "[o]f course, Lambatos' opinion would have lacked probative value if the prosecution had not introduced other evidence to establish the provenance of the profiles, but that has nothing to do with the truth of her testimony." 132 S Ct at 2239. Perhaps this dictum pertains only to opinions whose relevance *vel non* depends on the fulfillment of some condition of fact. Under Rule 104(b), there must be some evidence of the underlying condition. It is true that Lambatos's opinion about a match between the alleles she considered in querying the database and Williams's alleles could be seen to pose a conditional relevance issue. This opinion would be irrelevant in the absence of proof that the alleles she used had the proper provenance, i.e., that they were in the vaginal swabs from L. J. And, there was some "other evidence" of this in the form of the FedEx documents. But Lambatos also seems to have formed her own opinion about provenance. Even without the shipping documents, if it is reasonable for an ISP analyst to rely on the statements in reports from other laboratories to form opinions about provenance, then under Rule 703 the factfinder may rely on such an opinion to find, under Rule 104(b), the requisite relevance in an opinion about the database match.

In the wake of *Williams*, it would be both unfortunate and a violation of common sense if lower courts were simply to interpret the case as standing for the idea that expert basis evidence can be legitimately introduced for a purpose other than the truth of its contents, and hence, because the disclosure is for a nonhearsay purpose, the Confrontation Clause is not implicated.[113] First, at least five Justices disagreed with that view. Second, even those who adhered to the plurality opinion engaged in a set of justifications that were dramatically case-specific—that this was a bench trial rather than a jury trial and that there was some degree of circumstantial evidence to support the basis (albeit less than the plurality suggests). As a consequence, *Williams* cannot fairly be read as legitimating a mechanical and broad-brush application of a nonhearsay purpose under Rule 703—though we suspect that many courts will interpret it that way. Partly that will be because of the opacity of a case that has no shared conceptual basis of a majority of Justices for its resolution. Partly that will be because most of the lower courts have been resistant to *Crawford* and its progeny and will therefore likely jump at the chance to take a more permissive approach than the previous cases in the trilogy permitted. And partly that will be because the no-TMA argument, although often resting on a fictional basis, is an appealing way to treat science as special without appearing to engage in science exceptionalism for Confrontation Clause purposes.

Under this argument, experts can remain formally subject to the Confrontation Clause's strictures, just like any other kind of witness. But since laboratory reports will typically satisfy Rule 703, experts would be able to rely on them even though they are, per *Melendez-Diaz*, testimonial. Note that there is no explicit, overt science exceptionalism in this approach—the claim is that the Confrontation Clause applies to all evidence so long as it is offered for the truth of the matter asserted. Instead, Confrontation Clause jurisprudence simply builds on Rule 703's own ways for treating scientific evidence differently from other kinds of evidence—both in that experts can rely upon (and sometimes disclose) inadmissible evidence, and in that, for a set of context-specific reasons born in the previous Confrontation Clause era, there has been widespread

---

[113] Alas, some courts are already beginning to do precisely this. See, for example, *People v Viera*, No B230802, 2012 WL 2899343, *11 (Cal App Ct 2012); *McMullen v State*, 730 SE2d 151, 160 (Ga App Ct 2012).

acceptance of the no–TMA claim about basis evidence. Under the *Williams* approach, there is no need to exempt forensic science reports completely from the Confrontation Clause; instead, the no–TMA argument merely declaws the Clause in the forensic context.

To be fair, the plurality's arguments do have less reach than a total exemption of the sort seemingly favored by several Justices. After *Williams*, it is still not permissible to introduce a report without any expert as all, as was commonplace before *Melendez-Diaz*. Moreover, it would be strained to permit the testimony of a surrogate witness with no direct involvement in the testing, as in *Bullcoming*—but as much because of the limitations of the rules of evidence that prohibit one expert from merely serving as a mouthpiece for another[114] as because of the Confrontation Clause itself.

III. Confronting Science: The Future

The trilogy of laboratory cases marks the outer boundaries of what the Confrontation Clause allows for evidence on the findings of laboratory scientists or technicians whom the prosecution does not make available for cross-examination. At one pole are (*a*) highly formal reports or (*b*) testimony from an expert with no connection to the specific laboratory analyses to the effect that the contents of those solemn reports are true. The formal reports themselves are inadmissible. That is the teaching of *Melendez-Diaz*. In addition, the testimony about the truth of the contents is inadmissible if provided by experts unconnected to the specific test. That is the lesson of *Bullcoming*. At the other pole are written reports (*a*) not emblazoned with seals or attestations and (*b*) generated before a specific suspect or desired outcome was known to the laboratory staff. These reports the *Williams* majority should find acceptable even without a surrogate witness.

These latter outcomes follow from two unpopular theories— the *Williams* plurality's no-accusation theory, and Justice Thomas's no-formality theory. They are unpopular in that a majority of the *Williams* Court expressly rejected the no-accusation theory, and only a single Justice subscribed to the no-formality theory. Deciding more cases on theories that most of the Court rejects seems

---

[114] Kaye et al, *Expert Evidence* § 4.7.1 at 176–77 (cited in note 31).

perverse.[115] It may be the way things are for the moment, but without a more appealing doctrine, it may constitute an unstable equilibrium.

In between these extremes is a much larger and murkier zone of hypothetical questions (discussed in *Williams*), machine-generated results (mentioned in *Bullcoming* as possibly lying outside the Clause), and surrogate witnesses (left largely unresolved by *Williams*). As for hypothetical or conditional questions, the major *Williams* opinions allow that the Confrontation Clause is no barrier to asking a witness to draw expert inferences conditional on the truth of other experts' work. For example, a prosecutor seeking to introduce the ISP analyst's opinion in *Williams* could have posed questions that might have been answered as follows:

Q. Did you review the report that Cellmark sent back?

A. Yes.

Q. Did Cellmark report any alleles as being present in the vaginal swab and as not coming from L. J.'s DNA?

A. Yes.

Q. Could those alleles have come from the semen that your laboratory detected in the vaginal swabs that it shipped to Cellmark?

A. Definitely. Semen contains DNA, and it was present in the swabs.

Q. Did you search the Illinois database of DNA profiles from known individuals to see whether any of them were consistent with those DNA alleles that Cellmark attributed to the semen?

A. Yes.

Q. How many matches were there?

A. Only one.

Q. What is the name of that one and only matching individual?

A. Sandy Williams.

Q. Is there much of a chance of anyone else in the Chicago area besides Mr. Williams having a similarly matching profile?

A. This profile would be expected to occur in approximately 1 in 8.7

---

[115] But see Leo Katz, *Why the Law Is So Perverse* (Chicago, 2011).

> quadrillion black, 1 in 390 quadrillion white, or 1 in 109 quad-
> rillion Hispanic unrelated individuals.[116]

This line of questioning is entirely compatible with the Confron-tation Clause. The confrontation problem does not arise unless or until the prosecution presents evidence that would allow the factfinder to accept the unstated premise that Cellmark correctly deduced the alleles of the unknown rapist.

But skirting the confrontation problem in this way introduces the vexed evidentiary problem known as "conditional relevance."[117] This witness has said nothing about the truth of Cellmark's report that the alleles are attributable to the semen. Without proof that Cellmark's report is true, the expert opinion that builds on it may be irrelevant. To satisfy this relevance requirement, the prosecu-tion could try to introduce the Cellmark report into evidence— except that *Melendez-Diaz* bars that move unless the state also produces the Cellmark analysts. Could the prosecution establish the necessary condition through the ISP expert herself? If knowl-edgeable, she could testify to how wonderful and careful Cell-mark's work always is, giving the factfinder a reason to accept the statements in the report, and hence the ISP expert's finding of a very probative match.[118] This testimony about Cellmark resolves the conditional relevance problem, but it reintroduces the con-frontation problem of proving the facts on which the match and its associated probabilities rest without calling the witnesses to these facts. The sole testifying expert, like the one in *Bullcoming*, had no involvement in Cellmark's work, and, as we have seen, Rule 703 offers no way out because the statements are not admitted for the no-TMA purpose that sometimes, albeit rarely, legitimately applies.

To break out of this loop, the prosecution might try calling a

---

[116] The last answer is taken from the trial transcript. See Joint Appendix (cited in note 40). However, it is not quite responsive to the question because it does not account for relatives and because Sandy Williams's profile was not the only one that was consistent with the allele table in Cellmark's report. On the latter point, see Kaye, *Williams v. Illinois— Part II* (cited in note 83).

[117] See Richard D. Friedman, *Refining Conditional Probative Value*, 94 Mich L Rev 457 (1995); Dale A. Nance, *Conditional Relevance Reinterpreted*, 70 BU L Rev 447 (1990); David S. Schwartz, *A Foundation Theory of Evidence*, 100 Georgetown L J 95 (2011).

[118] The defense might object that Cellmark's past good acts are inadmissible to show a tendency to reach correct results. See Edward J. Imwinkelried and David H. Kaye, *DNA Typing: Emerging or Neglected Issues*, 76 Wash L Rev 413 (2001). This too is a relevance-prejudice issue rather than a constitutional question.

surrogate witness who is directly involved in at least one major step of the laboratory's testing and is familiar with the whole procedure. The Justices' opinions in *Williams* and *Bullcoming* display some nonspecific openness to the use of surrogate or synthesizing witnesses in this type of situation. When many workers contribute to the final conclusion and some of them perform rather mechanical procedures, tying up the entire team in court seems extravagant, at least to laboratory administrators as well as to some of the Justices.[119] And, of course, witnesses become unavailable for reasons beyond the control of the state. But the Justices have yet to coalesce on a workable and shared doctrine to effectuate this pragmatic compromise.

Notwithstanding the *Williams* plurality's efforts to rely upon Rule 703, we believe that this rule is more a source of confusion than a panacea for the problem of having to assemble an entire team of witnesses from the laboratory. The rule, as originally drafted, was not directed at the disclosure of underlying data. The rule's purpose is to allow an expert witness to testify to a conclusion that reasonably relies on the work of other experts without disclosing that underlying or related work. This expert's conclusion is the focus and gravamen of the rule. As a corollary, the rule allows disclosure of the other experts' out-of-court statements— but only for the limited and often fictional purpose of helping the factfinder evaluate the quality of the testifying primary expert's conclusion and only when the underlying statements are unusually probative of that reasoning.[120] In the settling dust of *Williams*, it seems that Justice Breyer was correct. If the Court is to avoid a regime in which every person who comes into contact with forensic science evidence must be produced for cross-examination,

---

[119] See generally *Williams*, 132 S Ct at 2244, 2248 (Breyer, J, concurring).

[120] A 2000 amendment to the rule specifies that "if the facts or data would otherwise be inadmissible, the proponent of the opinion may disclose them to the jury only if their probative value in helping the jury evaluate the opinion substantially outweighs their prejudicial effect." FRE 703. The Advisory Committee Note accompanying this amendment elaborates:

> When information is reasonably relied upon by an expert and yet is admissible only for the purpose of assisting the jury in evaluating an expert's opinion, a trial court applying this Rule must consider the information's probative value in assisting the jury to weigh the expert's opinion on the one hand, and the risk of prejudice resulting from the jury's potential misuse of the information for substantive purposes on the other.

Advisory Committee Note, FRE 703.

it will need to think hard about the function of confrontation and the nature of forensic science evidence.[121]

That takes us back to the still broader question that we suggested that the Court ought not to avoid: whether there is, in fact, a satisfactory justification for giving special treatment to forensic science evidence under the Confrontation Clause. We have seen how the Court has danced around this question, sometimes—as in Justice Kennedy's dissent in *Melendez-Diaz*—arguing explicitly that science needs to be treated differently from other kinds of evidence, and on other occasions—as in Justice Alito's opinion in *Williams*—building on the ways that the evidence rules already treat expert evidence differently to produce a doctrinal framework with the effect of creating special rules for forensic science.

The rules-of-evidence approach is not only unwieldy, but it fails to come to grips with the question of whether science testimony is meaningfully different from other testimony. Are there justifiable reasons for creating special rules in this context, and if so, what are they? On the one hand, some Justices, like Justice Scalia, seem determined both to deny that there is a critical difference and to assert that even if science testimony is different, it hardly matters. As he said in *Melendez-Diaz*, "the analysts who swore the affidavits provided testimony against Melendez-Diaz, and they are therefore subject to confrontation; we would reach the same conclusion if all analysts always possessed the scientific acumen of Mme. Curie and the veracity of Mother Theresa."[122] On the other hand, some other Justices, most notably Justice Kennedy, emphasize that forensic analysts are simply not like "ordinary" or "conventional witnesses" for myriad reasons.[123]

Notwithstanding Justice Kennedy's emphatic use of the term,

---

[121] Arguably, when a laboratory has no idea of whether its preliminary work (such as extracting DNA from a bloodstain, measuring the quantity extracted, and amplifying the extract with PCR) will incriminate anyone at all, statements about these preliminary steps fall short of the accusatory testimonial statements that demand confrontation. Perhaps this theory (which does not cramp the Confrontation Clause to the extent that the "targeted individual" requirement of Justice Alito's plurality opinion does) could deal with the problem of having to call a large number of individuals to prove the truth of every statement about every link in the chain of custody and every step in processing and testing forensic evidence. Additional proposals can be found in Kaye et al, *Expert Evidence* § 4.10 (cited in note 31); id § 4.12 (Supp 2013).

[122] *Melendez-Diaz v Massachusetts*, 557 US 305, 319 n 6 (2009). However, Justice Scalia also takes pains to suggest that the chance of incompetence, corruption, or mere mistake means that the confrontation of experts is not simply an empty formalism. Id at 319.

[123] Id at 345–46 (Kennedy, J, dissenting).

prior to *Melendez-Diaz* there was no category known as "conventional witnesses." It is true that expert witnesses are granted both certain kinds of special authorization under the evidence rules (such as the ability to give opinions and to rely on inadmissible evidence), and expected to face some special forms of regulation (such as *Daubert* and the provisos of Rule 702). It could even be said that "expert witnesses" are meaningfully their own category in some respects, a category sometimes used in relation to or in opposition to "lay witnesses," but a well-defined countercategory of "conventional witnesses" simply did not exist.[124] Still, he is right that there are differences. Nonexperts who appear in a criminal case are typically in court to testify about something atypical, have percipient knowledge of either a criminal act or some past events relating to it, and, for them, testifying itself is an exceptional occurrence. By contrast, as Justice Kennedy points out, forensic experts have standard protocols, are engaged in routine and regular activities, write their own reports rather than being the subjects of interrogation, and are taking written observations that are contemporaneous (or nearly so) with their scientific observations. These differences, in his view, should make a difference.

Although both *Crawford* and *Melendez-Diaz* emphasize that the Confrontation Clause is not supposed to be about reliability—even the evidence of saints is subject to its strictures—reliability still lurks in these opinions. And understandably so. First, it is hard to understand what the Confrontation Clause is for, if not reliability. It might be fair enough to say that a judicial determination of reliability ought not to deprive the factfinder of confrontation as a method for its own independent assessment of reliability, but it is difficult to understand the Confrontation Clause's purpose wholly disconnected from the idea of reliability. (Indeed, Justice Scalia recognizes as much, although he reads the Confrontation Clause as a procedural mechanism that tends toward greater reliability rather than a substantive check.) Moreover, when it comes to experts, the *Daubert* trilogy and its innumerable progeny in the lower courts have made reliability into the clear touchstone for the evaluation of scientific evidence, the evidentiary keyword that governs its assessment by the court. As Justice Black-

---

[124] Indeed, a LEXIS search indicates a total of four cases using the term "conventional witness" prior to 2009, the year *Melendez-Diaz* was decided. Kennedy defines his category as "one who has personal knowledge of some aspect of the defendant's guilt." Id at 330.

mun wrote in *Daubert*, "under the Rules the trial judge must ensure that any and all scientific testimony or evidence admitted is not only relevant, but reliable."[125]

Like most of the Justices in the science confrontation trilogy, we are dancing around the question of whether science is different. The difficulty is that expert witnesses, including forensic analysts, are neither entirely ordinary witnesses nor entirely unlike ordinary witnesses. Like ordinary lay witnesses, they can misperceive, make mistakes, misinterpret. They can be subject to cognitive biases. They can lie, mischaracterize, or overstate. As Justice Scalia recognizes,

> Nor is it evident that what respondent calls "neutral scientific testing" is as neutral or as reliable as respondent suggests. Forensic evidence is not uniquely immune from the risk of manipulation. According to a recent study conducted under the auspices of the National Academy of Sciences, "[t]he majority of [laboratories producing forensic evidence] are administered by law enforcement agencies, such as police departments, where the laboratory administrator reports to the head of the agency." And "[b]ecause forensic scientists often are driven in their work by a need to answer a particular question related to the issues of a particular case, they sometimes face pressure to sacrifice appropriate methodology for the sake of expediency." A forensic analyst responding to a request from a law enforcement official may feel pressure—or have an incentive—to alter the evidence in a manner favorable to the prosecution.[126]

But it is also true, as the dissent in *Bullcoming* explains, that forensic science reports are often

> prepared by experienced technicians in laboratories that follow professional norms and scientific protocols. In addition to the constitutional right to call witnesses in his own defense, the defendant in this case was already protected by checks on potential prosecutorial abuse such as free retesting for defendants; result-blind issuance of reports; testing by an independent agency; routine processes performed en masse, which reduce opportunities for targeted bias; and labs operating pursuant to scientific and professional norms and oversight.[127]

We will not here succeed in resolving to what degree forensic science witnesses are different from ordinary ones. But we do wish

---

[125] *Daubert*, 509 US at 589.

[126] *Melendez-Diaz*, 557 US at 318, citing National Research Council of the National Academies, *Strengthening Forensic Science in the United States: A Path Forward* 183 (National Academies, 2009).

[127] *Bullcoming*, 131 S Ct at 2726–27 (Kennedy, J, dissenting).

to suggest one extremely important feature of most science that has implications for how we think about science under the Confrontation Clause and that, as Justice Breyer recognized in *Williams*, will need to be confronted explicitly. In thinking about why scientific evidence might warrant some limited special treatment, it seems to us that the most important feature of science is that *it is a collective, rather than an individual enterprise.*[128] Most scientific experiments, research projects, analyses, and tests are not carried out by a single individual acting in isolation.[129] Certainly one can find instances of an individual experiment conducted by a scientist working alone (though even this solo scientist must rely on the contributions of others—purchasing reagents or laboratory equipment that embodies the expertise of others, or building on experimental results conducted by others). But most scientists simply do not operate solo. This is true across virtually all domains of science—from the high-energy physics experiment that involves hundreds or even thousands of collaborators, to the social psychology experiment conducted by a far smaller team. And it is also true of forensic science test procedures.

This reality is not lost on the Justices struggling with forensic science and the Confrontation Clause. In *Williams*, Justice Breyer wrote, "Experts—especially laboratory experts—regularly rely on the technical statements and results of other experts to form their own opinions. The reality of the matter is that the introduction of a laboratory report involves layer upon layer of technical state-

---

[128] The point is well established in the sociology of science. See Carlo Mongardini and Simonetta Tabboni, eds, *Robert K. Merton & Contemporary Sociology* (Transaction, 1998).

[129] Any broad-brush claim of this kind is an oversimplification, since "science" is a capacious category and includes substantial variation upon any given dimension, including this one. For an interesting book capturing the epistemic diversity of science, but also illustrating that knowledge is a collective enterprise, albeit to different degrees and in different ways, see, for example, Karien Knorr-Cetina, *Epistemic Cultures: How the Sciences Make Knowledge* (Harvard, 1999). The book contrasts the epistemic culture of high energy physics with that of molecular biology. Although she argues that high-energy physics is a collective culture and molecular biology an individual one, her examples actually illustrate that there are collective dimensions in both domains. See Ronald N. Giere, *Distributed Cognition in Epistemic Cultures*, 69 Phil Sci 637 (2002) (reviewing Knorr-Cetina).

Note also that we are going to bracket entirely the question of how to define science, and simply operate here with an imprecise but generally shared understanding. In doing so, we recognize that some critics—including us—have argued that forensic science is not always as scientific as it purports to be and operates within an inadequate research culture. Jennifer Mnookin et al, *The Need for a Research Culture in the Forensic Sciences*, 58 UCLA L Rev 725 (2011). Although there are significant limitations and problems with some forms of forensic science, we do not think that these weaknesses remove the enterprise from the realm of science, broadly defined.

ments (express or implied) made by one expert and relied upon by another."[130] As practiced in most laboratories, DNA analysis, for example, is a collaborative endeavor, involving multiple analysts, each of whom conducts one (or more) steps that subsequent analysis relies upon. Indeed, Justice Breyer's concurring opinion included an appendix describing, flow-chart style, the many different steps that may be taken by as many as a dozen different analysts, conducting a singular regular DNA profile comparison.[131] Must all of them testify in every case? Can it really be that the Confrontation Clause requires "turtles all the way down"?[132] Are we doomed to face a regress of experts, where each has relied upon the one before, who now must also testify?

By contrast, a "conventional witness," to borrow Justice Kennedy's nomenclature, does not usually testify about knowledge produced through such a collective, interconnected process. Usually such a witness testifies to firsthand, personal observations. While these may include the statements of others—which would be hearsay if introduced for their truth—this witness's testimony, beliefs, and observations typically do not intrinsically depend on a complex web of trusted activities conducted by others, or at least not to the same degree. Typically, a "conventional witness" may have seen or observed something that has probative value only in connection with other evidence. To borrow the evidentiary truism, a brick is not a wall; a given witness's testimony may be merely a modest brick that has to be integrated with other evidence to be persuasive on any matter of import to the case. But it is the factfinder who is asked to make these links, not the witness. When the conventional witness testifies to "bricks" within his firsthand knowledge, his knowledge does not depend on the other bricks in the same way that an expert's often does. To be sure, outside of the courtroom, he might think of himself as having knowledge of some of these other "bricks" as well, based on hunch, speculation, inference, or the testimony of others. But in court, his testimony is limited, as much as is practicable, to the matters that do not depend on factual knowledge that stems from sources outside his own observation.[133]

---

[130] *Williams*, 132 S Ct at 2246 (Breyer, J, concurring).

[131] Id at 2252–54.

[132] Stephen Hawking, *A Brief History of Time* 1 (Bantam, 1988).

[133] Of course, to paraphrase Quine, all knowledge depends on knowledge outside of

By contrast, the knowledge claims of forensic science witnesses are, intrinsically, strongly interlinked with the actions and knowledge production of others. Expert opinions and conclusions, inevitably and necessarily, require reliance on materials produced by others, data provided by others, and judgments and opinions reached by others. It is not an exaggeration to say that the knowledge that is produced through the exercise of expertise is inherently collective knowledge. It requires reliance on what others have done and what others know. This, of course, is precisely why Rule 703 permits experts, unlike lay witnesses, to rely on data and materials provided by others in forming their own conclusions. Doing so is part of what it means to engage in complex inference and knowledge production. Experts, in the course of their daily work, are engaged in a form of "collective" or "distributed cognition," in which they produce knowledge together that would not be available to any one of them standing alone. The knowledge is distributed across a group of experts, rather than being held by any single individual.[134] These individuals produce knowledge collaboratively that truly is not held by any one of them alone. In a sense, the knowledge belongs to the network rather than the individual. Collaborators create formal or informal procedures and mechanisms that both generate and rely upon trust, but there is inevitably an "epistemic dependence"[135] upon one another.

Returning to the Confrontation Clause conundrums, much of the time, the materials, data, and opinions upon which an expert relies, or the other individuals and elements within the expert's network of distributed cognition, will not itself be testimonial. The operator of a breathalyzer relies upon a machine he himself

---

specific observation in this case. For example, a witness can only put his observation into language because he already knows about language. He can testify that he smelled tobacco because he already has knowledge of what tobacco smells like. He can testify that the defendant had several drinks because he knows that Jim Beam contains alcohol, etc. Nonetheless, for "ordinary" witnesses, keeping observations as close as possible to the Lockean ideal of direct observation is the aspiration.

[134] See Ronald N. Giere, *Scientific Cognition as Distributed Cognition*, in Peter Caruthers et al, eds, *The Cognitive Basis of Science* 285 (Cambridge, 2002); P. D. Magnus, *Distributed Cognition and the Task of Science*, 37 Social Studies of Science 297 (2007); and, for a classic in the area, Edwin Hutchins, *Cognition in the Wild* (Bradford, 1995). For an article looking at the way humans can off-load knowledge and know-how to technology as well as to other experts, see Itiel E. Dror and Jennifer L. Mnookin, *The Use of Technology in Human Expert Domains: Challenges and Risks Arising from the Use of Automated Fingerprint Identification Systems in Forensic Sciences*, 9 Law, Probability & Risk 47 (2010).

[135] For an analysis of epistemic dependence focusing on the structure of expert knowledge, see John Hardwig, *Epistemic Deference*, 82 J Philosophy 335 (1985).

likely only partly understands—enormous technical knowledge is
literally built into it. But that knowledge is not testimonial under
any of the Court's definitions. The same goes for a forensic pathologist who relies on the deceased's medical records when ascertaining the cause of death. Those medical records are part of
the forensic pathologist's basis, but they are not themselves testimonial. So for many kinds of scientific evidence, distributed cognition does directly raise Confrontation Clause problems.

Because of the relatively limited definition of the testimonial,
it would be theoretically possible to require each and every testimonial declarant within a forensic science analysis to testify.
There is no inherent obstacle besides time and money. All of the
roughly dozen analysts who participated in a given DNA extraction
and comparison process could come to court to describe what they
did in turn. This might be highly impractical, but it *is* possible.[136]
Nonetheless, virtually no one who has thought about the intersection of forensic science and the Confrontation Clause thinks
this makes sense. Even Justice Scalia, who is perhaps prepared to
go furthest down that path, does not wish to go quite so far. He
wrote in *Melendez-Diaz*,

> Contrary to the dissent's suggestion, we do not hold, and it is not the
> case, that anyone whose testimony may be relevant in establishing the
> chain of custody, authenticity of the sample, or accuracy of the testing
> device, must appear in person as part of the prosecution's case. While
> the dissent is correct that "[i]t is the obligation of the prosecution to
> establish the chain of custody," this does not mean that everyone who
> laid hands on the evidence must be called. As stated in the dissent's
> own quotation, "gaps in the chain [of custody] normally go to the weight
> of the evidence rather than its admissibility." It is up to the prosecution
> to decide what steps in the chain of custody are so crucial as to require
> evidence; but what testimony is introduced must (if the defendant ob-
> jects) be introduced live.[137]

Justice Scalia tries to escape from the "turtles all the way down"
problem by distinguishing chain of custody evidence from substantive analysis, but as the dissent points out, this distinction does
not actually provide much assistance. Take the testimony about

---

[136] For years, the FBI's DNA laboratory sent all the technicians involved in a particular
analysis to testify at the later trial in capital cases if prosecutors insisted that the court
would not admit the DNA evidence otherwise. Frequently, the technicians would recite
the contents of their reports as to which they had no independent recollection. Interview
with Jenifer Smith, Jan 9, 2012.

[137] *Melendez-Diaz*, 557 US at 311 n 1 (citations omitted).

the chemical makeup of a drug in *Melendez-Diaz*. Justice Scalia implies that the person who establishes the accuracy of the testing device is not required. But why not? Is that not a prerequisite to being able to be confident about the accuracy of the result?[138] Arguably the person who interpreted the result is making the most central bottom-line judgment relevant to the defendant. Is this individual therefore the only one who needs to testify? What if the technician who prepared the sample somehow contaminated it? Should that technician be required to testify as well? None of these technicians is merely engaged in documenting the chain of custody. They are all taking steps that contribute to the final conclusion about the chemical composition of the substance at issue. They are, in other words, engaged in distributive cognition.

Thus, following to its logical conclusion the claim that testimonial evidence must be presented live would lead to the technically possible but worrisomely expensive and inefficient position that every testimonial link in the distributed cognitive chain of experts must be forged with a corresponding witness in court.

At the same time, however, understanding that distributed cognition and epistemic deference are part and parcel of what it means to be doing science may help justify a partial retreat from this unattractive result. This recognition could inform a coherent and constructive analysis of whether, when, and to what degree a form of science exceptionalism in the Confrontation Clause might be warranted. Recognizing that science is a *collective* mechanism for knowledge production, a process of *distributed* rather than individual cognition, and a set of methods that rely upon *both* skepticism and epistemic dependence should matter, at least to a limited degree. In making this claim, we appreciate that the legal system has its own methods for adducing knowledge. The procedures of science are not, ipso facto, adequate for legal purposes. The law is free to develop its own rules and requirements—even to the extent of requiring each and every forensic analyst to appear in court. Assertions of dire consequences and an end to forensic testing such as those made by New York City's Chief Medical

---

[138] There is a potentially persuasive argument that the calibrator's testimony is so far from being accusatorial that it should not be considered testimonial. See note 121. But that is a different theory than the one we are discussing here.

Examiner[139] might not sway judges, who might instead expect laboratories to consolidate tasks to require fewer analysts in each case. Surely, if pressed, laboratories could reduce the number of analysts involved in some tests. For example, a DNA analysis and comparison could revert to a process involving, say, three technicians and analysts, not twelve or more. But if we see distributed cognition as a defining feature of science, we recognize that this dilemma cannot—and indeed probably *should* not—be eliminated by expecting laboratories to restructure in fundamental ways to reduce or eliminated the collective nature of the knowledge produced.[140]

Given that the courtroom is a central operating theater for forensic science, draconian Confrontation Clause rules might well motivate laboratories to make such modifications. But if these modifications took laboratories in directions inconsistent with the practices of science more generally, it is far from clear that these would be positive developments. The general problem of forensic science has been inadequate incorporation of the norms and practices that govern scientific knowledge production in other settings. Creating incentives to reduce the degree of distributed cognition would push in the opposite direction. Thus, in the name of confrontation values, which, even if not about reliability per se, are intended as protections enhancing the reliability of evidence, forensic laboratories might instead develop practices that decreased accuracy, transparency, and the creation of a research culture.[141] Recognizing the valuable dimensions of the collective aspects of science suggests that this difficulty of potential expert witness regress cannot and should not be eliminated by expecting laboratories to change their practices. Asking for scientific knowledge to look like that of "conventional witnesses" in this respect is not a viable long-term solution.

Recognizing that there is a certain structural mismatch between

---

[139] Brief of Amici Curiae New York County District Attorney's Office and the New York City Office of the Chief Medical Examiner in Support of Respondent, *Williams v Illinois*, No 10-805, *6 (US, filed Oct 26, 2011) (available on Westlaw at 2011 WL 5125054) ("Requiring all of those technicians to appear in court for cross-examination would bring forensic work in the laboratory to a halt.").

[140] Forensic science is also, perhaps, transitioning from a craftsman approach to something closer to an assembly-line process. There may be both pluses and minuses to such a transition, discussion of which is beyond the scope of this article—but if a transition is under way, it also has the effect of increasing distributed cognition.

[141] See generally Mnookin et al, 58 UCLA L Rev at 725 (cited in note 129).

the atomized conception of knowledge provision that undergirds our approach to "conventional witnesses" and the operation of science may invite openness to some modifications to the Confrontation Clause with respect to expert witnesses.[142] At the same time, the fact that expert knowledge is, in some ways, different from lay knowledge does not justify abandoning the values underlying the Confrontation Clause altogether, nor treating science as if it is self-authorizing or infallible, for surely it is neither one. The question is whether the epistemic values of the Confrontation Clause can be melded with the epistemic realities at work in modern science.

We believe there is potential for such compromises. We conclude by briefly offering possible suggestions for such compromises—but we are less wedded to the particulars than to the larger points that (1) the right approach to the Confrontation Clause and forensic science is to ask whether, how, and to what extent science exceptionalism is warranted; and (2) to suggest that the key difference that Confrontation Clause jurisprudence needs to recognize and account for is that science is a collective phenomenon that both produces distributed knowledge and permits, and indeed requires, a certain bounded degree of epistemic deference to the findings of others.

What, then, might these compromises look like? We have mentioned that scientific practices involve a certain degree of trust, epistemic dependence, and deference. But they also often operate through procedures and modes of communication designed to enhance this trust and warrant this deference. Describing the origins of modern science in *Leviathan and the Air Pump*, Steven Shapin and Steven Shaffer described how Robert Boyle's scientific papers about experiments were self-consciously written to make the scientist readers of them into "virtual witnesses."[143] His hope was that by reading these immensely and self-consciously detailed accounts, complete with relevant visual depictions, other scientists could almost believe they were present at the experiment itself.

---

[142] While we have avoided discussing the originalist arguments contained in any of these cases, it is worth noting that this recognition of modern science as a process of distributed cognition might also provide a grounds for justifying treating expert statements differently from other testimonial statements. Arguably, testimony relying on distributed cognition is a modern phenomenon without clear Founding-era equivalents.

[143] Steven Shapin and Steven Shaffer, *Leviathan and the Air-Pump: Hobbes, Boyle, and the Experimental Life* 55–67 (Princeton, 1985).

Documentation that is both detailed and standardized is a "literary technology" that aids both epistemic deference and distributed cognition. Boyle did not simply ask his fellow scientists to believe him, or to defer to his authority—by documenting in vivid detail what he had done, he transmitted his knowledge partially to those readers sufficiently expert to understand, and thereby enhanced his authority and claims to being believed.[144]

A focus on the adequacy of documentation might be one place to bridge the Confrontation Clause and the practices of experts. For example, we have argued elsewhere that surrogate witnesses should not generally be permitted in lieu of the actual analysis, à la *Bullcoming*, but that in certain narrow circumstances they *should* be deemed permissible.[145] When the original analyst is unavailable through no fault of the state, when retesting of the evidence specimen is not possible, and when the documentation is sufficiently detailed to permit the surrogate to exercise independent judgment, we have suggested that surrogate witnesses should be allowed. This narrow compromise, we believe, respects both the Confrontation Clause and the processes of science. It is a second-best solution grounded on necessity (hence the requirement for unavailability, parallel to the second-best solution offered in *Crawford* itself of using a witness's prior testimony upon a showing of both unavailability and a prior opportunity to cross-examine). Given the confrontation value placed on having witnesses who were firsthand participants to the forensic process, if retesting is possible, that should be done rather than using a surrogate with no involvement. But if retesting is not possible, then the adequacy of documentation of the original test—a long-standing scientific strategy for enhancing communication across members of a distributed knowledge network—should permit the use of a surrogate witness who bases his conclusions on the original report coupled with the independent exercise of some degree of his own expertise. To be sure, the surrogate is still relying on the testimonial report. But he is also engaging in distributed knowledge production in ways commonplace within the scientific enterprise.

Assuming that they are all available, which members of a distributed knowledge network must testify to satisfy the Confron-

---

[144] See generally id.

[145] See Kaye et al, *Expert Evidence* § 4.10 (cited in note 31); Mnookin, 15 Brooklyn J L & Policy (cited in note 13).

tation Clause? This framework suggests no simple answer to this question, but it is nonetheless of some assistance. For no one at all to testify live—as in *Melendez-Diaz*—violates the Confrontation Clause's strong preference for live testimony. To have everyone involved testify is not only expensive, but it fails to take seriously the collective epistemic aspect of scientific evidence. It treats experts as if they were atomized knowledge producers instead of participants in a collective process that permits them a degree of deference, dependence, trust, and reliance upon each other's findings. How exactly to "split the baby" is not obvious. Should the focus be on the expert who exercised the greatest degree of independent judgment? Should the focus be on the expert at the top of the inferential chain who made the final interpretations and hence was in a position to describe, if not to warrant, the contributions that preceded his own? Should the inquiry be into which witnesses are "central" and which "peripheral," if such categories can be delineated?

We recognize that any determination along these lines will be somewhat arbitrary. We cannot truly argue that recognizing the collective nature of scientific knowledge yields a particular or simple answer. But it does suggest that permitting scientists to engage in some degree of epistemic deference toward the results of their collaborators is, in essence, to permit them to behave like scientists. Again, robust documentation norms may provide a partial palliative. More generally, this framework suggests that even though there may not be one right answer to the line-drawing question, drawing the line in some reasonable way is indeed justified, especially when coupled with robust documentation requirements that can improve the degree of justification for epistemic deference by other experts participating in the test process.

Finally, we come back to the facts of *Williams*. As we have indicated in great detail, we do not think that Justice Alito's no-TMA argument succeeds on the facts of the case, although we do think that on occasion this argument could work. Could the outcome in *Williams* have been justified on alternative grounds? The ISP's expert witness was engaged in a mixture of independent judgment and expertise *and* epistemic deference. She believed the Cellmark report not because she had participated in the analysis, but because it was the report of an accredited laboratory that she believed appropriate to trust unless provided with some reason not to, and no such reason was present in the case. We might reasonably say that the technicians at the ISP and the technicians at Cellmark were engaged in collective knowledge production, an example of distributed cognition.

We grant that this is a plausible argument. Frankly, we would have preferred to see the Court take up Justice Breyer's challenge and face directly this version of the "who must testify" question. Our view is that the better line drawing would have been to require *someone* from Cellmark to testify in addition to the witnesses from ISP. While it is certainly possible to draw a large circle of "collective cognition" around both laboratories at once, the two laboratories, hundreds of miles apart, have different protocols, different standard practices, and different internal cultures. The testifying witness knew nothing about these specific protocols. As Justice Kagan points out, the ISP analyst "had no knowledge at all of Cellmark's operations. Indeed, for all the record discloses, she may never have set foot in Cellmark's laboratory."[146] While the testifying expert's reliance may have been warranted from a scientific perspective, the high value placed by the Confrontation Clause on live testimony for any testimonial statements militates, we think, in favor of requiring someone from Cellmark to testify as well. We do recognize, however, that this conclusion is a judgment call, and that efforts to balance confrontation values with a sensitivity to what is distinctive about science might permit someone else to accept our general framework but reach a different conclusion about what was required under *Williams*'s facts.

We end, therefore, by returning to where we began. We have tried to show how the issue of science exceptionalism pervades the new expert-evidence trilogy. We do not believe that the Court will achieve a satisfying, persuasive, and workable approach until it forthrightly confronts the question of whether science is special in ways that warrant distinctive treatment under the Confrontation Clause. We have tried to show that this issue of science exceptionalism has been lurking within the various opinions in the trilogy—most explicitly in Justice Kennedy's dissent in *Melendez-Diaz*, but present to some degree throughout the trilogy.

We believe that the effort to resolve *Williams* through Rule 703 and the no-TMA argument was a wrong turn. Most of the time,

---

[146] *Williams*, 132 S Ct at 2268 (Kagan, J, dissenting).

as the dissent in *Williams* recognized, the no-TMA argument requires implausible mental gymnastics and operates as a legal fiction. There are some limited situations in which expert basis evidence might legitimately be said to be introduced for a purpose other than its truth, but *Williams* does not present one. In *Williams* there is some circumstantial evidence to provide independent support for the Cellmark reports' reliability, but this argument is less persuasive than Justice Alito believed. More fundamentally, it hardly provides a general Rule 703 exception in the Confrontation Clause setting because most of the time no such independent basis will be present.

At the same time, we believe that the issue lurking behind and in good part motivating Rule 703—the fact that experts almost inevitably do rely on information provided by others—is precisely what might justify a certain degree of special treatment of scientific evidence under the Confrontation Clause. When thinking about how to approach the Confrontation Clause, the distinctive feature of science that requires focused attention is that it is a collective enterprise: it produces distributed knowledge located across individuals rather than held by someone standing alone, and its participants engage in epistemic deference, deference that is supported by careful documentation. Only by confronting what these aspects of science ought to mean for the operation of the Confrontation Clause will the Court be able to develop an approach to this thorny set of issues that adequately respects both Confrontation Clause values and the practices of science.

HELEN NORTON

LIES AND THE CONSTITUTION

Is there a First Amendment right to lie? Although the Supreme Court declared almost forty years ago that "there is no constitutional value in false statements of fact,"[1] the Court in *United States v Alvarez*[2] ruled that the First Amendment protects at least some— and perhaps many—intentional lies from government prohibition.[3] In *Alvarez*, the Court considered the Stolen Valor Act, a federal statute that made it a crime for any person to state falsely that he or she had received a military decoration or medal.[4] Xavier Alvarez was convicted under that statute after he intentionally and falsely claimed to have received the Congressional Medal of Honor while introducing himself at a meeting as a newly elected water district

Helen Norton is Associate Dean for Academic Affairs and Associate Professor, University of Colorado School of Law.

AUTHOR'S NOTE: Thanks for very insightful comments to Geof Stone, Harold Bruff, John Carlson, Alan Chen, Caroline Mala Corbin, Melissa Hart, Sarah Krakoff, Steven Morrison, Seana Shiffrin, Harry Surden, Alex Tsesis, and the participants at the Loyola-Chicago Constitutional Law Colloquium as well as at University of Colorado Law School, Colorado Employment Law Faculty, and Chicago-Kent College of Law works-in-progress workshops. Thanks too to Tim Galluzzi and Genet Tekeste for outstanding research assistance.

[1] *Gertz v Robert Welch, Inc.*, 418 US 323, 340 (1974); see also *Virginia State Board of Pharmacy v Virginia Citizens Consumer Council, Inc.*, 425 US 748, 771 (1976) ("Untruthful speech, commercial or otherwise, has never been protected for its own sake."); *Garrison v Louisiana*, 379 US 64, 75 (1964) ("[T]he knowingly false statement and the false statement made with reckless disregard of the truth do not enjoy constitutional protection.").

[2] 132 S Ct 2537 (2012).

[3] Id at 2551.

[4] 18 USC § 704(b). The act imposed enhanced penalties on those who falsely claimed receipt of the Congressional Medal of Honor. 18 USC § 704(c).

board member.[5] Alvarez (who apparently did not seek or receive any material benefit from his lie[6]) challenged the constitutionality of the act, and a divided Court struck it down.[7] In three separate opinions, all of the Justices agreed that the First Amendment permits the government to punish at least some lies, but no majority approach emerged for determining more specifically which lies can be prohibited consistent with the Constitution.

This article addresses that issue. As a general matter, recall that the government cannot constitutionally prohibit speech because of its content unless the government can satisfy the exacting demands of strict scrutiny.[8] In some cases, however, a less rigorous standard of review applies to the government's punishment of speech that falls within a category of "low-value expression." *Alvarez* raises two related questions. First, when are lies of only low First Amendment value? Second, if a lie is of only low First Amendment value, when does the Constitution permit the government to prohibit it? It turns out that the answers to both questions are complicated.[9]

---

[5] *Alvarez*, 132 S Ct at 2542 ("For all the record shows, respondent's statements were but a pathetic attempt to gain respect that eluded him. . . . Here, the statement that the speaker held the Medal was an intended, undoubted lie."); id at 2543 ("Respondent's claim to hold the Congressional Medal of Honor was false. There is no room to argue about interpretation or shades of meaning.").

[6] Id at 2542 ("The statements do not seem to have been made to secure employment or financial benefits or admission to privileges reserved for those who had earned the Medal.").

[7] Id at 2543.

[8] See, for example, *Turner Broadcasting System, Inc. v FCC*, 512 US 622, 641 (1994); *R.A.V. v City of St. Paul*, 505 US 377, 391–92 (1992). Very few government efforts to punish lies could meet that standard. For the very rare exception in which the Court has upheld the government's regulation of speech under a strict scrutiny analysis, see *Holder v Humanitarian Law Project*, 130 S Ct 2705 (2010) (upholding federal law that criminalized the knowing provision of material support or resources to a foreign terrorist organization as applied to plaintiff's attempt to provide money, training, and advocacy to groups so characterized); see also *Burson v Freeman*, 504 US 198 (1992) (plurality) (upholding content-based ban on political speech within 100 feet of polling place).

[9] In addressing these questions I define a "lie" as a false statement known by the speaker to be untrue and made with the intention that the listener understand it as true. See Sissela Bok, *Lying: Moral Choice in Public and Private Life* 13 (Oxford, 1978) (defining a lie as "any intentionally deceptive message which is *stated*"); David Nyberg, *The Varnished Truth* 50 (Chicago, 1993) ("[W]e can say that lying means making a statement (not too vague) you want somebody to believe, even though you don't (completely) believe it yourself, when the other person has a right to expect you mean what you say."); Mark Tushnet, "Telling Me Lies": The Constitutionality of Regulating False Statements of Fact (Harvard Law Sch Pub Law & Legal Theory Working Paper Series, Paper No 11-02, 2011), online at http://ssrn.com/abstract=1737930 at *2 (defining a lie as a "false statement known by the person making it to be false and made with the intention that at least some listeners will believe the statement to be true, at least for some period before its falsity becomes evident to the listeners").

Part I of this article offers a brief taxonomy of falsehoods that reveals that some lies have First Amendment value in their own right, and that laws prohibiting lies that have no First Amendment value of their own may nonetheless sometimes present serious problems of government overreaching and chilling of valuable speech. The very ubiquity and diversity of lies thus supports a presumption that lies are fully protected by the First Amendment and that government therefore generally may not regulate them unless it satisfies strict scrutiny. That presumption, however, should not govern a specific category of low-value lies that themselves undermine First Amendment interests, and the First Amendment should therefore permit the government to regulate such lies to prevent certain types of harms. Justice Breyer's concurring opinion in *Alvarez* comes closest to this approach, insofar as it applies intermediate scrutiny to the government's regulation of a narrowly defined category of lies.[10]

Part II examines the circumstances in which low-value lies might cause harm of a sort that should permit government to prohibit them consistent with the First Amendment. More specifically, it urges that we can better assess the potential harm of the lies targeted by the Stolen Valor Act when we understand them as lies about a speaker's credentials that might cause significant second-party harms to listeners as well as third-party harms to the public trust on which certain important government processes (like the integrity of the military honors system) rely. Even so, however, First Amendment interests in checking the government's power to act as the ultimate arbiter of truth counsel that we take care when regulating such lies. Part II concludes that laws appropriately balance these competing concerns when they target lies that threaten second-party harms that take monetary or similarly tangible form, or lies that cause third-party harms when demonstrably material to high-stakes decisions in circumscribed settings.

I. IDENTIFYING "LOW-VALUE" LIES: A BRIEF TAXONOMY OF FALSEHOODS

Although the three *Alvarez* opinions agreed that some category of lies should be considered of low First Amendment value and thus subject to greater government regulation, each defined

---

[10] *Alvarez*, 132 S Ct at 2551–52.

that category differently. Justice Kennedy's plurality opinion (joined by Chief Justice Roberts and Justices Ginsburg and Sotomayor) identified this category as comprised of traditionally regulated lies that are associated with "legally cognizable harm."[11] Justice Breyer's concurring opinion (joined by Justice Kagan) identified the relevant category as including lies about "easily verifiable facts" that do not concern "philosophy, religion, history, the social sciences, the arts, and the like," and proposed to apply intermediate scrutiny to the government's regulation of lies within that category.[12] Finally, Justice Alito's dissenting opinion (joined by Justices Scalia and Thomas) defined all falsehoods as categorically unprotected by the First Amendment and thus entirely subject to government prohibition except when such regulation threatens to chill truthful speech.[13] In proposing these various categories, the three opinions discussed a wide range of lies that can help us sketch a rough taxonomy for thinking about various types of falsehoods and their implications for core First Amendment values.

A. SOME LIES HAVE FIRST AMENDMENT VALUE

Some lies have instrumental or even moral value. Justice Breyer's concurring opinion in *Alvarez* offered some examples:

> False factual statements can serve useful human objectives, for example: in social contexts, where they may prevent embarrassment, protect privacy, shield a person from prejudice, provide the sick with comfort, or preserve a child's innocence; in public contexts, where they may stop a panic or otherwise preserve calm in the face of danger; and even in technical, philosophical, and scientific contexts, where (as Socrates' methods suggest) examination of a false statement (even if made deliberately to mislead) can promote a form of thought that ultimately helps realize the truth.[14]

Indeed, even though many lies frustrate core First Amendment values, others may affirmatively further them.

---

[11] Id at 2545.

[12] Id at 2552.

[13] Id at 2561–62.

[14] Id at 2553; see also *United States v Alvarez*, 638 F3d 666, 673–75 (9th Cir 2010) (Kozinski concurring in denial of rehearing en banc) (listing multiple examples of harmless or even beneficial lies); David A. Strauss, *Persuasion, Autonomy, and Freedom of Expression*, 91 Colum L Rev 334, 355 (1991) ("One should not manipulatively deceive someone casually, but manipulative lying is certainly justified to prevent serious harms. It follows that a serious social problem could justify manipulation of the kind that the persuasion principle forbids.").

More specifically, although most lies directly undermine[15] the First Amendment's interest in furthering the search for truth and the dissemination of knowledge,[16] some lies may actually promote those goals. For example, lies that trigger confrontation and rebuttal may lead to increased public awareness and understanding of the truth,[17] lies by undercover law enforcement or journalists can help expose the truth,[18] and Socratic questioning in which a teacher knowingly asserts a falsehood can help a student to recognize and counter falsity.[19]

Lies can also both frustrate and facilitate First Amendment interests in promoting individual autonomy and self-expression.[20]

---

[15] See Steven Gey, *The First Amendment and the Dissemination of Socially Worthless Untruths*, 36 Fla St U L Rev 1, 9 (2008) ("The only purpose of the marketplace of ideas is to advance human understanding about the nature of the world and the best way to live within it; it directly contravenes that purpose if the marketplace is used to keep human society mired in socially dysfunctional misunderstandings about the nature of the world and its history.").

[16] See Ronald A. Cass, *The Perils of Positive Thinking: Constitutional Interpretation and Negative First Amendment Theory*, 34 UCLA L Rev 1405, 1411 (1987) (describing the values most often located at the heart of the First Amendment as including the search for truth and the discovery and dissemination of knowledge); Thomas I. Emerson, *First Amendment Doctrine and the Burger Court*, 68 Cal L Rev 422, 423 (1980) (same); Frederick Schauer, *The Boundaries of the First Amendment: A Preliminary Exploration of Constitutional Salience*, 117 Harv L Rev 1765, 1786 (2004) (same); see also Robert C. Post, *Democracy, Expertise, Academic Freedom: A First Amendment Jurisprudence for the Modern State* 6 (Yale, 2012) (summarizing and describing the three major proposed purposes of the First Amendment as "cognitive" (advancing knowledge and discovering truth), "ethical" (furthering individual autonomy and self-fulfillment), and "political" ("facilitating the communicative processes necessary for successful democratic self-governance")).

[17] See *New York Times*, 376 US at 279 n 19 ("Even a false statement may be deemed to make a valuable contribution to public debate, since it brings about 'the clearer perception and livelier impression of truth, produced by its collision with error.'"), quoting J. Mill, *On Liberty* 15 (Blackwell, ed 1947); Jonathan Varat, *Deception and the First Amendment: A Central, Complex, and Somewhat Curious Relationship*, 53 UCLA L Rev 1107, 1119 (2006) ("[C]onfronting the lie in the arena of public discussion may increase the likelihood that the truth will be clearer and more long-lived, so that the truth is not forgotten."). For a more skeptical view of the First Amendment's ability to uncover truth by protecting falsity, see Frederick Schauer, *Facts and the First Amendment*, 57 UCLA L Rev 897, 900 (2010) ("[T]he persistence of the belief that a good remedy for false speech is more speech, or that truth will prevail in the long run, may itself be an example of the resistance of false factual propositions to argument and counterexample.").

[18] See Varat, 53 UCLA L Rev at 1122 (cited in note 17).

[19] See *Alvarez*, 132 S Ct at 2553 (Breyer, J, concurring) (describing the Socratic method and similar pedagogical techniques as promoting "a form of thought that ultimately helps realize the truth").

[20] See *First National Bank of Boston v Bellotti*, 435 US 765, 777 n 12 (1978) ("The individual's interest in self-expression is a concern of the First Amendment separate from the concern for open and informed discussion."); *United States v Playboy Entertainment Group Inc.*, 529 US 803, 817 (2000) ("It is through speech that our personalities are formed and expressed."); C. Edwin Baker, *Scope of the First Amendment Freedom of Speech*, 25 UCLA

Lies told by speakers to manipulate their listeners obviously undermine those listeners' autonomy.[21] But lies can promote speakers' autonomy interests in a variety of ways.[22] For example, a speaker might lie about her sexual orientation or religion for privacy reasons or to protect herself from discrimination. More generally, autobiographical lies can further a speaker's ability to choose how to define and present himself, a fundamental exercise of self-expression. As David Han has observed,

> Choosing what we tell others about ourselves is a vital means by which we portray ourselves to the world; communicating truths, half-truths, and even falsehoods is essential to our ability to craft and calibrate the personas we present to others. . . . [I]f one takes seriously the Supreme Court's repeated assertions that the First Amendment is designed, at least in part, to preserve individual autonomy and self-realization, then courts should accord at least some constitutional weight to the interest in defining one's own public persona.[23]

Many lies frustrate First Amendment interests in facilitating democratic self-governance.[24] As the Supreme Court has explained,

---

L Rev 964, 966 (1978) (describing the First Amendment as seeking to protect "individual self-realization and self-determination"); Charles Fried, *The New First Amendment Jurisprudence: A Threat to Liberty*, 59 U Chi L Rev 225, 232–34 (1992) (identifying autonomy as the key First Amendment value).

[21] See Strauss, 91 Colum L Rev at 354–55 (cited in note 14) ("[L]ying is wrong because it violates human autonomy. Lying forces the victim to pursue the speaker's objectives instead of the victim's objectives. If the capacity to decide upon a plan of life and to determine one's own objectives is integral to human nature, lies that are designed to manipulate people are a uniquely severe offense against human autonomy.").

[22] See David S. Han, *Autobiographical Lies and the First Amendment's Protection of Self-Defining Speech*, 87 NYU L Rev 70, 115 (2012) (finding First Amendment autonomy value in "knowing, factual lies about oneself that are intended to influence one's public perception"); but see R. George Wright, *The Constitutional Status of Speech About Oneself*, 59 Cleve St L Rev 489, 511 (2011) (expressing skepticism about the First Amendment value of autobiographical speech on personal or private matters).

[23] Han, 87 NYU L Rev at 72–74 (cited in note 22); see also id at 107 ("At a certain point, the government cannot constitutionally interfere with an individual's right to define himself by his own speech."); *Alvarez*, 638 F3d at 674 (Kozinski concurring in the denial of petition for rehearing en banc) ("Alvarez's conviction is especially troubling because he is being punished for speaking about himself, the kind of speech that is intimately bound up with a particularly important First Amendment purpose: human self-expression. . . . Speaking about oneself is precisely when people are most likely to exaggerate, obfuscate, embellish, omit key facts or tell tall tales. Self-expression that risks prison if it strays from the monotonous reporting of strictly accurate facts about oneself is no expression at all.").

[24] See *Garrison*, 379 US at 77 (recognizing "the paramount public interest in a free flow of information to the people concerning public officials, their servants"); Alexander Meiklejohn, *Free Speech and Its Relation to Self-Government* 24–25 (Harper, 1948) ("The final aim of the [town] meeting is the voting of wise decisions. The voters, therefore, must be made as wise as possible. The welfare of the community requires that those who decide

That speech is used as a tool for political ends does not automatically
bring it under the protective mantle of the Constitution. For the use
of the known lie as a tool is at once at odds with the premises of
democratic government and with the orderly manner in which economic, social, or political change is to be effected.[25]

Even so, however, some contend that the government's punishment of lies about political matters itself undermines public discourse at the heart of the First Amendment. Robert Post, for
example, has argued that "[t]o the extent that law enforces claims
of truth, it suppresses 'political thinking' by excluding from participation those who embrace a different truth from the state."[26]

To be sure, reasonable people can disagree about the circumstances in which lies have value, and thus about the size of this

---

issues shall understand them. They must know what they are voting about. And this, in
turn, requires that so far as time allows, all facts and interests relevant to the problem
shall be fully and fairly presented to the meeting. . . . What is essential is not that everyone
shall speak, but that everything worth saying shall be said."); Robert Post, *Compelled
Subsidization of Speech: Johanns v Livestock Marketing Association*, 2005 Supreme Court Review 195, 213 (2005) (describing First Amendment values as "most conspicuously includ-
[ing] democratic self-governance and participation in the construction of public opinion");
Cass Sunstein, *Free Speech Now*, 59 U Chi L Rev 255, 263 (1992) ("[T]he First Amendment
is fundamentally aimed at protecting democratic self-government.").

[25] *Garrison*, 379 US at 75; see also Gey, 36 Fla St U L Rev at 10 (cited in note 15)
("The relevant point for present purposes is that the democratic self-actualization justification for free speech would not logically encompass the protection of those seeking to
disseminate empirically disprovable falsehoods. Those seeking to disseminate disprovable
falsehoods can in no way be viewed as acting in good faith with their fellow citizens.
Rather, they are seeking power through the duplicitous means of the Big Lie. The op-
timistic Brandeisian concept of democracy would not countenance this kind of collective
duplicity. . . . [T]he dissemination of false facts is much more likely to undermine democracy than it is to bolster democracy.").

[26] Post, *Democracy, Expertise, Academic Freedom* at 119 n 10 (cited in note 16); see also
id at 29 ("The difficulty is that government control over factual truth is in tension with
the value of democratic legitimation. Citizens who seek to participate in public discourse,
and who are penalized because they disagree with official versions of factual truth, are
excluded from the possibility of influencing public opinion. Although we might postulate
a world in which reasonable persons do not disagree about factual truth, we all know that
as a practical matter this is not the case. Intense and consequential disputes about factual
questions abound. Insofar as the state intervenes definitively to settle those disputes, it
alienates persons from participation in public discourse."); Brief of Amicus Jonathan D.
Varat, *United States v Alvarez*, No 11-210, *13 (filed Jan 19, 2012) (available on Westlaw
at 2012 WL 195302) ("To take one current example, assertions by segments of the population that the current President is not a United States citizen are fundamentally factual
statements, yet they are inextricably intertwined with the expression of subjective beliefs
concerning the trustworthiness and legitimacy of the current President. A regulation aimed
at the prohibition of such statements could, therefore, be a vehicle for idea suppression.
Many other types of false factual statements similarly are intertwined with the expression
of contested ideas, including statements regarding the threat of climate change or statements concerning the impact of legislation on the federal budget. For this reason, even
false factual speech may in certain circumstances have inherent worth and require protection for its own sake. . . .").

class of falsehoods.[27] Some commentators, like David Nyberg, argue that the universe of valuable lies is quite large.[28] Others, like Sissela Bok, maintain that it is very small.[29] For my purposes here, I simply contend that there is *some* set of lies that further First Amendment interests and thus deserve First Amendment protection for their own sake.[30]

---

[27] Philosophers have long struggled to define the size of this set for purposes other than First Amendment analysis. For example, even though St. Augustine viewed all lies as immoral, he identified a hierarchy of immorality among lies. Augustine, in Charles Lewis Cornish, Henry Browne, and Charles Marriot, trans, *On Lying* ¶ 42 (Oxford, 1847) ("In these eight kinds then, however, a man sins less when he tells a lie, in proportion as he emerges to the eighth: more, in proportion as he diverges to the first. But whoso shall think there is any sort of lie that is not sin, will deceive himself foully, while he deems himself honest as a deceiver of other men."); id at ¶ 25 (describing eight types of lying that vary in moral severity that include lies in religious teaching, lies that harm others and help no one, lies that harm others and help someone, lies told for the pleasure of lying, lies told to "please others in smooth discourse," lies that harm no one and that help someone, lies that harm no one and that save someone's life, and lies that harm no one and that save someone's "purity").

Aquinas also generated a taxonomy of lies according to their varying moral severity. St. Thomas Aquinas, in Fathers of the English Dominican Province, trans, *The Summa Theologica* 89–90 (Benziger Bros., 1922) ("Now it is evident that the greater the good intended, the more is the sin of lying diminished in gravity. Wherefore a careful consideration of the matter will show that these various kinds of lies are enumerated in their order of gravity: since the useful good is better than pleasurable good, and the life of the body than money, and virtue than the life of the body."); see also Bok, *Lying* at 78 (cited in note 9) ("Just as lies intended to avoid serious harm have often been thought more clearly excusable than others, so lies meant to *do* harm are often thought least excusable. And lies which neither avoid nor cause harm occupy the middle ground. Throughout the centuries, beginning with Augustine, such distinctions have been debated, refined, altered.").

[28] See Nyberg, *The Varnished Truth* at 24 (cited in note 9) ("My view, on the other hand, is that trust in others is a co-operative, life-preserving relationship that often depends upon the adroit management of deception, sometimes even lying, for its very subsistence."); id at 5 ("Deception is not merely to be tolerated as an occasionally prudent aberration in a world of truth telling: it is rather an essential component of our ability to organize and shape the world, to resolve problems of coordination among individuals who differ, to cope with uncertainty and pain, to be civil and to achieve privacy as needed, to survive as a species, and to flourish as persons.").

[29] See Bok, *Lying* at 45 (cited in note 9) ("I have to agree that there are at least *some* circumstances which warrant a lie. And foremost among them are those where innocent lives are at stake, and where only a lie can deflect the danger. But, in taking such a position, it would be wrong to lose the profound concern which the absolutist theologians and philosophers express—the concern for the harm to trust and to oneself from lying, quite apart from any immediate effects from any one lie. Individuals, these thinkers claimed, have to consider the long-range effects of lying on human communities; and even if liars have no such forethought, the risks that they themselves run from lying ought to matter to them perhaps most of all.").

[30] For these reasons, Justice Breyer concluded that some lies have First Amendment value. See *Alvarez*, 132 S Ct at 2553. Justice Kennedy's plurality opinion did not say this directly, although it perhaps did so implicitly by rejecting the government's claim that false statements of fact possess no First Amendment value. Id at 2547; see also id at 2544 ("Absent from those few categories where the law allows content-based regulation of

B. LIES AND THE CHILLING EFFECT

While some falsehoods may deserve constitutional protection because they have value in their own right, First Amendment interests may also sometimes require the protection of even valueless lies to prevent the chilling of truthful expression. In *New York Times Co. v Sullivan*,[31] the Supreme Court famously held that the First Amendment prohibits government from punishing harmful falsehoods when such punishment might chill truthful speech.[32] Examples of such harmful expression include negligent false statements about public officials or public figures,[33] which not only frustrate the First Amendment's truth-seeking goals[34] but can also inflict reputational damage or cause emotional distress.[35] Nonetheless, the Court held that such false statements are protected by the First Amendment, not because the speech itself is valuable, but because government efforts to regulate such speech might chill individuals' willingness to engage in valuable expression. As the Court explained, if speakers could be held liable for unintentionally false statements, "would-be critics of official conduct may be deterred from voicing their criticism, even though it is believed to be true and even though it is in fact true, because of doubt whether it can be proved in court or fear of the expense of having to do so."[36]

speech is any general exception to the First Amendment for false statements. This comports with the common understanding that some false statements are inevitable if there is to be an open and vigorous expression of views in public and private conversation, expression the First Amendment seeks to guarantee."). In his dissenting opinion, Justice Alito expressly rejected this proposition, insisting that "false statements of fact merit no First Amendment protection in their own right." Id at 2562. Interestingly, however, Justice Alito did not engage Justice Breyer's list of potentially valuable lies, except to note that it did not include lies of the sort targeted by the Stolen Valor Act. Id at 2562–63.

[31] 376 US 254 (1964).

[32] Id at 280 (concluding that the First Amendment prohibits the imposition of liability for a false statement about a public official unless made "with knowledge that it was false or with reckless disregard of whether it was false or not"); see also *Garrison*, 379 US at 73 ("[E]ven where the utterance is false, the great principles of the Constitution which secure freedom of expression . . . preclude attaching adverse consequences to any except the knowing or reckless falsehood.").

[33] See *New York Times*, 376 US at 279; *Gertz*, 418 US at 340.

[34] See *Hustler Magazine, Inc. v Falwell*, 485 US 46, 52 (1988) ("False statements of fact are particularly valueless [when] they interfere with the truth-seeking function of the marketplace of ideas.").

[35] See, for example, *Gertz*, 418 US at 347–48 (recognizing "the strength of the legitimate state interest in compensating private individuals for wrongful injury to reputation").

[36] *New York Times*, 376 US at 279; see also id at 271 ("[T]he erroneous statement is inevitable in free debate.").

All of the Justices in *Alvarez* agreed that the government's punishment even of intentional lies may sometimes unacceptably chill truthful, and thus valuable, speech.[37] For example, as Justice Alito explained in dissent:

> [T]here are broad areas in which any attempt by the state to penalize purportedly false speech would present a grave and unacceptable danger of suppressing truthful speech. Laws restricting false statements about philosophy, religion, history, the social sciences, the arts, and other matters of public concern would present such a threat. The point is not that there is no such thing as truth or falsity in these areas or that the truth is always impossible to ascertain, but rather that it is perilous to permit the state to be the arbiter of truth.[38]

To be sure, however, the Court has also long recognized that government's regulation of lies does not always create unacceptable chilling effects. As just one example, the Court has consistently held that the regulation of fraudulent commercial speech is unlikely to chill truthful speech for a variety of reasons.[39]

C. LIES AND GOVERNMENT OVERREACHING

Some lies should receive First Amendment protection even if they lack First Amendment value in their own right and even if their regulation would not appreciably chill valuable speech, but instead because their regulation offends First Amendment interests in constraining the government's power to impose its own version

---

[37] See *Alvarez*, 132 S Ct at 2545 (plurality); id at 2552 (Breyer, J, concurring); id at 2564 (Alito, J, dissenting). Ensuring a mens rea requirement—that is, prohibiting only knowing or intentional falsehoods and not those that are merely negligent or accidental—generally addresses these instrumental concerns. The Court, however, has also made clear that the First Amendment permits the regulation of negligently false statements under certain circumstances where chilling is less of a danger. See, for example, *Dun & Bradstreet, Inc. v Greenmoss Builders, Inc.*, 472 US 749 (1985) (holding that the First Amendment does not require showing of actual malice for recovery of presumed and punitive damages for false statements about private figures on matters of private concern).

[38] *Alvarez*, 132 S Ct at 2563–64. Justice Breyer shared this concern about potential chilling effect and thus limited his proposed category of low-value lies to those that do not fall within those subject matter areas. Id at 2552 ("Laws restricting false statements about philosophy, religion, history, the social sciences, the arts, and the like raise" chilling effect concerns.).

[39] See *Virginia State Board of Pharmacy*, 425 US at 772 n 24 ("[C]ommercial speech may be more durable than other kinds. Since advertising is the Sine qua non of commercial profits, there is little likelihood of its being chilled by proper regulation and forgone entirely. Attributes such as these, the greater objectivity and hardiness of commercial speech, may make it less necessary to tolerate inaccurate statements for fear of silencing the speaker.").

of the truth upon the public.[40] As the *Alvarez* plurality explained: "Our constitutional tradition stands against the idea that we need Oceania's Ministry of Truth. Were [the Stolen Valor Act] to be sustained, there could be an endless list of subjects the National Government or the States could single out."[41] Such subjects could include not only a range of relatively harmless lies, such as "bar stool braggadocio" or other casual forms of boasting, exaggeration, or puffery,[42] but also potentially more harmful lies, such as lies to loved ones to escape recrimination for one's bad behavior.[43] Either way, the government's regulation of such lies offends an anti-paternalistic understanding of the First Amendment that limits the government's power to declare itself the arbiter of truth.[44] Steven Gey has explained this view in terms of "structural rights," describing the First Amendment as focused on "constraining the collective authority of temporary political majorities to exercise their power by determining for everyone what is true and false

---

[40] See Gey, 36 Fla St U L Rev at 3 (cited in note 15) (explaining a "structural rights" view that characterizes the First Amendment as "primarily about constraining the collective authority of temporary political majorities to exercise their power by determining for everyone what is true and false, as well as what is right and wrong"). For a contrary view, see Tushnet at *25 (cited in note 9) ("[T]here is really no social value in the dissemination of falsehood, particularly knowing falsehood. If we can curb it without damage to other social values—including of course other statements covered by the First Amendment— we should. And the Constitution should not be interpreted to bar us from doing so.").

[41] *Alvarez*, 132 S Ct at 2547; see also id at 2555 (Breyer, J, concurring); id at 2563–64 (Alito, J, dissenting).

[42] Id at 2555 (Breyer, J, concurring); see id at 2547–48 (plurality) ("Permitting the government to decree this speech to be a criminal offense, whether shouted from the rooftops or made in a barely audible whisper, would endorse government authority to compile a list of subjects about which false statements are punishable. That governmental power has no clear limiting principle."); id at 2553 (Breyer, J, concurring) ("[T]he pervasiveness of false statements, made for better or for worse motives, made thoughtlessly or deliberately, made with or without accompanying harm, provides a weapon to a government broadly empowered to prosecute falsity without more. And those who are unpopular may fear that the government will use that weapon selectively . . . .").

[43] For examples of such lies both relatively harmless and potentially harmful, see *Alvarez*, 638 F3d at 673–75 (Kozinski concurring in denial of rehearing en banc) (listing multiple examples).

[44] See Paul Horwitz, *The First Amendment's Epistemological Problem*, 87 Wash L Rev 445, 451 (2012) (describing an antipaternalistic justification for the First Amendment as rooted "primarily on the grounds of distrust of government. . . . An anti-paternalistic approach would lead to a general refusal to regulate false statements—not because we value falsity, but because we are reluctant to hand over to the state the authority to make such determinations"); Nat Stern, *Implications of Libel Doctrine for Nondefamatory Falsehoods under the First Amendment*, 10 First Am L Rev 465, 503 (2012) ("To shelter ideas while leaving factual expression to plenary government control ignores an abiding First Amendment theme: wariness of government's capacity and motives when acting as arbiter of truth.").

. . . based on a deep skepticism about the good faith of those controlling the government."[45]

In sum, people lie frequently and for an astonishingly wide variety of reasons. Some lies have First Amendment value in their own right. In other instances, the government's regulation of even valueless lies threatens government overreaching or the chilling of valuable speech in ways that undermine important First Amendment interests. The very ubiquity and diversity of lies thus supports a presumption that lies are fully protected by the First Amendment such that government generally may not regulate them unless it satisfies strict scrutiny.[46]

D. LOW-VALUE LIES THAT CAN BE REGULATED SHORT OF STRICT
   SCRUTINY

Some lies may nevertheless sufficiently frustrate First Amendment interests such that they should be characterized as "low-value" speech and thus be subject to greater government regulation. Indeed, each of the *Alvarez* opinions suggested that some lies are of sufficiently low value that government should be permitted to prohibit them without satisfying the demands of strict scrutiny. The opinions, however, defined these categories in quite different ways.

Some background may be of help. The Supreme Court has over time identified several categories of speech as sufficiently "low value" to permit greater government regulation consistent with the First Amendment.[47] To be sure, the Supreme Court's First

---

[45] Gey, 36 Fla St U L Rev at 3, 21 (cited in note 15). Professor Gey further described the structural rights view of the First Amendment as "entirely negative" in that it "does not rest on the affirmative claim that free speech will lead to any particular social or political benefits" and instead emphasizes the dangers created "when collective entities are involved in the determination of truth." Id at 17.

[46] Of course, the First Amendment presumptively protects speech in general. See *Ashcroft v American Civil Liberties Union*, 535 US 564, 573 (2002) (explaining that the First Amendment generally permits the government "no power to restrict expression because of its message, its ideas, its subject matter, or its content") (citations and internal quotation marks omitted).

[47] For examples of commentators' pre-*Stevens* syntheses of the Court's approach to identifying categories of low-value speech, see Geoffrey R. Stone, *Sex, Violence, and the First Amendment*, 74 U Chi L Rev 1857, 1863–64 (2007) (identifying the key factors as whether the speech primarily advances political discourse, whether it is defined in terms of disfavored ideas or political viewpoints, whether it has a strong noncognitive aspect, and whether it has "long been regulated without undue harm to the overall system of free expression"); Cass R. Sunstein, *Pornography and the First Amendment*, 1986 Duke L J 589, 603–04 (1986) (suggesting that the Court considers the following factors in determining

Amendment doctrine generally applies strict scrutiny to content-based regulation of speech that is not of low value, an analysis that is almost always fatal to the government's restriction.[48] But as Geoffrey Stone has observed, "One obvious problem with a doctrine that presumptively holds all content-based restrictions unconstitutional is that there may be some types of content that do not merit such protection. Some speech might not sufficiently further the values and purposes of the First Amendment to warrant such extraordinary immunity from regulation."[49] To date, the categories of expression identified by the Court as "low value" include commercial speech, true threats, incitement to imminent illegal action, "fighting words," obscenity, defamation, fraud, child pornography, and speech that is integral to criminal conduct.[50]

Identifying a category of speech as low value is not, however, the end of the matter. The Court must then determine what test other than strict scrutiny should apply to government regulation of speech within that category.[51] Consider the example of commercial speech. The Court has held that commercial speech that is false, misleading, or related to an illegal activity is entitled to

---

whether speech is of low value: whether it is "far afield" from the central concerns of the First Amendment, whether there are important "noncognitive" aspects of the speech, whether the speaker seeks to communicate a message, and whether the speech is in an area in which the "government is unlikely to be acting for constitutionally impermissible reasons").

[48] See Geoffrey R. Stone, *Content Regulation and the First Amendment*, 25 Wm & Mary L Rev 189, 189 (1984) (explaining that content-based restrictions are subject to strict scrutiny unless they regulate speech that falls within a "low-value" category).

[49] Geoffrey R. Stone, *Free Speech in the Twenty-First Century: Ten Lessons from the Twentieth Century*, 36 Pepperdine L Rev 273, 283 (2009); see also Stone, 25 Wm & Mary L Rev at 189 n 24 (cited in note 48) ("The low value theory, or some variant thereof, is an essential concomitant of an effective system of free expression, for unless we are prepared to apply the same standards to private blackmail, for example, that we apply to public political debate, some distinctions in terms of constitutional value are inevitable.").

[50] See *Alvarez*, 132 S Ct at 2544. Indeed, the Supreme Court has noted "[n]umerous examples . . . of communications that are regulated without offending the First Amendment, such as the exchange of information about securities, corporate proxy statements, the exchange of price and production information among competitors, and employers' threats of retaliation for the labor activities of employees." *Obralik v Ohio State Bar Ass'n*, 436 US 447, 456 (1978) (citations omitted).

[51] See Stone, 25 Wm & Mary L Rev at 195 (cited in note 48) ("The conclusion that a particular class of speech has only low first amendment value does not mean that the speech is wholly without constitutional protection or that government may suppress it at will. Rather, the low value determination is merely the first step in the Court's analysis, for once the Court concludes that a particular class of speech is deserving of only limited first amendment protection, it then employs a form of categorical balancing, through which it defines the precise circumstances in which the speech may be restricted.").

no constitutional protection and thus can be banned altogether.[52] In contrast, the Court applies intermediate scrutiny to laws regulating other types of commercial speech based on its conclusion that such speech—although still of comparatively low value—can helpfully inform individuals about their choices in the commercial realm.[53]

The Court first set forth its approach to identifying categories of low-value speech in its 1942 decision in *Chaplinsky v New Hampshire*:[54]

> [I]t is well understood that the right of free speech is not absolute at all times and under all circumstances. There are certain well-defined and narrowly limited classes of speech, the prevention and punishment of which have never been thought to raise any Constitutional problem. These include the lewd and obscene, the profane, the libelous, and the insulting or "fighting" words—those which by their very utterance inflict injury or tend to incite an immediate breach of the peace. It has been well observed that such utterances are no essential part of any exposition of ideas, and are of such slight social value as a step to truth that any benefit that may be derived from them is clearly outweighed by the social interest in order and morality.[55]

The Court returned to and refined this explanation a half-century later in *R.A.V. v City of St. Paul*:[56]

> From 1791 to the present, however, our society, like other free but

---

[52] See *Central Hudson Gas & Electric Corp. v Public Service Comm'n of New York*, 447 US 557, 563–64 (1980) ("The First Amendment's concern for commercial speech is based on the informational function of advertising. Consequently, there can be no constitutional objection to the suppression of commercial messages that do not accurately inform the public about lawful activity. The government may ban forms of communication more likely to deceive the public than to inform it, or commercial speech related to illegal activity."); see also *Edenfield v Fane*, 507 US 761, 768 (1993) ("[T]he State may ban commercial expression that is fraudulent or deceptive without further justification."); *Zauderer v Office of Disciplinary Counsel*, 471 US 626, 638 (1985) ("The States and the Federal Government are free to prevent the dissemination of commercial speech that is false, deceptive, or misleading, or that proposes an illegal transaction.") (citation omitted).

[53] See *Central Hudson*, 447 US at 564 ("If the communication is neither misleading nor related to unlawful activity, the government's power is more circumscribed. The State must assert a substantial interest to be achieved by restrictions on commercial speech. Moreover, the regulatory technique must be in proportion to that interest. . . . First, the restriction must directly advance the state interest involved; the regulation may not be sustained if it provides only ineffective or remote support for the government's purpose. Second, if the governmental interest could be served as well by a more limited restriction on commercial speech, the excessive restrictions cannot survive.").

[54] 315 US 568 (1942).

[55] Id at 571–72.

[56] 505 US 377 (1992).

civilized societies, has permitted restrictions upon the content of speech in a few limited areas, which are "of such slight social value as a step to truth that any benefit that may be derived from them is clearly outweighed by the social interest in order and morality." We have recognized that "the freedom of speech" referred to by the First Amendment does not include a freedom to disregard these traditional limitations.[57]

Adopting a categorical approach to First Amendment protection requires a methodology for identifying the relevant categories. To this end, some understood *Chaplinsky* and *R.A.V.* to mean that the Court would characterize a category of expression as low value if the speech caused injury that outweighed its First Amendment value.[58] In its 2010 decision in *United States v Stevens*,[59] however, the Court insisted that historical tradition plays a central role in determining whether any category of expression has only low First Amendment value.[60] The *Stevens* Court struck down a federal law[61] that criminalized the commercial creation, sale, or possession of depictions of animal cruelty.[62] In so doing, the Court rejected as "startling and dangerous" what it characterized as the Government's proposed "free-floating test for First Amendment coverage . . . [based on] an ad hoc balancing of relative social costs and benefits."[63] Referencing *Chaplinsky*, the Court acknowledged that, "[a]s the Government correctly notes, this Court has often *described* historically unprotected categories of speech as being 'of such slight social value as a step to truth that any benefit that may be derived from them is clearly outweighed by the social interest in

---

[57] Id at 382–83, quoting *Chaplinsky*, 315 US at 572.

[58] See, for example, *R.A.V.*, 505 US at 400 (White, J, concurring) ("[T]he Court has held that the First Amendment does not apply to [certain content-based categories] because their expressive content is worthless or of *de minimis* value to society. We have not departed from this principle, emphasizing repeatedly that, 'within the confines of [these] given classification[s], the evil to be restricted so overwhelmingly outweighs the expressive interests, if any, at stake, that no process of case-by-case adjudication is required.'"), quoting *Chaplinsky*, 315 US at 571–72 and *New York v Ferber*, 458 US 747, 763–64 (1982).

[59] 130 S Ct 1577 (2010).

[60] Id at 1585–86. The *Stevens* majority thus described *Chaplinsky* and *R.A.V.* as emphasizing the long-standing nature of restrictions on such speech when characterizing it as of low value. Id.

[61] 18 USC § 48.

[62] *Stevens*, 130 S Ct at 1592.

[63] Id at 1585; id ("The First Amendment itself reflects a judgment by the American people that the benefits of its restrictions on the Government outweigh the costs.").

order and morality.'"[64] The Court continued, however:

> But such descriptions are just that—descriptive. They do not set forth
> a test that may be applied as a general matter to permit the Government
> to imprison any speaker so long as his speech is deemed valueless or
> unnecessary, or so long as an ad hoc calculus of costs and benefits tilts
> in a statute's favor. When we have identified categories of speech as
> fully outside the protection of the First Amendment, it has not been
> on the basis of a simple cost-benefit analysis . . . . [but we have instead]
> grounded [our] analysis in a previously recognized, long-established
> category of unprotected speech, and our subsequent decisions have
> shared this understanding.[65]

The Court found no historic tradition of banning depictions of
animal cruelty (as opposed to a tradition of banning animal cruelty
itself),[66] and thus concluded that the prohibited speech did not
constitute a low-value category. It then struck the law down as
substantially overbroad.[67]

The Court reiterated its emphasis on historical inquiry a year

---

[64] Id at 1585–86, quoting *R.A.V.*, 505 US at 383.

[65] Id at 1586; see also id (those decisions "cannot be taken as establishing a freewheeling
authority to declare new categories of speech outside the scope of the First Amendment.
Maybe there are some categories of speech that have been historically unprotected, but
have not yet been specifically identified or discussed as such in our case law. But if so,
there is no evidence that 'depictions of animal cruelty' is among them. We need not
foreclose the future recognition of such additional categories to reject the Government's
highly manipulable balancing test as a means of identifying them.").

[66] Id.

[67] Id at 1592. Some commentators quarreled with the majority's claim in *Stevens* that
its past decisions relied on historical tradition when identifying "low-value" categories of
speech. See Han, 87 NYU L Rev at 85–86 (cited in note 22) (criticizing as "fundamentally
illusory" *Stevens*'s claim that the Court had always engaged in historical analysis to identify
low-value categories of speech); Nadine Strossen, *United States v. Stevens: Restricting Two
Major Rationales for Content-Based Speech Restrictions*, 2010 Cato Sup Ct Rev 67, 78, and
81 (2009–10) (characterizing *Stevens* as "reformulat[ing]" *Chaplinsky* and concluding that
"[t]he *Stevens* approach is essentially backward-looking, treating the finite exceptions that
had been generally accepted since the First Amendment's adoption as a closed, fixed set
of all such exceptions. In contrast, *Chaplinsky* invites the very argument that the government made in *Stevens*: that the Court may now and in the future continue the process of
recognizing potentially unlimited new categories of unprotected expression, beyond those
with a longstanding historical pedigree, so long as the Court deems the expression at issue
to fail the open-ended, subjective balancing test that the last sentence of the *Chaplinsky*
passage sets out."); R. George Wright, *Electoral Lies and the Broader Problems of Strict
Scrutiny*, 64 Fla L Rev 759, 765 (2012) (finding "less than convincing" *Stevens*'s characterization of the Court's earlier approach to identifying low-value categories of speech).
For a pre-*Stevens* commentator who predicted the Court's emphasis on historical inquiry,
see Stone, 74 U Chi L Rev at 1863–64 (cited in note 47) (describing the Court's approach
to low-value speech as including an inquiry into whether it has "long been regulated
without undue harm to the overall system of free expression").

later in *Brown v Entertainment Merchants Ass'n.*[68] There it invalidated a state law restricting the sale or rental of violent video games to minors.[69] Again characterizing low-value speech categories as confined to those "well-defined and narrowly limited [classes of speech] the prevention and punishment of which have never been thought to raise any Constitutional problem,"[70] the Court emphasized the importance of history in deciding whether any particular category of expression can be held to be of low First Amendment value: "[W]ithout persuasive evidence that a novel restriction on content is part of a long (if heretofore unrecognized) tradition of proscription, a legislature may not revise the 'judgment [of] the American people,' embodied in the First Amendment, 'that the benefits of its restrictions on the Government outweigh the costs.'"[71] Finding no such tradition of restricting minors' access to depictions of violence,[72] the Court applied strict scrutiny to strike down the law because it was not necessary to achieve a compelling government interest.[73]

In neither *Stevens* nor *Brown* did the Court explain in any detail *why* historical tradition might be the appropriate means for identifying categories of low-value speech. But as Geoffrey Stone suggested long before those decisions, "[C]onfining the concept of 'low value' speech to those categories that have been recognized as 'low value' time out of mind lessens the risk that judges will conflate politically unpopular ideas with constitutionally low value speech."[74] Indeed, as applied in the First Amendment context, the Court's historical inquiry tends toward an expansive understanding of individuals' free speech rights.[75]

---

[68] 131 S Ct 2729 (2011).

[69] Id at 2734 ("[I]n *Stevens*, we held that new categories of unprotected speech may not be added to the list by a legislature that concludes certain speech is too harmful to be tolerated.").

[70] Id at 2733.

[71] Id at 2734, quoting *Stevens*, 130 S Ct at 1585.

[72] Id at 2736–37. In so doing, the majority continued its reluctance in recent decades to add to its list of less protected speech categories. See, for example, *FCC v Pacifica Foundation*, 438 US 726 (1978) (declining to characterize "indecent" speech that falls short of obscenity as low-value speech); *Cohen v California*, 403 US 15 (1971) (declining to characterize profanity as low-value speech).

[73] *Brown*, 131 S Ct at 2738–41.

[74] Stone, 36 Pepperdine L Rev at 284 (cited in note 49).

[75] See Strossen, 2010 Cato Sup Ct Rev at 71 (cited in note 67). Professor Strossen noted "a counterintuitive aspect of *Stevens*'s tightened criteria for recognizing a categorical ex-

Each of the *Alvarez* opinions suggested that some category of lies are of sufficiently low value that government should be permitted to prohibit them without satisfying the demands of strict scrutiny. The plurality and dissent both engaged in historical inquiry for these purposes, but each defined the relevant historical tradition—and thus the category of low-value lies—quite differently. Justice Breyer's concurring opinion, in contrast, relied on purpose-based and pragmatic arguments to identify another category altogether.

1. *Justice Kennedy's plurality opinion.* In his plurality opinion, Justice Kennedy (joined by Chief Justice Roberts and Justices Ginsburg and Sotomayor) found no long-standing tradition of punishing lies in general and thus rejected the government's contention that intentional lies, without more, comprise a broad category of low-value speech.[76] He distinguished the precedents proffered by the government to support its claim that falsehoods are categorically unprotected:

> [A]ll derive from cases discussing defamation, fraud, or some other legally cognizable harm associated with a false statement, such as an invasion of privacy or the costs of vexatious litigation. In those decisions

clusion from the First Amendment: by insisting that any such exclusion is not new but simply the explicit identification of historically unprotected speech—whose implicit exclusion is deeply rooted in history and tradition—the Court actually increases free speech protection. Typically, however—or at least stereotypically—anchoring the scope of constitutional rights, including freedom of speech, in history and tradition has had the opposite effect; it has restricted protection of these rights."); see also id at 87–88 ("Somewhat ironically, the justices who have most consistently stressed these prerequisites for recognizing a new substantive due process right are the justices who generally take the narrowest view of such rights. . . . In the substantive due process context, strictly enforcing these prerequisites for recognizing an implicit right has the effect of limiting the protection for the constitutional right at issue. In stark contrast, in the First Amendment context, strictly enforcing these same prerequisites for recognizing a categorical exemption from the right has the opposite effect: to maximize protection for the constitutional right at issue.").

[76] *Alvarez*, 132 S Ct at 2544. When engaging in this historical inquiry, the plurality did not focus on the narrowest applicable historical tradition—that is, a history of proscribing lies about military valor—perhaps because such a choice would have required it to acknowledge multiple separate categories of "low-value" lies. See Brief of Amici Eugene Volokh and James Weinstein, *United States v Alvarez*, No 11-210, *13–14 (filed Dec 27, 2011) (available on Westlaw at 2011 WL 6179424) (explaining the awkwardness of identifying a series of separate, narrow categories of unprotected lies of various types because to do so "would make it impossible for this Court to say, as it has before, that the exceptions to the general ban on content-based restrictions apply" in only a few situations); id at *17 ("[T]he creation of a large array of free speech exceptions ought to be avoided. Having a dozen exceptions for subcategories of knowingly false statements may seem more speech-protective than having a general exception for all knowingly false statements. But such a proliferation of exceptions may ultimately prove to be less speech-protective, because it may open the door to more exceptions that will not be limited to knowing falsehoods.").

the falsity of speech at issue was not irrelevant to our analysis, but neither was it determinative. The Court has never endorsed the cat-egorical rule the Government advances: that false statements receive no First Amendment protection. Our prior decisions have not con-fronted a measure, like the Stolen Valor Act, that targets falsity and nothing more.[77]

Justice Kennedy instead identified a long-standing tradition of restricting only a subclass of false statements of fact: those asso-ciated with "defamation, fraud, or some other legally cognizable harm."[78] Rather than defining the concept of "legally cognizable harm," he instead illustrated it with a discussion of various areas in which government had historically prohibited certain harm-causing lies. For example, he emphasized that perjury laws punish lies that inflict harm to the integrity of the legal system,[79] and he described statutes prohibiting a speaker from falsely representing herself to be a government official as punishing lies that inflict harms to the integrity of government processes.[80] After concluding that the Stolen Valor Act regulated lies that did not fall within this tradition, he then applied strict scrutiny and found that the act was not necessary to achieve a compelling government interest. Because the opinion did not specifically define the concept of historically recognized "legally cognizable harm," some uncer-tainty remains about precisely what sort of harms are sufficient to treat certain lies as falling within this category of "low-value" speech. The opinion left another area of uncertainty with its failure clearly to identify the analysis to be applied to government's efforts to regulate speech falling within this category (other than to make clear that the test would be something other than strict scrutiny).

2. *Justice Alito's dissenting opinion.* In contrast, Justice Alito's dis-senting opinion (joined by Justices Scalia and Thomas) identified the relevant historical tradition much more broadly as punishing false statements in general except where such punishment would chill truthful or other valuable speech (as would be the case, for

---

[77] *Alvarez*, 132 S Ct at 2545.

[78] Id.

[79] Id at 2546.

[80] Id. The plurality described statutory prohibitions on false statements to government officials not directly in terms of harm, but instead as distinguishable from the Stolen Valor Act because they are limited to lies told to certain audiences in certain settings. Id. Justice Breyer's concurrence, in contrast, explained such statutes as directed to "circumstances where a lie is likely to work particular and specific harm by interfering with the functioning of a government department." Id at 2554.

example, if the government were to punish lies about "philosophy, religion, history, the social sciences, the arts, and other matters of public concern").[81] Justice Alito rejected the plurality's efforts to describe long-standing practice more narrowly as restricting only certain harm-causing lies because he found that the asserted harms were often too diffuse or intangible to support such a theory.[82] He noted, for example, long-standing traditions of punishing lies that caused dignitary rather than pecuniary harm, that threatened likely rather than actual harm, and that caused generalized harm to government processes rather than to specific individuals.[83] He concluded that the historical tradition was better understood as prohibiting false statements without more, and thus that "false statements of fact merit no First Amendment protection in their own right."[84] In his view, lies do not have First Amendment value of their own, and are thus subject to government prohibition consistent with the Constitution except where their regulation would chill truthful speech.

3. *Justice Breyer's concurring opinion.* Justice Breyer (joined by Justice Kagan) relied on purpose-based and pragmatic—rather than historical—analysis to identify a category of low-value lies as including those "false statements about easily verifiable facts that do not concern" matters of "philosophy, religion, history, the social sciences, the arts, and the like."[85] Such lies frustrate core First Amendment truth-seeking and other values; moreover—and unlike lies about matters involving history, the social sciences, and related topics—their restriction is unlikely to chill truthful speech.[86]

Long attracted to balancing analyses that attend to the competing values on both sides of a constitutional question,[87] Justice

---

[81] Id at 2562–63.

[82] Id at 2563 n 14.

[83] Id.

[84] Id at 2562.

[85] Id at 2552.

[86] Id; see also id at 2564 (Alito, J, dissenting) ("[T]here are broad areas in which any attempt by the state to penalize purportedly false speech would present a grave and unacceptable danger of suppressing truthful speech. Laws restricting false statements about philosophy, religion, history, the social sciences, the arts, and other matters of public concern would present such a threat.").

[87] See, for example, *Bartnicki v Vopper*, 532 US 514, 536 (2001) (Breyer, J, concurring) ("I would ask whether the statutes strike a reasonable balance between their speech-restricting and speech-enhancing consequences. Or do they instead impose restrictions

Breyer then proposed to apply intermediate scrutiny—a type of balancing[88]—to laws regulating lies in this low-value category.[89] This analysis requires both an assessment of the weight of the government's interest in preventing the harms threatened by the targeted lies as well as an evaluation of the harms to First Amendment values posed by the government's regulation itself. He concluded that the lies prohibited by the Stolen Valor Act harmed both the government and legitimate medal recipients by diluting the value of military awards.[90] On the other hand, in language suggesting an antipaternalistic view of the First Amendment, he expressed concern that

> the pervasiveness of false statements, made for better or for worse motives, made thoughtlessly or deliberately, made with or without accompanying harm, provides a weapon to a government broadly empowered to prosecute falsity without more. And those who are unpopular may fear that the government will use that weapon selectively, say by prosecuting a pacifist who supports his cause by (falsely) claiming

---

on speech that are disproportionate when measured against their corresponding privacy and speech-related benefits, taking into account the kind, the importance, and the extent of these benefits, as well as the need for the restrictions in order to secure those benefits? What this Court has called 'strict scrutiny'—with its strong presumption against constitutionality—is normally out of place where, as here, important competing constitutional interests are implicated."); *Nixon v Shrink Missouri Government PAC*, 528 US 377, 402–03 (2000) ("In such circumstances—where a law significantly implicates competing constitutionally protected interests in complex ways—the Court has closely scrutinized the statute's impact on those interests, but refrained from employing a simple test that effectively presumes unconstitutionality. Rather, it has balanced interests. And in practice that has meant asking whether the statute burdens any one such interest in a manner out of proportion to the statute's salutary effects upon the others (perhaps, but not necessarily, because of the existence of a clearly superior, less restrictive alternative)."); see also Paul Gewirtz, *The Pragmatic Passion of Stephen Breyer*, 115 Yale L J 1675, 1689–90 (2006) (describing Justice Breyer's balancing analyses).

[88] See Kathleen M. Sullivan, *Post-Liberal Judging: The Roles of Categorization and Balancing*, 63 U Colo L Rev 293, 301 (1992) (Intermediate scrutiny "tends to make the articulation and comparison of competing rights and interests more explicit," "makes outcomes far less predictable," and "makes the Court more vulnerable to the charge of 'legislating from the bench.'").

[89] *Alvarez*, 132 S Ct at 2551–52 (Breyer, J, concurring) ("Those circumstances lead me to apply what the Court has termed 'intermediate scrutiny' here."); see also id at 2552 ("[S]ome such approach is necessary if the First Amendment is to offer proper protection in the many instances in which a statute adversely affects constitutionally protected interests but warrants neither near-automatic condemnation (as 'strict scrutiny' implies) nor near near-automatic approval (as is implicit in 'rational basis' review).").

[90] Id at 2555 ("To permit those who have not earned those honors to claim otherwise dilutes the value of the awards. Indeed, the Nation cannot fully honor those who have sacrificed so much for their country's honor unless those who claim to have received its military awards tell the truth.").

to have been a war hero, while ignoring members of other political groups who might make similar false claims.[91]

He found that the act failed intermediate scrutiny, concluding that the government's interest in preventing the harms caused by the targeted lies was outweighed by the statute's harms to First Amendment interests in empowering the government to prosecute lies told "in family, social, or other private contexts, where lies will often cause little harm"[92] as well as lies told in political contexts where the danger of selective government enforcement is high.[93]

4. *Assessing the three approaches.* Of the three *Alvarez* opinions, I find the dissent the least persuasive due to its failure to recognize that many lies have First Amendment value and that the regulation of even valueless lies often threatens government overreaching in a way inimical to important First Amendment interests.[94] Indeed, Justice Alito's approach would empower the government to regulate a breathtakingly wide variety of lies that include not only bragging and other relatively harmless lies but also potentially valuable lies told for a range of humanitarian, self-expressive, or other purposes.[95]

In contrast, both the plurality and the concurring opinions ap-

---

[91] Id at 2553; see also id ("The statute before us lacks any such limiting features. It may be construed to prohibit only knowing and intentional acts of deception about readily verifiable facts within the personal knowledge of the speaker, thus reducing the risk that valuable speech is chilled. But it still ranges very broadly. And that breadth means that it creates a significant risk of First Amendment harm.").

[92] Id.

[93] Id.

[94] For example, while Justice Breyer identified a relatively narrow category of lies as low value, id at 2552, Justice Alito indicated that the regulation only of a relatively narrow category of lies threatens instrumental harm to the First Amendment. Id at 2564.

[95] See notes 14–30 and accompanying text. Justice Alito identified the political process as the appropriate remedy for such concerns. See id at 2565 (Alito, J, dissenting) ("The safeguard against such laws is democracy, not the First Amendment. Not every foolish law is unconstitutional."). This response offers little comfort in light of the large universe of speech potentially at risk of government regulation under his approach. See Varat, 53 UCLA L Rev at 1109 (cited in note 17) ("[A]ccepting unlimited government power to prohibit all deception in all circumstances would invade our rights of free expression and belief to an intolerable degree, including most notably—and however counterintuitively—our rights to personal and political self-rule. A regime of zero tolerance for any form of deception, enforced at will by government officials or random opponents, undoubtedly would curtail unacceptably the willingness of the people to speak, especially in ways that might anger, or merely involve, the antideception police. Ironically, perhaps, but realistically, policing deception would tend to undermine the enlightenment function of free expression. Such a regime also could interfere with expressive autonomy and tend to inhibit creativity and experimentation, privacy, and the joys and solace that may come from spreading small, private, or otherwise benign delusions.").

propriately sought to cabin the category of low-value lies that are subject to greater government regulation.[96] To this end, Justice Kennedy concluded that the First Amendment permits the government to forbid lies that have been historically restricted because they cause or threaten to cause a "legally cognizable" harm. Justice Breyer, in contrast, concluded that the First Amendment permits the government to prohibit lies about "easily verifiable facts" that do not concern matters of "philosophy, religion, history, the social sciences, the arts, and the like" if the regulation satisfies intermediate scrutiny.

On balance, I prefer Justice Breyer's approach for several reasons. First, his opinion is more transparent than the plurality in acknowledging that some lies should be understood to have First Amendment value in their own right.[97] Second, by focusing on lies about "easily verifiable" facts in certain areas[98]—such as whether one received the Congressional Medal of Honor—Justice Breyer's proposed category lessens the risk of erroneous liability findings, and thus ameliorates chilling-effect concerns as well as the danger that the government will engage in partisan abuse or selective enforcement.[99]

Unlike the plurality opinion (which failed to identify the standard with which it would evaluate government's regulation of lies categorized as low value), Justice Breyer clearly identified intermediate scrutiny as the standard to be applied to laws regulating his proposed category of low-value lies. Of course, intermediate

---

[96] It remains unclear whether the Kennedy and Breyer approaches would generate different results in many cases. For example, one could certainly conclude that the First Amendment permits the government to regulate defamatory or fraudulent lies under both the plurality's historical analysis as well as the intermediate scrutiny proposed by the concurrence. Similarly, both analyses found that the First Amendment did not permit the government to punish the lies targeted by the Stolen Valor Act. On the other hand, historical analysis might well support the regulation of false statements to the government and false statements that one is a government official because such regulations have a long historical pedigree, while the fate of such statutes under intermediate scrutiny will likely depend on the degree to which the laws are tailored to address the relevant harm. See notes 139–66 and accompanying text.

[97] See *Alvarez*, 132 S Ct at 2553.

[98] Of course, just as we can anticipate uncertainty about what is and is not "legally cognizable harm" under the plurality's approach, we can also anticipate uncertainty about whether certain lies do or do not fall within the relevant subject matter areas under Justice Breyer's approach.

[99] See Stern, 10 First Am L Rev at 485 (cited in note 44) (noting that the objectivity of certain information "makes it subject to official review without fear of partisan overreaching by the state").

scrutiny and other forms of balancing analyses have both advocates and critics. Advantages include their flexibility and thus their ability to accommodate nuance and context.[100] Moreover, many see virtue in such analyses' transparency in acknowledging and assessing important competing interests.[101] Perhaps in recognition of these strengths, the Court has adopted intermediate scrutiny and other balancing analyses in a number of First Amendment contexts.[102] On the other hand, such approaches invite understandable concerns about unpredictability and judicial subjectivity.[103] Such unpredictability, however, may be unavoidable in this challenging context and perhaps in most judicial enterprises.[104] As just one example, the historical approach to identifying categories of low-value speech is not without its own subjectivity—as illustrated by the fact that the plurality and dissent both engaged in historical inquiry, only to identify very different categories of low-value lies.[105]

---

[100] See Joseph Blocher, *Categoricalism and Balancing in First and Second Amendment Analysis*, 84 NYU L Rev 375, 436–37 (2009); Pierre Schlag, The Legal Argument Project (unpublished manuscript, 2012, on file with the author) *24–25 (observing that indeterminacy has a number of virtues, including maintaining flexibility, accommodating future change, postponing decision making, and deferring to other decision makers).

[101] See *District of Columbia v Heller*, 554 US 570, 719 (2008) (Breyer, J, dissenting) (extolling balancing's "necessary transparency [which] lays bare the judge's reasoning for all to see and to criticize"); Schlag at *33 (cited in note 100) ("[E]ven if the choice is intuitionist or ungrounded, balancing may nonetheless contribute to the process of decision. When a court or other legal officials announce a balancing test, they often indicate what it is that is to be balanced—the factors or considerations that matter (and, by omission, those that don't). In this regard, balancing has the virtue of providing a checklist (things which a decisionmaker should consider).").

[102] See, for example, *Pickering v Board of Education*, 391 US 563, 568 (1968) (assessing public employees' First Amendment claims by weighing the individual employee's interest as a citizen in commenting on matters of public concern against the government's interest as an employer in efficiently providing public services); *Central Hudson*, 447 US at 564 (applying intermediate scrutiny to government's regulation of commercial speech that is neither false, misleading, nor related to illegal activity). Indeed, less flexible approaches can sometimes pose dangers to free speech rights precisely because of their rigidity. See Blocher, 84 NYU L Rev at 384–85 (cited in note 100) ("Justice Black's preference for categoricalism did not mean that he would give all speech-like acts complete immunity from regulation. Justice Black trimmed the most problematic results of his absolutist test by finding categorical exceptions to the categorical rule. Indeed, he was quicker than many balancing-inclined Justices to find that certain speech acts fell completely outside the bounds of the First Amendment.").

[103] See, for example, Stone, 36 Pepperdine L Rev at 275–76 (cited in note 49) (noting that balancing approaches can "produce a highly uncertain, unpredictable, and fact-dependent set of outcomes that would leave speakers, police officers, prosecutors, jurors, and judges in a state of constant uncertainty").

[104] See Stephen Breyer, *Active Liberty* 124–33 (Knopf, 2005).

[105] A number of thoughtful commentators suggested the manipulability of this test even

In sum, Justice Breyer's approach appropriately presumes that lies are fully protected by the First Amendment and that government therefore generally may not regulate them unless it satisfies strict scrutiny, while recognizing a specific category of low-value lies that remain subject to government regulation under certain circumstances. Part II examines the circumstances in which low-value lies might cause harm of the sort that should permit government to prohibit them consistent with the First Amendment.

II. ASSESSING THE HARMS OF LOW-VALUE LIES

Unless we are willing to protect all lies or no lies from government regulation, we must make some difficult judgments in determining when the Constitution permits government to punish intentional falsehoods. As David Strauss has observed, "If the category of false statements of fact is not defined very narrowly, [governmental efforts to prohibit lies] can, of course, become highly problematic. But there is a core area in which the harm of private manipulation seems great enough to justify government restrictions on speech."[106] Defining that core area poses a considerable challenge.

Both the Kennedy and Breyer approaches defined that core area largely in terms of harm. Justice Kennedy identified as low value those lies that have been historically restricted because they are associated with a "legally cognizable" harm.[107] Justice Breyer applied intermediate scrutiny to balance the government's interest

---

before the *Alvarez* decision. See Han, 87 NYU L Rev at 88 (cited in note 22) ("There is no purely 'neutral' means of historical analysis. A court can characterize the speech in question in multiple ways and craft analogies to 'longstanding tradition' at varying levels of generality and abstraction. In the end, the relative value and harm associated with the speech in question remains central to the analysis, since it is a court's sense of these values that will influence how it conducts the historical analysis."); Horwitz, 87 Wash L Rev at 461 (cited in note 44) ("Despite its emphasis on history, however, the Court has not rejected interest-balancing altogether. In order to determine whether false statements of fact fall within a traditional (albeit 'heretofore unrecognized') category, it will inevitably have to ask whether they share the fundamental characteristic of such categories."); Tushnet at *15 (cited in note 9) ("A purely historical inquiry cannot determine the level of generality at which the historically determined categories should be described."); id at *16 (suggesting that the relevant historical category is one in which legislatures have judged certain lies to trigger serious social problems); see also Allen Rostron, *Justice Breyer's Triumph in the Third Battle Over the Second Amendment*, 80 Geo Wash L Rev 703 (2012) (describing lower courts' struggles with the challenges of historical analysis in the Second Amendment context).

[106] Strauss, 91 Colum L Rev at 366 (cited in note 14).

[107] *Alvarez*, 132 S Ct at 2545.

in preventing the harms caused by certain low-value lies against the harm to First Amendment values caused by the government's regulation of such lies.[108] More specifically, although Justice Breyer concluded that the Stolen Valor Act failed intermediate scrutiny, he suggested that the outcome might have been different had the act required "a showing that the false statement caused specific harm or at least was material, or focus its coverage on lies most likely to be harmful or on contexts where such lies are most likely to cause harm."[109] Either approach thus requires us to consider more precisely when and how low-value lies cause harm.

Frederick Schauer has thoughtfully explored the relationship between harm and the First Amendment in other contexts, observing that

> We take an important first step when we recognize that much First Amendment argument is about consequential and often harmful speech, but the necessary second step is to understand the nature of those harms, for without that we cannot hope to evaluate (or generate) the data that would enable courts to determine the extent of the harms involved, and whether the doctrine should allow any redress against them.[110]

He thus suggests that we take care to disaggregate various speech-related harms "because free speech cases involving genuine harm seem far more likely to implicate or even require the kinds of empirical assessments that transparently preposterous claims of harm do not."[111] To this end, we might helpfully separate the second- and third-party harms of lies when thinking about whether and when such harms should justify government intervention.

More specifically, lies often harm second parties—that is, the listeners to whom the lie is told—in individualized ways that may or may not be tangible; compare, for example, fraudulent lies that cause monetary harm[112] to cruel lies that cause emotional

---

[108] Id at 2551–52.

[109] Id at 2553–54 (Breyer, J, concurring).

[110] See Frederick Schauer, *Harm(s) and the First Amendment*, 2011 Supreme Court Review 81, 107 (2011); see also id ("[I]t is impossible to evaluate these harms, or even to know which harms we are talking about, unless we have a better sense of exactly what kinds of harms are at issue, and thus what kind of evidence would bear, one way or another, upon their existence and extent.").

[111] Id.

[112] See *Illinois ex rel Madigan v Telemarketing Associates, Inc.*, 538 US 600, 619 (2003) (describing contexts in which the First Amendment permits the regulation of fraudulent speech); Gregory Klass, *Meaning, Purpose, and Cause in the Law of Deception*, 100 Geo L J 449, 449 (2012) (describing the [private] "law of deception" to include "the torts of

harm.[113] Lies can also harm individual third parties (i.e., someone other than the listener)—as is the case with defamation, where the harm is generally suffered not by the listener but by the subject of the lie.[114] Third-party harms can include more generalized harms to government institutions when, for example, lies undermine the public's confidence in important government processes that require the public's trust for their effectiveness. The more generalized and the less tangible the harms threatened by the targeted lies, however, the greater the concerns about selective or partisan enforcement. The remainder of this part thus explores in more detail the sorts of second- and third-party harms threatened by a speaker's lies about her credentials—that is, the sorts of lies prohibited by the Stolen Valor Act—and under what circumstances they should justify government punishment of such lies.[115]

A. SECOND-PARTY HARMS: LIES THAT HARM LISTENERS

Lies frequently cause second-party harms by undermining listeners' autonomy in a wide variety of ways, some considerably more tangible (and thus susceptible to proof) than others.[116] Sissela

---

deceit, negligent misrepresentation, nondisclosure, and defamation; criminal fraud statutes; securities law, which includes both disclosure duties and penalties for false statements; false advertising law; labeling requirements for food, drugs, and other consumer goods; and, according to recent scholarship, information-forcing penalty defaults in contract law and elsewhere").

[113] See, for example, *Cantrell v Forest City Publishing Co.*, 419 US 245 (1974) (upholding liability under false light tort for knowingly false and offensive statements); *Time, Inc. v Hill*, 385 US 374 (1967) (same).

[114] See *Gertz*, 418 US at 347–48 (recognizing "the strength of the legitimate state interest in compensating private individuals for wrongful injury to reputation"); id at 342, quoting *Rosenblatt v Baer*, 383 US 75, 92 (1966) (Stewart, J, concurring) (describing such harms as including "impairment of reputation and standing in the community, personal humiliation, and mental anguish and suffering"). Lies that cause both individualized and tangible harm to third parties include lies that threaten physical and financial injury by creating a public panic. See, for example, *Schenck v United States*, 249 US 49, 52 (1919) (anticipating the harms of falsely yelling "fire" in a crowded theater); *United States v Keyser*, 2012 WL 6052248 *6 (9th Cir 2012) (upholding defendant's conviction for communicating anthrax hoax: "False and misleading information indicating an act of terrorism is not a simple lie. Instead, it tends to incite a tangible negative response. Here, law enforcement and emergency workers responded to the mailings as potential acts of terror, arriving with hazardous materials units, evacuating buildings, sending the samples off to a laboratory for tests and devoting resources to investigating the source of the mailings.").

[115] See Helen Norton, *The Measure of Government Speech: Identifying Expression's Source*, 88 BU L Rev 587, 592 (2008) (describing studies confirming that the more credible a speaker, the more likely her message will persuade her listeners regardless of the message's content).

[116] See note 27 and accompanying text (describing philosophers' efforts to identify a hierarchy of lies based on their moral harm).

Bok, for example, has emphasized the moral threat to listeners' autonomy posed by lies, and characterized such a threat as a form of coercion akin to violence:

> Deceit and violence—these are the two forms of deliberate assault on human beings. Both can coerce people into acting against their will. . . . The knowledge of this coercive element in deception, and of our vulnerability to it, underlies our sense of the *centrality* of truthfulness. . . . [I]ts potential for coercion and for destruction is such that society could scarcely function without some degree of truthfulness in speech and action. . . . To the extent that knowledge gives power, to that extent do lies affect the distribution of power; they add to that of the liar, and diminish that of the deceived, altering his choices at different levels.[117]

Indeed, people generally resent being lied to precisely because such deception feels manipulative and disrespectful.[118]

Because individual self-fulfillment and autonomy are often identified as among the primary values served by the Free Speech Clause,[119] we might therefore understand lies that harm listener autonomy as themselves frustrating a core First Amendment interest.[120] For these reasons, David Strauss has concluded that ma-

[117] Bok, *Lying* at 18–19 (cited in note 9).

[118] Lies are morally wrong from a Kantian perspective, for example, when speakers undermine listener autonomy by seeking to use their listeners as a means to the speakers' own ends, rather than treating listeners as ends in themselves. See Immanuel Kant, trans James W. Ellington, *Grounding for the Metaphysics of Morals* 63–65 (3d ed 1993). Others are reluctant to find that many lies pose significant harms to their targets. See Nyberg, *The Varnished Truth* at 9 (cited in note 9) ("I know in my own case that I want neither to tell nor to hear all the truth that could be said about myself.").

[119] See Joseph Raz, *The Morality of Freedom* 372 (Oxford, 1980) ("[T]o be author of one's life, one's choices must be free from coercion and manipulation by others."); Tamara Piety, *Brandishing the First Amendment* 81 (Michigan, 2012) ("To be autonomous is not merely to be free of coercion by others. Rather, it encompasses some notion of a free mind as well as a free body, of self-possession."); Han, 87 NYU L Rev at 102–03 (cited in note 22) (describing a vision of autonomy "based on the simple and deeply rooted anti-paternalist principle that each person is entitled to a limited sphere within which she is free from external coercion or interference. . . .").

[120] Varat, 53 UCLA L Rev at 1108–09 (cited in note 17) ("[O]ther theories of the function of free expression—especially theories of autonomy—tend to support government restrictions on deception, at least when adopted to preserve the autonomy of those whom deceptive speakers otherwise might manipulate. . . ."). In this article I focus only on the regulation of affirmatively false statements—putting aside secrets, nondisclosure and the many other ways in which speakers may seek to deceive their listeners and thus offend their autonomy—in part because lying arguably poses the greater threat to listener autonomy. See Stuart P. Green, *Lying, Misleading, and Falsely Denying: How Moral Concepts Inform the Law of Perjury, Fraud, and False Statements*, 53 Hastings L J 157, 177 (2001) (distinguishing deception as "afford[ing] the listener the opportunity for more precise questioning, which bald-faced lies generally do not"); Strauss, 91 Colum L Rev at 356 (cited in note 14) ("Ordinarily, withholding information is not as effective as lying [in offending listener autonomy] because a lie affirmatively throws the hearer off the track.").

nipulative lies are unprotected by the First Amendment's fundamental "persuasion principle," which "holds that the government may not suppress speech on the ground that the speech is likely to persuade people to do something that the government considers harmful."[121] As he explained in more detail,

> The persuasion principle does not apply to government restrictions of false statements of fact because those restrictions do not manipulate or deny autonomy. No one wants to make decisions on the basis of false information. When the government prevents people from making decisions on the basis of false information, it does not manipulate their mental processes to serve the government's ends. Rather, it enables those processes to function as they should, to promote the ends of the listener.[122]

Under an autonomy-based approach, the decision in *Alvarez* might turn on whether the lie had the capacity to influence listeners' decision making in a way injurious to their autonomy. This view turns not only on the context in which the lies were told but also on how one defines the constitutionally relevant autonomy injury. For example, Mr. Alvarez's lies were told when he introduced himself at a meeting as a newly elected water district board member in a context in which he was unlikely to influence listeners' thinking on decisions with any material consequences. For this reason, the lie may not seem terribly manipulative.

To be sure, however, his lie inflicted *some* autonomy injury, as he likely sought to shape his listeners' opinion of him. Indeed, lies can undermine listener autonomy in a wide variety of ways, manipulating listeners' choices about how to spend their money, whom to recommend or hire for a job, with whom to spend their time, with whom to engage in an intimate relationship, and many other decisions. As Eugene Volokh has pointed out,

> [T]rying to affect private citizens' behavior through falsehoods creates

---

Such a distinction can also be defended on more instrumental grounds, on the theory that permitting the government to regulate the much larger universe of deception poses even greater chilling and overreaching concerns than those threatened by the government's regulation of lies. See Bok, *Lying* at 13–14 (cited in note 9) ("We can [deceive] through gesture, through disguise, by means of action or inaction, even through silence. . . . Deception, then, is the larger category, and lying forms part of it."); Nyberg, *The Varnished Truth* at 63–80 (cited in note 9) (describing the large universe of deception).

[121] Strauss, 91 Colum L Rev at 335, 339 (cited in note 14).

[122] Id at 357; see also id at 339 ("[B]ecause false statements of fact do not appeal to reason, their use does not constitute persuasion and they are therefore not protected by the persuasion principle.").

a significant harm—sometimes less significant, sometimes more significant, but significant nonetheless, because it involves manipulating
people through deception. And if there is a substantial government
interest in protecting people from being deceived into giving $50 to a
charitable fundraiser, there is likewise a substantial government interest
in protecting people from being deceived into giving others votes, respect, or attention.[123]

Indeed, lies that shape listeners' decision making about whether
to confer or withhold respect or affection can be among the most
painful. One might thus well choose to privilege listeners' First
Amendment autonomy interests throughout this wide range of
settings, as Volokh suggests.[124]

Doing so, however, would empower government to punish a
wide swath of lies and thus frustrate an antipaternalistic understanding of the First Amendment.[125] The less tangible the harms
threatened by prohibited lies, for example, the greater our concerns about government bias and partisanship in enforcing such
laws. For these reasons, some commentators would permit government to punish only lies that threaten monetary and similarly
material harm to the listener.[126] Others resist such a financial focus

---

[123] See Brief of Amici Eugene Volokh and James Weinstein at *31–32 (cited in note 76)
("[P]eople who lie about decorations generally do so for a reason: they may want to get
elected to public office, to get more credibility for their own statements in another's
election campaign, to get more credibility in some nonelectoral political debate, or even
just to get more respect from neighbors, acquaintances, potential business associates, or
potential romantic partners. They are thus trying to manipulate listeners' behavior through
falsehood, and their statements are quite likely to indeed affect listeners' behavior, particularly since having a military decoration is often seen as an especially important mark
of merit.").

[124] Sissela Bok, for these reasons, proposes a test of "publicity" for assessing whether
lies are justifiable. Bok, *Lying* at 93 (cited in note 9) ("The test of publicity asks which
lies, if any, would survive the appeal for justification to reasonable persons. It requires us
to seek concrete and open performance of an exercise crucial to ethics: the Golden Rule,
basic to so many religious and moral traditions. We must share the perspective of those
affected by our choices, and ask how we would react if the lies we are contemplating were
told to us.").

[125] See Varat, 53 UCLA L Rev at 1114 (cited in note 17) ("Lies to defraud someone
into parting with something of value might fit the account best: the one-to-one targeting
of the deception raises the concern not only about the unique control of the speaker over
the listener's reasoning process, but also about the deceived listener's direct response in
giving up something to the decisionmaker in a manner most akin to theft.").

[126] See *Alvarez*, 132 S Ct at 2547 (plurality) ("Where false claims are made to effect a
fraud or secure moneys or other valuable considerations, say offers of employment, it is
well established that the Government may restrict speech without affronting the First
Amendment."); Han, 87 NYU L Rev at 117 (cited in note 22) ("A significant factor in
evaluating the government's regulatory interest might therefore be whether the effect or
intended effect of the speech in question can be characterized as material or purely psychological in nature. In other words, was the lie in question aimed at procuring some sort

and instead seek a middle path that targets lies that cause individualized if potentially less tangible harms to listeners, such as
lies that may deprive the listener of "something of value" or may
cause the listener to change her course of conduct or otherwise
rely on the lie to her detriment.[127]

One could plausibly argue that each of these distinctions lacks
normative appeal or conceptual coherence or both.[128] On the one
hand, targeting only lies that threaten material harm understates
the many other ways in which lies can cause significant—if intangible—autonomy harm. On the other, choosing an approach that
targets less measurable harms invites slippery determinations of
"value" and "detriment." Indeed, any of these choices might be
criticized as reflecting a line drawn arbitrarily through what is a
very broad universe of autonomy-threatening lies.[129]

In short, none of these proposals is completely satisfying; indeed, I write in part to point out their deficiencies. But the conceptually coherent alternatives—that is, that the First Amendment
means that liars can never be punished because it protects all lies,
or that the First Amendment protects no lies and thus permits the
government to regulate them without constraint—are even less
appealing from a normative standpoint.[130] For these reasons, I still
prefer Justice Breyer's proposed balancing analysis, which more
transparently grapples with the important competing interests at

---

of material advantage, monetary or otherwise, or was it made solely in order to influence
the speaker's psychological standing with others?"); see also id at 119 (noting that choosing
the appropriate point on this autonomy spectrum at which to regulate lies is challenging
but also the sort of choice that courts are frequently called upon to make); Brief of Amicus
Jonathan D. Varat at *18–24 (cited in note 26) (arguing that only lies that inflict "targeted"
or "concrete" injury should be considered unprotected); id at *17 ("Using speech to gain
the respect of others, without harming the speaker's audience in any tangible or directed
way—such as by taking something from the listeners—is a normal and routine part of
self-expression that does include statements deliberately exaggerating or falsifying one's
accomplishments. The United States' ability to control how people express themselves in
their everyday lives as they negotiate their egos and insecurities should be extremely limited
and narrowly circumscribed.").

[127] See *United States v Lepowitch*, 318 US 702, 704 (1943) (interpreting 18 USC § 76
simply to require proof that the defendant "sought to cause the deceived person to follow
some course he would not have pursued but for the deceitful conduct"); Stern, 10 First
Am L Rev at 507 (cited in note 44) (suggesting the targeting of lies that "induce tangible
reliance and improper gain").

[128] See Schlag at *11–13 (cited in note 100) (identifying conceptual intelligibility and
normative appeal as among the criteria for "sound" legal distinctions). But as Schlag points
out, "ideal legal distinctions are elusive." Id at *16.

[129] See id at *14 (identifying frequent flaws of legal distinctions).

[130] See notes 46–47 and accompanying text.

stake.[131] When drawing those lines and managing this balance, however, I suggest that we err on the side of targeting lies that demonstrably threaten monetary and similarly tangible harms to listeners not because other lies are not deeply wounding to listener autonomy, but instead to accommodate our concerns about government bias and partisanship in enforcing such laws.

B. LIES THAT HARM THIRD PARTIES

A speaker's lies about her credentials can also threaten significant harm to third-party individuals or processes, sometimes in ways that are less individualized and even less tangible than the second-party harms discussed in the preceding section. Consider, for example, lies that undermine the public's willingness to participate in important government processes that require the public's trust for their effectiveness.[132] Ironically, some lies may enhance public trust (as Justice Breyer suggested with his list of socially valuable lies that include those "in public contexts, where they may stop a panic or otherwise preserve calm in the face of danger"[133]). But many others undermine it. As Sissela Bok explains:

> [Liars] often fail to consider the many ways in which deception can spread and give rise to practices very damaging to human communities. These practices clearly do not affect only isolated individuals. The veneer of social trust is often thin. As lies spread—by imitation, or in retaliation, or to forestall suspected deception—trust is damaged. Yet trust is a social good to be protected just as much as the air we breathe or the water we drink. When it is damaged, the community as a whole

---

[131] Note, however, that the plurality's approach does not avoid this challenge, in that it requires us to determine what is or is not "legally cognizable harm," a determination that ultimately requires similar assessments about when harm is and is not constitutionally sufficient.

[132] Indeed, the more legitimate (or trusted) a government institution is, the more public cooperation it will engender and the more effective it is likely to be. Jack Balkin has described legitimacy in this context as including "sociological legitimacy—whether people believe that the system is sufficiently fair and just that they can support it." Jack M. Balkin, *Plessy, Brown, and Grutter: A Play in Three Acts*, 26 Cardozo L Rev 1689, 1720 (2005). Legitimacy thus measures individuals' trust in leaders' authority and their willingness to comply with those leaders' directives. See Tom R. Tyler and Peter Degoey, *Collective Restraint in Social Dilemmas: Procedural Justice and Social Identification Effects on Support for Authorities*, 69 J Personality and Social Psychology 482, 483 (1995) (examining how authorities' actual or perceived legitimacy influences group members' decisions when facing social dilemmas).

[133] *Alvarez*, 132 S Ct at 2553. David Nyberg has more broadly contended that lies frequently add to the stability and success of a society. See Nyberg, *The Varnished Truth* at 80 (cited in note 9) ("To live decently with one another we do not need moral purity, we need discretion—which means tact in regard to truth.").

suffers; and when it is destroyed, societies falter and collapse.[134]

Perjury prohibitions offer perhaps the strongest examples of laws that bar lies that pose a range of third-party harms.[135] To be sure, such lies threaten individualized and concrete third-party harms to litigants when they lead to erroneous verdicts.[136] But these statutes also target such lies' more generalized third-party harms to the public's ability to trust in the integrity of the justice system.[137] Indeed, an earlier Court proclaimed perjury as "at war with justice."[138] By targeting lies that are material to high-stakes decisions in circumscribed settings, perjury laws rely on legal distinctions that are both normatively appealing and conceptually coherent.

Related but somewhat less targeted laws include the wide variety of statutes that prohibit lies to the government.[139] Consider, for instance, the Federal False Statements Act,[140] which began as a Civil War–era effort to protect the federal government from monetary scams by military contractors.[141] Congress expanded the statute's reach during World War I to prohibit any lie made with the intent to cheat or swindle the government out of money or prop-

---

[134] Bok, *Lying* at 26–27 (cited in note 9).

[135] See, for example, 18 USC § 1621; *United States v Debrow*, 346 US 374, 376 (1953) (explaining federal perjury law as prohibiting a "false statement willfully made as to facts material to the hearing" under an oath authorized by federal law and taken before a competent tribunal, officer, or person).

[136] See Geoffrey R. Stone, *A Free and Responsible Press*, 1993 U Chi Legal F 127, 132 (1993) ("The rules of evidence do not permit the presentation of knowingly false evidence. The reasons for this rule are clear. Such evidence serves no legitimate purpose in the effort to determine the truth. But it is worse than that, for such evidence is also destructive of the factfinding process. It attempts to distort, distract, and mislead. At best, such evidence will waste time and effort in requiring energy to be devoted to demonstrating that the testimony is false; at worst, the falsehood will not be revealed and the jury will reach the wrong substantive result.").

[137] See *Alvarez*, 132 S Ct at 2546 (explaining that perjury "undermines the function and province of the law and threaten[s] the integrity of judgments that are the basis of the legal system").

[138] *In re Michael*, 326 US 224, 227 (1945).

[139] See note 80.

[140] 18 USC § 1001 (prohibiting knowingly and willfully making "any materially false, fictitious or fraudulent statement or representation . . . in any matter within the jurisdiction of the executive, legislative, or judicial branch of the Government of the United States"). For a list of many other similar statutes, see *United States v Wells*, 519 US 482, 505–07 and nn 8–10 (1997) (Stevens, J, dissenting) (citing more than one hundred federal statutes prohibiting false statements to government officials in various settings).

[141] See Steven R. Morrison, *When Is Lying Illegal? When Should It Be? A Critical Analysis of the Federal False Statements Act*, 43 John Marshall L Rev 111, 125 (2009).

erty.[142] With the New Deal and its dramatic growth in regulatory programs that relied on self-reporting, however, "[t]he Government's concern was no longer merely with the direct loss of property or money; it now had a strong interest in preventing the loss of information through inaccurate and untruthful reporting."[143] Congress therefore expanded the act still further to prohibit any lie to the government without regard to whether the lie was intended to obtain a monetary benefit or whether it caused any material harm to the government.[144] To be sure, the act and similar statutes prohibit lies that may cause quite tangible harms by skewing government decisions that have material consequences. These laws, however, cast a wider net than perjury laws. For example, some target those lies that are "predictably capable of affecting" government decision making;[145] such decisions can take a wide variety of forms, including decisions to grant a benefit or contract, as well as decisions about whether and how to deploy the government's investigative resources.[146] Such statutes thus broadly target "material" falsity in communications with the government.[147] In an effort to tighten the connection between the targeted lies and demonstrable harm—and thus limit the potential for government overreaching—Justice Ginsburg is among those to suggest a more circumscribed focus for the act that targets lies "designed

---

[142] See id at 126.

[143] Green, 53 Hastings L J at 192 (cited in note 120).

[144] See Morrison, 43 John Marshall L Rev at 127 (cited in note 141); see also *United States v Yermian*, 468 US 63, 71 (1984) (describing how the act was originally interpreted to apply to lies intended to defraud the federal government out of its property or money, but was later amended to more broadly prohibit deceptive communications that interfered with or obstructed lawful government functions); id at 79–80 (Rehnquist, J, dissenting) (same); *Brogan v United States*, 522 US 398, 412 (1998) (same).

[145] See, for example, *Kungys v United States*, 485 US 759, 771 (1988) (explaining that a statement is "material" if "predictably capable of affecting" government decision).

[146] See *United States v Gilliland*, 312 US 86, 93 (1941) ("The amendment indicated the congressional intent to protect the authorized functions of governmental departments and agencies from the perversion which might result from the deceptive practices described."); Varat, 53 UCLA L Rev at 1114–15 (cited in note 17) ("Lies in the course of official government proceedings risk producing false beliefs in the minds of official investigators, risking perversion of the investigative process. Arguably, the deceptions in those instances also interfere with the reasoning processes of—and the respect owed to—the deceived parties, and are likely to influence their behavior.").

[147] See, for example, 18 USC § 1001 (prohibiting knowingly and willfully making "any materially false, fictitious or fraudulent statement or representation . . . in any matter within the jurisdiction of the executive, legislative, or judicial branch of the Government of the United States").

to elicit a benefit from the Government or to hinder Government operations."[148]

Recall too the wide range of laws that prohibit individuals from falsely representing that they speak on behalf of the government or from falsely impersonating a government official.[149] To be sure, such lies may cause second-party harms to listener autonomy, as listeners may make very different decisions in response to speech that they attribute to a government official.[150] But such laws also seek to address third-party harms by prohibiting lies that create doubt in the public's mind about who speaks for the government and thus whether purported government officials can be trusted. As the Supreme Court explained nearly a century ago,

> In order that the vast and complicated operations of the government of the United States shall be carried on successfully and with a minimum of friction and obstruction, it is important—or at least, Congress might reasonably so consider it—not only, that the authority of the governmental officers and employees be respected in particular cases, but that a spirit of respect and good will for the government and its officers shall generally prevail. And what could more directly impair this spirit than to permit unauthorized and unscrupulous persons to go about the country falsely assuming, for fraudulent purposes, to be entitled to the respect and credit due to an officer of the government?[151]

Under what circumstances do such lies threaten third-party harms to the public trust of the sort that would justify their regulation consistent with the First Amendment? Recall that each of the *Alvarez* opinions attended to the related possibility that the

---

[148] *Brogan v United States*, 522 US 398, 409 (1998) (Ginsburg, J, concurring); see also Morrison, 43 John Marshall L Rev at 139 (cited in note 141) (urging that the act be interpreted or amended to prohibit lies told to the government with the capacity to secure money, jobs, benefits, or "other things of value" or that "giv[e] false information which frustrates lawful regulation").

[149] See, for example, 18 USC § 912 (criminalizing the actions of those who "falsely assume[] or pretend[] to be an officer or employee acting under the authority of the United States or any department, agency, or officer thereof, and acts as such"); 18 USC § 709 (prohibiting a speaker's unauthorized use of federal agencies' names in a manner reasonably calculated to convey the impression that the speaker's message was approved or endorsed by the agency).

[150] See Norton, 88 BU L Rev at 592–94 (cited in note 115) (describing how a message's perceived governmental source may change the credibility with which listeners receive it).

[151] See *United States v Barnow*, 239 US 74, 78 (1915); id at 80 ("It is the aim of the section not merely to protect innocent persons from actual loss through reliance upon false assumptions of Federal authority, but to maintain the general good repute and dignity of the service itself.").

lies targeted by the Stolen Valor Act threatened generalized and intangible third-party harm by undermining the government's interest in the integrity of its military honor system.[152] Indeed, all three of the *Alvarez* opinions analogized the Stolen Valor Act to trademark law,[153] which provides a helpful (but by no means perfect) parallel for thinking about such harms.[154] More specifically, trademark infringement actions recognize the possibility that lies about the source of products and thus their perceived quality may not only cause second-party harms to listeners who may be deceived into making different purchasing decisions, but may also pose third-party harms to legitimate trademark holders.[155] Trademark infringement actions thus seek to prevent one party from capitalizing on the additional persuasive effects of having its message's (or product's) source misattributed to another, potentially more credible, party.[156] The Stolen Valor Act similarly sought to

---

[152] More specifically, the government claimed that Mr. Alvarez's lies about receiving the Medal of Honor damaged the public's trust in the government's program of awarding medals to individuals who in fact deserved them and that lies about the receipt of military medals thus undermine the message it seeks to convey by awarding such medals. See Reply Brief of the United States, *United States v Alvarez*, No 11-210, *13 (filed Feb 13, 2012) (available on Westlaw at 2012 WL 454625) ("The government employs military honors to convey a message to the public that the recipient has been endorsed by the government as part of a select group. The aggregate effect of false claims undermines this purpose, not by harming public opinion of the awards or true recipients, but by diluting the medals' message of prestige and honor. By creating the misimpression that the claimant has received a medal for fictitious conduct that likely bears no relation to the government's standards for awarding each medal, false claims undermine the government's efforts to maintain selectivity and to convey information about recipients' conduct.").

[153] See *Alvarez*, 132 S Ct at 2547 (plurality), citing *San Francisco Arts & Athletics, Inc. v United States Olympic Comm.*, 483 US 522, 539–40 (1987); id at 2554 (concurring opinion) ("Statutes prohibiting trademark infringement present, perhaps, the closest analogy to the present statute."); id at 2559 (dissent) (drawing analogy to trademark law).

[154] Trademarks are a form of speech about the source of products upon which consumers rely for information that gives them confidence that those products will have the qualities that they expect from that source. See, for example, Robert G. Bone, *Taking the Confusion Out of "Likelihood of Confusion": Toward a More Sensible Approach to Trademark Infringement*, 106 Nw U L Rev 1307, 1311–12 (2012).

[155] See id at 1312 ("[T]rademark law protects sellers as well as consumers."). Along the same lines, federal trademark law also gives rise to an action for "dilution by tarnishment," which refers to an "association arising from the similarity between a mark or trade name and a famous mark that harms the reputation of the famous mark." 15 USC § 1125(c)(2)(C); see also *Starbucks Corp. v Wolfe's Borough Coffee, Inc.*, 588 F3d 97, 110 (2nd Cir 2009) ("A trademark may be tarnished when it is linked to products of shoddy quality or is portrayed in an unwholesome or unsavory context, with the result that the public will associate the lack of quality or lack of prestige in the defendant's goods with the plaintiff's unrelated goods.").

[156] See Ann Bartow, *Likelihood of Confusion*, 41 San Diego L Rev 721, 745 (2004) ("Legal protections for trademarks are doctrinally justified by the need to prevent consumer confusion, which potentially disadvantages both individuals who are tricked by confusing or

prevent parties from wrongly capitalizing on the prestige of military honors in ways that might cause second-party harm by shaping listeners' decisions as well as third-party harms by undermining the value of the honors themselves to the medal winners and the government.

But such third-party harms are considerably less tangible and more diffuse than many other types of harm, raising especially challenging problems of proof and causation that may embolden government to punish lies for partisan or other illegitimate purposes.[157] Justice Kennedy's plurality opinion thus appropriately counseled caution in this regard.[158] In contrast to the concurring and dissenting opinions—which assumed such harm without requiring, much less evaluating, any evidence of its existence[159]— Justice Kennedy found that the government had not proven a causal connection between the regulated lies and its compelling interest in preventing the dilution of the value of military honors.[160] Although he did not identify the sort of proof he would

---

deceptive trademarks into purchasing goods and services other than those they intended to procure, and the providers of goods or services who lose sales when consumers are confused or deceived."); Barton Beebe, *Search and Persuasion in Trademark Law*, 103 Mich L Rev 2020, 2021 (2005) ("Trademarks exist only to the extent that consumers perceive them as designations of source. Infringement occurs only to the extent that consumers perceive one trademark as referring to the source of another.").

[157] For related reasons, a number of scholars have urged that trademark law focus not simply on consumer deception but instead more precisely on actual harm to consumers and trademark holders. See, for example, Bone, 106 Nw U L Rev at 1308 (cited in note 154) (criticizing multifactor test for assessing likelihood of confusion as "an open-ended and relatively subjective approach that generates serious litigation uncertainty, chills beneficial uses of marks, and supports socially problematic expansions of trademark law"); Mark A. Lemley and Mark McKenna, *Irrelevant Confusion*, 62 Stan L Rev 413, 414–16 (2010) (criticizing trademark law as undermining important speech interests by focusing on whether the allegedly infringing mark confuses consumers rather than on whether it materially affects consumers' purchasing decisions); Rebecca Tushnet, *Running the Gamut from A to B: Federal Trademark and False Advertising Law*, 159 U Pa L Rev 1305, 1344–45 (2011) (urging trademark law to focus on misleading communications that materially affect consumers' decision making).

[158] See *Alvarez*, 132 S Ct at 2549–50.

[159] See id at 2555 (Breyer, J, concurring) ("To permit those who have not earned those honors to claim otherwise dilutes the value of the awards. Indeed, the Nation cannot fully honor those who have sacrificed so much for their country's honor unless those who claim to have received its military awards tell the truth."); id at 2559 (Alito, J, dissenting) ("[T]he proliferation of false claims about military awards blurs the signal given out by the actual awards by making them seem more common than they really are, and this diluting effect harms the military by hampering its efforts to foster morale and esprit de corps").

[160] Id at 2549 ("The Government must demonstrate that unchallenged claims undermine the public's perception of the military and the integrity of its award system. This showing has not been made. . . . There must be a direct causal link between the restriction imposed and the injury to be prevented. The link between the Government's interest in protecting

have found probative of this causal connection, we might look for confirmation that such lies actually shaped meaningful decisions in specific contexts.[161]

For example, consider the many statutes that punish lies about a different type of credential: one's status as a law enforcement officer.[162] Because police officers' unusual power means that members of the public generally consider all interactions with law enforcement as potentially high-stakes in nature, such lies threaten not only significant second-party harms to their individual listeners[163] but also third-party harms to the public's trust in, and thus the effectiveness of, law enforcement. Members of the public who cannot be confident that police officers are who they claim to be will be less likely to cooperate with the police.[164] In light of the significant second- and third-party harms in play, courts have thus appropriately interpreted the statutory language—which generally prohibits lies about one's status as a law enforcement officer that seek to obtain "something of value"[165]—fairly broadly to prohibit a range of lies that shape the public's interaction with (purported) law enforcement. Examples include such lies as those told in an

---

the integrity of the military honors system and the Act's restriction on the false claims of liars like respondent has not been shown.").

[161] In contrast, the Stolen Valor Act was not limited to any particular context, nor did it focus on any specific decisions.

[162] See, for example, Va Code Ann § 18.2-174 (making it a crime to pretend or assume to be a law enforcement officer). Note that at least one federal judge has relied on *Alvarez* in dissent to cast doubt on such statutes, questioning whether lies about one's police officer status should be treated any differently for First Amendment purposes than about one's status as a Congressional Medal of Honor winner. *United States v Chappell*, 691 F3d 388, 402 (4th Cir 2012) (Wynn dissenting) (dissenting from majority decision that upheld constitutionality of state law that prohibits individuals from falsely assuming or pretending to be a law enforcement officer).

[163] Id at 392, 398 (majority) ("By protecting unsuspecting citizens from those who falsely pretend to be law enforcement officers, the statute serves the Commonwealth's critical interest in public safety. . . . In addition to promoting public safety, the statute deters individuals from pretending to be police officers in an attempt to evade fines, incarceration, and other state-imposed sanctions. . . .").

[164] See *Locurto v Guilani*, 447 F3d 159, 178–79 (2d Cir 2006) ("Police officers and firefighters alike are quintessentially public servants. As such, part of their job is to safeguard the public's opinion of them, particularly with regard to the respect that police officers and firefighters accord the members of that community. . . .").

[165] See, for example, 18 USC § 912 (criminalizing the actions of anyone who "falsely assumes or pretends to be an officer or employee acting under the authority of the United States or any department, agency, or officer thereof" and who "in such pretended character demands or obtains any . . . thing of value"); 18 USC § 76 (making it a crime to "demand or obtain from any person or from the United States . . . any money, paper, document, or other thing of value" while falsely assuming or pretending to be a federal government official or employee).

effort to avoid speeding tickets, or to convince a listener to share information she was otherwise unwilling to divulge.[166]

I close with a short note on campaign lies. To be sure, a political candidate's lies about her credentials pose an especially challenging First Amendment question. Such lies should fall into the category of low-value lies because lies about having a degree or a military decoration are "easily verifiable" and do not concern matters involving philosophy, religion, history, and similar areas that trigger substantial chilling effects and government overreaching. Moreover, such lies pose second-party autonomy harms to their listeners (especially if they can be shown as material to a voter's vote) and may also pose significant if intangible third-party harms if they undermine public confidence in the integrity of the political process.[167] On the other hand, such laws themselves threaten significant First Amendment harms because they regulate expression in a context in which we especially fear government overreaching and partisan abuse.[168] In short, such lies frustrate important First Amendment interests—but in a context where the countervailing First Amendment dangers are unusually acute. These competing and very substantial concerns illustrate why this is such a difficult constitutional issue, and I have little to add to the many commentators who have thoughtfully examined this question in detail.[169] As Frederick Schauer has observed, "this is an area in which it is easy to suspect that any cure could be substantially worse than

---

[166] See *Lepowitch*, 318 US at 705 ("[A] person may be defrauded although he parts with something of no measurable value at all," as the Court found to be the case where defendant's lie about being an FBI agent caused his listener to divulge information about another person's location); *United States v Ramos-Arenas*, 596 F3d 783 (10th Cir 2010) (interpreting the statute to prohibit the defendant's lie about being a federal law enforcement officer when told to prevent a state trooper from ticketing the defendant's friend for speeding); id at 788 (noting that such lie provided value to the liar "if only in elevating his status in [his girlfriend's] eyes").

[167] See William P. Marshall, *False Campaign Speech and the First Amendment*, 153 U Pa L Rev 285, 294–96 (2004).

[168] See *Alvarez*, 132 S Ct at 2556 (Breyer, J, concurring) ("expressing [no] view on the validity of those cases" rejecting First Amendment challenges to statutes prohibiting certain campaign lies); see also Marshall, 153 U Pa at 297–300 (cited in note 167).

[169] The many thoughtful discussions of these issues include Gerald G. Ashdown, *Distorting Democracy: Campaign Lies in the 21st Century*, 20 Wm & Mary Bill Rts J 1085 (2012); Richard L. Hasen, *A Constitutional Right to Lie in Campaigns and Elections?* (UC Irvine School of Law Research Paper No 2012-68, Sept 24, 2012), online at http://papers.ssrn.com/sol3/papers.cfm?abstract_id=2151618; Marshall, 153 U Pa L Rev 285 (cited in note 167).

the disease."[170] In short, I do not pretend that the approach suggested in this article will generate easy answers to hard First Amendment controversies about the regulation of lies, but I do hope that it offers a framework for transparently acknowledging and grappling with the relevant interests.

III. Conclusion

Is there a First Amendment right to lie? As is so often the case, the answer is "it depends." People lie frequently and for a wide variety of reasons. Some lies are morally and instrumentally more troubling than others; some lies may even be morally or instrumentally valuable. Because some lies may have First Amendment value in their own right and because the regulation of many other lies threatens government overreaching or the chilling of valuable speech, we should presume that lies are fully protected by the First Amendment such that government generally may not regulate them unless it satisfies strict scrutiny. On the other hand, a category of lies about certain objectively verifiable facts within the speaker's personal knowledge sufficiently frustrates First Amendment interests to justify their treatment as a "low-value" category in which greater government regulation may be permitted to prevent certain harms.

The great number and variety of lies thus undermine efforts to characterize all—or none—as fully protected by the First Amendment. This requires us to draw some uncomfortable distinctions. Justice Breyer's approach does not relieve us of this discomfort, but instead challenges us to confront it by transparently grappling with the important competing interests at stake. I have suggested that we can better assess the potential harm of the sorts of lies targeted by the Stolen Valor Act when we understand them as lies about a speaker's credentials that might cause significant second-party harms to listeners as well as third-party harms to the public trust on which certain important government processes rely. Even so, however, First Amendment interests in checking the government's power to act as the ultimate arbiter of truth counsel that we take care when regulating such lies. Laws appropriately balance

---

[170] Schauer, 57 UCLA L Rev at 915 (cited in note 17); see also Varat, 53 UCLA L Rev at 1131–32 (cited in note 17) ("When core speech on controversial matters of public concern is implicated in this way, there is great danger in leaving the ascertainment of truth so readily to judicial rather than public determination.").

these competing concerns when they target lies that threaten second-party harms that take monetary or similarly tangible form,
or lies that cause third-party harms when demonstrably material
to high-stakes decisions in circumscribed settings.

DOUGLAS G. BAIRD AND
ANTHONY J. CASEY

BANKRUPTCY STEP ZERO

In *RadLAX Gateway Hotel, LLC v Amalgamated Bank*,[1] the Supreme Court returned once again to interpreting the absolute priority rule, the foundational principle of the law of corporate reorganizations. The opinion itself, however, gives no hint that the Court was revisiting an issue that it has confronted many times over the last century. Rather than unpacking the contours of absolute priority, the Court focused on what has emerged as a central theme of the Court's recent bankruptcy jurisprudence: the proper domain of the bankruptcy judge.

One might expect the Court to approach that question of domain as it has for administrative agencies.[2] After all, both bankruptcy courts and administrative agencies are non-Article III tribunals.[3]

Douglas G. Baird is Harry A. Bigelow Distinguished Service Professor, University of Chicago Law School. Anthony J. Casey is Assistant Professor of Law, University of Chicago Law School.

AUTHORS' NOTE: The John M. Olin Foundation and the Jerome F. Kutak Faculty Fund provided research support to Baird and Casey, respectively. We thank Thomas Ambro, Donald Bernstein, Timothy Grinsell, Aziz Huq, Brian Leiter, Jennifer Nou, and Eugene Wedoff for their help. Michael Turkel provided excellent research assistance.

[1] 132 S Ct 2065 (2012).

[2] The Court's approach to administrative agencies of course finds its foundation in *Chevron USA v Natural Resource Defense Council, Inc.*, 467 US 837 (1984).

[3] Indeed, it has been noted that bankruptcy courts could just as well have been organized as administrative agencies had history played out differently. See Douglas G. Baird, *Blue Collar Constitutional Law*, 86 Am Bankr L J 3, 15 (2012). Others have gone further and suggested that bankruptcy administration *should* be transformed today into an executive-agency model where lawmaking is done by the agencies charged with administering the bankruptcy law. See, for example, Rafael Pardo and Kathryn Watts, *The Structural Exceptionalism of Bankruptcy Administration*, 60 UCLA L Rev 384 (2012).

But the Court sees them in an altogether different light. Administrative agencies are entrusted in the first instance with carrying out federal policies. They are parts of the executive, and a politically accountable legislature can delegate matters to them. And the scope of that delegation is often viewed quite broadly. They enjoy considerable leeway. In contrast, the Court has confined the space within which the bankruptcy judge may operate.

Some of the explanation for this contrast lies in the different relationship that agencies and bankruptcy courts have with Article III courts. Bankruptcy courts are entirely within the Judiciary. Article III judges themselves appoint bankruptcy judges. Article III judges can withdraw cases from bankruptcy courts, or refuse to refer them to bankruptcy courts in the first instance. Moreover, every bankruptcy judge's interpretations of law are reviewed de novo on appeal in the same fashion as those of any other inferior court. But in addition to and quite apart from the different structural relationship, the Court's own understanding of bankruptcy law itself shapes its view about the powers entrusted to the bankruptcy judge.

There are three principal strands to the Court's bankruptcy jurisprudence. The first, embodied in *Butner v United States*[4] and its progeny, centers on the idea that the bankruptcy forum must vindicate nonbankruptcy rights. In contrast to administrative agencies that give shape to federal policies, bankruptcy judges should not unsettle nonbankruptcy rights—rights that are largely creatures of state rather than federal law. In the absence of a clear directive from Congress, those nonbankruptcy rights trump a judge's impulse to advance federal policy. The second strand, beginning with *Northern Pipeline Construction Co. v Marathon Pipeline Co.*[5] and continuing last Term in *Stern v Marshall,*[6] focuses on the limits of bankruptcy in a different way. Unlike the public rights at the center of the administrative state, the traditional state rights at stake in bankruptcy lie at the heart of the judicial power and cannot be entrusted to non-Article III courts. Bankruptcy judges must therefore limit themselves to deciding issues central to the administration of the bankruptcy process. They cannot issue a final judgment with respect to those controversies in bankruptcy that are "the stuff of the tradi-

---

[4] 440 US 48 (1979).

[5] 485 US 50 (1982).

[6] 131 S CT 2594 (2011).

tional actions at common law tried by the courts at Westminster."[7]

RadLAX is the latest manifestation of a third strand, one driven in large measure by the frequent inability of Article III courts to review the decisions of bankruptcy judges before it is too late to give the losing party an effective remedy. Even with respect to matters properly entrusted to bankruptcy judges, *RadLAX* makes it plain that the Court reads ambiguous provisions of the Bankruptcy Code in a fashion that narrows the range of decisions over which the bankruptcy judge may exercise her discretion—at least when the exercise of that discretion might impact nonbankruptcy rights. Where the statute is ambiguous and nonbankruptcy rights might be compromised, the preferred reading in those cases is the one that is more rule-like. As the Court put it, "The Bankruptcy Code standardizes an expansive (and sometimes unruly) area of law, and it is our obligation to interpret the Code clearly and predictably using well established principles of statutory construction."[8] The Bankruptcy Code should be read narrowly to ensure that bankruptcy judges stay on a clearly demarcated path.

That view is in stark contrast to the Court's approach in administrative law. There the Court observed long ago that Congress has established non-Article III tribunals "to furnish a prompt, continuous, expert and inexpensive method for dealing with a class of questions of fact which are peculiarly suited to examination and determination by [those] specially assigned to that task."[9] But in bankruptcy the Court sees flexibility in the Bankruptcy Code as a potential source of mischief. The need to accommodate practical difficulties works as a thumb on the scale in assessing the operation of administrative tribunals, yet such pragmatism is not part of how the Court approaches bankruptcy courts.[10] Bankruptcy courts, it seems, need a disciplining hand that ordinary agencies do not. This article attempts to make sense of this state of affairs and proceeds in three parts.

RadLAX is, in the first instance, a straightforward question of statutory interpretation, and Part I sets out the statutory provision that *RadLAX* confronts and identifies the interpretative challenge

---

[7] Id at 2609.

[8] *RadLAX*, 132 S Ct at 2073.

[9] *Crowell v Benson*, 285 US 22, 46 (1932).

[10] See Troy A. McKenzie, *Getting to the Core of Stern v. Marshall: History, Expertise, and the Separation of Powers*, 86 Am Bankr L J 23, 42 (2012).

it poses. Part II links *RadLAX* to the foundational question of the domain of bankruptcy judges, and Part III explores the consequences that follow from having federal bankruptcy policy vindicated in a forum so different from those of the administrative state. The conclusion returns to the puzzle of why the Court perceives the need for oversight so differently.

I. The "Fair and Equitable" Benchmark

The law of corporate reorganizations has as its central requirement that plans of reorganization be "fair and equitable."[11] The core substantive meaning of that phrase has long been settled. The "fair and equitable" requirement imposes a regime of absolute priority.[12] A plan must provide for full payment to the senior creditors whenever it provides anything to anyone junior.[13] The Bankruptcy Code, however, does not set out clearly the discretion that the bankruptcy court enjoys in deciding how the senior creditor is protected.

The *RadLAX* case itself grew out of the financial failure of the Radisson Hotel at Los Angeles International Airport. The debtor borrowed to renovate the hotel and build a parking lot next to it. The economic downturn of 2008 unsettled these plans. The debtor filed a Chapter 11 petition in August 2009, with the parking lot incomplete and owing its senior lender $120 million. No one believed the property was worth that much. After extensive marketing, the debtor found a buyer willing to acquire substantially all of the assets for a much lower amount. The debtor used this bid as the basis for its plan of reorganization.[14]

The debtor proposed an open auction. Even though it seemed unlikely that another buyer would appear, others would have a chance to make higher bids. The senior lender would receive all the proceeds. The junior creditors received no immediate payment under the plan, but the buyer the debtor found was willing to fund some distributions to unsecured creditors from the future profits

---

[11] 11 USC § 1129(b).

[12] See Douglas G. Baird and Thomas H. Jackson, *Bargaining after the Fall and the Contours of the Absolute Priority Rule*, 55 U Chi L Rev 738, 744 n 20 (1988).

[13] See Walter J. Blum and Stanley A. Kaplan, *The Absolute Priority Doctrine in Corporate Reorganization*, 41 U Chi L Rev 651, 654 (1974).

[14] *RadLAX*, 132 S Ct at 2068–69.

of the hotel.[15] The senior lender could make its own bid, but it would have to bid in cash just like anyone else.

The debtor argued that this plan was "fair and equitable" and fully respected the rights of the senior creditor.[16] The senior creditor was receiving all the proceeds of the sale, and the value of an asset is what it yields in a regularly conducted sale.[17] The "fair and equitable" requirement demanded only that the senior creditor be given the value of its claim. Someone who both receives the proceeds of an open auction and who participates in the auction on the same terms as everyone else is necessarily receiving the entire value of her collateral. A secured creditor does not have the right to dictate the entire course of the reorganization, even when it is owed more than the firm is worth.

The senior creditor argued that this understanding of the "fair and equitable" principle offered it too little protection.[18] It was entitled to the entire hotel unless someone else was willing to put up more than $120 million to buy it. Hence, it should also have the right to "credit bid," the right to participate in the auction without putting up any cash. As the senior creditor, it was entitled to all the cash that the sale produced. Any cash it gave to the auctioneer would necessarily be immediately returned to it. Hence, unlike other bidders, it should be released from having to put up cash.

Forcing the senior creditor to turn over cash that would be immediately returned serves no purpose other than to place an obstacle in its way. Borrowing cash, even for a short time, is not costless. Among other things, the senior lender is often not a single entity, but rather a consortium of investors, some based overseas. Coor-

---

[15] Debtors' Joint Chapter 11 Plan, *In re: RadLAX Gateway Hotel, LLC*, No 09-B-30047, Docket No 205, *§ 3.09 (Bankr N D Ill June 4, 2010). This profit-sharing provision may have been problematic independent of the credit bidding dispute. The debtor, however, argued that the buyer's willingness to share some future profits with junior creditors was not of concern to the senior creditor as long as no such obligation was imposed on other bidders. Though not raised on appeal, this backdoor distribution to the junior creditors might violate the "fair and equitable" requirement. While such "gifting" has become common practice in the wake of sales, it has been questioned regularly by appellate courts. See, for example, *In re DBSD North America, Inc.*, 634 F3d 79 (2d Cir 2011).

[16] See, for example, Brief of Petitioner, *RadLAX v Amalgamated Bank*, No 11-166, *9–10 (S Ct, Jan 28, 2012) ("Petitioner's Brief").

[17] *BFP v Resolution Trust Corp.*, 511 US 531 (1994).

[18] See, for example, Brief for Respondent, *RadLAX v Amalgamated Bank*, No 11-166, *19–20 (S Ct, March 2, 2012) ("Respondent's Brief").

dinating actions among them is hard.[19] Regulations may limit the ability of some to contribute new cash, even for a few minutes. The frictions such coordination difficulties present should not keep the senior creditor from taking its collateral when it prefers the collateral to the highest cash offer. So ran the secured creditor's argument.[20]

To resolve these competing arguments about whether a plan could provide for a sale without giving the secured creditor a right to credit bid, the Court in *RadLAX* turned to the part of the Bankruptcy Code that spells out what it means for a plan to be "fair and equitable" with respect to secured creditors.[21] This provision requires that the plan must provide the secured creditor with (1) a lien on its collateral and a note equal to the value of its secured claim; (2) a sale subject to credit bidding; or (3) "for the realization by such holders of the indubitable equivalent of such claims."[22]

This language contains an ambiguity. On the one hand, the provision is written in the disjunctive. As long as a sale without credit bidding provides the secured creditor with the "indubitable equivalent" of its claim, a plan is fair and equitable. Each of the avenues is an alternative to the other.[23] The provision that explicitly provides

---

[19] See, for example, *In re Metaldyne Corp.*, 09-13412 (Bankr S D NY 2009) (approving credit bid at the motion of 97 percent of the creditors in the consortium to overcome objections of 3 percent hold-out group).

[20] Respondent's Brief at 20–21.

[21] Section 1129(b)(2)(A) provides:

> (i) that the holders of such claims retain the liens securing such claims, whether the property subject to such liens is retained by the debtor or transferred to another entity, to the extent of the allowed amount of such claims; and (II) that each holder of a claim of such class receive on account of such claim deferred cash payments totaling at least the allowed amount of such claim, of a value, as of the effective date of the plan, of at least the value of such holder's interest in the estate's interest in such property;

> (ii) for the sale, subject to section 363(k) of this title, of any property that is subject to the liens securing such claims, free and clear of such liens, with such liens to attach to the proceeds of such sale, and the treatment of such liens on proceeds under clause (i) or (iii) of this subparagraph; or

> (iii) for the realization by such holders of the indubitable equivalent of such claims.

Section 363(k) gives secured creditors a right to credit bid in the absence of cause in those cases in which assets are sold outside of a reorganization plan.

[22] Id.

[23] *In re Phila Newspapers, LLC*, 599 F3d 298 (3d Cir 2010). The Third Circuit invoked the familiar cannon of textual interpretation that focuses on the meaning of disjunctive

that a sale with credit bidding is fair and equitable is not dispositive.
It does not exclude the possibility that giving the secured creditor
the proceeds of a sale without credit bidding might also provide
the indubitable equivalent of the secured claim and therefore also
be fair and equitable.

Of course, one can take a different view. While each section stands
as an alternative to the others, each sheds light on the other. Because
the provision explicitly provides that a sale with credit bidding is
"fair and equitable," one can infer that a sale without credit bidding
is not "fair and equitable." It cannot provide the secured creditor
with the "indubitable equivalent" of its claim. Inferring exclusions
of some things because of the inclusion of others is a well-recog-
nized part of how ordinary people understand language.[24] Called
"scalar implicatures," linguists have studied them closely for the last
fifty years.[25]

Consider the following two statements.

> An apartment building limits the pets tenants may have. It permits "cats,
> small dogs, or pets that are apartment friendly."
>
> Your nephew has asked you for a video game that has "big scary mon-
> sters, robots, or cool stuff."

Both these examples have the same structure as the provision of
the Bankruptcy Code the Court confronted in *RadLAX*. There is
a mandate and three avenues to satisfying it. In the first case, the
rule identifies the sorts of pet that a tenant may have; the second
example identifies the types of video game that your nephew will
like; the Bankruptcy Code identifies the plans that are "fair and
equitable." In all three cases, there are specifically blessed types
("cats" and "small dogs"; "big scary monsters" and "robots"; notes
secured by liens on the collateral and sales subject to credit bidding).
There is also a general category ("apartment friendly" pets; "cool
stuff"; plans that provide the "indubitable equivalent"). Each list
puts forward two discrete options, and leaves a large category that

---

lists containing the word "or." Id at 304–10; see also Antonin Scalia and Bryan A. Garner,
Reading Law: The Interpretation of Legal Texts 116–25 (West, 2012) (explaining the "Con-
junctive/Disjunctive Canon"). The Third Circuit based its adoption of this statutory canon
in part on 11 USC § 102(5), which provides that "'or' is not exclusive."

[24] The basic ideas are based on the work of Paul Grice. See Paul Grice, *Studies in the
Way of Words* 22–40 (Harvard, 1989).

[25] See generally Ryan Doran et al, *A Novel Experimental Paradigm for Distinguishing
Between What Is Said and What Is Implicated*, 88 Language 1, 124 (2012) (reviewing theoretical and experimental literature on scalar implicatures).

lacks a hard definition. What exactly is an apartment friendly pet? What exactly is cool stuff? What provides the indubitable equivalent?

The linguistic question we face in each case is the extent to which the meaning of the larger and more general category is informed by the inclusion of the other more specific ones. Does the reference to small dogs implicitly exclude large ones and tell us, by implication, that large dogs are not apartment friendly? Does the reference to big scary monsters exclude small ones, and, by implication, exclude the possibility that small scary monsters might be cool? Does the reference to sales subject to credit bidding exclude sales that are not, and, again by implication, exclude the possibility that sales without credit bidding can provide the indubitable equivalent?

Items on such a list can serve different roles. A specific item on a list might be understood as a specific illustration or a safe harbor, and not as serving to exclude others of the same type. The owner of a cat or a small dog is spared the effort of arguing that a particular cat or a particular small dog is apartment friendly. Specific items can provide context that enables the rule provider to understand the more general mandate. The nephew might list a specific type of video game that is acceptable without any intent that you exclude other games or draw inferences about what is not cool. Instead, he may have pointed to big scary monsters to make vivid what sorts of games are cool.[26]

It is axiomatic among modern linguists that one cannot determine how an ordinary speaker understands any of these statements merely by resorting to abstract principle. Instead, one must engage in empirical inquiry. As it happens, most ordinary native speakers of English think that the apartment building does not permit large dogs.[27]

---

[26] In the case of the nephew, another force may be at work. The ability to infer the exclusion of one thing from the inclusion of another is underdeveloped in young children. See Ira Noveck, *When Children Are More Logical Than Adults: Experimental Investigations of Scalar Implicature*, 78 Cognition 165 (2001); Anna Papafragoua and Julien Musolino, *Scalar Implicatures: Experiments at the Semantics-Pragmatics Interface*, 86 Cognition 253, 267 (2003). A speaker of English may infer a young age for the nephew from the way the preferences are spelled out and take this into account in trying to understand what is being said.

[27] We surveyed 2,000 individuals using Mechanical Turk, and 74 percent of the native English speakers opted for this interpretation. We ran an alternative survey of 2,000 different individuals using the word "and" in place of "or." The results were not meaningfully different: 77 percent of the native English speakers opted for the interpretation excluding large dogs. Web-based surveys, of course, rely on samples that, while diverse, are not randomly drawn. There are other potential sources of bias as well. Alternative

By listing small dogs as among the pets that are permitted, the speaker is understood to exclude large dogs. The speaker is telling us both that she judges small dogs to be apartment friendly, and that she has reached the opposite conclusion for large dogs. The purpose of an open-ended category is to allow for certain apartment-friendly pets that are neither cats nor dogs. It is still open whether canaries are apartment friendly, but the issue is resolved as far as dogs are concerned. Small ones are; large ones are not. In this example, the use of the adjective "small" is functioning as a scalar implicature for the typical native speaker.

Implicatures can be expected to be used in accordance with certain linguistic maxims.[28] For example, the two Gricean maxims of quantity suggest that a speaker will make his statement (1) as informative as necessary, but (2) no more so.[29] A speaker who includes the word "small" would, under the first maxim, be expected to include the word "large" if both small and large dogs were allowed.[30] The word's absence violates the first maxim of quantity if large dogs were allowed. The statement thus implies the exclusion of large dogs. As with other linguistic maxims, this one was anticipated by one of the standard Latin maxims of statutory interpretation. In this case, it is *expressio unius est exclusio alterius*.[31]

The same analysis could apply to the nephew's request. But ordinary native speakers of English believe that the nephew is perfectly open to the possibility that small scary monsters, like robots and big scary monsters, might be cool.[32] The nephew refers to large scary monsters to illustrate what might constitute cool stuff, not to create an excluded category of scary monster. This is consistent

methodologies, however, are not likely to produce qualitatively different results for questions such as this. See Adam J. Berinsky, Gregory A. Huber, and Gabriel S. Lenz, *Evaluating Online Labor Markets for Experimental Research: Amazon.com's Mechanical Turk*, 20 Pol Analysis 351 (2012); Laura Germine et al, *Is the Web as Good as the Lab? Comparable Performance from Web and Lab in Cognitive/Perceptual Experiments*, 19 Psychonomic Bulletin & Rev 847 (2012).

[28] See generally Grice, *Studies in the Way of Words* (cited in note 24).

[29] Id at 26.

[30] Of course, just "dogs" would have sufficed as well.

[31] The close connection between maxims of statutory interpretation and Gricean maxims has, of course, been long recognized. See, for example, Geoffrey P. Miller, *Pragmatics and the Maxims of Interpretation*, 1990 Wis L Rev 1179 (1990).

[32] Again we surveyed 2,000 individuals using Mechanical Turk, and 76 percent of the native English speakers opted for this interpretation. An alternative survey of 2,000 different individuals using the phrase "or any other cool stuff" in place of "or cool stuff" did not produce meaningfully different results (74 percent).

with an application of Grice's second maxim of quantity. The parallel maxim of statutory interpretation at work here is *eiusdem generis*. The specific examples (big scary monsters and robots) illuminate the large category ("cool stuff"). "Cool stuff" has to be like big scary monsters or robots in some way, but it does not have to *be* big scary monsters or robots.

Linguistic theory alone is still too primitive to explain when ordinary speakers will draw different inferences from statements that have the same grammatical structure. Much ink continues to be spilled over words such as "some" and "or." Linguists are not yet able to explain the difference between using the word "big" in asking for a video game with "big scary monsters" and using the word "small" in permitting tenants to have "small dogs" as pets. The best one can do is to observe that ordinary listeners understand these statements differently.

The understanding of ordinary speakers can change with only small changes in context. Even when we limit ourselves to an apartment's pet policy, different items on the same list can serve different functions. If goldfish are added to the list of permitted pets, ordinary speakers are not inclined to think that all other types of fish are excluded. They might think that goldfish are on the list not to exclude other types of fish, but rather to provide an example with which others might be compared.[33] There is more room to argue that tropical fish are permitted than there is room to argue that large dogs are apartment friendly.

This is simply to say that linguistic maxims, like their counterparts in statutory interpretation, can be helpful in identifying the dynamics at work, but they are less useful in pinning down the meaning of a specific statement. In understanding whether a particular adjective (small, gold, or big) implicitly excludes the others (large, tropical, or small) that are within the larger category (of dogs, fish, or scary monsters), context matters. Ordinary speakers may be familiar with apartments that have weight limits on dogs. They may also have listened enough to young children to know that they are not as attuned to the way that the use of adjectives may implicitly exclude what is not described. They may also think that young children make their illustrations vivid ("big scary monster") to convey what constitutes "cool stuff."

---

[33] In our surveys, a majority of the native English speakers opted for this interpretation (60 percent in one survey and 69 percent in the other).

All that being said, even context leaves matters unclear. The inference that the majority of native speakers of English draw will not be universal. One in four native English speakers thinks that the apartment permits large dogs if apartment friendly. For this minority, if someone wants to prohibit large dogs, their rules should not have open-ended categories. Exclusions should be explicit. Similarly, one in four speakers of English understands the nephew to exclude small scary monsters. He wants a video game with big scary monsters because these are the only sorts of monsters that are cool.

Even if linguistics were more advanced, one can progress only so far in interpreting a statute by relying on the understanding of native speakers. Legislation is not understood in the same fashion as ordinary language. The way statutes are drafted is so radically different from the way language is typically used that one has to be careful about focusing on the common understanding. The balance between clarity and redundancy is likely to be struck differently. Less may be left to implication, and ambiguity may arise for altogether different reasons.

Statutes are written in a special language and often with special care. Sometimes this makes the task of statutory interpretation easier. The drafters of the Bankruptcy Code, for example, created a concordance and ensured that when the same words and phrases were used in different places in the text, they had the same meaning. But precisely because they are trying to be clear, drafters may leave less to implication. Inferences that might be reasonable with respect to regular speech might not make sense with respect to legislation.[34]

At the same time, statutes contain language that is ambiguous in ways that ordinary speech is not. Drafting of legislation reflects the product of competing interests. Accommodating these may itself result in ambiguities that arise not by virtue of carelessness, but because each competing interest finds itself better off living with the ambiguity (and with its belief about how such ambiguity will be resolved) than continuing to struggle over text.[35]

As it happens, the difficulties we face in interpreting the section

---

[34] Grice's maxims, for example, emphasize concision. An ordinary speaker avoids redundancy. As a result, listeners draw inferences in order to give each word meaning. Grice, *Studies in the Way of Words* (cited in note 24). The drafter of a statute does not value and does not expect her listeners to value concision, at least not in the same way. Hence, inferences one would ordinarily draw make less sense.

[35] On the sources of legislative ambiguity, see Saul Levmore, *Ambiguous Statutes*, 77 U Chi L Rev 1073 (2009).

of the Bankruptcy Code at the center of *RadLAX* arise for just this reason. The provision itself reflects a compromise between those who favored credit bidding in all cases and those who did not. The provision was drafted in the mid-1970s in the shadow of a recent real estate bankruptcy case. A group of investors put up a modest amount of capital, formed a limited partnership, and had it borrow $1.45 million from an insurance company to build Pine Gate, an apartment complex outside of Atlanta. The lender agreed to look only to this real property in the event of default.[36]

After a short time the investors filed a bankruptcy petition.[37] The bankruptcy judge estimated the value of the property and confirmed a plan of reorganization in which the insurance company was given a note that the bankruptcy judge found was worth the value of the property.

The plan, in his view, provided the "indubitable equivalent." The empirical evidence suggests that bankruptcy judges provide unbiased valuations of assets, but these valuations are subject to wide variance and this variance alone may give the debtor an ability to capture value.[38] The debtor does not have to go forward with any particular plan before it learns the judge's valuation. If the judge provides a value that is too high, the debtor could walk away from the property. By contrast, if the judge announces a value that is too low, the investors could put in place a plan of reorganization and then flip the property, paying the senior creditor the artificially low amount set by the bankruptcy judge and pocketing the difference.

Guarding against this sort of strategic behavior on the part of the debtor is one of the things that a bankruptcy judge must do in trying to craft rules that vindicate the "fair and equitable" requirement. Bankruptcy lawyers and judges are aware of the *Pine Gate*

---

[36] See *In re Pine Gate Associates, Ltd.*, No B75-4345A, 1976 US Dist LEXIS 17366 (N D Ga Oct 14, 1976); *In re Pine Gate Associates, Ltd.*, 12 Collier Bankr Cas (MB) 607 (Bankr N D Ga Mar 4, 1977); see also Douglas G. Baird, *Remembering Pine Gate*, 38 John Marshall L Rev 5 (2004).

[37] Pine Gate turned out to be too far from Atlanta to attract the tenants willing to pay the rent the investors expected. Indeed, it attracted few renters of any kind. The property was not going to do well until there was more development in the area, and it became clear this would not happen for a long time. The property was no longer worth what the insurance company was owed. Moreover, if the insurance company foreclosed, the investors would be saddled with enormous tax liabilities. They took advantage of accelerated depreciation rules so that their basis in the property was much lower than its foreclosure value. Baird, 38 John Marshall L Rev at 7 (cited in note 36).

[38] See Douglas G. Baird and Donald S. Bernstein, *Absolute Priority, Valuation Uncertainty, and the Reorganization Bargain*, 115 Yale L J 1930 (2006).

problem and indeed know it by that name. One can argue that such cases provide a reason to entrust these issues to the bankruptcy court in the first place. Like much else in bankruptcy practice, the *Pine Gate* problem is not especially visible to outsiders. The case itself cannot be found in any of the standard reporters, nor is it in Westlaw; but bankruptcy judges and lawyers know it, worry about it, and talk about it.

The drafters of the Bankruptcy Code trusted the ability of bankruptcy judges to implement the fair and equitable rule through case-by-case development. The drafters, however, had to contend with representatives of real estate lenders who had the ear of some of the legislators and who took a different lesson from *Pine Gate*. For them, *Pine Gate* showed a downside to giving bankruptcy judges discretion over too broad a domain. In the course of vindicating other goals, bankruptcy judges will slight the fair and equitable requirement, even while giving lip service to it. These representatives wanted to corral the scope of bankruptcy judges' discretion and limit their ability to develop the "fair and equitable" rule.[39]

The compromise that emerged is the Bankruptcy Code's elaboration of fair and equitable with its two specific provisions—notes supported by liens and sales subject to credit bidding—and one general one—providing the indubitable equivalent. The drafters consciously left tension between them unresolved.[40] In other words, the legislative compromise itself introduced the ambiguity. We face a difficulty that does not arise when one person attempts to convey meaning to another.

The kind of ambiguity that emerges in these environments depends on what background rule of interpretation the contending interests think the courts will ultimately adopt. To put the point somewhat more formally, a compromise such as the one here is a Bayesian equilibrium in which neither party to the negotiations thinks it can improve its position given the position of the other and given its beliefs about how a court will interpret the ambiguity.

---

[39] See generally Baird, 38 John Marshall L Rev at 5 (cited in note 36).

[40] Complex statutes passed many decades ago are usually the work of many forgotten hands. Hence, most discussions of what the drafters believed they were doing are abstract and somewhat artificial. Whether an ambiguity was deliberate is a matter for speculation. Not so with bankruptcy. Its world is small, and everyone in it knows the two individuals who drafted the Bankruptcy Code. It is easy enough to ask one of them about such things, and we have. This is not to say, of course, that the drafters' awareness of the ambiguity should itself have any effect on how the language is interpreted.

The method that resolves the ambiguity, or at least beliefs about this method, is part of the background against which the statute is drafted in the first place.[41]

That the drafters themselves understood they were leaving matters ambiguous should caution against thinking that the text itself provides a clear answer.[42] Instead of adopting an interpretative rule that tries to resolve the meaning of the text, it may make more sense to adopt an interpretative rule that vindicates other objectives and assume that, over time, those who bargain over legislative language will negotiate with this rule in mind. *RadLAX* and the sequence of cases leading up to it may be understood as an effort to articulate such a background rule. We explore the rule that seems to be emerging and trace its origins in the next part.

II. Bankruptcy's Domain

In confronting the ambiguity in *RadLAX*, the Court could have leaned toward expanding the scope of the bankruptcy judge's discretion. One can argue that, in the absence of an unambiguous statute, much is sensibly left to case-by-case adjudication. Reviewing courts have little expertise with respect to reorganizing large corporations. Congress may have intended for bankruptcy judges to enjoy considerable discretion when it provided a general directive that plans be "fair and equitable" and allowed them to confirm plans of reorganization without staying them pending review by an Article III court.

---

[41] Others, of course, have made this point. See, for example, McNollgast, *Positive Canons: The Role of Legislative Bargains in Statutory Interpretation*, 80 Georgetown L J 715 (1992). The compromises that force courts to confront statutory ambiguity arise in many environments. See, for example, *United States v Taylor*, 487 US 326 (1988) (Speedy Trial Act); *Board of Education v Mergens*, 496 US 226 (1990) (interpreting provisions of Equal Access Act, statute forbidding discrimination against religion-based student groups). For a general discussion of the problem, see Courtney Simmons, *Unmasking the Rhetoric of Purpose: The Supreme Court and Legislative Compromise*, 44 Emory L J 117 (1995).

[42] See Levmore, 77 U Chi L Rev at 1083 (cited in note 35). The question of intentional ambiguity provides interpretative challenges in other contexts as well. Contract cases are full of examples where the parties have intentionally left it to a later court to determine the precise meaning of a provision. The interpretative role of courts in those cases is quite different from interpreting intentional ambiguity in a statute. See, for example, Omri Ben-Shahar, *Agreeing to Disagree: Filling Gaps in Deliberately Incomplete Contracts*, 2004 Wis L Rev 389 (2004) (discussing how courts deal with intentional ambiguity); see also UCC §2-204(4) (providing that contracts with open terms are valid if there is a basis for an appropriate remedy); *United Rentals Inc. v RAM Holdings Inc.*, 937 A2d 810 (Del Ch 2007) (adopting a "forthright negotiator" rule where only one party intended the provision to be ambiguous).

Credit bidding is, from this perspective, one of the many issues facing bankruptcy judges who supervise corporate reorganizations. It is their job to assess the value of credit bidding and weigh it against the competing objectives of the Bankruptcy Code. Although there may not be many situations in which restrictions on credit bidding make sense,[43] it is possible to imagine a narrow set of cases where obstacles to a secured creditor's bid are valuable because that creditor's participation in an auction might scare away other less informed bidders—even those who might place a higher value on the property.[44] Judges sensibly developing jurisprudence around the idea of "fair and equitable" should be attuned to such issues.[45] The Supreme Court, however, hardly looked at the merits of credit bidding at all. To understand the course it took, it is necessary to step back from the narrow question of statutory interpretation and connect it to the Court's other bankruptcy opinions.

---

[43] Indeed, Vince Buccola and Ashley Keller and Adam Mortara argued in an amicus brief in *RadLAX* that these situations were indeed so rare that a plan that prohibits credit bidding cannot be "fair and equitable." In making this argument, however, they focused on how credit bidding vindicated the absolute priority rule, not on general principles of statutory interpretation. Amicus Brief, *RadLAX Gateway Hotel, LLC v Amalgamated Bank*, No 11-166 (S Ct, March 8, 2012).

[44] The presence of the senior creditor and its ability to credit bid might chill the bidding and junior creditors would suffer part of the cost. This effect matters only when the asset's true value hovers close above the face value of the senior lien. The ability of the senior creditor to credit bid costlessly may aggravate the problem of the "winner's curse," the idea that a bidder who wins an auction has overpaid for the asset because she was willing to pay more than the market for the asset. This effect is magnified when one of the bidders has asymmetric information—all the worse to pay more than the amount that the party who knows the true value is willing to pay. The equilibrium is often that the other bidders anticipate this and therefore make no bid. This in turn pushes down the price the informed bidder pays. Paul Klemperer, *The Wallet Game and Its Applications*, 42 Eur Econ Rev 757 (1998) (noting that a very small information advantage can greatly increase a bidder's chance of winning and "greatly reduce the price he pays"); Paul Klemperer, *What Really Matters in Auction Design*, 16 J Econ Persp 169, 173 (describing how asymmetric information can depress auction bids as bidders attempt to avoid the "winner's curse").

[45] As our interest is in locating where the decision making about credit bidding resides, we are not focused on the merits of this argument. We do not want to overstate the argument for limitations on credit bidding. Among other things, limiting credit bidding is a particularly ineffective and crude way of eliminating the potential winner's curse (assuming the problem is real to begin with). Auction theorists have suggested more direct ways of designing nonascending auctions to deal with this situation. But very little work has been done to apply those design theories to bankruptcy. One notable exception is Paul Povel and Rajdeep Singh, *Sale-Backs in Bankruptcy*, 23 J L Econ & Org 710 (2007) (discussing ways to bias auctions against informationally advantaged bidders to increase the expected final bid). Povel and Singh note that while it may be optimal to exclude the informationally advantaged bidders in ascending auctions, it is "optimal to *always* let [them] participate" when the sale procedures can be freely designed. Id at 712. Nothing in the Bankruptcy Code requires ascending auctions or prohibits free auction design. See, for example, *In re Texas Rangers Baseball Partners*, 431 BR 707, 710 (Bankr N D Tx 2010) (noting the court's clear power to "author and adopt bidding procedures").

RadLAX is part of a family of cases in which the Court has limited the domain over which the bankruptcy judge may exercise her discretion. The most prominent of these is the sequence of cases beginning with *Northern Pipeline Construction Co. v Marathon Pipeline Co.*[46] and *Granfinanciera SA v Nordberg*[47] that continued with *Stern v Marshall* in 2011.[48] Those cases dealt directly with the fact that bankruptcy judges are not Article III judges and do not possess judicial power. As a result, they can issue final judgments only with respect to matters that are central to the administration of the bankruptcy process. *RadLAX*—and other cases not usually included in the *Marathon*-to-*Stern* list—embrace an analogous principle.

RadLAX provides a gloss on how the Court understands Congress to have exercised its bankruptcy power. Principles like "indubitable equivalent" allow for "unruly"[49] exercises of discretion. Hence, Congress intended that the boundaries within which such discretion is available should be narrow—particularly when the results of that discretion are unreviewable as a practical matter. The confirmation of a plan puts in place a sequence of events that is hard to reverse. Assets have been sold and new securities have been issued. The senior creditor no longer has a right to protest because the dispute is "equitably moot." The amount of free rein the bankruptcy judge enjoys must be seen in this light. Between two interpretations of the Bankruptcy Code that are otherwise plausible, the one to be preferred, at least when nonbankruptcy rights are in issue, is the one that limits the power of the bankruptcy judge to depart from objective benchmarks such as those that the market provides. This idea has long been an undercurrent in the Court's bankruptcy jurisprudence. Indeed, it is fundamental to the evolution of the "fair and equitable" doctrine itself.

The Supreme Court's first clean take on the meaning of "fair and equitable" came in *Case v Los Angeles Lumber Products*.[50] The Court treated these words as terms of art that meant absolute priority. The relevant precedent did not compel this understanding of the language. The Court could have picked instead an interpretation

---

[46] 458 US 50 (1982).

[47] 492 US 33 (1989).

[48] 131 S Ct 2594 (2011).

[49] *RadLAX*, 132 S Ct at 2073 ("The Bankruptcy Code standardizes an expansive (and sometimes unruly) area of law.").

[50] 308 US 106 (1936).

that gave bankruptcy judges greater freedom to decide whether a particular plan of reorganization could be confirmed. By choosing the absolute-priority meaning, the Court significantly limited the scope of discretion available to the lower courts in reorganization cases.

The Court's answers to other questions about the meaning of "fair and equitable" follow in the same spirit. In spelling out the "fair and equitable" test as it applies to unsecured creditors, the Bankruptcy Code prohibits junior interest holders from receiving any property on account of their existing claim or interest when those senior to them are not paid in full.[51] On its face, this provision adds little. If the firm owes the senior lender $200, and the firm is worth $100, there is no way to give anything to the junior stakeholders and comply with the absolute priority rule. When they are not being paid in full, the seniors are entitled to everything.

The old junior stakeholders, however, sometimes offer to make a new contribution to the firm. They insist that they are not receiving anything on account of their old interest. They are receiving a share of the reorganized firm on account of the new value they are putting in. In principle, acquiring an interest in the firm in return for such contributions does not violate absolute priority. The question, however, is whether the bankruptcy judge can even entertain such an argument. In *Los Angeles Lumber*, the Court suggested in dictum that, when senior stakeholders were not paid in full, participation by the junior stakeholders required new value from them in "money or money's worth."[52] Sweat equity was not good enough—regardless of the value a bankruptcy court might place on it.

When the Court confronted this question again in *203 N LaSalle*,[53] it found that giving the old stakeholders any kind of exclusive right to a share of the reorganized business, even in return for cash, was suspect. It was not permissible for the bankruptcy judge to rely on experts to determine that the old stakeholders were paying enough. The junior stakeholders could participate, but only if their contribution was market tested. It was not enough that the bankruptcy judge found it sufficient. The key issue was not the sub-

---

[51] 11 USC § 1129(b)(2)(B).

[52] 308 US at 122.

[53] *Bank of America Nat'l Trust & Savings Ass'n v 203 N LaSalle Street P'Ship*, 526 US 434, 437 (1999).

stantive right of the junior stakeholders, but whether the bankruptcy judge had been delegated the power to decide whether the junior stakeholders were entitled to exercise it and what it is worth.[54]

RadLAX follows in the same spirit. The substantive right of the senior creditors was not open to doubt. Because the assets were worth less than they were owed, they were entitled to whatever value the assets had. No one argued otherwise. The question rather was whether the bankruptcy judges had been delegated the power to choose the form in which senior creditors were given that value. Like her determination that a junior stakeholder is providing new value, the bankruptcy judge's determination that the senior creditor is receiving the "indubitable equivalent" is essentially unreviewable. The Court limited the impact of this unreviewable discretion to confirm a plan of reorganization by holding that it did not include plans that provided for sales without credit bidding. In the face of an ambiguous statute, the court opted for the reading that narrowed the options of the bankruptcy judge to reshape nonbankruptcy rights.

Limiting the domain of the bankruptcy judge's decision protects nonbankruptcy rights from dilution. We can see this at work in *In re River East*,[55] a case decided while *RadLAX* was before the Court. The issue in that case can be put simply. Debtor owes Bank $100 and owns Blackacre, which the bankruptcy court finds is worth $50. Bank demands it be given a lien on Blackacre for $100 and a note that has a discounted present value of $50. Debtor proposes a plan that it claims provides Bank with the "indubitable equivalent" of its claim. It offers to give Bank a stream of payments backed by a treasury bill that is worth $50. There is no doubt that the stream of payments that Bank is being offered is in fact worth the value of its secured claim as measured by the bankruptcy judge. Unlike the note secured by the building, the note secured by the treasury bills has a readily ascertainable market value and this value is $50.

---

[54] Id at 457–58. There was nothing novel about the idea that discretionary valuation can interfere with substantive rights or about using the market as a solution. Peter Leeson notes that even eighteenth-century pirates recognized this problem and applied a similar solution. Peter Leeson, *An-arrgh-chy: The Law and Economics of Pirate Organization*, 115 J Pol 1049, 1073 (2007). (Noting that the elected quartermaster would auction off items with uncertain value to prevent conflict and "constrain[] the discretion of the quartermaster, who might otherwise be in a position to circumvent the terms of compensation").

[55] *In re River East*, 669 F3d 826 (7th Cir 2012).

Hence, the debtor argues, the secured creditor is getting the indubitable equivalent of a $50 claim.[56]

Confirming such a plan, however, runs contrary to the spirit of *RadLAX* and the cases leading up to it. A plan that gives Bank a lien on Blackacre for the amount of its claim gives it a chance to capture upside in the event that the property proves to be worth more than the bankruptcy judge decides it is worth. The ability to enjoy liens provides a cushion against undervaluation—as does the ability to credit bid. We cannot be confident that a bankruptcy judge will guard against the problem of valuation variance in assessing "indubitable equivalence." Hence, we want to limit the range of circumstances in which the debtor can satisfy the "fair and equitable" requirement using this test.

Nothing in the provision setting out what it means for a plan to be "fair and equitable" explicitly bars the debtor from proposing a plan in which the secured lender receives only equity in the reorganized business, but those who do not trust the judge's discretion will resist readings of the Bankruptcy Code that allow such license.[57] When the secured creditor is provided with senior secured debt under a plan, it is more likely to be paid the true value of what it is owed even when the bankruptcy judge misvalues the underlying assets.

Together these cases start to form a pattern. On certain questions, the market and Congress are the only competent arbiters. To the extent Congress is unclear in addressing those questions, the Court will view it as providing as narrow a rule as is reasonably consistent with the Code's language.

This presumption arises not from ordinary understanding or some general interpretative canon, but rather from an interpretative principle indigenous to bankruptcy. From this view, bankruptcy policy is best vindicated when, even with respect to the business properly entrusted to them, bankruptcy judges are limited in their freedom to make factual decisions that may impact nonbankruptcy entitlements. It is for this reason, and not the understanding of the ordinary speaker, that a sale subject to credit bidding is more like a small dog than a big scary monster.

---

[56] 668 F3d at 832–33.

[57] See *203 N LaSalle*, 26 US at 457 ("[I]t was, after all, one of the Code's innovations to narrow the occasions for courts to make valuation judgments.").

III. Bankruptcy through a Chevron Lens

In bankruptcy, the threshold question is similar but covers a different type of power than the one at issue in administrative law. In the case of an administrative agency, there is a threshold inquiry about the extent to which Congress has effectively delegated lawmaking power to the agency in the first place.[58] That is to say, the "step-zero" question of administrative law is about which legal decisions fall under the agency power.[59] The answer determines when courts will defer to an agency.[60] In the case of bankruptcy, on the other hand, the threshold question concerns not the delegation of law making but the delegation of discretion to the bankruptcy judge to apply legal principles to the facts before her. Here the Court has consistently found that, when the underlying statutory language is unclear, there should be a presumption in favor of interpretations that limit the extent to which the bankruptcy judge can exercise her discretion where it may impact nonbankruptcy rights.[61]

The different issues at stake caution against pressing the analogy between bankruptcy and administrative law too far. Nevertheless, many of the factors that incline the Court to think an agency should be entrusted with an interpretation of a statute seem to suggest a

---

[58] Cass R. Sunstein, *Chevron Step Zero*, 92 Va L Rev 187 (2006); Thomas W. Merrill and Kristin E. Hickman, *Chevron's Domain*, 89 Georgetown L J 833 (2001).

[59] One should not confuse the decision at step zero with a decision about the *level of deference* being granted to the agencies once an issue is delegated. At step zero the decision it is about the *scope of delegation*. See Frank H. Easterbrook, *Judicial Discretion in Statutory Interpretation*, 57 Okla L Rev 1, 4–5 (2004) (lamenting the tendency of the Court and scholars to conflate the scope of delegation with the level of deference). The same is true in the bankruptcy context. There, the level of deference is set in large part by the unreviewable nature of the decisions. But the question of the scope of delegation is the one that was before the court in *RadLAX*, and the question of interest to us.

[60] The answer is a source of deep division among the Justices. Sunstein, 92 Va L Rev at 199 (cited in note 58). Justice Breyer has advocated a case-by-case inquiry looking at what "a sensible legislator would have expected given the statutory circumstances." Id. Justice Scalia has advocated an across-the-board presumption of delegation. Under this view, Congress is presumed to have delegated authority any time it creates ambiguities. Put another way, for Justice Scalia all the action occurs at step one. The Court has accepted neither view outright and has vacillated from points between them. Sunstein suggests that Breyer's view gained considerable (though not absolute) traction in the trilogy of step-zero cases of *Christensen, Mead,* and *Barnhart*. Id. In these cases the standard for step zero has blurred a little (at least rhetorically) into the inquiry for subsequent steps. See *Christiansen v Harris County*, 529 US 576 (2000) (considering the procedural exercise of discretion as a factor relevant to the inquiry of whether the discretion was delegated in the first place).

[61] As we have suggested, there is no deference to the bankruptcy court in its interpretation of the ambiguous statute itself. Such interpretations are reviewed de novo.

posture toward interpreting the Bankruptcy Code that is different. Instead, bankruptcy judges, when the statute is ambiguous, should be able to apply a general standard to a given set of facts. A bankruptcy court makes its decision by formal adjudications[62] with the force of law.[63] Moreover, the arguments about flexibility, expertise, and institutional competence that have been put forward to support the delegation of authority to administrative agencies apply similarly to bankruptcy courts.[64] The bankruptcy court possesses an expertise in administering the Bankruptcy Code, and that administration—especially when it turns on the facts of a particular case—is highly complex and not particularly amenable to inflexible rules. Case-by-case adjudication allows for the natural evolution of sound practices, practices that may not be particularly amenable to top-down directives.[65]

It is in part the accountability of agencies—because they are appointed by an elected branch—that justifies giving them room to maneuver,[66] and bankruptcy courts are among the least politically accountable entities. They are neither elected, nor appointed by an

---

[62] *Christensen*, 529 US at 587 (distinguishing "a formal adjudication or notice-and-comment rulemaking" from opinion letters in holding that the latter did not have the markings of legislative delegation of the former); *United States v Mead*, 533 US 218, 230 (2001) (noting the "overwhelming number" of cases applying *Chevron* deference dealt with "the fruits of notice-and-comment rulemaking or formal adjudication").

[63] *Mead*, 533 US at 226–27 ("We hold that administrative implementation of a particular statutory provision qualifies for *Chevron* deference when it appears that Congress delegated authority to the agency generally to make rules carrying the force of law, and that the agency interpretation claiming deference was promulgated in the exercise of that authority."). Of course, some rulings of the bankruptcy court no longer have the force of law after *Stern* and *Marathon*. But matters not excluded by those cases are still understood to be decided with the force of law.

[64] But see *Stern*, 131 S Ct at 2615 ("This is not a situation in which Congress devised an 'expert and inexpensive method for dealing with a class of questions of fact which are particularly suited to examination and determination by an administrative agency specially assigned to that task.' *Crowell*, 285 U.S. at 46; see *Schor*, supra, at 855–856."). Of course others have argued that any reference to the expertise of administrative agencies is a fiction itself. See Easterbrook, 57 Okla L Rev at 3 n 6 (cited in note 59).

[65] *Barnhart v Walton*, 535 US 212, 222 (2002) ("[T]he interstitial nature of the legal question, the related expertise of the Agency, the importance of the question to administration of the statute, the complexity of that administration, and the careful consideration the Agency has given the question over a long period of time all indicate that *Chevron* provides the appropriate legal lens through which to view the legality of the Agency interpretation here at issue."). For an interesting game theoretic analysis of the delegation choice in a context that involves only agencies and Article III courts, see Dennis W. Carlton and Randal C. Picker, *Antitrust and Regulation* (forthcoming 2013) online at http://www.nber.org/chapters/c12565.pdf.

[66] The degree to which accountability actually exists for administrative agencies is open to debate.

elected branch. But accountability is a much less weighty factor when the discretion is being exercised over factual findings than over legal interpretations. Legal interpretations are a form of law making.[67] That is traditionally a function of elected government. Factual determinations are not.

The explanation for the Court's reluctance to find that Congress entrusted bankruptcy courts to apply broad standards to the facts before her may lie in the way that *RadLAX* is connected to other parts of the Court's bankruptcy jurisprudence. *Butner* stands for the idea that nonbankruptcy rights create a baseline. The law of corporate reorganizations is designed to help investors solve the collective-action problem they face when their firm encounters financial distress. Bankruptcy provides a forum in which they can sort out conflicting claims when the assets are insufficient to pay everyone off in full. Nothing in this policy requires altering the priority that one creditor enjoys over another outside of bankruptcy.[68]

Once one accepts this principle, it is only a short step to assume that Congress is similarly reluctant to expand the discretion that bankruptcy courts enjoy. Discretion with respect to questions such as the value of a nonbankruptcy entitlement can result in this entitlement being slighted. As *203 N LaSalle* suggests, when markets are available to assess the value of nonbankruptcy entitlements, there is no need for a bankruptcy judge to do so.

The need to guard the nonbankruptcy rights closely might seem to lead to limiting the power of bankruptcy judges to reshape them. But it is not a necessary response. Adherence to *Butner* might not require limiting the power of bankruptcy judges. Taking *Butner* seriously only means that whoever is entrusted with the power to affect the nonbankruptcy rights of parties should be well aware of and respect that principle. Indeed, there is no reason to think bankruptcy judges will systematically slight nonbankruptcy rights or that rules are needed to rein them in. Not only are bankruptcy courts likely to be aware of the importance of the *Butner* principle, they are likely to have a comparative advantage (over Congress and Article III courts) in identifying which factual issues and decisions are prone to raise *Butner* concerns and go astray of nonbankruptcy rights. For what it's worth, the bankruptcy courts in *RadLAX* and

---

[67] See Margaret Lemos, *The Other Delegate: Judicially Administered Statutes and the Non-delegation Doctrine*, 81 S Cal L Rev 405 (2008).

[68] Thomas H. Jackson, *The Logic and Limits of Bankruptcy Law* 10 (Harvard, 1986).

Philadelphia Newspapers found that plans that denied senior creditors the ability to credit bid were not fair and equitable. It was the circuit judges who were divided.[69] Similarly, the bankruptcy judge in *River East* limited the breadth of plans allowed as indubitably equivalent to protect the value of nonbankruptcy rights.[70] Moreover, limiting the power of the bankruptcy court in these cases will not protect the nonbankruptcy rights in all cases. In particular factual scenarios, the bankruptcy court's discretion might be exercised precisely to protect the nonbankruptcy rights where the narrow rule-like reading is sometimes underprotective.[71]

Of perhaps even greater importance is the posture that the Court has taken to the constitutional problems inherent in delegating so much power to non-Article III judges. While one can trace some of the limits on judicial discretion in bankruptcy to an era in which judges in reorganization cases were Article III judges, today a large part of the rationale derives from the fact that bankruptcy judges are not Article III judges and that their decisions are hard to review. Indeed, in *Stern* the majority squarely rejected the dissent's argument that the implicit control that the judiciary has over bankruptcy courts by means of appointment, oversight, and appellate review somehow alleviates balance-of-power structural concerns.

Congress has the power to create substantive bankruptcy provisions that may alter state law rights, but any grant of discretion that allows the bankruptcy court to apply a general directive to achieve that same outcome begins to look like a traditional adjudication of private rights at common law. And those adjudications are the special province of Article III judges. Precisely because bankruptcy law is, by its nature, both vindicating and altering nonbankruptcy (often state law) rights, the Court worries more about those nonbankruptcy rights. The more Congress entrusts discretion of any kind to bankruptcy judges or anyone else who lacks the

[69] *In re River Rd Hotel Partners LLC*, 2010 Bankr Lexis 5933, *1 (Bankr N D Ill 2010) (denying motion to approve bidding procedures); *In re Phila Newspapers, LLC*, 418 BR 548, 552 (E D Pa 2009) (reversing bankruptcy court's rejection of bidding procedures).

[70] See *In re River East*, 669 F3d at 829 ("The bankruptcy judge rejected the plan, lifted the automatic stay, and dismissed the bankruptcy proceeding.").

[71] For an example of a case in which a rule-like interpretation slights nonbankruptcy rights, see *United Savings Ass'n of Texas v Timbers of Inwood Forest Ass'n*, 484 US 365 (1988) (rejecting the bankruptcy court's power to include the value of postpetition use of collateral in a secured creditor's adequate protection, even where it arguably was entitled to as much outside of bankruptcy).

attributes that Article III requires, the more constitutionally questionable the system becomes.

Put simply, Congress can alter nonbankruptcy rights but the bankruptcy judge cannot. The less rule-like the bankruptcy law, the greater the danger that the bankruptcy judge will be shaping bankruptcy policy rather than applying the one Congress has created. Moreover, the more one relies on the discretion of the bankruptcy judge, the more likely the bankruptcy judge will be adjudicating nonbankruptcy rights, a function exclusive to Article III judges. *RadLAX* puts in place an avoidance presumption that reads ambiguities in the Bankruptcy Code in a way that limits the ability of the bankruptcy judge either to alter nonbankruptcy rights or adjudicate them.

Unlike most areas of federal law, bankruptcy law has as its guiding principle the vindication of rights that exist independent of itself. It is one thing to allow a non-Article III tribunal to alter state law rights to achieve a uniform federal environmental policy, but quite another to allow it to alter those rights in the name of a statute that has the vindication of those very rights as one of its foundational principles. If Congress intends to change that nonbankruptcy law, it does so explicitly; if it intends to point to that law as a guide for application, interpretation, or gap filling, an Article III court may be required to adjudicate the matter.

This understanding of bankruptcy law embedded in *Butner* and *Marathon* naturally leads to *RadLAX*. If Congress wants a bankruptcy judge to vindicate some bankruptcy policy (and thus risk undermining *Butner* or running afoul of *Marathon*), it should speak clearly. If Congress wants debtors to be able to pay creditors in exotic coin that is hard to value, it must say so. If it wants to allow sales without credit bidding, it must be clear. Congress must be explicit if it wants to give bankruptcy judges the power to make subjective judgments (valuations, approval of sale procedures, approval of the form of payment) about what is "fair and equitable."

RadLAX is unlikely to have much direct impact on the way that bankruptcy judges apply the absolute priority rule. There are few cases where limits on credit bidding make sense.[72] In the vast majority of cases, the effect of limits on credit bidding is to deny the secured creditor some of the value of its claim. Hence, a plan with-

---

[72] See above at notes 44 and 45.

out credit bidding will rarely offer secured creditors the indubitable equivalent of their claim, and today's bankruptcy judges would be most unlikely to approve such plans. To limit the bankruptcy judge's discretion in these cases is to mandate the result they almost always reach anyway. But *RadLAX* matters because the presumption it brings to interpreting the Bankruptcy Code whenever deferring to the bankruptcy court's discretion might compromise the principles at work in *Butner* and *Marathon*.

In this way, the arc from *Los Angeles Lumber* to *203 N LaSalle* to *RadLAX* and its relationship to *Butner* and *Stern* give some meaning and direction to the Supreme Court's repeated admonition to adhere strictly to the text of the Bankruptcy Code. The opinion should not be understood as a general mandate to apply strong maxims of statutory interpretation to the Bankruptcy Code. Nor should it be read as an instruction to be narrow across all ambiguities, but rather only where those ambiguities intersect with the application of nonbankruptcy rights.

The importance of understanding that *RadLAX* is not a general mandate for mechanical application of the canons of interpretation can be seen in two examples. Courts have struggled with the appropriate treatment of executory contracts for intellectual property rights in bankruptcy. A provision of the Bankruptcy Code provides for special protections for holders of copyrights and patents, but not for trademarks. Contested is whether the treatment of trademarks is different when the more general provisions of the Code are applied.

If *RadLAX* were read simply as giving a thumb on the scale in favor of the interpretative canon of *expressio unius*, then it would suggest that, by giving special protection to patent and copyright, Congress has determined that patent and copyright deserved this sort of protection and trademarks did not. If Congress had wanted this protection for trademarks, they could have easily provided it. Hence, one should incline away from an interpretation of general principles to reach the same result. This approach seems wrong across several dimensions. The question about the consequences that flow from the rejection of an executory contract in bankruptcy has nothing to do with the domain of the bankruptcy judge's discretion over nonbankruptcy rights. Indeed, inferring that the debtor enjoys a greater power to reject trademark licenses than patent licenses expands the domain of bankruptcy and runs counter to the *Butner* principle.[73]

Another example can be found in a question that has divided a number of courts.[74] In drafting a series of amendments to the Bankruptcy Code in 2005, Congress enacted a number of provisions that had the effect of ensuring that individuals received comparable treatment regardless of which chapter of the Bankruptcy Code they filed under. Under the most literal reading, however, the various sections in combination appear to abolish the absolute priority rule in individual Chapter 11 cases. Apart from unmoored literalism, however, this reading of the Bankruptcy Code has little to recommend it. Nothing about *RadLAX*, however, pushes in favor of such a reading. The amount of discretion delegated to bankruptcy judges is not implicated. None of the concerns about bringing order to the unruly world of bankruptcy push toward excluding ordinary prepetition assets from the bankruptcy estate.

More importantly, the substantive presumption of *RadLAX* is not a blanket presumption of narrowness. When viewed in connection with *Butner* and *Marathon*, the *RadLAX* presumption is about limiting discretion where its exercise may alter nonbankruptcy rights. If the ambiguity in the statute does not involve altering nonbankruptcy rights or exercising anything akin to the judicial power with respect to nonbankruptcy rights, there is no reason to gravitate toward the narrow interpretation. Neither *Butner* nor *Marathon* is implicated.

As noted above, much of the Bankruptcy Code does involve the adjudication of nonbankruptcy rights, but that is not uniformly true. Some provisions are pure bankruptcy law. When Congress has left ambiguity over these provisions and where the bankruptcy court's discretion impacts only the federal rights created by the Bankruptcy Code, courts must look elsewhere for interpretative guidance. For example, when courts are interpreting the boundaries of voidable preferences and good-faith filing requirements, they should recall that each is a statutory matter that exists only as a function of

---

[73] Judge Easterbrook looks beyond mechanical rules of statutory interpretation to reach this result in *Sunbeam Products, Inc. v Chicago American Mfg, LLC*, 686 F3d 372 (7th Cir 2012).

[74] Compare *In re Shat*, 424 Bankr 854 (Bankr D Nev 2010 (Markell, J)), with *In re Stephens*, 2013 WL 151193 (10th Cir 2013) (in face of ambiguity, court will not read the Bankruptcy Code to erode absolute priority rule "absent a clear indication that Congress intended such a departure").

bankruptcy law and independently of nonbankruptcy rights. Voidable preferences exist only in bankruptcy and protect the integrity of the collective proceeding.[75] Similarly, the application of discretionary principles such as good faith filing can only be answered by resort to bankruptcy law principles.[76]

Ambiguities in these provisions do not implicate the *RadLAX* presumption. A question of how broadly a court can define a voidable preference should be viewed with the policy of bankruptcy in mind rather than some imported state law directive.[77] The same is true for ambiguities that may exist as to the breadth of anti-ipso-facto-clause provisions of the Bankruptcy Code. These are not provisions intended to vindicate nonbankruptcy rights but rather to further specific bankruptcy principles and bring coherence to the Code.[78] In none of these cases is there a question of the interpretation, adjudication, or discretionary application of nonbankruptcy rights.[79]

III. CONCLUSION

While *Stern* makes it clear that bankruptcy courts are not Article III courts, *RadLAX* adds the message that they are also not administrative agencies or anything like them.[80] The former narrows

---

[75] HR Rep No 595, 95th Cong, 1st Sess 177–78 (1977).

[76] See, for example, *In re Integrated Telecom Express, Inc.*, 384 F3d 108, 120 (3d Cir 2004) (noting the focus for good-faith filing is on whether the petition serves a valid bankruptcy purpose of either preserving going concern or maximizing the value of the estate).

[77] But see *In re PA Bergner & Co.*, 140 F3d 1111, 1118–19 (7th Cir 1998) (focusing preference inquiry on state law of letters of credit).

[78] For an example of where the interpretation of pure bankruptcy law can become unnecessarily mixed up with state law adjudication, see *In re Haire Ford, Inc.*, 403 BR 740 (MD Fla Bankr 2009). There the bankruptcy court was faced with the question of whether a third party could terminate an at-will contract with the debtor at the time of filing. The court found the termination to violate the clear policy but not the language of the Bankruptcy Code. Rather than resolving this ambiguity, the court created a state-law implied covenant to bar the exercise of the otherwise valid contract right in violation of bankruptcy policy.

[79] An example of this distinction can be found in the personal bankruptcy context in *Marrama v Citizens Bank of Mass*, 549 US 365 (2006). There the Court allowed the bankruptcy court to exercise discretion over decisions about who is eligible to convert a Chapter 7 bankruptcy to Chapter 13. The discretion there was over a decision about pure bankruptcy rights. Id; but see *Marrama*, 549 at 376 (Alito, J, dissenting) (arguing that the relevant statute unambiguously restricted the scope of discretion).

[80] An alternate approach in a world outside the constraints of *Butner*, *Stern*, and *RadLAX* would be to organize the bankruptcy system entirely in the administrative law model. It has been noted that it may be a historical accident that this did not happen. Baird, 86 Am Bankr L J at 15 (cited in note 3). And several scholars have toyed with the idea. See, for

the range of legal issues that they may decide; the latter limits the domain of factual discretion they may exercise in deciding those issues.

RadLAX crystallizes a substantive interpretive principle that has been in the background of the Court's bankruptcy jurisprudence for decades: in interpreting the Bankruptcy Code, courts should start with the presumption that the range of discretion a bankruptcy judge enjoys over issues that affect the application of substantive nonbankruptcy rights is narrow. Between two interpretations of the Bankruptcy Code that are otherwise plausible, the Court will incline toward the one that limits the power of the bankruptcy judge to unsettle those rights.

From the perspective of those deeply immersed in bankruptcy, the Court's opinion in *RadLAX* is unsettling. It embraces an approach to bankruptcy that, quite apart from its logical coherence, is divorced from reality. Someone reading the Court's bankruptcy opinions over the last three decades would have no idea of the extent to which the world it is trying to regulate has changed.

The bankruptcy world the Court confronted in *Marathon* was dysfunctional. The judges were former bankruptcy referees, sometimes corrupt and often of limited competence. Debtors ran roughshod over the rights of creditors, and firms often entered Chapter 11 only to bleed to death slowly. The bankruptcy world today is altogether different. Its judges are among the best in the federal judiciary. Bankruptcy judges as a general matter quickly dispose of cases that do not belong in Chapter 11. In large business cases, the judges are typically the equal of any Delaware Chancellor. They oversee the restructuring of multi-billion-dollar corporations with consummate skill. As a matter of sound judicial administration, it would make sense to give them more discretion rather than less.

Those who work on the ground view the bankruptcy court as creating an umbrella that protects a space within which interested parties can plot a future course for a distressed business. The process is necessarily a fluid one and works best with a decent measure of flexibility and pragmatism. There is no recognition of this state of affairs in *RadLAX* or indeed in any of the Court's bankruptcy opinions. The pragmatic imperatives at work when the court assesses

---

example, Pardo and Watts, 60 UCLA L Rev 384 (cited in note 3). The centrality of nonbankruptcy rights discussed above may make this more complicated than has been recognized—or at least may require a great deal more china to be broken. In any event, *RadLAX* is a significant move in the opposite direction.

tribunals for everything from workers' compensation to securities trading are altogether absent when it comes to bankruptcy. One can, of course, take the view that, when it comes to interpreting the Constitution or a bankruptcy law passed in 1978, today's realities are irrelevant. Nevertheless, the failure to recognize these realities is in the end the most striking difference when viewing bankruptcy through an administrative law lens.

DANIEL ABEBE

ONE VOICE OR MANY? THE POLITICAL QUESTION DOCTRINE AND ACOUSTIC DISSONANCE IN FOREIGN AFFAIRS

A common theme in foreign affairs law is the importance of the US speaking with "one voice" to the international community. Speaking with one voice, so the story goes, ensures that the US is not embarrassed by multiple, inconsistent pronouncements from the several states or the different branches of the national government when it takes a position on a foreign affairs issue.[1] Such acoustic dissonance from the US could potentially result in a loss of credibility, a reduced capacity to achieve foreign policy goals, and a greater chance of conflict with other countries. So, when the Constitution is unclear about the allocation of decision-making authority on an issue, but the President or the national government speaks first, the presumption in favor of speaking in one voice reduces the possibility of multiple governmental decision makers and permits the US to act clearly and decisively in foreign affairs. While it reduces acoustic dissonance, the presumption in favor of one voice

---

Daniel Abebe is Assistant Professor of Law, The University of Chicago Law School.

AUTHOR'S NOTE: Many thanks to Aziz Huq and David Strauss for comments, and to Stephanie de Padua and Lee Deppermann for excellent research assistance. All mistakes are mine.

[1] See *Baker v Carr*, 369 US 186, 211 (1962) ("Not only does resolution of such [foreign affairs] issues frequently turn on standards that defy judicial application, or involve the exercise of a discretion demonstrably committed to the executive or legislature, *but many such questions uniquely demand single-voiced statement of the Government's views.*") (emphasis added).

has two other effects as well: the centralization of foreign affairs decision making in the federal government vis-à-vis the states[2] and centralization of foreign affairs decision making in the President vis-à-vis Congress.

The Supreme Court applies several doctrines to effectuate the one-voice preference in foreign affairs. For example, the Court has developed preemption doctrines to limit the capacity of the states to interfere with the national government's prerogatives in foreign affairs. In several cases,[3] the courts have struck down state laws that purport to interfere with congressional statutes or touch upon Congress's Commerce Clause or Dormant Commerce Clause authority. In each, the Court relied on a notion of speaking with one voice in the face of potentially inconsistent state laws.[4] Crudely stated, when the federal government and the states act on the same foreign affairs issue—even if the state acts first—the one-voice presumption tends to protect federal government decision making.

In regulating the President's relationship with Congress, the Court's one-voice vehicle has been the political question doctrine. As elucidated by the Court in *Baker v Carr*,[5] the political question doctrine serves to insulate the courts from adjudicating cases that implicate issues that the Court views as properly resolved by the political branches. In *Baker*, the Court outlined a six-factor test, and this article focuses on one of special relevance for foreign affairs: "the potentiality of embarrassment from multifarious pronouncements by various departments on one question":[6] in other words, when adjudicating the case would lead to the possibility of embarrassment by inhibiting the ability of the US to speak with one voice.

In effect, the political question doctrine, at least as applied in the foreign affairs context, creates a first-mover bias: since the first mover is generally the first "voice" to speak authoritatively on a foreign affairs issue, its voice benefits from the presumption that one voice is preferred. And, since the first mover is most often the President instead of Congress, the political question doctrine typically serves to insulate the President's decision making from judicial

---

[2] For a discussion of foreign affairs federalism, see Daniel Abebe and Aziz Z. Huq, *Foreign Affairs Federalism: A Revisionist Approach*, Vand L Rev (forthcoming 2013).

[3] For a review of the cases, see id at 7–14.

[4] See notes 19–23.

[5] See 369 US 186, 217 (1962).

[6] See *Baker*, 369 US at 217.

review. At bottom, one factor of the political question doctrine's multifactor test suggests that one voice is almost always preferred and, given the President's capacity to act more quickly than Congress, it effectively means that the one voice will likely belong to the President.

Of course, the courts do not apply the political question doctrine in every case that touches and concerns foreign affairs, and the President does not always succeed in cases where the political question doctrine might be applicable—mostly because it is difficult for courts to weigh the political question factors. Sometimes, as a result, the courts perhaps unwisely exercise jurisdiction over the most complicated and sensitive of foreign policy issues. For example, in *Zivotofsky v Clinton*, the Supreme Court declined to apply the political question doctrine when confronted with the issue of whether Congress or the President had the authority to record the country of birth on a US passport for naturalized US citizens born in Jerusalem.[7] In vacating the decision of the US Court of Appeals for the DC Circuit, the Court held that a congressional statute permitting the designation of Israel as the country of birth for those persons born in Jerusalem did not present a political question,[8] despite the fact that the statute directly conflicted with the State Department's "longstanding policy of not taking a position on the political status of Jerusalem."[9] Rather, the Court held that the conflict was indeed justiciable because it only "demands careful examination of the textual, structural, and historical evidence put forward by the parties regarding the nature of the statute and of the passport and recognition powers"[10] normally associated with judicial review, rather than any consideration of delicate issues of international politics or the merits of US foreign policy.

While *Zivotofsky* demonstrates that the President does not always succeed in political question doctrine cases, the general operation of the doctrine combined with the political economy of foreign affairs decision making—the President as first mover—provides lat-

---

[7] See *Zivotofsky v Clinton*, 132 S Ct 1421, 1430 (2012) ("Recitation of [the parties'] arguments—which sound in familiar principles of constitutional interpretation—is enough to establish that this case does not 'turn on standards that defy judicial application.'") (quoting *Baker*, 369 US at 211).

[8] Id at 1430–31.

[9] Id at 1424.

[10] Id at 1430.

itude to the President to engage in activities that might not be per se constitutional but are later insulated by the Supreme Court's desire to avoid adjudication on the matter. What is less clear, however, is the wisdom of the one-voice presumption built into the political question doctrine. Even with this presumption, the courts lack a framework to distinguish between those foreign affairs issues where speaking with one voice is particularly important and those for which it is not. The political question doctrine, as currently applied, sweeps too broadly and lacks a useful, workable metric for distinguishing among foreign affairs cases, treating some as political questions but failing to draw a principled or meaningful line. This article begins that project.

This article examines the merits of the one-voice presumption of the political question doctrine. It has two goals. First, it aims to unpack the underlying assumptions supporting a presumption in favor of one voice in foreign affairs to determine the conditions under which the presumption holds. The traditional account about speaking with one voice focuses on the benefits of centralizing decision making in foreign affairs.[11] The creation of foreign policy and the provision of national security, among other things, are public goods best provided by the national government, rather than the states. Relative to the national government, the states are not as well placed to coordinate national policy and maximize social welfare for all Americans; in fact, they are more likely to pursue narrow, parochial policies that might be welfare enhancing for the state, but not for the nation as a whole. Beyond that, the benefits of centralization in foreign affairs decision making are plainly obvious in the context of the national government and the fifty states; the possibility of dozens of inconsistent pronouncements from various sovereigns justifies, to some degree, limits on foreign affairs federalism. In fact, exactly this lack of centralization in foreign affairs substantially contributed to the collapse of the Articles of Confederation.

But while this traditional account might justify limits on foreign affairs federalism and support a one-voice presumption for the relationship between the national government and the various states, it is not as convincing when applied to the relationship between President and Congress. Here, there are only two actors rather than

---

[11] See Jenna Bednar, *The Robust Federation: Principles of Design* 25–52 (Cambridge, 2009) (providing an account of the costs and benefits of decentralization).

potentially dozens, reducing the concern about problematic acoustic dissonance. Moreover, Congress, unlike the states, is well placed to engage in precisely the kind of trade-offs necessary to promote the public good. Congress also has much more foreign affairs expertise than the states, and the competency gap between Congress and the President is much smaller than that between the national government and the states. It's simply easier for Congress to solve collective action problems and reach decisions than the states. Along each of these dimensions, the traditional account justifying the Supreme Court's one-voice presumption is much weaker among the branches of the national government.

Despite the weakness of the traditional account in this context, it does not lead inexorably to the conclusion that the political question doctrine's emphasis on speaking with one voice is inappropriate at all times. Rather, it suggests that the one-voice presumption likely obtains only under certain external conditions. My second goal is to tease out those conditions under which speaking with one voice is most likely to produce the benefits associated with the centralization of foreign affairs decision making for the US, and those when the one voice might be unnecessary. Since we don't know how the courts weigh the different factors of the political question doctrine, measure the potential for embarrassment, or evaluate risks from multiple, inconsistent pronouncements, it might seem like a fool's errand to try to determine the conditions when these factors are more or less salient. Nonetheless, we know that the courts, in applying the political question doctrine, must engage in some ad hoc analysis of these factors when deciding to apply the doctrine or adjudicate the issue on the merits.

Building on prior scholarship on the role of international political factors and the use of polarity as a metric in foreign affairs institutional design,[12] I argue that the political question doctrine's presumption for speaking with one voice should vary with the position of the US in international politics. In simple terms, when the US is in a highly competitive international political environment—for example, when there are multiple powerful states or great powers in the world—the courts should apply a presumption in favor of speaking in one voice. Under this condition, speaking with one voice

---

[12] See generally Daniel Abebe, *The Global Determinants of U.S. Foreign Affairs Law*, 49 Stan J Int'l L (forthcoming 2013) (developing a theory of foreign affairs law based on the concept of polarity and changing geopolitical conditions).

is likely more important because the costs of multiple inconsistent pronouncements from the President, Congress, and the courts increase. Some of the values associated with the centralization of foreign affairs decision making—for example, clear communication of policy to the international community, speed of decision making, and determination of the national interest—are of greater importance when the US is navigating a complicated international political environment and has less freedom to pursue its objectives.

In contrast, when the US is a superpower or the dominant state in international politics—when it is the unipolar power—the necessity of rigidly adhering to a one-voice presumption diminishes. Under this condition, the benefits of centralization of foreign affairs are still present, but not as salient, because the US is pursuing its interests in a less challenging political environment. Stated simply, the more complicated the environment, the higher the cost of acoustic dissonance between the branches. As the environment becomes less complicated, the costs of acoustic dissonance decrease. Moreover, acoustic dissonance promotes transparency and public deliberation, values that are often sublimated in the multipolar world. Using the concept of polarity as a metric,[13] the wisdom of the political question doctrine's one-voice presumption is contingent on or a function of the position of the US in international politics.

How would the courts operationalize this as a doctrinal matter? The President certainly has institutional expertise in foreign affairs relative to the courts, and the political question doctrine, at least in the foreign affairs context, serves to ensure that the courts do not weigh in on issues properly committed to the political branches. At the same time, the political question doctrine requires the courts to make a threshold foreign affairs determination, namely, whether adjudication of the issue would cause the US embarrassment or create foreign affairs problems. Since the courts have to make an inquiry into geopolitical conditions anyway, the courts should simply apply a presumption in favor of speaking with one voice when the international political environment is most challenging (multipolar worlds) and relax the presumption when the environment is less challenging (the US as the superpower in the unipolar world). Shifting the presumption in this way would align the political question doctrine's rationale of centralizing decision-making authority

---

[13] Id (developing this argument at length).

when necessary, while still maintaining a role for the courts to adjudicate issues properly before them when the costs of doing so are likely to be lower. Moreover, it ensures that the political branches—most likely the President—are still tasked with making the foreign affairs determinations for which they are best suited. And it provides much more reasoned guidance to the ad hoc application of the political question doctrine today.

Part I of this article examines the implicit assumptions underlying the political question doctrine's one-voice presumption. Part II proposes a metric to determine the conditions under which the one-voice presumption obtains and describes its operation. It concludes by discussing the merits of the status quo in comparison to varying the one-voice presumption based on changing geopolitical conditions.

I. The Political Question Doctrine in Foreign Affairs

A. THE ONE-VOICE PRESUMPTION

At its core, the political question doctrine is a justiciability limitation on federal court jurisdiction.[14] Beginning with *Marbury v Madison*,[15] the Supreme Court has suggested that there are some questions or issues that properly come before the courts that, by their nature, are somehow political, and thus outside of the traditional scope of judicial review. When a court determines that the matter before it presents a political question and thus applies the political question doctrine, it refuses to adjudicate the matter and in effect provides absolute discretion to the political branches to resolve the matter.

Until the 1960s, the courts generally adopted a categorical approach to the political question doctrine in which some foreign affairs questions were deemed to presumptively or automatically require the application of the doctrine, removing them from the

---

[14] See *Baker v Carr*, 369 US 186, 210 (1962) ("Deciding whether a matter has in any measure been committed by the Constitution to another branch of government, or whether the action of that branch exceeds whatever authority has been committed, is itself a delicate exercise in constitutional interpretation, and is a responsibility of this Court as ultimate interpreter of the Constitution.").

[15] See *Marbury v Madison*, 5 US 137, 164 (1803) ("Is the act of delivering or withholding a commission to be considered as a mere political act belonging to the Executive department alone, for the performance of which entire confidence is placed by our Constitution in the Supreme Executive, and for any misconduct respecting which the injured individual has no remedy?").

purview of the courts. The categorical approach designated particular questions like those relating to the cessation of hostilities, the territorial boundaries of the US, or whether the US should recognize a government as the legitimate representative of a foreign nation as questions more appropriately resolved by the political branches. The categorical approach's rule-like quality, however, meant that it lacked the flexibility to deal with more nuanced foreign affairs questions that touch and concern war or national security but do not warrant the rigid application of the political question doctrine.

The Supreme Court moved away from the categorical approach in *Baker v Carr*.[16] Though *Baker* addresses a wholly domestic question concerning a denial of equal protection in Tennessee relating to legislative apportionment, Justice Brennan's opinion for the Court discusses the various applications of the political question doctrine in the domestic and foreign affairs context and elucidates a multifactor test to determine when the political question should be applied.[17] The most important factors include determining whether there is textually demonstrable constitutional commitment of the issue to a coordinate federal branch or a lack of judicially discoverable or manageable standards for resolving the issue. Although these two factors are most salient for the application of the political question doctrine, perhaps the factors of greatest relevance in foreign affairs are concern about a lack of respect for the coordinate branches of government and, most important, the possibility of embarrassment to the US from the lack of "one voice."

One way of characterizing the "one-voice" factor in the political question doctrine is a concern that if the President, Congress, and the courts each try to speak authoritatively to resolve a foreign affairs issue, the possibility or likelihood of embarrassment for the US would increase. To put it concretely, if, for example, the na-

---

[16] See *Baker v Carr*, 369 US 186 (1962) (outlining the factors to be considered by courts in applying the political question doctrine).

[17] Id at 217 ("[A] textually demonstrable constitutional commitment of the issue to a coordinate political department; or a lack of judicially discoverable and manageable standards for resolving it; or the impossibility of deciding without an initial policy determination of a kind clearly for non judicial discretion; or the impossibility of a court's undertaking independent resolution without expressing lack of the respect due coordinate branches of government; or an unusual need for unquestioning adherence to a political decision already made; or *the potentiality of embarrassment from multifarious pronouncements by various departments on one question*" (emphasis added).

tional government cannot speak clearly and articulate its position on which government is the legitimate representative of Syria, the US would suffer some embarrassment in the eyes of both the domestic and international audience. Thus, the one-voice factor serves to prevent or at least reduce the likelihood of embarrassment for the US in foreign affairs.

But what does embarrassment mean? The one-voice factor assumes that if the US speaks in multiple voices on an issue, the possibility of embarrassment increases. But in fact the US regularly and consistently speaks with multiple voices on many highly sensitive foreign affairs law questions. For example, just in the past ten years the President, Congress, and the Supreme Court have each spoken—and disagreed—on the President's authority to create and set the standards for military commissions during the War on Terror.[18] The President, the Supreme Court, and the state of Texas spoke with different voices on the President's authority to order a state to enforce a decision of the International Court of Justice.[19] The courts often consider and reject Statements of Interest by the Executive Branch regarding the foreign policy complications of international human rights litigation in Alien Tort Statute cases.[20] The truth is that the US often fails to speak in one voice on many highly salient foreign affairs questions, making concerns about potential embarrassment in the political question doctrine seem somewhat antiquated.

Perhaps the one-voice factor and the concern about the possibility of embarrassment actually refer to something else, namely, the important social welfare effects of concentrating or centralizing decision making in the political branches because of their greater competency or expertise in foreign affairs.[21] The wisdom

---

[18] See *Hamdan v Rumsfeld*, 548 US 557 (2006) (invalidating the President's military commissions on grounds that it violated the Uniform Code of Military Justice and the Geneva Conventions).

[19] See *Medellin v Texas*, 552 US 491 (2008) (invalidating a memorandum from President Bush purporting to order the state of Texas to enforce a judgment by the International Court of Justice and set aside its procedural default rules for certain alien nationals). See also *Sanchez-Llamas v Oregon*, 548 US 331 (2006) (holding that the Vienna Convention on Consular Relations did not oust a state's procedural default rules).

[20] For a discussion on the Bush Administration's use of statements of interest in Alien Tort Statute cases, see generally Beth Stephens, *Upsetting Checks and Balances: The Bush Administration's Efforts to Limit Human Rights Litigation*, 17 Harv Hum Rts J 169 (2004).

[21] For a discussion of institutional competency and the political question doctrine in foreign affairs, see generally Jide Nzelibe, *The Uniqueness of Foreign Affairs*, 89 Iowa L Rev 941 (2004).

of speaking with one voice rests on the benefits of centralization over decentralization in foreign affairs. On this reading, the one-voice factor in the political question doctrine represents not a concern about embarrassment but rather the Supreme Court's view that the political branches are more competent in foreign affairs than the courts, and its implicit assumption that centralization of decision making in the President should be generally preferred. Rather than a concern about embarrassment, the logic of one voice is better understood as resting on the merits of centralized decision making in foreign affairs.

B. ONE VOICE AND CENTRALIZATION

The Supreme Court's emphasis on centralized decision making in foreign affairs is perhaps best exemplified in its foreign affairs federalism jurisprudence. The Constitution specifically limits the participation of states in foreign affairs[22] and, in the event of conflict between a federal statute and state law, the Supremacy Clause ensures that the state law is preempted. But the Supreme Court has also developed several preemption doctrines to ensure the primacy of the national government over the states on a range of foreign affairs questions, including field preemption,[23] obstacle preemption,[24] dormant foreign affairs preemption,[25] and executive preemption.[26] In each of these areas, the Supreme Court's emphasis on speaking with one voice has resulted in the centralization of foreign affairs decision-making authority in the national government over the states.

What is the logic of this centralization? Much of it rests on general understandings of the merits of centralization in institutional design. The common functionalist account justifying cen-

---

[22] US Const, Art I, § 10, cl 11.

[23] See *Hines v Davidowitz*, 312 US 52, 56 (1941) (invalidating a Pennsylvania statute where Congress passed legislation to occupy the field).

[24] *Crosby v National Foreign Trade Council*, 530 US 363, 373 (2000) (invalidating a Massachusetts "Burma" statute for creating "an obstacle to the accomplishment of the Congress's full objectives under the federal act.").

[25] *Zschernig v Miller*, 389 US 429, 432 (1968) (striking down an Oregon statute as "an intrusion . . . into the field of foreign affairs which the Constitution entrusts to the President and the Congress.").

[26] See *American Insurance Association v Garamendi*, 539 US 396, 420 (2003) (striking down a California insurance statute because the "likelihood that [it] will produce something more than incidental effect in conflict with express foreign policy of the National Government would require preemption of the state law.").

tralization of decision making in the national government focuses on collective action problems and the provision of public goods. National governments are best placed to coordinate public policy, determine national interests, and engage in the necessary trade-offs to promote national public welfare. Perhaps most central to the responsibilities of the national government is the provision of national security, the maintenance of a domestic market for trade, and the generation of economic wealth. For example, in the security context, the national government can act as a single, integrated institutional actor to determine the national interest; develop US foreign policy; coordinate the military, diplomatic, and intelligence resources of the nation; swiftly pursue national objectives; and prosecute wars. If the several states were tasked with such responsibilities, it does not take much to imagine the difficulties in coordinating among a large number of heterogeneous subnational governments, each with its own interests and desire to pass on the cost of national defense, when possible, to its co-sovereigns.

The same logic applies to the development and maintenance of a common economic market and the promotion of policies to encourage economic prosperity. The national government can aggregate information and coordinate policy to ensure that the US can benefit from international trade, encourage the production of goods for which it has a competitive advantage, protect the national market from foreign anticompetitive behavior, and redistribute wealth, if necessary, to ameliorate the unequal distribution of wealth across particular regions, states, or demographic groups. The states, by contrast, will tend to be focused narrowly on their own economic prosperity, and will produce economic policies that allow them to reap the benefits and externalize the costs. We can imagine Alaska, Texas, and Louisiana, for example, adopting policies with respect to resource extraction that might impose environmental costs on the US as a whole, just as we can imagine Massachusetts, California, and New York adopting regulatory policies that might limit the ability of the US as a whole to benefit from its resource endowment. In these contexts—national security, trade, and economic prosperity—the benefits of centralization over vast decentralization among dozens of subnational entities are clear.

Beyond this traditional account, there are less obvious but similarly important justifications for centralization in foreign affairs. One is the clarity of the ensuing foreign policy. Even if there is substantive disagreement over policy, clarity ensures at least in theory that there is a clear communication of the US national interest to friend and foe alike. Another is the designation of a clear decision-making authority in foreign affairs. Among other things, it reduces the likelihood of constitutional impasses over key issues, provides an accountable governmental entity for the domestic voting public, and encourages specialization over time. Finally, to the extent the national government is working with other countries on an issue of global concern, centralization designates the US representative for international policy coordination.

But if the logic of centralization in foreign affairs in the form of speaking with one voice obtains in the context of the national government vis-à-vis the states, it is not as clear that the same logic holds with respect to Congress. In fact, the logic is not as persuasive for at least two important reasons. First, the competency gap in foreign affairs between the national government and the states far exceeds the gap between the President and Congress, and even the gap between the political branches and the courts. The states are very poorly placed to coordinate policy and make foreign affairs determinations. The centralization of decision making and speaking in one voice are, accordingly, much more important when the institutional expertise of the national government is weighed against that of the state. But the President and Congress both have significant institutional resources to coordinate foreign policy and act decisively in foreign affairs, and are specifically empowered by the Constitution to do so. Unlike the states, Congress has institutional structures like the Senate Foreign Relations Committee, the House Armed Services Committee, and dozens of subcommittees dedicated to foreign affairs and international politics, with each generating valuable information and developing Congress's foreign policy expertise. Thus, the necessity of centralization and a unified voice between Congress and the President is not as strong, and that perhaps weakens the common justifications for the one-voice factor in the political question doctrine.

The same analysis applies to the gap between the political branches and the courts. While in the aggregate the political branches are probably better placed to act in foreign affairs than the courts, the courts certainly adjudicate many sensitive matters that touch and concern foreign affairs, while the states are, for the most part, uninvolved in such issues. From adjudicating delicate issues regarding the War on Terror[27] to determining the constitutionality of international human rights litigation under the Alien Tort Statue,[28] the Supreme Court is not only involved in foreign affairs but also has developed some expertise in dealing with politically sensitive issues. On institutional competency grounds, the importance of centralization for purposes of limiting foreign affairs federalism outweighs the salience of centralization in foreign affairs decision making among the different branches of the national government.

In addition, the concerns about the provision of public goods, the coordination of national policy, and the potential collective actions problems disappear when dealing with the President and Congress. Both branches have the necessary institutional capacity to determine the national interest and ameliorate collective action concerns, far beyond anything the states could muster. Again, while centralization makes sense when dealing with national government and the states, the logic is certainly weaker with respect to the President and Congress. At bottom, the political question doctrine's one-voice factor rests on a conception of centralized foreign affairs decision making that, while appropriate with respect to the states, seems inapt for the coordinate branches of the national government.

II. ONE VOICE AND INTERNATIONAL POLITICS

A. EFFECT OF THE ONE-VOICE FACTOR IN FOREIGN AFFAIRS

The political question doctrine's one-voice factor demonstrates the Supreme Court's concern with the potential embarrassment for the US of failing to speak in a unified manner. On balance, this factor privileges centralization of decision making in foreign

---

[27] See *Boumediene v Bush*, 128 S Ct 2229, 2277 (2008) ("Within the Constitution's separation-of-powers structure, few exercises of judicial power are as legitimate or as necessary as the responsibility to hear challenges to the authority of the Executive to imprison a person.").

[28] See *Sosa v Alvarez-Machain*, 542 US 692 (2004) (upholding the constitutionality of international human rights litigation under the Alien Tort Statute under limited circumstances).

affairs. However, as we have seen so far, it is not clear what constitutes embarrassment for the US, as the US often speaks with multiple voices in foreign affairs. Conceptually, it is not clear to whom or to what the embarrassment attaches, or how the embarrassment affects the future pursuit of foreign affairs objectives. And the justifications for centralization that appear so persuasive with respect to limits on foreign affairs federalism and preemption are much less convincing in the political question doctrine context.

Yet the one-voice factor, for reasons I will explain, may very well serve to insulate the President's foreign affairs decision making from judicial review. As we know from *Curtiss-Wright*[29] and *Belmont*,[30] the President is at least the chief representative of the US in foreign affairs. While the President does not act alone—Congress has foreign affairs authority as well—he tends to be the "first mover" in foreign affairs. The President has access to the institutional resources of the Departments of State, Defense, and Homeland Security and can respond more quickly to any foreign affairs concerns. More concretely, in the face of particular foreign affairs issues for which the Constitution isn't clear and Congress has not acted, or when the foreign policy interests of the US are triggered in litigation properly before the courts, the President generally moves first on behalf of the US.

Since the President tends to be the first mover, the political question doctrine's one-voice factor effectively creates a presumption in favor of the President's action, even if it might very well push the outer bounds of the President's Article II authority. Why? The incentive structure for members of Congress will likely discourage them from acting to challenge the President, even if they might think that he has surpassed his constitutional authority. As an initial matter, the President's party might very well control Congress or be able to block legislation invalidating the President's action. If so, Congress would be unable to act and protect its institutional prerogatives. In addition, Congress rarely gets the credit for foreign affairs successes or failures. Since the public

---

[29] See *United States v Curtiss-Wright Export Corp.*, 299 US 304, 320 (1936) (characterizing "the very delicate, plenary and exclusive power of the President as the sole organ of the federal government in the field of international relations . . .").

[30] See *United States v Belmont*, 301 US 324, 330 (1937) ("Governmental power over external affairs is not distributed, but is vested exclusively in the national government. And in respect of what was done here, the Executive had authority to speak as the sole organ of that government.").

generally perceives the President as the dominant actor in foreign affairs, there is little benefit to challenging the President until it becomes clear that his policies have failed. Thus, the President in theory can act, and if his actions or policies are successful—even if the actions are beyond his constitutional authority—Congress is unlikely to respond.[31]

The one-voice factor in the political question doctrine exacerbates this dynamic. The courts, worried about their capacity to make foreign affairs determinations, sensitive to their relative weakness in enforcing their decisions, and lacking contrary legislation from Congress upon which to base a decision, are likely to weigh heavily the political question doctrine's emphasis on speaking with one voice. Thus, to the extent the courts rely on the one-voice factor in applying the political question doctrine, they essentially validate the President's action. Since the President generally moves first and Congress is disincentivized to act, the one-voice factor creates a first-mover bias and insulates the President's action from judicial review.

B. ONE VOICE OR ACOUSTIC DISSONANCE?

Some might immediately ask why this is a problem. After all, the President is the chief actor in foreign affairs and likely has the deepest institutional knowledge and expertise in the area: if the political question doctrine creates a bias in favor of the President, the bias is running in the right direction. This bias, however, creates two kinds of problems.

First, the logic of speaking with one voice, whether resting on concerns about embarrassment for the US or drawn from the merits of centralization in another context, is not as powerful as the political question doctrine suggests. Despite this weak edifice, the first-mover bias almost always privileges the President's foreign affairs decision making whether or not it is consistent with the Constitution. Though it doesn't mean that the President will always prevail—there are other political question factors that the courts consider—the first-mover bias may very well overprivilege the President's actions because it unrealistically assumes that a

---

[31] William G. Howell and John C. Pevehouse, *While Dangers Gather: Congressional Checks on Presidential War Powers* (Princeton, 2007) (describing the conditions under which Congress influences the President's use of force).

more vigorous and active Congress would be willing to challenge him. Since we don't know how courts weigh the different factors in applying the political question doctrine, the first-mover bias combined with the one-voice factor might be doing much more work than it should.

Second, the first-mover bias doesn't vary; speaking with one voice is always privileged. But speaking with one voice might be especially important under some conditions, and much less important under others. Consider a crude distinction between high-stakes and low-stakes foreign affairs issues. For example, when the US is at war, or trying to determine whether a mutual-defense treaty requires it to come to the aid of an ally, or even deciding whether to exercise its veto on the United Nations Security Council, we might think that speaking with one voice is especially important. The resolution of foreign affairs questions relating to war, the defense of treaty partners, and other potential national security concerns requires the kind of quick, clear, and decisive action generally associated with the political branches—specifically the President—rather than the courts. We might characterize these as exactly the high-stakes foreign affairs issues for which speaking in a unified voice, on balance, makes sense; the benefits of centralizing decision making in the more competent political branches will likely generate better outcomes than a more ponderous decision-making process by the courts.

But just as we can imagine the type of high-stakes issue for which the one-voice presumption is appropriate, we can also imagine low-stakes issues for which centralizing decision making might be less urgent. Take the seemingly important question of the US position on which government is the legitimate representative of a country. Some might view this as a complicated foreign affairs issue for which speaking with a unified voice through the President is absolutely necessary. However, not all foreign affairs questions of this kind require the quick, decisive action that centralization in the President provides. For example, it is hard to see why the delicate question of whether the US should recognize the recently ousted President Nasheed or the current incumbent President Waheed as the legitimate representative of the government of the Republic of the Maldives necessarily requires the exclusion of Congress or the courts. We can imagine that there are geographically concentrated interest groups with both foreign affairs expertise and strong policy preferences about the appropriate US policy outcome, giving Congress a legitimate interest in creating policy. In fact, careful deliberation by the political branches together, buttressed by judicial review, might be beneficial in determining the appropriate policy outcome. In other words, acoustic dissonance, in some cases and under certain conditions, may have value.

So when will acoustic dissonance—or speaking with multiple voices—be beneficial and when will it create costs? Acoustic dissonance in foreign affairs will, at times, reduce the ability of the US to react clearly and decisively. As described above, when the US is dealing with a core foreign affairs issue that implicates national security or a sensitive foreign policy objective, the benefits of centralizing decision making are clearer. The one-voice factor in the political question doctrine makes most sense when the US is dealing with vital foreign policy concerns for which acting with speed and dispatch is necessary. For high-stakes or exigent foreign affairs issues, a presumption in favor of one voice seems appropriate.

However, when the US is dealing with a foreign affairs issue for which the speed and dispatch associated with centralized decision making is not as crucial, the one-voice presumption might be less important. Again, the discussion above of high-stakes and low-stakes foreign issues illustrates exactly this concern. In low-stakes cases, we might find that acoustic dissonance improves decision making by encouraging Congress to engage the President in foreign affairs. Open, careful deliberation about foreign affairs questions leads to greater transparency and democratic legitimacy. Since greater congressional involvement in foreign affairs in low-stakes questions will likely lead to more opportunities for judicial review, acoustic dissonance prevents the atrophy of oversight that the one-voice factor creates. The courts' willingness to adopt a one-voice presumption in low-stakes cases could reduce the judiciary's future capacity to engage in a meaningful review of the President in foreign affairs, concretize the first-mover bias in favor of the President, and disincentivize the President, over time, to employ his own intrabranch review mechanisms. This phenomenon is exacerbated by a dynamic effect, whereby the President's expertise and decision-making preeminence become self-affirming over time, and congressional enfeeblement becomes increasingly pathological. In low-stakes foreign affairs cases, the presumption in favor of one voice is weaker and acoustic dissonance may be appropriate.

C. ACOUSTIC DISSONANCE AND INTERNATIONAL POLITICS

All of this might make sense in theory. But when courts consider whether or not to apply the political question doctrine and weigh the various factors, they will struggle to distinguish the high-stakes cases that might warrant a one-voice presumption from the low-stakes cases where acoustic dissonance might be useful. While courts have experience adjudicating foreign affairs questions, it is not clear that they have the necessary foreign policy expertise to make fine-grained distinctions between seemingly high-stakes and low-stakes foreign affairs questions. Nonetheless, courts routinely make those determinations when they apply the political question doctrine. For example, in order to determine whether there is a possibility of embarrassment to the US by failing to speak with one voice, the courts must make some threshold inquiry about the importance of the foreign affairs issue, the likelihood of embarrassment, and the consequences of that embarrassment on US foreign policy objectives. Yet we don't know how the courts make this inquiry or assessment in deciding whether the application of the political question doctrine is merited. Thus the courts—or, perhaps more accurately, individual judges—engage in an ad hoc analysis without the benefit of a framework to guide their reasoning.

While a more categorical approach to the political question doctrine would carry the benefits commonly associated with rules—clarity, ease of administration, and low decision costs—it is probably too rigid to deal with the great variety of foreign affairs issues commonly before the courts. The late-twentieth-century rise of international human rights litigation under the Alien Tort Statute,[32] for example, implicates sensitive foreign affairs issues that make a rule-like approach to the political questions doctrine a poor fit with the complex transnational litigation seen in US courts today. The increasing intermingling of foreign and domestic issues and the collapse of any meaningful definitional dis-

---

[32] See *Sosa v Alvarez-Machain*, 542 US 692 (2004) (upholding international human rights litigation under the Alien Tort Statute under limited circumstances).

tinction between the two only weakens the value of the categorical approach. But if courts lack the institutional competency to assess complicated foreign affairs questions, and the nature of modern litigation so routinely implicates foreign affairs that it makes a categorical issue-by-issue approach unworkable, how should courts determine when speaking with one voice (or acoustic dissonance) is appropriate?

Courts can gain traction on this question by assessing the background conditions of international politics to understand when a presumption in favor of speaking with one voice is warranted, and when such a presumption is unnecessary. As I have argued in prior scholarship,[33] the courts can adopt a parsimonious framework, based on the international relations concept of polarity, to assess background international political conditions and the role of the US in the world. Based on this assessment, the courts would not decide whether a particular foreign affairs question required the application of the political question doctrine; rather, the assessment would assist the courts in weighing the benefits of speaking with one voice.

International theorists often describe the structure of international politics in terms of polarity.[34] Polarity is a heuristic that permits a simple, if somewhat crude, measure of the material power of the most influential states in international politics. By looking at a rough measurement of a state's economic wealth and military strength, scholars and judges can identify the most powerful countries in the world and focus attention on them. Such identification is particularly important in the foreign affairs context because, on average, the most powerful countries are best placed to influence international politics.

Polarity refers to the number of great powers (powerful states in the world). A multipolar system reflects a world in which there are three or more great powers. Similarly, a bipolar system is a world with two great powers, and a unipolar system is one with only one great power or hegemon in international politics. Each of these systems presents different challenges or background con-

---

[33] See Abebe, 49 Stan J Int'l L (cited in note 12).

[34] For a general discussion about polarity in international politics, see John J. Mearsheimer, *The Tragedy of Great Power Politics* (Norton, 2001); Kenneth N. Waltz, *Theory of International Politics* (McGraw-Hill, 1979).

ditions, and these conditions are relevant for understanding the importance of speaking with once voice.

To make the illustration simple, let's imagine that it is the year 2030 and the US is one of three great powers in a multipolar world, along with Germany and China. Each of these great powers will have different and often competing economic goals, security interests, and national objectives, drawn from their respective cultures, histories, and resource endowments. Each will develop policies designed to achieve their goals and will look to build relationships with other states to advance their interests. In a world with finite resources, these great powers will compete, conflict, and perhaps even clash as they pursue their foreign policy objectives.

The multipolar world presents a complex and challenging international political environment for the US. Since it is competing with China and Germany as a relative equal, the US incurs great costs in trying to achieve its objectives. In a multipolar world, the returns to speaking with one voice and centralizing foreign affairs decision making will likely be high. The US is not a global superpower and lacks the material power and political influence to ignore China and Germany as it pursues its policies. In fact, the US has to be careful to calibrate its foreign policy goals and the means to achieve them to minimize conflict with China and Germany, just as China and Germany exercise care vis-à-vis the US. Here, the President's foreign affairs expertise, institutional knowledge, and capacity to marshal resources and act quickly are especially beneficial given the particularly challenging international political environment that the US must navigate. To put it differently, the benefits of acoustic dissonance that emerge from careful, open, and deliberate consideration of policy are unlikely to be realized in a more complicated world requiring high levels of expertise and decisive action. Under this condition, a presumption in favor of speaking with one voice—through the one-voice factor in the political question doctrine—is appropriate. Such a presumption links the centralization of foreign affairs decision making through speaking with one voice with the international political environment in which it is most useful.

In contrast, consider a unipolar world with the US as the hegemon or the unipolar power in international politics. Here, the US stands alone; by definition, there are no other great powers that can approximate the material power and political influence of the US. Of course, there are other powerful states in the world, but none of them is a peer of the US, the sole superpower. In the unipolar world, the President still has valuable foreign affairs expertise useful for the pursuit of the national interest, but the necessity of acting with speed, secrecy, and dispatch is not as urgent. Since the US is dominant, it has greater latitude to develop foreign policy, define more broadly the national interest, and pursue national objectives because the potential for serious conflict with peer states is reduced. Stated slightly differently, the error costs tend to be lower. This does not mean that the US is free to do what it wants in international politics—it simply suggests that relative to a multipolar world, the unipolar world reduces some of the concerns that speaking with one voice or centralization address.

It also leads to a different reading of the one-voice factor in the political question doctrine. Again, the structure of international politics is simply a background condition that helps inform the merits of centralization. In the unipolar world, the need for centralization in foreign affairs is not as acute as it is in the multipolar world. And, in the same unipolar world, the benefits of acoustic dissonance increase. Since the US is a superpower, the international political environment is not as complicated or taxing as the more challenging multipolar world. This permits the US to act with greater transparency and less haste, engage in more open deliberation, and encourage greater participation of Congress and the courts. At the same time, centralizing decision making still has some role to play; the President still maintains a high level of expertise regardless of whether the US is in a multipolar or unipolar world. Thus, to ensure that the President's expertise and the value of centralization are captured by the doctrine, while still profiting from the virtues of some acoustic dissonance, the one-voice presumption should be relaxed when the US is the dominant power in a unipolar world. That is, the burden of demonstrating the necessity of speaking with one voice on a particular foreign affairs question should rest with the first mover, generally the President.

D. CONCLUSION: STATUS QUO VERSUS SHIFTING PRESUMPTIONS

Treating the one-voice factor as presumption that shifts according to international political conditions represents an improvement on the status quo for several reasons. First, it is information generating and only applies under the conditions when the costs of deliberation and information production are likely to be lowest. In practice, the President enjoys the presumption in a multipolar world, when the benefits of speaking with one voice and centralization of foreign affairs decision making are most important to the US. Similarly, the President bears the burden of showing that the one-voice presumption is necessary in a unipolar world, when the benefits of acoustic dissonance are more apparent. Either way, the President has the opportunity, in both the unipolar and multipolar world, to insulate his decision making from review by making a showing that speaking with one voice is appropriate.

Second, the information-generating component of the shifting presumption will likely result in a better-informed judiciary on foreign affairs issues and, in some instances, result in better policy outcomes. At the very least, it encourages greater participation by Congress and the courts in foreign affairs when such participation will likely produce the most benefits and the least cost: in a unipolar world. Third, this approach brings some clarity to the current operation of the one-voice factor as part of the political question doctrine's multifactor balancing test. It is less manipulable than traditional standards, but more flexible than rules. Finally, rather than leaving judges without guidance in weighing the multiple factors or determining whether to use the political question doctrine to insulate the President's action from review, the approach outlined here provides the courts with a more rigorous, parsimonious, and easily applicable framework for thinking about the merits of speaking in one voice in foreign affairs.

BARRY FRIEDMAN AND
GENEVIEVE LAKIER

"TO REGULATE," NOT "TO PROHIBIT":
LIMITING THE COMMERCE POWER

Despite universal acknowledgment that Congress's power to regulate interstate commerce does not constitute an unbounded police
power, the difficulty has been in distinguishing "what is truly national and what is truly local."[1] Since the New Deal, the effort to

Barry Friedman is the Jacob D. Fuchsberg Professor of Law at New York University
School of Law. Genevieve Lakier is a 2011 graduate of the New York University School
of Law, and a law clerk to the Honorable Martha Craig Daughtrey, United States Court
of Appeals for the Sixth Circuit.

AUTHORS' NOTE: This work is the product of many conversations and much assistance,
for which the authors would like to thank Bobby Ahdieh, Lynn Baker, Jack Balkin, Randy
Barnett, Lisa Bressman, Rebecca Brown, Michael Dorf, Richard Epstein, Willy Forbath,
Rick Hills, Calvin Johnson, Susan Klein, Maggie Lemos, Robert Mikos, Ricky Revesz,
Larry Sager, Eric Segall, and Dick Stewart. The authors also are grateful for the comments
received at workshops at Emory Law School, Georgia State Law School, and the University
of Texas School of Law. Valuable research assistance was provided by Christina Dahlman,
Kevin Friedl, Kylie Hoover, and Andrew Ward. This research was funded in part by a
grant from the Filomen D'Agostino and Max E. Greenberg Research Fund.

[1] *Lopez v United States*, 514 US 549, 567–68 (1995). For cases insisting such limits must
exist see, for example, *United States v Morrison*, 529 US 598, 608 (2000) ("[E]ven under
our modern, expansive interpretation of the Commerce Clause, Congress' regulatory authority is not without effective bounds."); *NLRB v Jones & Laughlin Steel Corp.*, 301 US
1, 37 (1937) ("Undoubtedly the scope of [the commerce] power . . . may not be extended
so as to embrace effects upon interstate commerce so indirect and remote that to embrace
them, in view of our complex society, would effectually obliterate the distinction between
what is national and what is local and create a completely centralized government."};
Gibbons v Ogden, 22 US 1, 194 – 95 (1824) ("The enumeration [in the Commerce Clause]
of the particular classes of commerce, to which the power was to be extended, would not
have been made, had the intention been to extend the power to every description. The
enumeration presupposes something not enumerated.").

do so has been notably unsuccessful. The Supreme Court has identified only two limiting principles, and neither has or is likely to
affect congressional power much in the end. Commencing with
United States v Lopez, the Supreme Court drew a line resting on
the distinction between "economic" and "non-economic" activity.[2]
That line quickly withered.[3] Then, there was the decision in *National
Federation of Independent Business v Sebelius*, distinguishing between
economic "activity," which Congress can regulate, and "inactivity,"
which it cannot.[4] Whatever one thinks of the decision on its merits,
this is not a line Congress has needed to cross for over two hundred
years, which is reason enough to doubt it will have much significance.[5]

Yet, there is one aspect of the commerce power—the question
of what it means "*to regulate*" commerce—in which line-drawing
might better foster federalism, but any attempt to do so has been
abandoned. The Supreme Court is taken to have held, in its 1903
decision in *Champion v Ames* sustaining a congressional law banning
the interstate transportation of lottery tickets, that Congress's power
"to regulate" commerce includes the power to prohibit it altogether.[6] Based on that assumption, Congress has exercised free rein
to shut down interstate markets, even if the states would have it
otherwise. For over one hundred years, few commentators, and even
fewer court decisions, have questioned Congress's power to enact
market bans as a "regulation" of interstate commerce.[7]

---

[2] *Lopez*, 514 US at 567.

[3] See Jonathan H. Adler, *Is Morrison Dead: Assessing a Supreme Drug (Law) Overdose*, 9
Lewis & Clark L Rev 751, 765 (2005) (arguing that the distinction between economic
and noneconomic activity no longer represents "a meaningful limit on federal power");
Thomas W. Merrill, *Rescuing Federalism after Raich: The Case for Clear Statement Rules*, 9
Lewis & Clark L Rev 823, 826 (2005) (arguing that "*Lopez*'s prohibitory rule [has been]
watered down to the point where it may have little continuing significance").

[4] 132 S Ct 2566, 2589 (2012) (Roberts, CJ); id at 2648 (Scalia, Kennedy, Thomas, and
Alito, JJ, dissenting).

[5] Immediate responses to the decision certainly suggested as much. See, for example,
Jonathan Cohn, *Did Roberts Gut the Commerce Clause?*, New Republic (June 28, 2012),
online at http://www.tnr.com/blog/plank/104455/did-roberts-gut-the-commerce-clause;
Kevin Drum, *Obamacare Ruling Doesn't Limit Congress Much*, Mother Jones (June 28, 2012),
online at http://www.motherjones.com/kevin-drum/2012/06/obamacare-ruling-doesnt-
limit-congress-much.

[6] 188 US 321, 357–58 (1903).

[7] There are, however, notable exceptions to this general rule. See Richard A. Epstein,
*A Most Improbable 1787 Constitution: A (Mostly) Originalist Critique of the Constitutionality
of the ACA*, in Nathaniel Persily, Gillian E. Metzger, and Trevor W. Morrison, eds, *The
Health Care Case: The Supreme Court's Decision and Its Implications* 28 (Oxford, 2013) (ar-

Gonzales v Raich is endemic of the problem.[8] The plaintiffs in *Raich* were California residents who wished to cultivate and use marijuana for medicinal purposes, which was legal under California's Compassionate Use Act, but illegal under the federal Controlled Substances Act (CSA).[9] Relying on *Lopez* and its progeny, *United States v Morrison*, the plaintiffs argued that the CSA was unconstitutional as applied to the purely intrastate, noncommercial use of marijuana.[10] The *Raich* majority disagreed. Holding that Congress may regulate even purely intrastate noncommercial activity that, in the aggregate, might "undercut [its] regulation of the interstate market in that commodity," it found the application of the CSA to the plaintiffs' conduct entirely constitutional, given the risk that medical marijuana would seep into the interstate marijuana market and thereby impede Congress's efforts to shut that market down.[11] But what no one asked in *Raich* was where Congress got the power to shut down the interstate market in marijuana in the first place.[12] Instead, relying on *Champion*, the majority simply asserted that "[i]t has long been settled that Congress' power to regulate commerce includes the power to prohibit commerce in a particular commodity."[13]

The impact on federalism of blithely assuming that Congress has the power to shut down interstate markets is readily apparent. Roughly eighteen states have legalized the use of marijuana for medicinal purposes, and in 2012 two states—Colorado and Washington—legalized the recreational use of marijuana as well.[14] This

guing that Congress cannot prohibit interstate commerce "at least absent some strong justification in some particular case"); Randy E. Barnett, *The Original Meaning of the Commerce Clause*, 68 U Chi L Rev 101, 139 (2001) (arguing that "[t]he power to regulate does not generally include the power to prohibit"); Donald H. Regan, *How to Think About the Federal Commerce Power and Incidentally Rewrite United States v. Lopez*, 94 Mich L Rev 554, 576–77 (1995) (arguing that Congress should not usually have the power to ban goods that the states would allow). See also *Hammer v Dagenhart*, 247 US 251 (1918).

[8] 545 US 1 (2005).

[9] Id at 6–7.

[10] Brief for Respondents, *Gonzales v Raich*, No 03-1454, *12 (US filed Oct 13, 2004) (available on Westlaw at 2004 WL 2308766), citing *United States v Morrison*, 529 US 598 (2000).

[11] *Raich*, 545 US at 18.

[12] Seeking to minimize the import of the relief they were seeking, the plaintiffs in *Raich* did not challenge Congress's power to pass the Controlled Substances Act under the commerce power. Id at 15.

[13] Id at 19 n 29.

[14] Jack Healy, *Voters Ease Marijuana Laws in 2 States, but Legal Questions Remain*, NY Times P15 (Nov 7, 2012); *18 Legal Medical Marijuana States and DC: Laws, Fees, and*

sort of state-by-state choice is often thought emblematic of the real virtues of a federal system. It encourages experimentation, localized democracy, and maximization of individual choice.[15] Yet, under the Supremacy Clause, if Congress has the power to adopt the CSA, congressional will prevails.[16] End of story.

The problem transcends marijuana of course—although, given the seemingly unending, expensive, yet equally unsuccessful war on drugs, one might think the cost of granting Congress the power to enact total bans of this sort to be particularly evident in this context.[17] Nevertheless, Congress's ability to shut down interstate markets impedes the values of federalism whenever there is a good that some states wish to allow their citizens but the federal government prohibits. At times this has been an issue with regard to alcohol, gambling, and prostitution. Today there is a similar conflict between state and federal power with respect to products made of raw milk.[18] And recent calls for federal bans on assault weapons and high-volume ammunition magazines may raise related concerns.

This article calls for a reexamination of the long-standing, yet inadequately examined, assumption that Congress's power to regulate interstate commerce necessarily includes the power not only

Possession Limits (ProCon.org, updated Feb 22, 2013), online at http://medicalmarijuana .procon.org/view.resource.php?resourceID=000881.

[15] See Barry Friedman, *Valuing Federalism*, 82 Minn L Rev 317, 389–400 (1997).

[16] Robert Mikos argues that states retain authority to allow marijuana even in the face of the federal ban, but most other scholars disagree. Compare Robert A. Mikos, *On the Limits of Supremacy: Medical Marijuana and the States' Overlooked Power to Legalize Federal Crime*, 62 Vand L Rev 1421, 1423 (2009) (arguing that "states retain both de jure and de facto power to exempt medical marijuana from criminal sanctions, in spite of Congress's uncompromising—and clearly constitutional—ban on the drug"), with Robert J. Pushaw Jr., *The Medical Marijuana Case: A Commerce Clause Counter-Revolution?*, 9 Lewis & Clark L Rev 879, 912 (2005) (arguing that in the face of the federal ban, "no state may help its citizens who are enduring constant pain that can be relieved only through the controlled use of marijuana"); Susan R. Klein, *Independent-Norm Federalism in Criminal Law*, 90 Cal L Rev 1541, 1563 (2002) (suggesting state efforts to legalize marijuana will "never succeed" in the face of the federal ban); Caleb Nelson, *Preemption*, 86 Va L Rev 225, 261 (2000) ("If state law purports to authorize something that federal law forbids . . . then courts [] have to choose between applying the federal rule and applying the state rule, and the Supremacy Clause requires them to apply the federal rule.").

[17] See generally Steven B. Duke and Albert C. Gross, *America's Longest War: Rethinking Our Tragic Crusade Against Drugs* (Putnam, 1993); Doug Bandow, *War on Drugs or War on America?*, 3 Stan L & Pol Rev 242, 245 (1991) (arguing that "drug prohibition is, at best, an imperfect, and at worst, a counterproductive vehicle for" protecting the public).

[18] Although federal law bans the interstate transport of unpasteurized milk products, thirty states allow raw milk, under a variety of regulations. See 21 CFR § 1240.61 (banning raw milk); National Conference of State Legislatures, *Raw Milk*, NCSL.org (Oct 2012), online at http://www.ncsl.org/issues-research/agri/raw-milk-2012.aspx (detailing the various state regulatory schemes).

to (as the *Raich* Court put it) "protect" interstate markets but also to "eradicate" them.[19] Nothing in the analysis advanced here is easy or definitive. Nevertheless, it suggests that there are very good reasons to resist an unthinking adherence to the assumption that under its power to regulate commerce, Congress also can shut it down.

The case for limiting congressional power is grounded in history, albeit history that unfortunately has been lost to us over the years. At the Founding and for more than one hundred years thereafter, Congress's power to regulate commerce was *not* thought to include the power to prohibit it. Nor, in fact, did *Champion v Ames* hold otherwise. Rather, *Champion* simply countenanced a federal regulatory ban on the interstate shipment of lottery tickets in a situation in which all states already had banned the lottery.[20] The federal statute at issue in *Champion* was a "helper" law facilitating state choices, not barring them. It was only after the decision in *Champion* that the dam of federal power burst open. And even then, the extension of federal power to issues such as gambling and narcotics was left unjustified by anything other than a (misplaced) citation to *Champion* and a highly formal test that deemed anything crossing state lines a "regulation" of commerce.

But the case here rests as well on constitutional structure and the theory of American federalism. If this article accomplishes nothing else, it seeks to force a debate, and require a justification—beyond a simple citation to *Champion*—when Congress seeks to shut down a market some states would allow. Constitutional limits govern not only the courts but members of Congress as well. Under the interpretation of the Commerce Clause offered here, Congress must justify its decision to privilege the preferences of some states over others when in fact both sets of preferences could be respected. Once the question is analyzed, rather than the answer simply assumed, the case for congressional power to prohibit markets becomes notably weaker and the argument for state autonomy concomitantly greater.

This article ultimately concludes that restricting Congress's ability to shut down markets would not render either the states or the

---

[19] *Raich*, 545 US at 19 n 29 (2005) (asserting that the difference between regulations that seek "to protect and stabilize" interstate markets and those that seek "to eradicate" them is "of no constitutional import").

[20] See notes 85–93, and accompanying text.

federal government unable to act in the face of moral, physical, or environmental threats to the public welfare. First, Congress retains the power "to regulate" commerce, even if it cannot prohibit it altogether. Second, Congress can enact "helper" statutes like the one at issue in *Champion*, to assist states in enforcing their own choices. Third, Congress can ban individual products from the market when doing so would be "in service" of the broader market. (A classic example is the federal ban on the interstate transportation of diseased cattle that Congress passed in 1884 not out of antipathy to the possession of diseased cattle but in order to protect and foster a vibrant national livestock market.[21]) What Congress may not do, however, is determine that it will shut down trade that some of the states would allow.

In Part I, we advance the argument in terms both originalist and grounded in one hundred years of subsequent historical practice. The evidence from the Constitutional Convention and the ratification debates makes clear that Congress's power "to regulate Commerce . . . among the several States" was meant to foster the free flow of interstate commerce, not curtail it. For over one hundred years after the Founding, the country adhered to this view of Congress's interstate commerce power. Few even argued otherwise, and at no point did Congress act as if it possessed the power to ban markets in goods that the states would allow. This history calls into question any easy assumption that the power "to regulate" commerce necessarily includes the power to eradicate it.

In Part II, we explore why this long-standing interpretation of Congress's interstate commerce powers changed around the turn of the twentieth century. We explain that, following *Champion*, Congress increasingly came to rely upon its power to prohibit the movement of things in commerce for two reasons. First, prohibiting the circulation of goods in commerce provided Congress a means by which to regulate an increasingly integrated national economy without appearing to regulate the purely intrastate activities that the Court, in 1895, declared to be beyond the reach of federal power.[22] But once the Court adopted the now-familiar "substantial effects" test of commerce power, this first use of the power to prohibit commerce became entirely vestigial—it is altogether unnecessary

[21] Animal Industry Act, 23 Stat 31 (1884).
[22] *United States v E. C. Knight Co.*, 156 US 1, 21 (1895).

today.[23] Second, Congress used its power to ban interstate markets to restrict consumers' access to the vice goods that many believed posed a serious threat to social progress and stability in an industrializing age. Yet, the cases sustaining such use of congressional power were remarkably candid in stating that, in going after vice, Congress effectively was exercising a police power of the sort historically reserved to the states. If prohibiting commerce—rather than fostering it and regulating it—is nothing but an exercise of the power of police, then the existence of that power in Congress requires squaring up with long-standing notions of federalism.

In Part III, we argue that there are structural reasons, grounded in principles of American federalism, why the states should have primary responsibility for determining what kinds of goods can legally circulate in domestic markets. Filling out Framing-era understandings of the proper division between the national and state governments with modern economic analysis of the values of federalism, we explain in Part III.A that the only conceivable justification for allowing Congress to ban markets—other than simply granting Congress a generalized police power—is to control the spillover costs of state diversity. We conclude that although the matter is not entirely free from doubt, the spillover rationale standing alone is insufficient justification to allow Congress to prohibit commerce, in large part because it either cannot work, or proves too much.

In Part III.B, we specify what it would mean to deny Congress the power to "prohibit" commerce. We make clear that, although Congress would not under this interpretation of the Commerce Clause have the power to ban interstate markets, it would still be able to ban goods when doing so serves, rather than restricts, the interstate market. "In-service" laws of this kind have a long genealogy that significantly predates the *Champion* rule. Because they do not work to shut interstate commerce down, but instead typically help enforce the rules by which interstate commerce operates, they do not represent prohibitions of commerce in the sense used here or in the nineteenth-century debates. Congress would also have the power to adopt "helper" statutes. Helper statutes do what the name

---

[23] *United States v Darby*, 312 US 100, 122 (1941) (upholding the Fair Labor Standards Act based on its effect on interstate commerce); *NLRB v Jones & Laughlin Steel Corp.*, 301 US 1, 37 (1937) (adopting the substantial effects test for exercises of the Commerce Clause).

suggests: they lend federal enforcement authority to states that have chosen through their own democratic processes to ban certain goods. Because statutes of this kind leave it to each state to determine what goods to ban or allow, they also do not constitute prohibitions of commerce, in the sense of the term used here.

Finally, in Part III.C we take up possible objections to our reading of the Commerce Clause. We argue that because Congress would still be able to enact in-service laws and helper statutes, restricting Congress's ability to prohibit markets would not undermine its ability to regulate the national economy, or to protect the environment or public health. It would simply keep Congress from prohibiting interstate trade that "states themselves" would allow. We also defend against the objection that drawing a line between regulation and prohibition would be, in practice, unworkable or too difficult to enforce. Although the distinction is not always an easy one to draw, we conclude that it is neither incoherent nor impossible to maintain—particularly if we recognize that it need not only be the courts that bear responsibility for enforcing the rule, but members of Congress themselves.

Many truths that seem universal at one time, turn out not to be at another. So it was with lottery tickets, and alcohol, and may ultimately prove the case with marijuana. State divergence on these issues necessarily calls into question the universality of such truths. When states diverge, it suggests uniform regulation may not only be unnecessary, but that it may be inappropriate or even counterproductive. The simple fact is that Congress's power to regulate commerce was not thought to encompass the power to prohibit it for the first half of the country's history. The claim here is not novel—it just has been lost to us. At the least, recovering it requires us to ask provocative but important questions about the scope of federal power, particularly when the states disagree among themselves.

I. The Founding and the Nineteenth Century

Although it is commonly assumed today that Congress's power "to regulate" commerce necessarily includes the power to prohibit it, this was not how the Commerce Clause was always understood. At the Founding, and for roughly 115 years thereafter, the dominant view was that Congress did not possess the authority to ban goods merely because they crossed state lines. This is not to say that there was no disagreement on the question. There was, particularly as it related to the domestic slave trade.[24] But as late as 1886, a report prepared by the House Judiciary Committee could assert that a proposed bill to ban the interstate sale of oleomargarine was "plainly unconstitutional" and declare itself entirely ignorant of any arguments to the contrary. As the report explained (and it is worth reading this carefully):

> Your committee are not aware that it has ever been asserted for the power to regulate commerce that it involved a power to prohibit the free transportation of the products of each State through and into every other; and it could hardly have been within the minds of the framers of the Constitution to give to Congress the power to do so, when history shows that the purpose of giving the power to Congress and taking it from the States was to prevent the very result which this construction of the clause would involve and bring about. . . .
> It may be within the meaning of this clause such needful regulations as to articles transported from State to State as will conserve the safety and well-being of the transportation, but the right to say what articles shall and what shall not be the subject of commerce is not included in the regulation of the commerce in such articles.[25]

Congress agreed, ultimately choosing to regulate oleomargarine under its taxing rather than its commerce powers.[26]

In this part, we show that the Judiciary Committee report was correct in its reading of constitutional history from the Founding to the end of the nineteenth century. This history calls into question any easy assumption that Congress's power to regulate commerce inevitably or necessarily includes its prohibition.

A. FOUNDING ASSUMPTIONS

While there was a paucity of discussion at the Constitutional Convention about the domestic commerce power, extant evidence suggests the Framers neither imagined nor intended Congress to possess the power to determine, via prohibition, what kinds of goods could move in interstate markets. Congress's power over foreign commerce received far more attention, and here it was clear that the power "to regulate" foreign commerce included the power to ban it. No doubt, the relative lack of conversation about

[24] See note 60 and accompanying text.
[25] *Adulteration of Food*, HR Rep No 49-1880, 49th Cong, 1st Sess 2 (1886).
[26] Oleomargarine Act of 1886, 24 Stat 209.

the domestic power makes drawing certain conclusions more difficult.[27] Still, the Framers clearly intended the domestic commerce power to serve very different purposes than the foreign commerce power. The authority to ban commerce made much more sense in the context of the foreign commerce power, and silence about a like authority in the context of domestic commerce is telling.

The primary reason for granting Congress the domestic commerce power was *to facilitate* interstate trade and protect it against the sort of protectionist state trade policies that occurred all too frequently under the Articles of Confederation. Such laws proliferated in the weak economic climate of the post-Revolutionary period, as states attempted to protect local manufacturers by discriminatorily taxing and regulating domestic imports, and by restricting the access of other states' vessels to local ports.[28] These measures generated increasing concern about their effect on the national economy, and political unity. As Alexander Hamilton argued in Federalist No. 22:

> The interfering and unneighbourly regulations of some States, contrary to the true spirit of the Union, have, in different instances, given just cause of umbrage and complaint to others, and it is to be feared that examples of this nature, if not restrained by national controul, would be multiplied and extended, till they become not less serious sources of animosity and discord than injurious impediments to the intercourse between the different parts of the confederacy.[29]

The Framers plainly sought to take from the states the power to pass "interfering and unneighbourly regulations" of this kind. They also sought to empower Congress to make uniform rules for trade, so that what James Madison described as "the perverse-

---

[27] See Albert S. Abel, *The Commerce Clause in the Constitutional Convention and in Contemporary Comment*, 25 Minn L Rev 432, 443, 446, 470 (1941) ("The first thing that strikes one's attention in seeking references directed to interstate commerce is their paucity."). See also Grant S. Nelson and Robert J. Pushaw Jr., *Rethinking the Commerce Clause: Applying First Principles to Uphold Federal Commercial Regulations but Preserve State Control over Social Issues*, 85 Iowa L Rev 1, 35 n 138 (1999) (noting that "during the Convention and Ratification debates, many participants declared, without challenge, that everyone agreed that the Commerce Clause would be especially beneficial" without elaborating further what it meant).

[28] Cathy D. Matson and Peter S. Onuf, *A Union of Interests: Political and Economic Thought in Revolutionary America* 70–74 (Kansas, 1990); Barry Friedman and Daniel T. Deacon, *A Course Unbroken: The Constitutional Legitimacy of the Dormant Commerce Clause*, 97 Va L Rev 1877, 1884–85 (2011).

[29] Federalist 22 (Hamilton), in Jacob E. Cooke, ed, *The Federalist* 135, 137 (Wesleyan, 1961).

ness" of the states would not hamper "concert in matters where common interest requires it."[30] In both cases, the ultimate aim was to facilitate what Hamilton described in Federalist No. 11 as the "unrestrained intercourse between the States" that he, and other Federalists, believed would promote both economic prosperity and political unity.[31]

No one suggested, during the framing or ratification of the Constitution, that in addition to facilitating an unrestrained intercourse between the states, Congress also would be empowered to *restrain* such intercourse, by restricting what goods could cross state lines or be sold in interstate markets. When delegates referred to Congress's interstate commerce powers, they referred to them exclusively as a solution to the problem of burdensome or discriminatory state legislation.[32] On the few occasions in which participants discussed Congress's domestic commerce powers, they depicted them along the lines Hamilton and Madison suggested in the Federalist papers: as a mechanism for "preserv[ing] . . . a beneficial intercourse among [the states]."[33]

An absence of debate alone hardly provides irrefutable evidence of constitutional meaning, but this particular silence speaks loudly given the quite explicit acknowledgment that under its *foreign* commerce power, Congress would possess the power not only to regulate—that is, to set rules for—trade with foreign nations, but also to limit it. Indeed, there was wide agreement among the delegates in Philadelphia that Congress would have the authority to pass what were colloquially referred to as "navigation acts," restricting what kinds of ships could legally bring goods into and out of the United States, and what kinds of goods they could carry.[34]

---

[30] James Madison, *Vices of the Political System of the United States*, in Jack N. Rakove, ed, *James Madison: Writings* 69, 71 (Library of America, 1999).

[31] Federalist 11 (Hamilton), in Jacob E. Cooke, ed, *The Federalist* 65, 71 (Wesleyan, 1961). Hamilton argued that "[a]n unrestrained intercourse between the States themselves" would advantage all the states, and disadvantage none, by promoting "the trade of each, by an interchange of their respective productions, not only for the supply of reciprocal wants at home, but for exportation to foreign markets." Id.

[32] See Abel, 25 Minn L Rev at 470 (cited in note 27) (describing each mention of the domestic commerce power during the Constitutional Convention).

[33] Roger Sherman, *Observations on the New Federal Constitution*, New-Haven Gazette 1 (Dec 25, 1788).

[34] The term was borrowed from Great Britain, which beginning in 1651 passed a number of Navigation Acts to protect British ships and manufacturers from foreign competition. In many cases the acts also restricted foreign goods themselves. See Roger J. Delahunty,

Empowering Congress to limit foreign trade in this manner was believed necessary to defend U.S. interests against the exclusionary trade policies that Great Britain imposed in the wake of the Revolution.[35] These laws barred U.S. ships and most kinds of U.S. goods from access to British ports and caused significant damage to U.S. industries, which depended heavily on trade with Britain and Britain's colonies. Yet the states proved incapable of a coordinated response and Congress was not able to get the supermajority approval necessary under the Articles of Confederation to respond in kind.[36]

Congress's power to ban goods in foreign commerce was the subject of quite explicit debate; the power was not granted unknowingly or without challenge. Federalists promoted the view that, as a major benefit of union under the new constitution, Congress would be able to enact "prohibitory regulations . . . capable of excluding Great Britain . . . from all our ports."[37] Southern delegates, in contrast, expressed considerable concern that Congress would unduly limit foreign trade in order to protect northern industries, and northern ships, to the detriment of the much more import-dependent southern states.[38] They also expressed anxiety about the possibility that Congress would use its foreign commerce power to ban the importation of slaves. Representatives of Georgia and South Carolina even threatened to walk out of the convention if their concerns on this score were not addressed—which they were, eventually, by the agreement to include in the Constitution

---

Federalism Beyond the Water's Edge: State Procurement Sanctions and Foreign Affairs, 37 Stan J Intl L 1, 18 (2001).

[35] See id at 17 ("Courts and legal scholars have long recognized the desire for an effective national authority to regulate foreign commerce—more specifically, an authority that would enable the states to take concerted action to resist and retaliate against exclusionary British trade practices—was one of the primary causes of the agitation for the Constitution of 1787."). See also Nelson and Pushaw, 85 Iowa L Rev at 22, 25 (cited in note 27).

[36] See Delahunty, 37 Stan J Intl L at 17–19 (cited in note 34) (discussing the federal response); Jacques LeBoeuf, *The Economics of Federalism and the Proper Scope of the Federal Commerce Power*, 31 San Diego L Rev 555, 595–98 (1994) (discussing the state response).

[37] Federalist 11 (Hamilton) at 66–67 (cited in note 31).

[38] Abel, 25 Minn L Rev at 454 (cited in note 27) ("This objection, that the power to regulate commerce, by a mere majority, would facilitate adoption of a navigation act beneficial to the shipping states and prejudicial to the South, was a favorite subject of complaint with the Southern opponents of the constitution."). See also Max Farrand, ed, 2 *The Records of the Federal Convention of 1787* 449–53 (rev ed 1937) (discussing the possibility that a northern-dominated Congress would use its foreign commerce powers to pass "oppressive regulations" harmful to the southern states).

the Migration or Importation Clause, barring any restriction on the importation of slaves until 1808.[39]

In contrast to their expressed worries about Congress foreclosing the foreign slave trade, southern delegates were noticeably silent about the possibility that Congress would use its power over interstate commerce to restrict or prohibit the interstate sale or transport of commodities, including the most controversial of commodities, slaves.[40] Nor did anyone else suggest that Congress's interstate commerce powers were equivalent to its foreign commerce powers in this respect. As the historian David Lightner notes, "[a]lthough the Antifederalists racked their brains to conjure up every possible objection to the Constitution, not one of them ever suggested that it opened the way for Congress to restrict the interstate movement of slaves."[41] Any number of historians have interpreted the silence of the southern states on this issue as decisive proof that Congress's interstate commerce powers were not intended by the Framers to empower Congress to prohibit the interstate sale or transport of slaves, or anything else.[42]

Southern delegates and Antifederalists also failed to raise any concern about the possibility that Congress might limit what goods traveled in interstate markets in order to advance certain

---

[39] US Const, Art I, § 9, cl 1. See David L. Lightner, *Slavery and the Commerce Power: How the Struggle Against the Interstate Slave Trade Led to the Civil War* 17–19 (Yale, 2006) (discussing the deal).

[40] Walter Berns, *The Constitution and the Migration of Slaves*, 78 Yale L J 198, 205–06 (1968) ("[I]t is surprising how little was said in the South concerning [the Interstate Commerce Clause], surprising because the clause obviously affected commerce in slaves in *some* manner and because, just as obviously, Congress was being given authority to regulate domestic as well foreign commerce."); Abel, 25 Minn L Rev at 476 (cited in note 27) (noting that, in Philadelphia, "the possibility of federal restraints on the movements of slaves in interstate commerce was not once mentioned").

[41] Lightner, *Slavery and the Commerce Power* at 32 (cited in note 39).

[42] See David Brion Davis, *The Problem of Slavery in the Age of Revolution, 1770–1832* 128–29 n 33 (Cornell, 1975) (concluding that there is "no reason to believe that the framers intended or could have agreed upon" giving Congress the power to interdict the interstate slave trade); Abel, 25 Minn L Rev at 475–76 (cited in note 27) (invoking the "deep" and "significant silence" of the southern states as "striking proof of the relatively limited scope of the power over interstate, as compared with foreign, commerce"); Alan N. Greenspan, Note, *The Constitutional Exercise of the Federal Police Power: A Functional Approach to Federalism*, 41 Vand L Rev 1019, 1023 (1988) ("If the power over commerce among the states was intended by the Framers to be an independent grant of affirmative power over domestic affairs . . . the southern states would have perceived the interstate commerce power as a potential threat to the institution of slavery."); Lightner, *Slavery and the Commerce Power* at 36 (cited in note 39) ("[T]he vast majority of white southerners would never have accepted the Constitution if they had thought that it granted such power.").

commercial interests over others. Delegates did worry that the Commerce Clause empowered Congress to establish "mercantile monopolies"—that is, to dictate that only certain persons or entities could provide certain kinds of goods and services to the interstate market.[43] That was as far as it went, however. It seems to have occurred to no one that Congress might act not only to limit who could provide goods and services to the interstate market but also to limit what kinds of interstate markets could exist.

In short, both positive and negative evidence suggests that the Framers did not intend—and probably did not even imagine— that the Interstate Commerce Clause would be read in such a way as to give Congress the power to "restrain" interstate intercourse, as well as to promote it.

Critics of this view make primarily a textual argument. Because Congress's power "to regulate" interstate commerce appears in the same clause granting that power over foreign commerce, critics argue that the two powers must be read *in pari materia*. In other words, if Congress's power "to regulate" foreign commerce includes the power to ban the import of foreign goods—as everyone at the convention agreed it did—then the same must be true of domestic goods as well.[44] But there is no evidence from the Found-

---

[43] One of the reasons that Elbredge Gerry of Massachusetts provided for refusing to sign the Constitution draft was that "[u]nder the power over commerce, monopolies may be established." Farrand, ed, 2 *Records of the Convention* at 633 (cited in note 38). See also Abel, 25 Minn L Rev at 459–60 (cited in note 27).

[44] See, for example, Jack M. Balkin, *Commerce*, 109 Mich L Rev 1, 28 (2010); Nelson and Pushaw, 85 Iowa L Rev at 46 n 185 (cited in note 27). Proponents of this view also sometimes point to the Migration or Importation Clause as textual evidence of the Framers' intent. They argue that the fact that the clause refers to both the migration and the importation of "such Persons as any of the States now existing shall think proper to admit" suggests that it was meant to apply to both the foreign slave trade—which involved the "importation" of slaves into the United States—and the interstate slave trade—which involved their "migration" across state lines. See, for example, Berns, 78 Yale L J at 214 (cited in note 40); see also Robert J. Pushaw Jr. and Grant S. Nelson, *A Critique of the Narrow Interpretation of the Commerce Clause*, 96 Nw U L Rev 695, 702 (2002). The historical evidence does not appear to support this interpretation of the clause, however. Instead, as David Lightner has argued, evidence from the drafting debates suggests that "migration" was either intended to refer to the immigration of free whites or was included in the clause to avoid the ire of antislavery delegates who might object to referring to slaves as property subject to "importation." Lightner, *Slavery and the Commerce Power* at 27, 36 (cited in note 39) (noting that the "preponderance of evidence is against the Berns thesis"). See also Paul Finkelman, *Slavery and the Founders: Race and Liberty in the Age of Jefferson* 204 n 87 (Sharpe, 2d ed 2001) (arguing that Berns's thesis "defies all understanding of the Convention" and that "Berns . . . provides no evidence that anyone at the Constitutional Convention or in any of the state ratifying conventions believed this. . . . At no time before 1861 did any president, leader of Congress, or majority in either house of Congress accept this analysis.").

ing to support this position, other than the language of the clause itself, and there is no reason the verb "to regulate" must mean the same thing in different contexts.

First, when the Constitution invoked the power "to regulate," it did not always encompass the power to prohibit. For example, Article I, Section 8 gives Congress the power "to coin money, [and] *regulate* the Value thereof." One might respond that, given the context, it simply makes no sense to read the clause as granting Congress the power to "coin money [and] to prohibit its value."[45] But that's the very point—to the Framing generation it also seems not to have made sense to read the power "to regulate" interstate commerce to include the power to prohibit it. It is difficult to believe that if it had occurred to them, it would not have engendered discussion similar to what occurred regarding the foreign commerce power.

Second, and perhaps more important, the foreign and interstate commerce powers were understood as aimed at distinct evils, suggesting that the power "to regulate" each must be read to address distinct problems. James Madison certainly argued as much. In 1819, when debates about the introduction of slavery into the Missouri territories broke out, Madison expressly denied that Congress had the authority to ban the interstate sale of slaves, notwithstanding its clear authority to ban their foreign import and export.[46] In a letter he wrote to Virginia state senator Joseph Cabell in 1829, Madison made even more explicit his view that the interstate and foreign commerce clauses were neither intended, nor should be construed, as vesting Congress with equivalent power. "I always foresaw that difficulties might be started in relation to [the interstate commerce power]," Madison stated.

> Being in the same terms with the power over foreign commerce, the same extent, if taken literally, would belong to it. Yet it is very certain that it grew out of the abuse of the power by the importing states in taxing the non-importing, and was intended as a negative and preventive provision against injustice among the States themselves, rather than as a power to be used for the positive purposes of the General Government, in which alone, however, the remedial power could be lodged.

---

[45] Randy Barnett makes this point, even while remaining committed to a textualist interpretation of the clause as a whole. Randy E. Barnett, *The Original Meaning of the Commerce Clause*, 68 U Chi L Rev 101, 140 (2001).

[46] Letter from James Madison to Robert Walsh (Nov 27, 1819), in Max Farrand, ed, 3 *The Records of the Federal Convention of 1787* 437 (rev ed 1937).

> And it will be safer to leave the power with this key to it, than to extend
> it all the qualities and incidental means belonging to the power over
> foreign commerce.[47]

Madison hardly stands alone on this point; a number of commentators since have made precisely the same point: that despite
the similarity of constitutional language, the two powers should
be interpreted differently, in light of the very different problems
to which they were addressed.[48]

B. SUBSEQUENT INTERPRETATIONS

This interpretation of the Founders' intentions is reinforced by
the first century of postratification practice. Although Congress
regularly passed laws prohibiting foreign trade, it did not pass any
laws to prohibit interstate trade for well over one hundred years.
On a few occasions it passed laws that restricted what goods could
travel across state lines, but only when doing so was necessary to
safeguard a domestic market or helped enforce the diverse domestic policies of the states. Still, Congress did not pass a ban on
commerce that was neither an in-service law nor a helper law for
the country's first century.

1. *No breach during the first century.* Following ratification, in
the area of *foreign* commerce, Congress passed a number of what
Hamilton referred to as "prohibitory regulations." In 1794, for
example, it passed a law banning the export from the United States
of "any cannon, muskets, pistols, bayonets, swords, cutlasses, mus-
ket balls, lead, bombs, grenados, gunpowder, sulphur or salt-
petre."[49] In 1806, it banned the importation of any silk, leather,
hemp, tin, or brass goods from Great Britain or Ireland.[50] In 1807,
it banned the importation of slaves, effective January 1, 1808.[51]

---

[47] Letter from James Madison to Joseph C. Cabell (Feb 13, 1829), in Farrand, ed, 3 *Records of the Convention* at 478 (cited in note 46).

[48] See Regan, 94 Mich L Rev at 577–78 n 95 (cited in note 7) (arguing that the verb "regulate" "has a different most natural meaning as applied to foreign and to interstate commerce, given that the situations of the union and the individual states are quite different in these two arenas"); Abel, 25 Minn L Rev at 475 (cited in note 27) ("Despite the formal parallelism of the grants, there is no tenable reason for believing that anywhere nearly so large a range of action was given over commerce 'among the several states' as over that 'with foreign nations.'").

[49] Act of May 22, 1794, 1 Stat 369.

[50] Act of Apr 18, 1806, 2 Stat 379.

[51] Act of Mar 2, 1807, 2 Stat 426.

Most dramatically, three days before Christmas 1807, it passed an Embargo Act, prohibiting all ships in the United States from traveling to foreign ports, save with the express permission of the President.[52] The Act, and supplementary Embargo Acts passed the following year, made "virtually everything that moved in commerce in the United States potentially subject to seizure."[53]

In contrast, although Congress passed many regulations of domestic commerce, it enacted no prohibitions of what kinds of goods could travel in interstate commerce. The First Congress almost immediately set about establishing rules for the licensing of ships that participated in coastal (that is, interstate) trade.[54] It funded the building of lighthouses, beacons, buoys, and public piers.[55] In later years, Congress remained heavily involved in regulating and improving the waterways and other channels of interstate commerce, and the ships that traveled along them.[56] It also passed, very early on, a number of helper laws, designed to lend federal muscle to the enforcement of state trade regulations and restrictions. In 1799, for example, Congress enacted "An Act respecting Quarantines and Health Laws."[57] The Act "authorized and required [officers of the Unites States] faithfully to aid in the execution of [state] quarantines and health laws, according to their respective powers and precincts, and as they shall be directed, from time to time, by the Secretary of the Treasury of the United States."[58] At no point, however, did Congress establish its own restrictions on what goods could travel across state lines.

Indeed, where prohibitions targeted at foreign trade appeared likely to affect the domestic market, Congress expressly carved out exemptions for those engaged in interstate trade. Hence, a proviso to the Embargo Acts exempted from its prohibitions any ships that engaged in purely domestic trade. The only caveat was

---

[52] Embargo Act of 1807, 2 Stat 451.

[53] Jerry L. Mashaw, *Reluctant Nationalists: Federal Administration and Administrative Law in the Republican Era, 1801–1829*, 116 Yale L J 1636, 1654 (2007).

[54] See, for example, Act of Sept 1, 1789, 1 Stat 55.

[55] Act of Aug 7, 1789, 1 Stat 53.

[56] Hence, for example, in 1838 and 1852 Congress passed a series of ambitious statutes, setting rules for the construction and maintenance of steamboat boilers. Robert L. Rabin, *Federal Regulation in Historical Perspective*, 38 Stan L Rev 1189, 1196 (1986).

[57] Act of Feb 25, 1799, 1 Stat 619.

[58] Id. See also Act of Apr 2, 1790, 1 Stat 106 (directing federal customs officers to "pay due regard to the inspection laws of the states in which they may respectively act").

that "the owner, master, consignee, or factor of the vessel" had to give bond to guarantee that "the ship's cargo would be re-landed in some port of the United States, 'dangers of the sea excepted.'"[59]

It was not until the 1818–19 debates about whether slavery would be permitted in the new state of Missouri that slavery abolitionists came up with the argument that Congress had the constitutional authority to ban the interstate sale as well as the importation of slaves.[60] The fact that it took thirty years for abolitionist groups to recognize that the Commerce Clause could be interpreted to vest Congress with the same power to prohibit the interstate as the foreign slave trade suggests how strongly the assumptions of the Founding generation dictated the opposite conclusion.

Outside of the immediate context of the slavery debate, no one suggested that Congress could or should impose any restraints on what goods circulated in interstate markets. Instead, it appears to have been widely accepted that, as the House Judiciary Committee report put it, Congress did not have the power "to prohibit the free transportation of the products of each State through and into every other."[61] This helps explain why, in 1849, a report examining the efficacy of a federal law that banned the importation, but not the domestic sale or interstate transport, of adulterated medicines could note without elaboration that the bill would be far more effective if it also banned domestic manufacture or sale of drugs, but that under the constitutional system, only the states had the power to enact such a ban.[62]

To the extent Congress wanted to ban articles of commerce in the first hundred years, it relied on other Article I powers. In 1867, Congress passed a law banning the sale, and the possession with intent to sell, of a particular kind of "illuminating oil."[63] But

---

[59] Mashaw, 116 Yale L J at 1651 (cited in note 53) (citing Embargo Act § 1).

[60] Lightner, *Slavery and the Commerce Power* at 37–38, 48–52 (cited in note 39). The first suggestion Congress might have such power was made by worried southerners in 1807 in the context of Congress exercising its power to ban the importation of slavery in 1808. Id at 37.

[61] HR Rep No 49-1880 at 2 (cited in note 25).

[62] *Report of the Secretary of the Treasury*, S Exec Doc No 30-16, 30th Cong, 2d Sess 8 (concluding that "[t]he general government has done all in its power, and it is incumbent on the several States, by special statute, to render penal the conduct that endangers the lives and health of the citizens").

[63] Revenue Act of 1867 § 29, 14 Stat 471, 484.

those who passed the law apparently believed that they were exercising their taxing, rather than their Commerce Clause authority—or at least hoped to make it appear that way. Hence, the ban was included in the Internal Revenue Act of March 2, 1867, and applied generally, rather than to just the sale or possession with intent to sell across state lines.[64] The Supreme Court nevertheless struck the statute down as an unconstitutional attempt to use the Commerce Clause to enact a "police regulation, relating exclusively to the internal trade of the States."[65] Suitably chastened, Congress did not repeat the mistake. When, in the 1860s and 1870s, it got increasingly involved in the moral policing of domestic markets—for reasons we explore below—it relied on the Postal Clause, rather than its Commerce Clause powers, to do so. In 1868, Congress passed a law banning the distribution of lottery tickets in the mail.[66] In 1873, it passed the Comstock Act, which made it illegal to send obscene material (including material about contraception) through the mail.[67] And when it finally passed the Oleomargarine Act in 1886, it imposed a tax rather than a ban, to avoid any constitutional difficulties.[68]

2. *No breach despite industrialization.* By the late nineteenth century, industrialization and the nationalization of the market were putting increasing pressure on Congress to enact commercial regulations. As many scholars have noted, industrialization contributed to economic growth but also posed a serious challenge to local and state systems of regulation by rendering an increasing amount of economic life beyond their jurisdiction and control.[69] In addition, in an increasingly nationalized marketplace, clashing state regulations of matters such as food quality and labeling troubled manufacturers seeking to do business on a national scale,

---

[64] Robert L. Stern, *That Commerce Which Concerns More States Than One*, 47 Harv L Rev 1335, 1357–58 (1934). See also *United States v Dewitt*, 76 US (9 Wall) 41, 43 (1869) (noting the claim that, in passing the statute, Congress intended to exercise its power under the Taxing Clause).

[65] *Dewitt*, 76 US at 43–44.

[66] Act of July 27, 1868 § 13, 15 Stat 194, 196.

[67] 17 Stat 598.

[68] 24 Stat 209.

[69] See, for example, Rabin, 38 Stan L Rev at 1194 (cited in note 56) (explaining how the interconnectedness of railroads obligated Congress to regulate them).

leading industry groups to lobby Congress in the 1880s and 1890s to act.[70]

Yet, when Congress responded to the pressures of industrialization with legislation, it largely adhered to the original understanding of the interstate commerce power as more limited in scope than the foreign commerce power. Hence, although in the late nineteenth century, Congress passed a number of bills prohibiting the import and export of adulterated or otherwise inferior food and drugs, it refused to similarly regulate the domestic food and drug markets.[71] Congress's reluctance was due largely to concerted opposition by states' rights advocates who argued that such legislation would amount to "virtually a regulation of [ ] manufacture within the state" and therefore exceeded Congress's power under the Commerce Clause.[72]

On several occasions, Congress did in fact pass legislation that prohibited the transport of goods across state lines, but these laws were plainly "in service" of the well-being of the national economy, rather than an attempt to dictate to the states what goods were proper subjects of commerce. In 1884, for example, Congress passed the Animal Industry Act, which banned the transport of diseased cattle across state lines.[73] The purpose of the Act was to ensure that the "great transcontinental lines of railways, and their network of branches . . . [that were then] rapidly penetrating to all the valleys and grazing ranges of the West" did not threaten the health of the domestic cattle industry by carrying disease to all the states through which they passed.[74] Similar justifications

---

[70] Charles Wesley Dunn, *Original Food and Drugs Act of 1906: Its Legislative History*, 1 Food Drug Cosm L J 297, 306, 303 (1946) ("[W]hen the 1906 act was enacted the state food and drug laws were in an irreconcilable condition of divergent and conflicting provisions, e.g., with respect to food standards" and that as a result "organizations of the food and drug industries and trades . . . supported the enactment of th[e federal] law from the beginning to the end of its legislative career.").

[71] Examples of import laws regulating food and drugs that Congress passed during this period include the Tea Importation Act, 29 Stat 604 (1897), the Meat Inspection Act, 26 Stat 1089 (1891), and the Import Drugs Act, 9 Stat 237 (1848). For discussion of Congress's failure to pass similar regulations of the domestic market, see Thomas A. Bailey, *Congressional Opposition to Pure Food Legislation, 1879–1906*, 36 Am J Soc 52, 52 (1930) (noting that during this period "it was comparatively easy to pass a measure governing the importation of foreign goods, less easy to regulate exported goods, less easy to improve food conditions in the District of Columbia, and exceedingly difficult to prohibit adulterated foods in interstate commerce").

[72] Dunn, 1 Food Drug Cosm L J at 307 (cited in note 70).

[73] Animal Industry Act, 23 Stat 31 (1884).

[74] *Bureau of Animal Industry*, HR Rep 48-119, 48th Cong, 1st Sess 4 (1884).

were invoked in support of the 1893 National Quarantine Act, which authorized the Secretary of the Treasury to make rules and regulations to prevent the introduction of disease into any state or territory whose own regulations were deemed to be insufficient to do so.[75]

In-service laws of this kind had an established lineage. The Steamboat Boiler Act of 1838, for example, prohibited the transportation of any goods "upon the bays, lakes, rivers or other navigable waters of the United States" on any steamboats that had not satisfied the inspection requirements set up by the Act.[76] It did so to ensure the safety of what was at the time one of the most important instruments of interstate trade and transportation in the United States. It thus provides a very early example of an in-service law that included a prohibition.

Despite the existence of precedents like the Steamboat Boiler Act, however, it is notable that both the Animal Industry Act and the National Quarantine Act generated considerable constitutional debate. Opponents challenged the constitutionality of what appeared at the time to be the unprecedented use of federal power to limit what goods could travel across state lines.[77] (Earlier statutes, like the Steamboat Boiler Act, targeted only the vehicles that carried goods across state lines, not the goods themselves.) The fact that even what appears today to be federal regulation of the most obvious and necessary kind engendered stiff opposition when it involved a ban on commerce emphasizes the original understanding that it was the states, and the states alone, that determined

---

[75] National Quarantine Act, 27 Stat 449 (1893); Edwin Maxey, *Federal Quarantine Laws*, 23 Pol Sci Q 617, 622 (1908) ("recurring epidemics of yellow fever in the sixties, seventies and eighties created a popular sentiment which forced Congress to do something more than 'second the motion.'"). Maxey notes, however, that "[e]ven under pressure, Congress moved very cautiously." Id.

[76] Steamboat Boiler Act of 1838 § 2, 5 Stat 304.

[77] See, for example, 15 Cong Rec 938–39 (Feb 6, 1884) (statement of Rep Gibson) (calling the Animal Industry Act a "fraud" and objecting to the fact that the bill gives to a federal agent the power to "adopt rules and methods and say in what kind of cars you shall carry your cattle, . . . and that no man shall transport cattle otherwise than according to the rules adopted by [the agent]"; arguing also that, by vesting a federal agent with the power to "build a wall of fire around" any state that it found to possess diseased cattle, the bill "invade[s] constitutional rights . . . [and] invade[s] every idea and every principle of good government"); Carleton B. Chapman and John M. Talmadge, *Historical and Political Background of Federal Health Care Legislation*, 35 L & Contemp Probs 334, 339 (1970) (noting that the Quarantine Act passed but only "after lively debate" and significant opposition from states' rights advocates, who argued that Congress had "no jurisdiction to enact quarantine or health laws overruling the laws of the states").

what goods were fit subjects of commerce in their markets.

Legislative debates over the Wilson Act of 1890 also demonstrate the strength of Congress's commitment in the late nineteenth century to the view that it belonged to the states to determine what goods circulated in their markets—though Congress could pass "helper laws" to assist with enforcement. The Wilson Act provided that all liquor transported into a state or territory "shall upon arrival . . . be subject to the operation and effect of the laws of such State or Territory . . . to the same extent and in the same manner as" domestically produced liquor.[78] The Act was a direct response to the Supreme Court's holding in *Leisy v Hardin*, handed down earlier that year, that states could not constitutionally ban the sale of alcohol imports—at least so long as they remained in their original packaging.[79] The opinion did suggest, however, that states like Iowa could ban the sale of such goods if and when Congress gave them permission to do so.[80] The Wilson Act was Congress's attempt to do just that.

In adopting the Wilson Act, members of Congress went out of their way to make clear that it was a helper law, and as such did not trench on the states' police powers. Senator James Wilson argued, for example, that the bill was intended only "to grant to the states what may be called a local option, to allow them to do as they please in regard to the liquor question."[81] Senator James George, a states-right Democrat from Mississippi, confessed that he was "constrained to support the bill, since only through such legislation can the States, under the decision of the Supreme Court, exercise their rightful and necessary jurisdiction over" the liquor question.[82] Indeed, like the 1799 "Act respecting Quarantines and Health Laws"[83]—and many other helper statutes Congress passed subsequently—the Wilson Act supported, rather than supplanted, state policymaking by providing federal muscle and federal legitimacy to help enforce state regulations. Thus it is that

---

[78] Wilson Act, 26 Stat 313 (1890).

[79] 135 US 100, 125 (1890).

[80] Id at 123–24.

[81] Richard F. Hamm, *Shaping the Eighteenth Amendment: Temperance Reform, Legal Culture, and the Polity, 1880–1920* 80 (North Carolina, 1995).

[82] 21 Cong Rec 4957–58 (May 20, 1890); see also id at 5325–30 (May 27, 1890) (statement of Sen George) (elaborating on this point).

[83] Act of Feb 25, 1799, 1 Stat 619.

throughout the nineteenth century, Congress adhered to the view that its power over interstate commerce did not include the power to prohibit that commerce, at least when doing so was not an in-service law necessary to conserve the safety and well-being of the channels of interstate commerce, or a helper law necessary to help ensure the effectiveness of state policymaking. Views on this limitation were about to change, however, in the aftermath of the Supreme Court's decision in *Champion v Ames*.

II. Of Vestigial Virtue and Vice: The Champion Power

The 1903 decision in *Champion v Ames* was taken by some to signal a decisive shift away from the view—dominant through the end of the nineteenth century—that Congress lacked the power under the Commerce Clause to prohibit interstate commerce that the states would allow.[84] But, as we make clear below, a far narrower reading of *Champion* was available, one that was perfectly consistent with earlier understandings of the scope of Congress's commerce power. In this part, we explain why views of Congress's commerce power changed in the wake of *Champion*, and show how the decision came to be interpreted to allow Congress to exercise a police power akin to that of the states.

A. CHAMPION, ON ITS OWN TERMS

At issue in *Champion* was the constitutionality of an 1895 law, "An Act for the suppression of lottery traffic through national and interstate commerce," conventionally known as the Lottery Act.[85] The Act made it a crime to bring lottery tickets into the United States or to carry them "from one State to another in the United States."[86] The defendant, Charles F. Champion, was arrested after he used the Wells Fargo Express Company to ship Paraguayan

---

[84] *Champion v Ames*, 188 US 321 (1903). In 1911, for example, Frederick H. Cooke interpreted *Champion* to mean that "under the power to regulate commerce, Congress may likewise interfere by way of prohibition or otherwise with transportation between points in different states." Frederick H. Cooke, *The Source of Authority to Engage in Interstate Commerce*, 24 Harv L Rev 635, 638–39 (1911). See also Alfred Russell, *Three Constitutional Questions Decided by the Federal Supreme Court During the Last Four Months*, 37 Am L Rev 503, 505–07 (1903) ("So the court decided [in *Champion*] . . . that the power to regulate does involve the power to prohibit interstate commerce altogether").

[85] Lottery Act, 28 Stat 963 (1895).

[86] Id.

lottery tickets from San Antonio, Texas, to Fresno, California.[87] Champion argued that his arrest was illegal because Congress lacked the constitutional authority to prohibit the interstate circulation of lottery tickets.[88] After hearing argument in the case twice, the Court, in a 5–4 decision, sustained Congress's power to enact the Lottery Act under the Commerce Clause.

Although *Champion* was later read to grant Congress broad power to prohibit the interstate transport of goods, Justice Harlan's opinion made perfectly clear that he viewed the Lottery Act as a helper statute, an attempt by Congress to shore up state police power, not to trench upon it. He was quite explicit on this point:

> In legislating upon the subject of the traffic in lottery tickets, as carried on through interstate commerce, *Congress only supplemented the action of those States*—perhaps all of them—which, for the protection of the public morals, prohibit the drawing of lotteries, as well as the sale or circulation of lottery tickets, within their respective limits. *It said, in effect, that it would not permit the declared policy of the States, which sought to protect their people against the mischiefs of the lottery business, to be overthrown or disregarded by the agency of interstate commerce.*[89]

Congressional power was necessary to aid the states, Justice Harlan explained, because "Congress alone has the power to occupy, by legislation, the whole field of interstate commerce."[90] As one commentator explained, "The power was exercised it was said, not in hostility to the State, but supplementing the actions of those States which had for the protection of public morals prohibited the drawing of lotteries or the circulation of lottery tickets within their respective limits."[91]

This reading of the decision is supported by the fact that, when Congress passed the Lottery Act in 1895, all forty-four states already banned lotteries.[92] The statute thus merely reflected the widely shared view that lotteries were a "pestilence" that had to be exterminated. Unlike the Wilson and Animal Industry Acts, the Lottery Act was passed with almost no constitutional debate

---

[87] Herbert F. Margulies, *Pioneering the Federal Police Power: Champion v. Ames and the Anti-Lottery Act of 1895*, 4 J Southern Legal Hist 45, 46 (1996).

[88] Id.

[89] *Champion*, 188 US at 357 (emphasis added).

[90] Id.

[91] Paul Fuller, *Is There a Federal Police Power?*, 4 Colum L Rev 563, 584 (1904).

[92] G. Robert Blakey and Harold A. Kurland, *The Development of the Federal Law of Gambling*, 63 Cornell L Rev 923, 941 (1978).

whatsoever, suggesting that members of Congress did not believe they were doing anything novel.[93] Undoubtedly many members of Congress viewed the statute as nothing more than a helper statute that lent federal muscle to help enforce the state prohibitions on the sale of lottery tickets.

In this context, the *Champion* majority's conclusion that the Lottery Act was a legitimate exercise of Congress's commerce power may stand for something much less than a blanket authority to ban. Indeed, Justice Harlan was careful to narrow the scope of the holding. He did state that "regulation may sometimes appropriately assume the form of prohibition," but this assertion was made in the specific context of a discussion of Court decisions upholding in-service and helper statutes.[94] Furthermore, responding to the dissenters' complaints about the possible reach of the opinion, Justice Harlan made clear that he was deciding what needed to be decided, and no more:

> *It is said*, however, that if, in order to suppress lotteries carried on through interstate commerce, Congress may exclude lottery tickets from such commerce, *that principle leads necessarily to the conclusion that Congress may arbitrarily exclude from commerce among the states any article, commodity, or thing, of whatever kind or nature, or however useful or valuable*, which it may choose, no matter with what motive, to declare shall not be carried from one state to another. *It will be time enough to consider the constitutionality of such legislation when we must do so. The present case does not require the court to declare the full extent of the power that Congress may exercise in the regulation of commerce among the states.*[95]

Thus *Champion* need not be, and perhaps should not be, read—despite some loose language in Justice Harlan's opinion—to hold

---

[93] Margulies, 4 J Southern Legal Hist at 50–51 (cited in note 87).

[94] *Champion*, 188 US at 358. As support for this claim, Justice Harlan pointed specifically to *In re Rahrer*, 140 US 545 (1891), which affirmed the constitutionality of the Wilson Act, the helper statute discussed in Part II, and *Reid v Colorado*, 187 US 137 (1902), which recognized federal power to enact the Animal Industry Act, the in-service law discussed also in Part II. See 188 US at 359–60. Justice Harlan also invoked the Sherman Antitrust Act, 26 Stat 209 (1890), as "an illustration of the proposition that regulation may take the form of prohibition." *Champion*, 188 US at 360. As Justice Harlan himself noted, the object of the Sherman Act was "to protect trade and commerce against unlawful restraints and monopolies." Id. The Sherman Act was therefore, like the Animal Industry Act but unlike the Lottery Act, an in-service law that aimed to protect interstate markets from the problems associated with monopolization, rather than to limit what markets could exist.

[95] Id at 362 (emphasis added).

that Congress's power to regulate commerce necessarily includes the power to prohibit it.

B. WHY THE BREACH AFTER CHAMPION?

Despite Justice Harlan's careful qualifications, Congress was quick to read *Champion* as granting it broad authority to prohibit the transport of articles of commerce across state lines, and in subsequent cases the Court upheld Congress's authority to do so.[96] Only once thereafter, in *Hammer v Dagenhart*, did the Court impose any limits on Congress's authority to prohibit the interstate movement of goods—and even then, the Court quickly abandoned its own limitation.[97]

Two factors appear to have motivated Congress, as well as the Court, to affirm a broad federal power to ban interstate commerce. First, industrialization, and the increasingly integrated nature of the national economy, led industry groups and others to place increasing pressure on Congress to regulate the national marketplace. Because the Commerce Clause jurisprudence of the late nineteenth century made it impossible for Congress to regulate economic production directly, it embraced a broad interpretation of *Champion* to justify its regulation of products (as well as persons) crossing state lines. This use of *Champion* quickly became vestigial, however, once the Court—in cases such as *NLRB v Jones & Laughlin Steel Corp.* and *United States v Darby*—recognized Congress's authority to regulate activities that, even if not commerce themselves, have a "substantial effect" on interstate commerce.[98] Sec-

---

[96] See, for example, *Hoke v United States*, 227 US 308 (1913) (affirming Congress's power to prohibit the interstate transportation of women for purposes of prostitution); *United States v Sullivan*, 332 US 689 (1948) (affirming Congress's power to prohibit the sale of unlabeled goods that had at one point in their life cycle crossed state lines); *Gonzales v Raich*, 545 US 1 (2005) (affirming Congress's power to prohibit the intrastate possession and sale of drugs). See generally Diane McGimsey, *The Commerce Clause and Federalism after Lopez and Morrison: The Case for Closing the Jurisdictional-Element Loophole*, 90 Cal L Rev 1675, 1685–1701 (2002) (chronicling the evolution of the *Champion* line of cases).

[97] 247 US 251 (1918). The *Hammer* Court held that, although Congress could prohibit goods when the fact of transportation itself was necessary to the harm that the federal prohibition aimed to prevent—when, in other words, the harm came about either during or after the transportation of the good—it could not constitutionally prohibit goods in order to prevent harms that occurred prior to transportation. Id at 271. Whether or not this distinction was a plausible one, the Court quickly lost its commitment to enforcing it. See *United States v Darby*, 312 US 100, 116 (1941) (noting that "*Hammer v. Dagenhart* has not been followed" and citing cases).

[98] *NLRB v Jones & Laughlin Steel Corp.*, 301 US 1, 37 (1937); *United States v Darby*, 312 US 100, 119–20 (1941).

ond, the social changes taking place in early twentieth-century America led to the growth of popular movements aimed at the prohibition of vices such as alcohol and gambling. These movements increasingly focused their demands on the federal, rather than the state, governments. *Champion*'s potentially expansive view of federal power over goods moving across state lines allowed Congress to respond to both sets of demands.

1. *Regulating the national economy—until the rise of "substantial effects."* Although *Champion* was itself ambiguous on whether, and to what extent, Congress could prohibit the interstate transportation of goods when those goods did not themselves pose a direct threat to the instrumentalities of commerce, it was quickly seized on to justify federal regulation of the interstate food and drug markets. *Champion* was cited in the congressional debates over the Pure Food and Drug Act of 1906, for example, and when a unanimous Court upheld the law, it expressly invoked *Champion* as authority.[99]

Champion was soon put to even broader purposes yet; it was relied upon as justification for the federal regulation of economic production and other purely intrastate economic activities that previously had been understood to be beyond the scope of Congress's power. In *United States v E. C. Knight*, the Supreme Court had held that Congress was powerless under the Sherman Antitrust Act to criminalize the establishment of a monopoly power in sugar production.[100] The Court famously drew a line between the regulation of "manufacturing"—a purely intrastate activity beyond Congress's authority—and the regulation of interstate commerce itself:

> The fact that an article is manufactured for export to another state does not of itself make it an article of interstate commerce, and the intent of the manufacturer does not determine the time when the article or product passes from the control of the state and belongs to commerce.[101]

Champion allowed Congress to work around the restrictions that

---

[99] See, for example, 40 Cong Rec 2762 (Feb 21, 1906) (statement of Sen Knox) (quoting heavily from *Champion*); *Hipolite Egg Co. v United States*, 220 US 45, 57–58 (1911) (citing *Champion* as support for Congress's power not only to prohibit the transportation of adulterated food and drugs across state lines, but also to seize food and drugs shipped in contravention of the law "wherever [they are] found").

[100] 156 US 1, 16–18 (1895).

[101] Id at 13.

the decision in *E. C. Knight* imposed on its ability to regulate production and manufacturing. Although Congress could not, under *E. C. Knight*, regulate intrastate commercial activity directly, it could achieve the same result by banning the products of that activity from interstate commerce. In 1938, for example, in *Electric Bond & Share Company v SEC*, the Court cited *Champion* to support the constitutionality of provisions of the Public Utility Holding Company Act that punished holding companies that failed to register with the Securities and Exchange Commission by barring them from the use of the instrumentalities of commerce.[102] Similarly, in *NLRB v Fainblatt*, in 1939, the Court invoked *Champion* to uphold the application of the National Labor Relations Act to employers who were not themselves engaged in interstate commerce but who received and shipped goods in interstate commerce.[103]

This first novel use of the *Champion* rule served as a stopgap measure between the "spatialized" conception of federal commerce power of the nineteenth-century cases, and the "consequentialist" model of congressional power that would emerge from the New Deal cases. Under the earlier model, the boundary between federal commerce power and state police power was drawn with reference to the location of the regulated goods and their position in a stream of commerce. Under the rule first articulated by Chief Justice Marshall in *Brown v Maryland*, federal power attached to goods that traveled in interstate markets only while they remained in transit.[104] The decision in *E. C. Knight* made clear how strongly this spatialized model continued to dominate constitutional jurisprudence at the turn of the century. Indeed, the central justification that the *E. C. Knight* Court provided for why federal power did not reach manufacturing was a temporal one: namely, that "[c]ommerce succeeds to manufacture, and is not a part of it."[105]

By continuing to identify federal commerce power with the movement of goods across state lines, *Champion*, and the cases that followed after it, managed to adhere to this essentially spatialized conception while at the same time expanding federal power to regulate the national economy. Decisions such as *Electric Bond &*

---

[102] 303 US 419, 442 (1938).

[103] 306 US 601, 608–09 (1939).

[104] 25 US 419, 441–42 (1827).

[105] *E. C. Knight*, 156 US at 12.

Share Company and *Fainblatt* demonstrate how the *Champion* rule allowed Congress to evade at least some of the restrictions imposed on its authority by the commerce-manufacturing distinction. But under this approach the test of federal power became increasingly formal, requiring only that some kind of interstate movement take place, at some point in the life of the regulated object or entity.[106]

Beginning with the decision in *Jones & Laughlin*, however, the Court moved away from its spatialized approach and toward a new consequentialist logic of "effects."[107] The "effects" test focused not on the location of the regulated activities but instead on their connection to, and effect upon, the integrated interstate economy. This approach took the integrated nature of the national economy as a given, and asked whether the regulated activity had an impact on it.

Wickard v Filburn is emblematic of the new consequentialist approach.[108] The facts of *Wickard* are familiar. Filburn, who grew wheat for consumption on his family farm, exceeded his congressionally authorized allotment. The question was whether Congress had the power to regulate Filburn's purely intrastate, noncommercial cultivation of wheat.[109] The Supreme Court answered in the affirmative: "Even if appellee's activity be local and though it may not be regarded as commerce, it may still, whatever its nature, be reached by Congress if it exerts a substantial economic effect on interstate commerce."[110]

Wickard is controversial among those who today fret over the extent of congressional power, but if the substantial effects test makes sense, then so does *Wickard*.[111] The law at issue in *Wickard*—

---

[106] In later cases, the Court explicitly held as much. See *Scarborough v United States*, 431 US 563 (1977) (finding the fact that a gun had at some point in its life cycle traveled across state lines sufficient to vest Congress with the authority to regulate it under the Commerce Clause); *United States v Bass*, 404 US 336, 350 (1971) (suggesting same); McGimsey, 90 Cal L Rev at 1700 (cited in note 96) ("In sum, after *Bass* and *Scarborough*, . . . Congress could regulate any person or good that had ever crossed state lines, even if that line crossing was entirely unconnected with the regulated activity, as long as Congress included a jurisdictional element in the statute.").

[107] *Jones & Laughlin*, 301 US at 37.

[108] 317 US 111 (1942).

[109] Id at 113–14.

[110] Id at 125.

[111] See, for example, Richard A. Epstein, *The Proper Scope of the Commerce Power*, 73 Va L Rev 1387, 1450–51 (1987) (criticizing *Wickard* as "stand[ing] a clause of the Constitution upon its head").

the Agricultural Adjustment Act of 1938—was intended to stabilize
wheat prices by limiting the domestic production of the crop.[112]
Although Filburn intended to use his above-quota wheat on his
own farm rather than selling it on the open market—and even if
he had, what he produced was, in terms of the national market,
only a miniscule amount of wheat—what the *Wickard* Court recognized was that if everyone did what Filburn did, demand for
wheat on the open market would drop and so would prices, thereby
undermining the congressional scheme.[113] *Wickard* thus gave birth
to the notion that in evaluating substantial effects, any given activity must be considered in the aggregate.[114] One might disagree
with the law at issue in *Wickard* on policy terms, but if Congress
was going to have regulatory control over the national economy,
then Filburn's conduct was logically within that power.

Once cases like *Wickard* made clear that Congress no longer
needed to rely upon interstate movement to justify its regulation
of the national economy, but could regulate activities that were
themselves not interstate commerce so long as they had a substantial effect on interstate commerce, the first novel use of *Champion* became entirely vestigial. The pivot point was *United States
v Darby*, the decision that (*a*) gave the substantial-effects line of
cases its name, but (*b*) also still relied heavily upon the now unnecessary *Champion* rationale to sustain the legislation there at
issue.[115] *Darby* involved a challenge to provisions of the Fair Labor
Standards Act, which set minimum wages and maximum hours for
employees who engaged in the production of goods for interstate
commerce.[116] In his opinion for a unanimous Court, Justice Stone
invoked *Champion* both to affirm the constitutionality of the pro-

---

[112] 317 US at 115, citing Agricultural Adjustment Act of 1938, § 331, 52 Stat 52 (codified
at 7 USC § 1331).

[113] See *Wickard*, 317 US at 128–29 ("It is well established by decisions of this Court
that the power to regulate commerce includes the power to regulate the prices at which
commodities in that commerce are dealt in and practices affecting such prices. . . . It can
hardly be denied that a factor of such volume and variability as home-consumed wheat
would have a substantial influence on price and market conditions. . . . This record leaves
us in no doubt that Congress may properly have considered that wheat consumed on the
farm where grown, if wholly outside the scheme of regulation, would have a substantial
effect in defeating and obstructing its purpose to stimulate trade therein at increased
prices.").

[114] Id at 127–28.

[115] *Darby*, 312 US at 119–20.

[116] Id at 108–09.

hibition on the interstate shipment of goods made in violation of the Act and to affirm the constitutionality of the wage and hour provisions.[117]

The Court's first basis for upholding the FLSA relied on the logic of *Champion*, applied in what can only be characterized as an "inside-out" way. The prohibition on interstate shipment was constitutional, Justice Stone argued, because "Congress . . . is free to exclude from the commerce articles whose use in the states for which they are destined it may conceive to be injurious to the public health, morals or welfare, even though the state has not sought to regulate their use."[118] Note the oddness of the reasoning here. Congress's power to regulate what ultimately crosses state lines was used to reach backward to allow it to control what eventually will cross state lines. Obedience to *Champion* required the Court effectively to turn the FLSA on its head, construing the regulations that were its primary purpose—the wage and hour provisions—as merely necessary and proper means of effectuating the border-crossing prohibition.

Darby is a landmark case, however, because of the entirely separate argument Justice Stone made to justify the constitutionality of the FLSA wage and hour provisions: the logic of substantial effects. Specifically, Justice Stone held that the FLSA's wage and hour regulations were constitutional because they were a necessary and proper means, not to effectuate the ban on interstate circulation, but to protect the market against "unfair competition." As he explained:

> [T]he evils aimed at by the Act are the spread of substandard labor conditions through the use of the facilities of interstate commerce for competition by the goods so produced with those produced under the prescribed or better labor conditions; and the consequent dislocation of the commerce itself caused by the impairment or destruction of local businesses by competition made effective through interstate commerce. The Act is thus directed at the suppression of a method or kind of competition in interstate commerce which it has in effect condemned as "unfair," as the Clayton Act has condemned other "unfair methods of competition" made effective through interstate commerce. . . . The means adopted by § 15(a)(2) for the protection of interstate commerce by the suppression of the production of the condemned goods for in-

---

[117] Id at 113–16, 124.

[118] Id at 114.

terstate commerce is so related to the commerce and so affects it as to
be within the reach of the commerce power.[119]

In other words, Congress could directly regulate wages and hours,
not because those goods would someday cross state lines, but because their manufacture affected commerce, and the regulation of
interstate commerce now was understood in an integrated national
economy to include commercial activity in one state that might
indirectly affect commercial activity in the others.

As *Darby* demonstrated, once courts had available to them the
consequentialist vocabulary of substantial effects, they no longer
needed to rely upon the formal logic of the *Champion* cases to
uphold Congressional regulations of production. It was within this
substantial effects rubric that the Court justified most of the major
Commerce Clause regulations Congress passed in the post-New
Deal period, such as the loansharking measure at issue in *Perez v
United States*.[120] With regard to federal regulation of the interstate
market—even federal regulations aimed, like the Civil Rights Act
of 1964, at moral ends—*Champion* became, therefore, entirely unnecessary: a remnant of an era before it was possible to justify
federal power using the logic of substantial effects.[121]

2. *Regulating vice—Congress's power of police.* This is not to say
that *Champion* became entirely vestigial. In the early twentieth
century, Congress began to shut down markets simply because it
disapproved of particular goods or services—also relying upon
Champion to do so. These laws included the Mann Act, barring
the interstate transportation of women for immoral purposes, the
Wire Act of 1961, an antigambling statute banning the interstate
transmission of wagers and bets in interstate commerce, and—of
course—the CSA, which although technically upheld by the Court
in *Raich* under the substantial effects test, was in fact premised on
Champion.[122] These laws could not be justified by the logic of
"substantial effects." Rather, they point to the other primary mo-

---

[119] Id at 122–23.

[120] 402 US 146, 146–47, 151–54 (1971) (upholding Title II of the Consumer Credit
Protection Act under a logic of "substantial effects").

[121] Civil Rights Act of 1964, Pub L No 88-352, 78 Stat 241, codified as amended at 42
USC §§ 1981–2000h6.

[122] White Slave Traffic (Mann) Act, 36 Stat 825 (1910), codified as amended at 18 USC
§§ 2421–24; Wire Act, Pub L No 87-216, 75 Stat 491, codified as amended at 18 USC
§ 1084; Controlled Substances Act, Pub L No 91-513, 84 Stat 1242 (1970), codified as
amended at 21 USC § 801 et seq.

tivation behind the Court and Congress's embrace in the early twentieth century of the expansive *Champion* power: namely, the intense political mobilization taking place at the time around the problem of vice.

During the last few decades of the nineteenth century and the first few decades of the twentieth century, social progressives joined forces with Christian reformers to spearhead national campaigns to suppress vices such as alcohol, gambling, and prostitution, which they saw as posing a serious problem to social progress in the industrial age.[123] These laws were aimed in part at the waves of immigrants who were then entering the country.[124] As William Howard Moore, summarizing a generation of scholarship on the morals policing side of progressivism, noted:

> [T]he campaigns against prostitution, the saloon, and gambling constituted important elements of national progressivism. Reformers saw these institutions as part of the social disorder resulting from rapid expansion and industrialization. Not only would Progressives seek to tame the forces of growth itself but they would also seek to ameliorate its immediate impact on the community. The brothel, saloon, and gambling parlor seemed to many Progressives distinct threats to home, the work ethic, and even to the political process.[125]

Champion was read, by Congress and the Court alike, as justifying these new anti-vice laws; the simple fact that something crossed a state line was deemed sufficient to allow a federal ban. The Mann Act of 1910, for example, prohibited the interstate transportation of women "for the purpose of prostitution or debauchery, or for any other immoral purpose."[126] Proponents of the law argued that it was necessary to protect women from the

---

[123] See generally David Langum, *Crossing over the Line: Legislating Morality and the Mann Act* (Chicago, 2007); Gaines M. Foster, *Moral Reconstruction: Christian Lobbyists and the Federal Legislation of Morality, 1865–1920* (North Carolina, 2002); Nicola Kay Beisel, *Imperiled Innocents: Anthony Comstock and Family Reproduction in Victorian America* (Princeton, 1997); Paul Boyer, *Urban Masses and Moral Order in America, 1820–1920* (Harvard, 1978); David J. Pivar, *Purity Crusade, Sexual Morality, and Social Control: 1858–1900* (Greenwood, 1973); Jason H. Timberlake, *Prohibition and the Progressive Movement, 1900–1920* (Harvard, 1963).

[124] See, for example, Jerry L. Mashaw, *Federal Administration and Administrative Law in the Gilded Age*, 119 Yale L J 1362, 1370–71 (2010) ("Immigrants challenged the economic position of skilled workers, the political control of the Republican Party, and the moral authority of dominant protestant religious groups.").

[125] William Howard Moore, *Progressivism and the Social Gospel in Wyoming: The Anti-gambling Act of 1901 as a Test Case*, 15 Western Hist Q 299, 301 (1984).

[126] White Slave Traffic Act, 36 Stat 825 (1910), codified as amended at 18 USC §§ 2421–24.

dangerous prostitution rings that were believed to forcibly conscript women into prostitution by plying them with liquor and carting them across state lines.[127] Opponents of the law pointed out, however, the lack of evidence that state laws were inadequate to prohibit either the forcible conscription or the resulting prostitution of women, and argued that the proposed federal law neither protected nor promoted interstate commerce.[128] Thus the only justification for federal intervention, as Representative William C. Adamson of Georgia noted to applause, was that the interstate transportation of women for immoral purposes polluted the channels of commerce, like the diseased animals prohibited by the Animal Industry Act or the lottery tickets in *Champion*.[129] This was not an argument that proponents (for obvious reasons) pressed too hard. Nevertheless, the Act passed with a sizable majority.

Despite the speciousness of the commerce argument regarding the Mann Act—that women crossing state lines for commercial sex were polluted in the same way as diseased cattle—the Court, in *Hoke v United States*, upheld the law without dissent, citing *Champion*.[130] Four years later, in *Caminetti v United States*, the Court held the Mann Act constitutional even as applied to defendants who traveled across states lines to engage in purely noncommercial sex and who therefore lacked any connection to interstate "commerce."[131]

The difficulty was that, in truth, these statutes were really noth-

---

[127] See Langum, *Crossing over the Line* at 4 (cited in note 123) (describing these arguments).

[128] See, for example, 45 Cong Rec 1033 (Jan 26, 1910) (statement of Rep Adamson).

[129] Id ("Now, the present proposition is that a general ticket unlimited to the use of any person shall be tabooed and the man shall be imprisoned for buying it if it is to be used by a woman to go into another State for the purpose of prostitution. Now, in order to be parallel with either of the cases cited, in order for the proponents of this legislation to find in either of these cases a single leg to stand on, much less a case going on all fours, they must show either, as in the quarantine case, that the woman's condition of vileness and immorality is contagious by contact, and that by using the ticket in paying for transportation on the train there is danger of contagion and contamination to the other persons and things being transported, or they must show, in order to parallel the case of the lottery ticket, the horrible falsehood that women are creatures per se vile and immoral, designed and intended in nature for no other than immoral purposes.").

[130] 227 US 308, 321 (1913).

[131] 242 US 470 (1917). The Court cited *Champion* as support for the proposition that "the authority of Congress to keep the channels of interstate commerce free from immoral and injurious uses has been frequently sustained, and is no longer open to question." Id at 491–92.

ing other than police power regulations masquerading as regulations of interstate commerce, a fact acknowledged with remarkable candor in the Supreme Court opinions upholding them. In *Champion* itself, Justice Harlan observed: "If a State, when considering legislation for the suppression of lotteries within its own limits, may properly take into view the evils that inhere in the raising of money, in that mode, why may not Congress, invested with the Power to regulate commerce among the several States, provide that such commerce shall not be polluted by the carrying of lottery tickets from one State to another?"[132]

When the Court upheld laws under this understanding of *Champion* it frequently resorted to describing congressional power as akin to the state police power. In *Hoke*, the Court explicitly acknowledged that "Congress [could] adopt not only means necessary but convenient to its exercise," including laws that "have the quality of police regulations."[133] Later opinions freely endorsed this view. In *Brooks v United States*, for example, the Court affirmed the constitutionality of the Stolen Motor Vehicles Act, which made it a federal crime to transport stolen vehicles across state lines, by noting that "Congress can certainly regulate interstate commerce to the extent of forbidding and punishing the use of such commerce as an agency to promote immorality, dishonesty or the spread of any evil or harm to the people of other States from the State of origin."[134] In acting in such a manner, the Court noted, Congress "is merely exercising the police power, for the benefit of the public, within the field of interstate commerce."[135]

Of course, no one—then or now—really believed Congress possessed a general power of police. Rather, the logic of the cases was implicitly premised on the following reasoning: (*a*) Congress is banning something crossing state lines; (*b*) congressional power over commerce is "plenary"; therefore (*c*) Congress may use its power to regulate interstate commerce to enact what are in essence simple police regulations. As the Court said in *Caminetti*: "the authority of Congress to keep the channels of interstate commerce free from immoral and injurious uses has been frequently sus-

---

[132] *Champion*, 188 US at 356.
[133] *Hoke*, 227 US at 323.
[134] 267 US 432, 436 (1925).
[135] Id at 436–37.

tained, and is no longer open to question."¹³⁶ In *Raich*, the Court went even further. It did not even pretend to justify the state border-crossing part of the rationale. Instead it simply cited *United States v Lopez* citing *Champion*.¹³⁷

In short, the reasoning of these cases became strained and completely formalistic. The mere fact that a good or a person crossed a state line was deemed sufficient to give Congress the power to ban it. Indeed, at the same time it decided *Champion* and *Caminetti*, the Court—for what now must seem obvious reasons—took the position that Congress's motive in adopting a law was simply irrelevant.¹³⁸ After all, looking too closely at motive would reveal that in these cases Congress was "regulating" commerce in only the most superficial sense. Line-crossing became but a hook to justify congressional intrusion into matters that heretofore would plainly have been deemed beyond congressional ken.

Moreover, it added absolutely nothing to the calculus to insist that congressional power was "plenary." Although Congress's power has long been deemed plenary, that conclusion still applies only to what properly is a regulation of commerce in the first place. "Plenary" is a description of Congress's power within its proper realm; it does not expand that realm. This much was clear from *Gibbons v Ogden*, which itself established the plenary power doctrine. Even as Chief Justice Marshall said in *Gibbons* that federal power was "plenary" and "complete in itself" he acknowledged that it did not extend to "commerce, which is completely internal, which is carried on between man and man in a State, or between different parts of the same State, and which does not extend or affect other States."¹³⁹

The difficulty is that the formalism required by the use of *Champion* in these vice cases ran smack against the entire point of the nineteenth-century distinction between Congress's power to reg-

---

¹³⁶ *Caminetti*, 242 US at 491.

¹³⁷ *Raich*, 545 US at 19 n 29, citing *United States v Lopez*, 514 US 549, 571 (1995) (Kennedy, J, concurring).

¹³⁸ See, for example, *McCray v United States*, 195 US 27, 55 (1904) (explaining that there is "no authority in the judiciary to restrain a lawful exercise of power by another department of the government, where a wrong motive or purpose has impelled to the exertion of the power"). In reaching this conclusion, the *McCray* Court relied in part on *Champion* itself, and specifically on dicta in Justice Harlan's opinion that suggested that the only remedy for the "unwise or injurious" use of federal power was the democratic process, not judicial review. Id, quoting *Champion*, 188 US at 363.

¹³⁹ Id at 194.

ulate and its power to prohibit, which was intended to provide a means of drawing a line between what properly was a matter within the states' police power, and what Congress could properly tackle as a national matter. As counsel for the individuals accused of transporting lottery tickets explained in *Champion*:

> If the present question had arisen in the days of Marshall, when the public opinion of the country was not as hostile to lotteries as it is to-day, and if the Federal government had sought to prevent the people of any State from dealing as they saw fit in the lottery issues of other States, it would have been held that Congress had gone outside of the powers which had been conferred on it by the terms of the Constitution, and that the legislation was unconstitutional and void because it was not a regulation of commerce, but an unwarranted interference with the police power reserved to the States.[140]

Case after case after case from the nineteenth century relied on the police power to explain why decisions regarding the morality or even the dangerousness of goods or conduct remained with the states and outside congressional control. Because they involved questions regarding the health, safety, and welfare of citizens, they were thought to be matters exclusively for the states. In *Brown v Maryland*, in 1827, Chief Justice Marshall said, "The power to direct the removal of gunpowder is a branch of the police power, which unquestionably remains, and ought to remain, with the states. . . . The removal or destruction of infectious or unsound articles [from trade] is, undoubtedly, an exercise of that power."[141] In *Patterson v Kentucky*, in 1878, the Court held that a state ban on certain illuminating oil trumped its use pursuant to a congressional patent.[142] "By the settled doctrines of this court the police power extends, at least, to the protection of the lives, the health, and the property of the community against the injurious exercise by any citizen of his rights. . . . Hence the States may, by police regulations, protect their people against the introduction within their respective limits of infected merchandise."[143] In *Mugler v Kansas*,[144] in 1887, the Court asked the apt question: "But by whom, or by what authority, is it to be determined whether

---

[140] Brief for Appellant, *Champion*, 188 US 321.

[141] *Brown*, 25 US at 443.

[142] 97 US 501 (1878).

[143] Id at 504–05.

[144] 123 US 623 (1887).

the manufacture of particular articles of drink, either for general use or for the personal use of the maker, will injuriously affect the public?"[145] The answer was that it was within "the police powers of the State . . . to determine, primarily, what measures are appropriate or needful for the protection of the public morals, the public health, or the public safety."[146] Indeed, it is instructive to note that on the two occasions in the nineteenth and early twentieth centuries when the federal government acted to ban trade that some states wanted to permit—that being slavery, and alcohol—a constitutional amendment was believed necessary, given the limits on federal power.[147]

Of course, simply because the power to prohibit or ban commerce was considered part of state police power, and beyond federal commerce power, in the nineteenth century does not mean that conclusion must remain static. There is almost universal agreement that Congress's commerce powers necessarily expanded in the twentieth century in response to industrialization and the integration of the national economy. In light of these changes, one must ask whether it also follows that Congress's commerce power should be expanded to enable it to ban products or activities merely because they cross a line. Fidelity to principles of precedent and federalism require at a minimum that the necessity of expanded congressional power in this regard be justified by changed circumstances that demonstrate that it is unworkable today to leave such matters to the states.

This difficulty within our system of federalism of simply assuming Congress has the power to ban commerce is brought into focus when the states differ over the wisdom of banning the product or activity. In the early *Champion* police power cases, the states tended to hold similar views, which is why this facet of *Champion* went down rather easily at the time. Although constitutional purists like the *Champion* dissenters bemoaned what they saw as an extension of the commerce power in *Champion*, it was not seriously disruptive of federalism because these federal laws mirrored what the states already were doing on their own. But what if the states *do* disagree about the legality of the underlying product or activity?

---

[145] Id at 660.

[146] Id at 661.

[147] See US Const, Amend XIII; US Const, Amend XVIII.

To what extent may the national government resolve the issue for them under the guise of its authority to regulate interstate commerce? It is to this question that we now turn.

III. In Defense of a Ban on Congressional Bans

This part suggests that it is time to reconsider the broad, post-*Champion* view that Congress's power "to regulate" commerce includes the power to ban it entirely. Here, we explain that under legitimate principles of federalism, the only plausible justification for allowing congressional market bans is to mitigate the spillover costs of a checkerboard regulatory scheme, and it is doubtful that this rationale justifies giving Congress the power to arbitrate between disagreeing states. Although our approach would deny Congress the authority to adopt bans merely because it disapproves of the product or activity, most of the remainder of congressional power would remain untouched.

A. BEYOND FORMALISM: THE PROBLEM OF SPILLOVERS AS A JUSTIFICATION FOR FEDERAL POWER

Most authorities today accept that the transformation in Congress's power under the Commerce Clause reflected in the "substantial effects" test set out in *Jones & Laughlin* and *Darby* was a necessary response to the changing nature of the national economy. But can the same be said of Congress's power to shut down markets, as exercised in statutes such as the Mann Act and the Controlled Substances Act? This is not so vexing when the states coalesce on a set of policy choices that federal action then supports, as was the case with the Lottery Act. But what about when states do not agree? This is the central question, and it cannot be answered simply by noting that the articles or conduct Congress forbids might—at some point—cross a state line. Some rationale beyond formalism is required, and until now none has been offered.

There is, in federalism's birth logic, a starting place for evaluating the question of whether Congress ought to possess the power to ban markets. The enumerated congressional powers in Article I, Section 8 of the Constitution—including the Commerce Clause—arose out of Resolution VI of the Constitutional Convention. That resolution held that there should be national power "in all Cases for the general Interests of the Union, and also in those Cases to which the States are separately incompetent, or in which the Harmony of the United States may be interrupted by the Exercise of individual Legislation."[148]

Scholars differ over the role Resolution VI should play in interpreting the Constitution, but there is a sensible middle position. Some today—typically those who would expand federal authority—believe Congress's enumerated powers should be interpreted through the lens of Resolution VI.[149] Others (generally those who would limit federal authority) insist this is mistaken; they argue that, despite some agreement in the Convention on the general principles reflected in Resolution VI, what the Convention in fact adopted, and the country ratified, was the specific text of Article I, Section 8. It is therefore only the text, they argue, that should govern.[150] The middle ground here seems both apparent and sensible: quite obviously it is the enumeration itself that is determinative, but interpretation of that enumeration is illuminated by the problem it was understood to address. This is particularly the case when Resolution VI is used as a limiting principle. It would be difficult to maintain that Congress should act when the "general interest" does *not* require it, when states *are* competent to act on their own, and when their doing so *does not* affect the "harmony" of the United States.

Of course, the rub remains in figuring out when a state-by-state solution is plausible, and when the exercise of national power is

---

[148] Kurt T. Lash, *"Resolution VI": The Virginia Plan and Authority to Resolve Collective Action Problems under Article I, Section 8*, 87 Notre Dame L Rev 2123, 2126 (2012).

[149] See, for example, Robert D. Cooter and Neil S. Siegel, *Collective Action Federalism: A General Theory of Article I, Section 8*, 63 Stan L Rev 115, 123–24 (2010) (tracing the Framers' concerns about collective action problems to Resolution VI and arguing more broadly for the resolution's value in interpreting Section 8); Balkin, 109 Mich L Rev at 8–12 (cited in note 44) (arguing that "all of Congress's powers were designed to realize the structural principle of Resolution VI"); Regan, 94 Mich L Rev at 570–71 (cited in note 7) (arguing for Resolution VI's value in interpreting "the vaguer of the grants of power, like the Commerce Clause").

[150] See Lash, 87 Notre Dame L Rev at 2145–52 (cited in note 148) (citing evidence that the Framers considered Resolution VI a mere placeholder and that it later played no role in the ratification debates); Robert J. Pushaw Jr., *Obamacare and the Original Meaning of the Commerce Clause: Identifying Historical Limits on Congress's Powers*, 2012 U Ill L Rev 1703, 1721–25 (2012) (arguing that Resolution VI was not "implicitly enacted" because it was replaced by a set of more specific, enumerated powers). See also Randy E. Barnett, *Restoring the Lost Constitution: The Presumption of Liberty* 155 (Princeton, 2004) (characterizing the Committee on Details' response to Resolution VI as a rejection of the resolution's "open-ended grant of power to Congress").

necessary. If there were no downside to letting each state go its own way, both history and the values of federalism would mandate doing so. But the Constitution was adopted precisely because allowing complete state autonomy was thought to be undesirable and unworkable. Thus, the question is: Can and should we tolerate a checkerboard, or must all our squares be red (or black)?

Although Resolution VI is ambiguous, economics can help shed light on the matter. An economic approach allows us to identify with some greater specificity when, with regard to market bans, "the States are separately incompetent" or the "harmony of the United States would be interrupted." Economic terminology is neither determinative nor essential here—the argument largely is intuitive—yet it helps frame and analyze the relevant question with some precision.

1. *Of collective action problems, first movers, and spillovers.* In the language of economic analysis, individuals and firms should be left free to make decisions for themselves unless there are collective action problems associated with individual choices.[151] Collective action problems are those in which actors would be better off if they adopted a common approach, but barriers of one sort or another prevent them from doing so. Overgrazing of the commons is the classic example.

When it comes to federalism—and, in particular, the regulatory choices made by the states—two sorts of collective action problems are commonly identified. Although often spoken of in one breath, it is useful to keep them distinct. One form of collective action problem is implicated by the rule barring Congress from shutting down markets; the other is not.

The first federalism collective action problem travels by many names, but generally describes a situation in which paralysis or partial paralysis might well take hold if the central government could not act despite the contrary preferences of some states. *Wickard* provides an example: any state could develop its own system of price supports to assure an adequate supply of wheat, but if wheat were available on the open market from other states, those price supports will collapse.[152] Sometimes states that would be

[151] See Cooter and Siegel, 63 Stan L Rev at 137–44 (cited in note 149) (arguing that power should be allocated to the smallest social unit internalizing its effects).

[152] This was because, as the Court noted, wheat grown outside the system of price supports "tends to flow into the market and check price increases." *Wickard v Filburn*,

first-movers decline to do so out of fear of suffering a competitive loss. *Darby* provides an example of this.[153] If some states adopt higher labor standards, their products will be more expensive on the market and they will lose out to states with lower standards. This can lead to races to the bottom, or holdouts. As Justice Cardozo explained when upholding the Social Security pension tax in *Steward Machine Co. v Davis*:

> inaction [on the part of the States] was not owing, for the most part, to the lack of sympathetic interest. Many held back through alarm lest in laying such a toll upon their industries, they would place themselves in a position of economic disadvantage as compared with neighbors or competitors.[154]

As an example, Justice Cardozo pointed to a Massachusetts pension law that would not go into effect unless and until either the federal government passed a law on the subject, or eleven of twenty-two designated states did so.[155] This type of collective action problem maps onto that aspect of *Champion* that was rendered vestigial by the logic of the "substantial effects" test. Although people may disagree about whether the collective action problems at issue in the post-*Champion* cases dealing with such issues as wage and hour regulations were sufficiently grave to warrant federal regulation, it was a concern with these problems that underscored Justice Cardozo's opinion in *Steward Machine Co.*

However, this sort of federalism collective action problem is *not* implicated by a rule that would prohibit Congress from shutting down markets in particular goods or activities. Indeed, it is hard to imagine that a state would decide to allow trafficking in a good or service, or feel compelled to disallow it, simply to stay in line with other states. And, in fact, when given the opportunity for divergence, this sort of collective action problem has not kept states from going their own way. To the contrary, from alcohol, to marijuana, to prostitution, to gambling, a checkerboard has

---

317 US 111, 128 (1942). The Court also noted that of the four large exporting countries that had (at the time the decision was handed down) taken measures to prop up domestic wheat prices against the global downturn, all four had enacted such legislation at the national rather than the local or state level—presumably because of the difficulties of enforcing and rendering local legislation of this sort effective. Id at 126 n 27.

[153] See *United States v Darby*, 312 US 100 (1941).

[154] *Steward Machine Co. v Davis*, 301 US 548, 588 (1937).

[155] Id at 588 n 9.

often prevailed—particularly when the national government has not interfered.

On the other hand, the second form of collective action problem—that of negative externalities, or spillovers—*is* implicated by, and provides some justification for, congressional market bans. Externalities are costs (or benefits) that are not captured within any given state, and so spill over to other states. The classic example here is environmental pollution. If State A benefits in taxation or otherwise from a factory whose harmful pollutants are swept away on the wind to State B, State A maximizes its benefits and minimizes its costs by doing nothing about the pollution. One obvious solution is national legislation that either compels states to internalize the costs of their policies or prohibits spillovers altogether. Here, national power is generally thought to be appropriate, even at the expense of state autonomy.[156]

Spillovers are common in the realm of market bans, and undoubtedly provide the strongest rationale for national decision making in the face of state disagreement. Indeed, they seem to provide the only *sound* rationale for federal market bans. Spillovers are undoubtedly real. As the *Raich* Court observed, if marijuana is grown and possessed legally in California, some of it inevitably will bleed into the interstate market.[157] Similarly, when police chiefs testified in 1994 in favor of a federal ban on assault weapons, they argued that a national ban was essential given the ease with which guns flowed across state lines.[158]

2. *Are spillovers enough?* Although a concern with spillovers might provide a rational basis for action by the national government, it may not be sufficient justification to overcome the competing interest in federalism when the states do not agree on the merits of the policy. There are a number of problems with relying on spillovers as a basis for federal action.

The first problem is that spillovers are ubiquitous. If the existence of a spillover allows federal action, then state choice over most things could be eliminated. Any time two states adopt dif-

---

[156] Cooter and Siegel, 63 Stan L Rev at 138 (cited in note 149).

[157] *Gonzales v Raich*, 545 US 1, 19 (2005).

[158] Assault Weapons: A View from the Front Lines: Hearing on S 639 and S 653 before the Senate Committee on the Judiciary, 103d Cong, 1st Sess 49, 62 (1993) (statements of Fred Thomas, Chief, DC Police Department, and Johnny Mack Brown, President, National Sheriffs' Association).

fering regulatory or policy regimes, there will be some incentive to arbitrage them. Some persons inclined to commit burglaries in State A will shift their crime to neighboring State B if State A's penalties for burglary are more severe. Can the federal government then dictate uniform state penalties for burglary?[159] It is necessary, in other words, to determine which sorts of spillovers justify national action and which do not.

The second problem is that when the national government steps in to arbitrate between state choices, it does not necessarily eliminate spillovers; it simply replaces one spillover problem with another. The national ban on marijuana is a good example. Some states favor legalization, at least for medicinal purposes. Other states, and the national government, do not. The latter policy generally has prevailed, but the inevitable consequence of this has been the creation of a black market, with its own spillover costs. As Craig Bradley points out, the United States created organized crime when it adopted a policy of alcohol prohibition.[160] Marijuana policy fosters such organized crime. When it comes to marijuana, the negative externalities of the national ban are breathtaking in terms of lives lost, money spent, and people incarcerated.[161]

The problem with market bans is that when people disagree about them spillovers cannot be eliminated easily, if at all. There will always be a border across which the banned good can travel. The national ban on marijuana has only emphasized the complete inability of the national government to shut its international borders.[162] Black markets, with their attendant costs, *are* inevitable.

Some suggest that the right move in the face of trade-offs in spillovers like these is cost-benefit analysis, but it is unclear that cost-benefit analysis would or should settle the question. Trade-

---

[159] See Doron Teichman, *The Market for Criminal Justice: Federalism, Crime Control, and Jurisdictional Competition*, 103 Mich L Rev 1831, 1842 (2005) (making this point).

[160] Craig M. Bradley, *Racketeering and the Federalization of Crime*, 22 Am Crim L Rev 213, 226 (1984).

[161] See, for example, Jeffrey A. Miron, *The Budgetary Implications of Marijuana Prohibition* *1 (report, Taxpayers for Common Sense, 2005), online at http://www.prohibitioncosts .org/wp-content/uploads/2012/04/MironReport.pdf (estimating the cost of federal and state marijuana enforcement at $7.7 billion annually); Duke and Gross, *Longest War* at xxi (cited in note 17) (estimating the total cost of the "drug problem" to be up to $200 billion annually, when the costs of drug-related crime are factored in).

[162] See Federal Research Division, Library of Congress, *Marijuana Availability in the United States and Its Associated Territories* *12, *23 (report, 2003), online at http://www .loc.gov/rr/frd/pdf-files/MarAvail.pdf (noting that 50 percent of marijuana in the United States is imported and that no more than 10 percent of imported marijuana is intercepted).

offs in this area abound, which is precisely why states disagree—as they have come to over the issue of marijuana. Some states may worry that if they legalize certain drugs, addiction will rise, or use of the drug by youths will skyrocket. Others may decide they will bear these risks in order to halt the black market, or better prioritize law enforcement resources.

Deciding among trade-offs like these is precisely what federalism leaves to the states. If spillovers could be eliminated, or seriously curtailed, federal action might be justified. But given the trade-offs in the real world and the nature of the competing values, it is hard to believe that cost-benefit analysis will yield either a persuasive or uniform answer that would justify overriding the legitimate interests of the states.[163]

The third problem with allowing spillovers to justify congressional action is that the difficulty of enforcing national bans in the face of state disagreement typically leads to temporizing by the federal government, which in turn undercuts the spillover rationale that justified federal regulation in the first place. Consider raw milk and marijuana. In theory the national government has taken a hard-line absolutist stance with respect to both.[164] In practice, however, national regulators recognize the difficulty with this position, and in each area have tempered the national policy with a more pragmatic approach to enforcement. For example, the Food and Drug Administration (FDA) recently stressed that it would not prohibit individuals from drinking raw milk, or from transporting it across state lines for personal consumption.[165] Similarly, the Department of Justice has instructed federal drug enforcement agencies that they should "not focus federal resources . . . on individuals whose actions are in clear and unambiguous compliance with existing state laws providing for the medical use of

---

[163] As Richard Hamm notes, prohibitionists targeted the federal government only after their efforts to enact state-level prohibition laws failed, or achieved only temporary success. Hamm, *Shaping the Eighteenth Amendment* at 123–24 (cited in note 81) (noting that, after a decade of success, "[t]emperance progress, as measured by the adoption of state prohibition laws, halted abruptly" and that even among the prohibition states, enforcement "ranged from sporadic to nonexistent").

[164] 21 CFR § 1240.61(a) (banning raw milk from interstate commerce); 21 CFR § 1308.11(d) (classifying marijuana as a Schedule I drug).

[165] FDA, *Food Safety and Raw Milk* (press release, Nov 1, 2011), online at http://www.fda.gov/Food/GuidanceRegulation/GuidanceDocumentsRegulatoryInformation/Milk/ucm277854.htm.

marijuana."[166] But it is difficult to square these decisions with the rationale for the national bans in the first place. The FDA claims not only that raw milk is unwholesome, but that it may contain E. coli, and that consuming it may cause communicable disease.[167] If this is true, it is hard to see why the FDA allows anyone to possess raw milk that surely will bleed into the interstate market. So too with marijuana. The federal government has classified it as a Schedule I drug. This is the highest category of regulation, reserved for items having absolutely no therapeutic value.[168] But if marijuana has no therapeutic value, why tolerate consumption of marijuana for medicinal purposes, given the inevitable bleed that plainly is occurring from the medical marijuana market to other markets?[169]

Fourth, allowing spillovers as a rationale for a national ban has lock-in effects that prevent the sort of experimentation that federalism is lauded for fostering.[170] In the absence of a national ban, states can choose themselves to limit or prohibit certain markets. But once a national ban is in place, it becomes very difficult for states to diverge from the federal policy, limiting states from trying various regulatory frameworks to see if they deal better with negative externalities than a complete ban. This was precisely the point of Justice Kennedy's concurrence in *United States v Lopez*, which struck down the Gun Free School Zones Act. States might reasonably have believed that guns would most effectively be kept out of schools by encouraging people to turn their guns in voluntarily, or by implementing an amnesty, or by encouraging tattle-telling by reducing the penalties imposed on violators.[171] The fed-

[166] See David W. Ogden, Deputy Attorney General, DOJ (memorandum to US attorneys, Oct 19, 2009), online at http://www.justice.gov/opa/documents/medical-marijuana.pdf.

[167] *The Dangers of Raw Milk: Unpasteurized Milk Can Pose a Serious Health Risk* (FDA Aug 2012), online at http://www.fda.gov/downloads/Food/FoodborneIllnessContaminants/UCM239493.pdf.

[168] 21 USC § 812 (defining the five drug schedules). It is possible, of course, that the DOJ policy is simply one of enforcement priorities, but that is a little hard to comprehend. If marijuana is properly a Schedule I drug, then its widespread use ought to be a problem.

[169] See Adam Nagourney, *Marijuana, Not Yet Legal for Californians, Might as Well Be*, NY Times A1 (Dec 21, 2012), online at http://www.nytimes.com/2012/12/21/us/politics/stigma-fading-marijuana-common-in-california.html.

[170] See Ilya Somin, *Gonzales v. Raich: Federalism as a Casualty of the War on Drugs*, 15 Cornell J L & Pub Pol 507, 540–42 (2006) (citing the marijuana ban as an example of national policy decision undercutting the benefits of federalism).

[171] *United States v Lopez*, 514 US 549, 581–83 (1995) (Kennedy, J, concurring).

eral ban that the Court struck down in *Lopez* prevented all this from occurring.

In light of these difficulties with spillovers, the final—and especially perplexing—problem is how courts should decide when the federal government should be allowed to regulate spillover effects at the expense of state diversity. If ten states want to legalize marijuana, and forty do not, may the national government impose a ban? If twenty states prefer raw milk and thirty would bar it, is that enough to justify national action?

Note that when the first sort of collective action problem exists—the one discussed above that is not germane to market bans—it can be so severe that some advocate empowering the national government to act to solve it, even if only a single state has the same preference as the national government. But even scholars who support the exercise of federal power in response to the first sort of collective action problem even when there is widespread disagreement among the states reach the opposite conclusion when spillovers are the issue. Because of their ubiquity and lock-in effects, these scholars conclude that the federal government may act to prevent spillovers only in the face of widespread state agreement. Only then is it appropriate, they maintain, to curtail the activities of outliers.[172] But how does one decide as a matter of constitutional law where to place the line that allows national action, short-circuiting state choice?

In answering the question of whether spillover costs justify market bans when state preferences diverge, it is worth recalling why our federal system exists in the first place. One answer, of course, is that it was but the price for Union—although there were some then and now who preferred erasing state lines altogether, this never was a remote possibility. But federalism is believed to exist for reasons other than historical path dependence. Federalism fosters local governance and permits experimentation. Most impor-

---

[172] See Balkin, 109 Mich L Rev at 33 (cited in note 44) (requiring widespread agreement among the states before Congress acts to address claimed spillover effects); Cooter and Siegel, 63 Stan L Rev at 138, 140–42 (cited in note 149) (calling for federal intervention to address externality problems only where there are "significant" spillovers, and only where a majority of states are in favor); Richard B. Stewart, *Pyramids of Sacrifice? Problems of Federalism in Mandating State Implementation of National Environmental Policy*, 86 Yale L J 1196, 1229 (1997) ("Recognizing the legitimacy of state autonomy values, the spillovers required to justify federal coercion of the states should be substantial—more stubstantial than those required to support the exertion of the federal commerce power against private firms or individuals.").

tantly, the belief is that allowing states to go their own way except when national uniformity demands it maximizes utility.[173] If eighty citizens of State A prefer policy X and twenty oppose it, whereas twenty citizens of State B prefer policy X while eighty oppose it, more people will be satisfied with policy if a checkerboard prevails.

At the least, the democratic and utilitarian benefits that flow from allowing independent and divergent state choices should not be displaced casually. Congress should not act on the spillover justification except when a small number of outlier states impose significant spillovers on most others. But even here, caution is warranted, in light of the many difficulties with using national power to control spillovers by way of a market ban, and in view of the lock-in effect that then keeps states from changing their minds. This is particularly so given that, as we will show, the costs of limiting Congress's ability to prohibit interstate commerce are lower than they may seem initially.

B. SPECIFYING THE CLAIM

What would be the consequence of denying Congress the power to shut down viable markets? In exploring this question, it is both useful and necessary to specify with some precision what it means to say that Congress may not prohibit commerce, only regulate it. Specifying the claim allows us to see what is within it—that is, what Congress may not do—but also what is outside the claim, that is, the extent to which Congress's power would remain untouched.

Clarifying the claim is important because, as we have seen, Congress's power to adopt such bans rests ultimately on *Champion v Ames*, but in the years since *Champion*, that opinion has been given exceptionally broad scope. Today, *Champion* is used to justify the federal regulation—and prohibition—of not only anything traveling in commerce, but anything that has so traveled, at any point in its life or life cycle.[174] Thus, in addition to the sort of "morals"

---

[173] See John O. McGinnis and Ilya Somin, *Federalism vs. States' Rights: A Defense of Judicial Review in a Federal System*, 99 Nw U L Rev 89, 106–07 (2004); Michael W. McConnell, *Federalism: Evaluating the Founders' Design*, 54 U Chi L Rev 1484, 1493–94 (1987) ("So long as preferences for government policies are unevenly distributed among the various localities, more people can be satisfied by decentralized decision making than by a single national authority.").

[174] McGimsey, 90 Cal L Rev at 1698–99 (cited in note 96).

legislation that was prominent at the turn of the twentieth century, *Champion* has provided a basis for much additional federal legislation, most notably an explosion in federal criminal laws. These include racketeering laws, child support laws, gun laws, obscenity laws, and child pornography laws, to name but a few.[175]

Many are critical of the broad reach of national power *Champion* has engendered. As Donald Regan states, "The idea that Congress can regulate whatever has moved across a state line has become a popular 'hook' for federal legislation. . . . But it is none the better argument for that."[176] Some propose limitations on the use of the sort of extended "nexus" test that was used to justify the reenactment of federal legislation banning guns near schools.[177] Others decry the expansion of federal criminal law premised on a broad reading of *Champion*, and urge cutting back on that authority.[178]

No matter what the general controversy over *Champion*, however, our focus is decidedly narrower. Limiting Congress's power to prohibit commerce says nothing about the vast majority of federal laws enacted pursuant to *Champion* (or otherwise). It is aimed at a very specific kind of federal law, and leaves most others—whether enacted pursuant to *Champion* or not—wholly untouched.

1. *The claim.* Our claim is straightforward. Congress's power "to regulate Commerce . . . among the several States" does not encompass the power to prohibit that commerce. Congress may regulate markets, but it may not eliminate them. The choice of what goods citizens may or may not consume is one for the citizens of each state to make.

Still, that straightforward claim requires definition. In particular, it is necessary to distinguish "regulation" from "prohibition," and

---

[175] See, for example, 18 USC § 228 (imposing criminal penalties on anyone who travels in interstate commerce with the intent to evade the obligation to provide child support); 18 USC § 922(g) (prohibiting any person convicted of a felony from transporting, possessing, or receiving any firearm or ammunition that has been transported across state lines); 18 USC § 1462 (prohibiting the receipt of "any obscene, lewd, lascivious, or filthy" book, film, or recording or any "thing designed, adapted, or intended for producing abortion, or for any indecent or immoral use" that has traveled in interstate or foreign commerce); 18 USC § 2252A (prohibiting the interstate transport, receipt, or distribution of material constituting or containing child pornography).

[176] Regan, 94 Mich L Rev at 600 (cited in note 7).

[177] See McGimsey, 90 Cal L Rev at 1731–35 (cited in note 96).

[178] See Bradley, 22 Am Crim L Rev at 213–15 (cited in note 160).

to think about how to define a market. As acknowledged below, there may be hard questions at the margin; nonetheless, the broader principle properly frames the debate about where the margin should be located.

2. *Congress may enact regulations that are not bans.* To begin, regulations that do not involve prohibitions would not be implicated at all by reading Congress's power to regulate commerce as denying it the power to prohibit. A great deal of environmental regulation, for example, is justified on the basis of spillovers, but does not involve banning any article of commerce. This is true of laws that regulate smokestack emissions or set clean air or water standards.[179] These laws regulate the ill effects of commerce, but they do not ban commerce, so nothing here speaks to them.

3. *Congress can enact "helper" laws.* Congress also retains full authority to adopt bans (and related regulations) to the extent that they are "helper statutes" designed to assist states in the enforcement of their own domestic prohibitions. The Wilson Act of 1890, which mandated that domestically imported liquor be subject to state law, and the Webb-Kenyon Act of 1913, which made it a federal crime to transport liquor into a state with the intent or knowledge that it would be received, sold, or otherwise used in violation of state law, both imposed federal restrictions on commerce.[180] But rather than reflecting a *federal* judgment that commerce in the targeted good—for example, alcohol—should be prohibited, they merely assisted in enforcing choices the citizens of each state had made for themselves about what kinds of goods were proper subjects of commerce. Such statutes support rather than limit the autonomy of the individual states.[181]

4. *Congress may enact laws "in service" of the national market.* Congress can also prohibit the possession, transportation, or sale

---

[179] See, for example, Clean Air Act, 42 USC § 7401 et seq (regulating pollution sources and setting emission standards without regulating goods or movement per se); Clean Water Act, 33 USC § 1251 et seq (prohibiting the addition of pollutants to U.S. water without a permit).

[180] Webb–Kenyon Act, 37 Stat 699 (1913) (similar to 27 USC § 122); Wilson Act, 26 Stat 313 (1890).

[181] Although helper statutes are permissible, they should be written clearly as support for state choices, rather than flat prohibitions. The Lottery Act at issue in *Champion* was in effect a helper statute, but it was framed as a flat prohibition. When states began to permit lotteries again in the middle of the twentieth century, Congress was forced to enact exceptions before states could do so lawfully. See 5 Stat 304. This is the sort of lock-in effect that should be avoided by the wording of helper statutes to allow states to move in and out of Congress's regulatory ambit.

of a particular article if it does so in service of the functioning of
a national market (as opposed to shutting down the market altogether). As we showed in Part I, in-service laws have a well-
established history that significantly predates *Champion*. Such laws
operate to enforce the rules by which markets operate, not to shut
those markets down. In-service laws may be aimed at two distinct
problems. First, like the ban on the transport of diseased cattle in
the Animal Industry Act of 1884, they can serve the market by
keeping it safe and well functioning. Second, like the Steamboat
Boiler Act of 1838, they can protect the instrumentalities of commerce themselves.[182] In both situations, in-service laws operate on
the assumption that well-regulated markets will encourage participation and minimize externalities.

Today there are many analogues to the Steamboat Boiler Act
and the Animal Industry Act. As to the former, 18 USC § 842
prohibits the unlicensed carrying of explosives on interstate instrumentalities like airplanes.[183] As to the latter, many environmental and public health laws serve the market by making it safe
and transparent, so that consumers are eager to participate. Examples include the Federal Food, Drug & Cosmetic Act (FFDCA)
and the Toxic Substances Control Act, which prohibit—respectively—the transport and distribution of adulterated food and cosmetics, and unduly dangerous chemicals.[184] Laws that seek to
counter the negative externalities of a well-functioning market also
can be understood as in-service laws. For example, the federal ban
on the sale of asbestos-containing products serves the market in
those goods by ensuring that its operation does not entail unnecessary public health costs.[185]

As these examples suggest, some in-service laws can be understood as a form of public good. When the EPA, under authority
delegated from Congress, decides that certain pesticides, rather

---

[182] 5 Stat 304.

[183] 18 USC § 842(a)(3)(A) (prohibiting anyone but licensees to "transport, ship, cause
to be transported, or receive any explosive materials").

[184] 21 USC § 331(a) (prohibiting adulterated and misbranded food and drugs); 15 USC
§ 2605 (prohibiting certain injurious substances).

[185] 16 CFR § 1304.4 (banning consumer patching compounds containing intentionally
added asbestos because of the danger they pose to the public health); 16 CFR § 1305.4
(banning for the same reason artificial fireplace ash and embers containing asbestos); 40
CFR § 763.169 (banning the distribution in commerce of asbestos-containing flooring
felt, commercial paper, corrugated paper, rollboard, and specialty paper).

than others, are too dangerous to be offered for sale in domestic markets, it performs a cost-benefit analysis.[186] States could perform the same cost-benefit analysis and make individual determinations about what goods to allow, but it would be costly—perhaps too costly—to have each state do so, and in any event the market requires some minimal regulatory uniformity. That said, states remain free to perform their own cost-benefit analyses if they wish, and in many cases are permitted to set regulatory standards that exceed the federal floor. Statutes of this kind do not as a result typically take from the states the authority to regulate the targeted markets, although they clearly constrain state power in certain respects. Moreover, they do not bring all commerce in the targeted market to a halt.

C. OBJECTIONS

Finally, we address possible objections to our approach.

1. *Difficulties of line-drawing.* Some may argue that the critical distinction we draw between in-service laws and market bans is unworkable. In both cases, federal power is being used to prohibit the movement, sale, or possession of goods or persons who have, are, or will travel across state lines. But there is a real distinction here, and although hard cases may arise, for the most part the distinction can and should be made.

Line-drawing efforts under the Commerce Clause have frequently come under attack, but the reason may not be so much that lines are inherently difficult to draw.[187] Rather, there are political stakes in drawing the lines and so they come under pressure. It is thus important to distinguish between principles about which it is inherently difficulty to draw lines, and principles about which the difficulty derives instead from resistance to the principle itself.

In theory, there is a clear difference between bans on particular products that are adopted in service of a well-functioning com-

---

[186] See Federal Insecticide, Fungicide, and Rodenticide Act, USC § 136(bb) (defining the term "unreasonable adverse effects on the environment" to mean "any unreasonable risk to man or the environment, taking into account the economic, social, and environmental costs and benefits of the use of any pesticide").

[187] See, for example, Gil Seinfeld, *The Possibility of Pretext Analysis in Commerce Clause Adjudication*, 78 Notre Dame L Rev 1251, 1282–84 (2003) (criticizing the economic-noneconomic line-drawing in *Lopez*); Lawrence Lessig, *Translating Federalism: United States v Lopez*, 1995 Supreme Court Review 125, 161 (explaining that line-drawing under the Commerce Clause is difficult in our presently functionalist jurisprudence).

merce, and those bans that simply seek to shut down trade and transport entirely. The former are a means to a healthy market; the latter attempt to squelch all market activity. Justice Marshall noted in *Gibbons v Ogden* that "the power to regulate . . . is to prescribe the rule by which commerce is to be governed."[188] The power to prohibit, in contrast, is the power to bring commerce to an end. The first presupposes the continuation of the regulated activity; the second presupposes its cessation. It is only when the federal government enacts prohibitions that work to bring all commerce in a given market to a halt that it bans commerce, in the sense used here, rather than "regulates" it.

Moreover, in-service laws further the purposes of the Commerce Clause and federalism, as described in Parts I and II, whereas market bans frustrate those purposes. Congress was given the power over interstate commerce to foster a vibrant commerce, not to shut it down. In-service laws attempt to protect commerce and to encourage participation in well-functioning markets. They do not trench on state choices about which commodities their citizens may (or may not) possess and use. Market bans do the opposite.

One way to think of operationalizing the distinction is to ask whether there would be an identifiable market in the product that is banned in the absence of the federal law. If so, the law is a ban; if not, it may be in service of the market. Compare, for example, the Mann Act's ban on the interstate transportation of prostitutes with the prohibition in the FFDCA on the interstate transport and sale of adulterated drugs.[189] In the latter case, there is no independent market in adulterated drugs that the federal law prohibits. To the extent people know a product is adulterated, we may assume that they will not want to buy or use it. (And indeed, historically, supporters of the federal ban on adulterated drugs promoted it primarily as necessary to safeguard consumers against fraud and abuse.[190]) In the former case, however, there is a viable

---

[188] 22 US 1, 196 (1824).

[189] White Slave Traffic Act, 36 Stat 825 (1910), codified as amended at 18 USC § 2421; 21 USC § 331 (prohibiting the transport or receipt in interstate commerce of adulterated or misbranded food, drugs, devices, or cosmetics).

[190] See C. C. Regier, *The Struggle for Federal Food and Drug Legislation*, 1 L & Contemp Probs 3, 5–10 (1933) (describing the popular agitation around the problem of consumer fraud in the food and drug markets); Richard Curtis Litman and Donald Saunders Litman, *Protection of the American Consumer: The Muckrakers and the Enactment of the First Federal Food and Drug Law in the United States*, 36 Food Drug Cosm L J 647, 647 (1981) ("The Pure Food and Drug Act of 1906 was passed in response to the demand of the public for

interstate market that the federal ban prohibits. It thus comes as little surprise that the legislative history of the Mann Act is brimming with evidence that moral antipathy toward a particular kind of product (namely, prostitution) was what drove the bill's enactment, rather than a desire to protect consumers against fraud and abuse.[191]

Congressional laws requiring labeling of food and other products are interesting in this regard. They often are written as market bans on unlabeled goods, posing the question whether such bans are permissible in-service laws or impermissible prohibitions. The answer is that they are the former. Congress's intention in requiring the (proper) labeling of goods is to inform people of what they are purchasing, thereby facilitating the operation of the market rather than shutting it down. The assumption is that if consumers know what they are buying they can make wise decisions when they consume, thus enhancing market efficiency.[192] The labeling requirements provided by laws as diverse as the FFDCA, the Fair Packaging and Labeling Act, and the Federal Insecticide, Fungicide, and Rodenticide Act therefore all rather straightforwardly represent permissible in-service laws.[193]

In some cases, however, determining whether a given statute is

---

protection from the deception practiced upon consumers by manufacturers of and dealers in foods and drugs.").

[191] Although proponents of the law justified it as necessary to protect women themselves from exploitation at the hands of the criminal cartels that allegedly sold them into what was called at the time "white slavery," the legislative debates make clear that behind this concern with the welfare of the women targeted by the Act was a distaste for their "degraded" profession in which they were forced, or voluntarily participated. See White Slave Traffic, HR Rep No 61-47, 61st Cong, 2d Sess 10–11 (discussing the "degraded life" of the prostitute); Langum, *Crossing over the Line* at 17 (cited in note 123) (noting how, in the early twentieth century, the "'problem' of prostitution became a flash point for . . . social tensions [arising from] immigration, urbanization [and changing social mores relating to] the sexuality of women"). The extent of the moral antipathy placed states' rights opponents of the law into a difficult position. Representative William Richardson of Alabama, who opposed the bill, noted, for example, that "a man puts himself in a position . . . to be criticized by standing up here on the floor of this House and undertaking to resist a bill of this kind." 45 Cong Rec 810 (1910). Another southern representative, before criticizing the bill on states' rights grounds, reassured his audience that he was not speaking "in defense of prostitution of women. We are all opposed to that." 45 Cong Rec 823 (1910) (Rep Adamson).

[192] Indeed, to the extent the health or safety aspects of a particular problem are contested, this is reason for Congress to adopt a labeling requirement rather than a ban.

[193] 7 USC § 136(a), (c)(9) (prohibiting the distribution of unlabeled pesticides); 21 USC § 331(a) (prohibiting the "misbranding of any food, drug, device, tobacco product, or cosmetic in interstate commerce"); 21 USC § 331(a) (prohibiting the "misbranding of any food, drug, device, tobacco product, or cosmetic in interstate commerce").

a ban or an in-service regulation will raise more difficult questions. For example, if Congress were to enact a ban on assault weapons similar to the assault weapons ban that expired in 2004, would that legislation represent a permissible in-service regulation or an impermissible market ban?[194] The same questions can be asked about the federal ban on marijuana enacted in the CSA and upheld in *Raich*: does it regulate the broader market in drugs, or does it impermissibly shut down the market in marijuana? These statutes pose a more difficult question of line-drawing because, unlike the Mann Act, they prohibit goods that could conceivably participate in a larger, legal market (the market in remedial drugs, in the case of marijuana, or the market in guns, in the case of assault weapons) but, unlike other congressional statutes, nevertheless reflect an a priori judgment on the part of Congress that certain kinds of goods are simply unfit or inappropriate for use or consumption.

In the face of hard cases, it may prove instructive to ask—as is often asked in antitrust cases, where market definition is extremely important—whether the targeted goods are substitutable.[195] If consumers can easily find a nonbanned substitute for the prohibited good, then the prohibited good does not compose a distinct market, and therefore it is likely that Congress is not seeking to ban the good but is attempting to foster, or otherwise regulate, the broader market of which the banned good forms only one part.[196] It is only when Congress bans a good for which there are

---

[194] Violent Crime Control and Law Enforcement Act of 1994, Pub L No 103-322, § 110102, 108 Stat 1796, 1996, codified at 18 USC § 922, expired Sept 13, 2004. See David Jackson and Aamer Madhani, *Obama Calls for Assault-Weapons Ban, Background Checks*, USAToday.com (Jan 16, 2013), online at http://www.usatoday.com/story/news/politics/2013/01/16/obama-gun-violence-plan-assault-weapons-ban-background-checks/1837793/.

[195] The leading case setting out the substitutability test of market definition in the antitrust context is *United States v E. I. Du Pont de Nemours and Co.*, 351 US 377, 395 (1956) ("In considering what is the relevant market for determining the control of price and competition, no more definite rule can be declared than that commodities reasonably interchangeable by consumers for the same purposes make up that part of the trade or commerce, monopolization of which may be illegal.") (internal punctuation omitted). See also *National Collegiate Athletic Association v Board of Regents of University of Oklahoma*, 468 US 85, 111 (1984) (noting that the "correct test for determining whether" particular products "constitute a separate market" is "whether there are other products that are reasonably substitutable" for them).

[196] One might argue that under this logic Congress can ban marijuana, viewing alcohol as a safe substitute in a general market for intoxicants or mood-altering substances. Note, however, that this is not what Congress has done or purported to do. Marijuana only has been considered (and banned) for its supposedly therapeutic values. (Of course, not all would agree that alcohol and marijuana are in fact substitutes, or that alcohol is safe in some way marijuana is not when used recreationally.)

no legal substitutes that the federal prohibition amounts to a market ban. Indeed, it is only in the latter case that Congress attempts to dictate the purposes that may be served by market activity. In the former case, Congress merely regulates which specific kinds of goods may serve the ends consumers seek from them. For example, consumers use leaded and unleaded gasoline for precisely the same purposes—to fuel their cars—suggesting that they are substitutable products, even if some may differ on which kind of gasoline they find more effective. For this reason, the federal ban on the sale of leaded gasoline represents a permissible in-service regulation of the gasoline market, not a prohibited market ban.[197]

Of course, the question of when a product is or is not substitutable becomes complex when there are multiple uses that a product does or can serve. Consider, for example, the proposed ban on assault weapons. In surveys, gun owners cite three primary reasons why they own guns: hunting, sport shooting, and self-defense.[198] Gun advocates also cite another purpose for owning guns that is less commonly mentioned in surveys: namely, protection against tyrannical government. (This is also a purpose that was historically associated with the Second Amendment right to bear arms.[199]) And, of course, guns are used to commit crime.

With respect to some of these uses, an argument could be made that there are no reasonable substitutes for the banned goods. In defending against tyrannical government, a revolver will certainly not prove as effective as an assault weapon. One could argue, on that basis, that the two weapons are not reasonably substitutable and that a congressional ban on assault weapons would therefore be impermissible under our reading of the Commerce Clause. The problem with this argument, however, is that it proves too much. Semiautomatic pistols will certainly prove more effective than revolvers in defending against tyranny, but tanks will prove far more

---

[197] 42 USC 7545(n).

[198] See, for example, Philip J. Cook and Jens Ludwig, *Guns in America: National Survey on Private Ownership and Use of Firearms* *2–3 (report, National Institute of Justice, DOJ, May 1997), online at https://www.ncjrs.gov/pdffiles/165476.pdf *2–3 (reporting that, in a national survey of gun owners, the most common reason for owning a gun was self-protection (46 percent) and the second most common reason was recreation—not only hunting but sport shooting (35 percent or 50 percent). More recent polls report similar results. See, for example, *Guns*, Gallup.com, online at http://www.gallup.com/poll/1645/guns.aspx.

[199] Calvin Massey, *Guns, Extremists, and the Constitution*, 57 Wash & Lee L Rev 1095, 1100–25 (2000).

effective still, as will nuclear weapons, and yet neither the states nor the federal government permit civilian use of these kinds of weapons, and no one within their right mind thinks they should. Defense against tyranny may therefore play an important role in the rhetoric of the gun rights movement, but it is not a use that federal or state law appears to legitimate. For that reason, it is unclear how important a role it should play in defining the market.

On the other hand, if we consider the other uses for which consumers possess or purchase guns—namely, hunting, sport shooting, and self-defense—a reasonable argument can be made that other guns *are* substitutes for assault weapons, and that a federal ban on assault weapons would therefore not represent a ban of the market in assault weapons but instead would represent an in-service regulation of the larger market in guns. One could argue, in other words, that in banning assault weapons, Congress is not enacting a moral judgment about the use of those kinds of guns but merely seeking to minimize the negative externalities associated with the legal, and constitutionally protected, interstate gun market. Gun advocates themselves argue, in critiquing the proposed ban, that little distinguishes the weapons referred to as "assault weapons" in contemporary debates from other guns not designated as such, and that both assault and nonassault weapons are equally useful when it comes to hunting and self-defense.[200] Evidence from the 1994 assault weapons ban suggests that, at least at that time, the banned guns were quickly replaced by other nonbanned weapons—and thereupon used, for both legitimate and illegitimate purposes.[201] If this characterization of the uses of assault weapons and the availability of substitutes is correct (though there may well be those who disagree), then just as Congress may ban particularly harmful pesticides as a means of regulating the

---

[200] See Sarah Jones, *In 2004 the NRA Called the Assault Weapons Ban Nonsense, Here's Why They're Wrong*, Politicususa.com (Dec 17, 2012), online at http://www.politicususa.com/wayne-lapierre-2004-its-question-harm-question-meaningless-ban-involved-cosmetics.html (quoting NRA CEO Wayne LaPierre as saying "there's no difference in the performance characteristics").

[201] Christopher S. Koper, *An Updated Assessment of the Federal Assault Weapons Ban: Impacts on Gun Markets and Gun Violence, 1994–2003* *10–11 (report, National Institute of Justice, DOJ, June 2004), online at https://www.ncjrs.gov/pdffiles1/nij/grants/204431 .pdf (noting that manufacturers produced legal substitutes for the banned weapons and that "[r]elatively cosmetic changes . . . [were] sufficient to transform a banned weapon into a legal substitute"). Of course, some of this substitutability reflects the shortcomings of the law itself and might be avoided in future legislation.

broader pesticide market, it may ban assault weapons as a means of regulating the broader gun market.

The legislative history and purposes of the bill can also help resolve the question of whether it constitutes a permissible in-service regulation or an impermissible market ban. Consider the example of the congressional ban on the possession or use of marijuana. Given the extensive evidence of the drug's therapeutic uses as a painkiller and antinausea medication, one could argue that the drug is both substitutable for, and substitutable by other, legal pain and antinausea medications and that its prohibition is merely an in-service regulation of the broader drug market.[202] Congress may have determined that, among a variety of products with similar uses, marijuana was less safe than the alternatives (and perhaps less effective). But there are two problems with this argument. First, there is also a recreational market for marijuana. As with the gun market, there are alternatives here too, such as alcohol, but also—as with assault weapons—disagreement about how substitutable these are. Second, perhaps more importantly, the federal government has actively discouraged research into marijuana's medical safety and therapeutic efficacy by imposing onerous procedural requirements that apply to no other drugs.[203] There is thus good reason to doubt that the federal government has taken the question of substitutability very seriously, or that marijuana is banned because of its specific, scientifically demonstrated, risks.

The history of the drug laws certainly suggests that what lies behind the federal ban is a moral, rather than a technical or scientific, judgment about the uses that consumers make of the drug, and about the kinds of persons associated with its use.[204] If so, the

---

[202] See, for example, Janet E. Joy, Stanley J. Watson Jr., and John A. Benson Jr., eds, *Marijuana and Medicine: Assessing the Science Base* *137–92 (report, Institute of Medicine, National Academy of Sciences, 1999), online at http://www.nap.edu/openbook.php ?record_id = 6376 (explaining the therapeutic uses of marijuana).

[203] See *Federal Obstruction of Medical Marijuana Research* *1 (report, Marijuana Policy Project), online at http://www.mpp.org/assets/pdfs/library/Federal-Obstruction-of-MMJ-Research-1.pdf (noting that "[i]n addition to the standard FDA and DEA approvals needed for all research using Schedule I drugs, researchers conducting trials with marijuana must receive approval through a National Institute on Drug Abuse/Public Health Service (NIDA/PHS) protocol review process that exists for *no other drug*").

[204] See Erik Grant Luna, *Our Vietnam: The Prohibition Apocalypse*, 46 DePaul L Rev 483, 491–95 (1997) (noting the extent to which the early drug laws were motivated by, and justified in terms of, racist stereotypes of Chinese immigrants, African Americans, and Hispanics); Duke and Gross, *Longest War* at 82–83, 90–94 (cited in note 17).

ban cannot be justified as an in-service regulation. Of course, supporters of the ban could contest that conclusion; but in so doing, they would have to engage in a serious discussion about the purposes of the federal prohibition, and about the ways in which it serves those purposes. This would be a welcome discussion that the formalism of the *Champion* rule largely has foreclosed.

This last point—focusing on what the legislative history and past practice tell us about congressional purposes in adopting a ban—raises the question of what to do with congressional motives. In general, looking to congressional motives is disfavored under the Commerce Clause.[205] Thus, perhaps the analysis here runs the risk of slipping into an impermissible examination of motive and pretext.

Note, however, that our thesis is directed as much to members of Congress as to the courts. Even if courts ought not take congressional motives into account—and recall that the ban on examining motives finds its root in *Champion*—it does not mean members of Congress should not examine their own motives. The judiciary may be unwilling to examine congressional motives for reasons of institutional competence or interbranch respect. Whether the disfavoring of these tests makes sense or not, something that is debatable, members of Congress ought themselves to take the Constitution into account and cast votes in good-faith compliance with the best conception of its requisites. Even if judicial line-drawing is complicated, members of Congress ought to know whether they are trying to shut down a market because of ideological disfavor, or whether they are instead attempting to foster a broader market.

2. *The "tying Congress's hands" objection.* One might also object that limiting congressional power in the way we suggest here could tie Congress's hands in undesirable ways. Consider for example the Endangered Species Act. The Act functions to shut down the interstate market in endangered animals not as a means of regulating a broader market, but—as the congressional statement of purposes indicates—as a means of protecting endangered and

---

[205] See, for example, *United States v Orito*, 413 US 139, 144 (1973), citing *McCray v United States*, 195 US 27 (1904) ("The motive and purpose of a regulation of interstate commerce are matters for the legislative judgment upon the exercise of which the Constitution places no restriction and over which the courts are given no control.").

threatened species of animals and wildlife from extinction.[206] In this respect, it constitutes, under the rule articulated above, an impermissible market ban that is beyond Congress's power to enact under its commerce power. And yet the Endangered Species Act addresses a problem that appears to be genuinely interstate. Animal habitats and ecosystems cross state lines, which means that leaving primary enforcement of the prohibition on the sale of endangered animals to the states may seriously undermine the purpose of enacting such a prohibition in the first place: that is, to protect particular species against commercial exploitation.

Or consider the federal prohibition on the production, transfer, and possession of biological weapons such as anthrax.[207] Given the tremendous harm that weapons of this sort can impose on the general population, and the significant threat they may pose to national security, as well as to public health, one could argue that it is perfectly appropriate for the federal government to ban markets in them—particularly given the slim probability that there will be any significant divergence among the states about the propriety of such a ban. And yet an argument could be made that the federal biological weapons prohibition goes beyond what is necessary simply to protect the channels and instrumentalities of commerce from harm because it bans not only the use and transport of biological weapons across state lines but even their purely intrastate production, manufacture, and sale. As such, the ban may constitute an impermissible market ban.

Statutes like the Endangered Species Act and the federal biological weapons ban suggest that there may be real costs associated with limiting Congress's ability to prohibit commerce. Given the significant role that the federal government assumes not only over the regulation of the economy but also in protecting national security and advancing other ends, one might fear that such a limit—however well grounded in history and theory—constrains federal power too much.

There are, however, good reasons to believe that federal power will not be unduly constrained by a ban on congressional market bans. First, as explained in Part III.B, Congress remains free to

---

[206] 16 USC § 1531(b) ("The purposes of this [Act] are to provide a means whereby the ecosystems upon which endangered species and threatened species depend may be conserved.").

[207] 18 USC § 175.

regulate in ways that do not result in the prohibition of the market. In service of the uninterrupted functioning of the national market, Congress could (as it in fact already does) prohibit the transportation in interstate commerce of explosive or dangerous materials.[208] Similarly, although Congress may lack the power to ban the market in endangered species, nothing in our reading of the Commerce Clause limits Congress's power to intervene to protect these species in a number of other ways—including by enacting prohibitions on the destruction of their habitats.[209]

Second, to the extent that these limitations on the commerce power are a problem, it sometimes will be the case that Congress can act in the face of genuinely interstate problems on the basis of another of its enumerated powers. The Treaty Power, Congress's power over foreign commerce, and Congress's war powers may empower Congress to act even when the Commerce Clause does not.[210] For example, when Congress banned the markets in

---

[208] 18 USC § 842(a)(3)(A) (prohibiting anyone but licensees to "to transport, ship, cause to be transported, or receive any explosive materials").

[209] Courts have found that Congress can constitutionally prohibit the killing of endangered animals, as well as activities that result in the destruction of the habitats in which endangered species live, under its authority to regulate activities that have a "substantial effect" on interstate commerce. Activities that target endangered animals or their habitats have a substantial effect on interstate commerce, courts conclude, because they threaten the potentially significant economic resources that these species, and their biodiverse habitats, represent. See *GDF Realty Investments, Ltd. v Norton*, 326 F3d 622, 638–41 (5th Cir 2003); *Gibbs v Babbitt*, 214 F3d 483, 492 (4th Cir 2000); *National Association of Home Builders v Babbitt*, 130 F3d 1041, 1050–52 (DC Cir 1997). Because these cases do not rely on Congress's power to prohibit commerce, nothing in our reading of the Commerce Clause should prevent Congress from prohibiting activities of this sort. They also suggest that a federal ban on the sale of endangered species might be justifiable, as a necessary and proper means of enforcing the federal regulation of endangered species.

This raises, however, the interesting and perhaps difficult question of how the Necessary and Proper Clause fits into our analysis. There are two possibilities. The first is to say that congressional bans are not appropriate under the Necessary and Proper Clause for all the federalism reasons rehearsed above. The second position is that although interstate market bans are not acceptable under the Commerce Clause, they may be permissible under the Necessary and Proper Clause. Without resolving this question, it is useful to note that under the second position, market bans still must be necessary and proper to some *other* permissible goal of Congress's. So, for example, could a ban on the interstate (or intrastate) possession and use of marijuana be justified under the Necessary and Proper Clause? The only justification that conceivably would work is one maintaining that Congress—under the Commerce Clause—can prohibit the consumption of particular commodities to protect public health and thereby lower costs in the national health care market. It goes without saying, especially in light of the controversy over the Affordable Care Act, that such a position—which would seem to apply equally to issues such as alcohol consumption and obesity—would trigger quite a national debate. It is difficult to see such a position being adopted anytime soon.

[210] US Const, Art II, § 2, cl 2 (treaties); US Const, Art I, § 8, cl 3 (foreign commerce); US Const, Art I, § 8, cl 11 (war).

endangered species and biological weapons, it made clear that in each case, one of the goals of the legislation was to implement the United States's various treaty obligations.[211] Courts have affirmed the constitutionality of the biological weapons ban under the Treaty Clause, and commentators have suggested that the Endangered Species Act is similarly sustainable under the treaty power.[212]

In the absence of a treaty, Congress's war powers may also allow it to prohibit goods that pose a significant threat to national security, such as nuclear materials and other goods that may be used as weapons. Congress's war powers have been invoked to justify broad prohibitions of other kinds of activities that implicate national security. There is no obvious reason why any limits should be imposed on Congress's ability to enact other kinds of national security bans.[213] And of course Congress may always use its power to ban foreign commerce to limit what kinds of goods circulate in domestic markets. This means that, in many cases in which there is a pressing justification for a market ban, and even in some cases where there is not, Congress will be able to enact the ban,

---

[211] Endangered Species Act, 16 USC § 1531 (noting that "the United States has pledged itself as a sovereign state in the international community to conserve to the extent practicable the various species of fish or wildlife and plants facing extinction" and enumerating the many treaties and conventions which the Act is intended to implement); Biological Weapons Anti-Terrorism Act of 1989, Pub L No 101-298 § 2, 104 Stat 201 (1990) (noting that "the purpose of the [biological weapons act] is to implement the Biological Weapons Convention, an international agreement unanimously ratified by the United States Senate in 1974" as well as to "protect the United States against the threat of biological terrorism"). See also Migratory Bird Treaty Act, 16 USC §§ 703–12 (prohibiting the killing, as well as the sale, of migratory birds, their nests, eggs, and products, as an implementation of the Migratory Bird Treaty of 1916); Chemical Weapons Convention Implementation Act, 22 USC § 7601–71 (implementing the Chemical Weapons Convention in the United States by prohibiting the development, production, acquisition, transfer, receipt, possession, as well as use of chemical weapons).

[212] *United States v Bachner*, 2011 WL 1743427, *2 (ND Ill) (recognizing the biological weapons prohibition enacted in 18 USC § 175 to be a "valid exercise of Congress' [treaty] power under the framework of [*Missouri v*] *Holland*"). See also *United States v Bond*, 681 F3d 149, 166 (3rd Cir 2012) (affirming the constitutionality of a similar ban on chemical weapons under Congress's treaty powers), cert granted, 133 S Ct 978 (2013). See also Gavin R. Villareal, Note, *One Leg to Stand On: The Treaty Power and Congressional Authority for the Endangered Species Act After United States v. Lopez*, 76 Tex L Rev 1125, 1153–62 (1998).

[213] See *Holder v Humanitarian Law Project*, 130 S Ct 2705, 2731 (2010) (rejecting challenges under the First and Fifth Amendments to a statute prohibiting material support to terrorist organizations). See also *In re Consolidated U.S. Atmospheric Testing Litigation*, 820 F2d 982, 990 (9th Cir 1987) (recognizing 42 USC § 2212, which limits contractor liability for harms arising from domestic nuclear testing, as a constitutional exercise of Congress's war and commerce powers); *Hammond v United States*, 786 F2d 8, 13 (1st Cir 1986) (same).

if not under its Commerce Clause authority, then under one of its other enumerated powers.

3. *The no-effect objection.* The fact that Congress will retain the power to enact market bans under its other powers—while of comfort to those who might worry about imposing undue constraints on the federal government—might prompt others to wonder whether, in practice, the interpretation of the Commerce Clause advocated here will have too little effect on the overall scope of federal power. A related objection might be that Congress, even if it is genuinely barred from banning the market in a particular good, and cannot use its other powers as a means of running around the limitations on the Commerce Clause, will be able to get around the limitation nonetheless by enacting regulations that function in effect like bans.

We have two responses to this objection. First, our approach is functionalist, not formalist. Our claim is that, when acting under its interstate commerce powers, Congress may not attempt, either in form or in effect, to shut a market down when it is not acting in service to the market as a whole. What is decisive, in other words, is not whether the law *looks* like a prohibition or a regulation but whether it *functions* like a prohibition or a regulation. Congress should not therefore be able to cloak prohibitions as regulations by imposing such onerous requirements that effectively make it impossible to buy or sell a particular good. Nor should it be able to tax those goods out of existence—as it has tried on multiple occasions in the past—although it can legitimately tax goods in order to influence market behavior.[214]

Second, there are significant structural and subject-area con-

---

[214] As the Court noted only last term in *National Federation of Independent Business v Sebelius*, Congress's power under the Taxing Clause is limited to the regulation, rather than the prohibition, of behavior—just as is true, we argue, of Congress's power under the Commerce Clause. See 132 S Ct 2566, 2600 (2012), quoting *Oklahoma Tax Commission v Texas Co.*, 336 US 342, 364 (1949) (noting that "[t]he power to tax is not the power to destroy"). Congress cannot therefore rely upon its taxing power to evade the limitations imposed on its commerce powers, as it can rely, when appropriate, on its treaty or foreign commerce powers. Nevertheless, as the Court has long recognized, Congress can use its taxing power to influence the behavior of customers who participate in a market. See Robert D. Cooter and Neil S. Siegel, *Not the Power to Destroy: An Effects Theory of the Tax Power*, 98 Va L Rev 1195, 1209 (2012) (noting that both "constitutional text and political history suggest that Congress possesses ample power to alter individual behavior by using taxes much like it uses many regulations"). Therefore, Congress can certainly influence consumer behavior, either by means of its taxing or by means of its commerce powers. What it cannot do is pass taxes—or regulations—that function in effect to shut the market down.

straints on the exercise of Congress's other powers that limit the
extent to which they can enable Congress to evade the limitations
on its authority under the Commerce Clause. Consider, for example, Congress's power over foreign commerce: although Congress may enact bans on imported and exported goods, that provides no justification for federal bans of domestically produced
goods; nor, under existing precedents, does it justify federal power
to restrict imported goods that are no longer in their original
packaging and have been assimilated into the mass of property
properly under the control of the states.[215] Similarly, bans justified
under Congress's war powers can and should relate only to products that are genuinely relevant to the national security because
of their use or potential use as weapons of war. Because it takes
two-thirds of the Senate to ratify a treaty, Congress also should
not be able to use the Treaty Power to evade the limitations on
its power under the Commerce Clause. The fact that, as Oona
Hathaway has noted, it takes an "extraordinary level of consensus
. . . to conclude an Article II treaty," makes it unlikely that Congress will be able to ban the market in a particular good or class
of goods using its treaty powers unless there is widespread agreement among the states about the importance of the ban.[216]

4. *Facilitating diversity: the change-over-time objection.* Our approach thus *will* limit federal power. But the constraint it will
impose will matter only in cases where there is a difference of
opinion among the states about whether any particular product
or activity should be prohibited. This suggests that congressional
power might ebb and flow over time with respect to specific commodities. While some may see this as a problem, we believe it is
a virtue.

To see why this is so, consider the example of child pornography.
Federal law has prohibited the transportation, receipt, and possession of child pornography since 1977, when it passed the Protection of Children Against Sexual Exploitation Act.[217] It seems
clear that this law constitutes a market ban, given strong evidence

---

[215] See *Brown v Maryland*, 25 US 419, 441–42 (1827).

[216] See, for example, Oona A. Hathaway, *Treaties' End: The Past, Present, and Future of
International Lawmaking in the United States*, 117 Yale L J 1236, 1310, 1312 (2008) (noting
that senators representing about 8 percent of the country's population can halt a treaty
and that "an extraordinary level of consensus is required to conclude an Article II treaty").

[217] Protection of Children Against Sexual Exploitation Act of 1977, Pub L No 95-225,
92 Stat 7 (1978), codified as amended at 18 USC § 2251 et seq.

that child pornography is not reasonably substitutable by another, nonbanned good—for example, adult pornography—and that Congress's intent when passing the law was to curb the nationwide demand for these materials, rather than to ensure the safety or transparency of a broader market.[218] There is therefore a good argument to be made that, under our analysis, Congress may not constitutionally enforce the prohibition.

Because there is widespread unanimity among the states about the importance of enacting a ban on child pornography, however, little would be lost by redrafting the federal prohibition as a helper statute.[219] In this situation, the helper statute would function in effect much like a total ban, insofar as it would effectively make the interstate transport or distribution of child pornography a federal crime. Of course, enforcement of the federal prohibition would depend in part on the vagaries of the various states' statutory schemes. But presumably this is to the good, because it would allow variation and experimentation among the states, while still ensuring that federal muscle is available to help prevent spillovers. On the whole, then, the transport, sale, and possession of child pornography would still be banned nationally—albeit under a somewhat more complex and diverse regulatory scheme than is currently the case.

But what if this state consensus on child pornography were to break down, rendering the federal helper law ineffective or at least limited in its ability to combat something that many believe is a great evil? It is, of course, almost unimaginable that child pornography will ever be acceptable. But sometimes, as is obvious with regard to the cases of marijuana and alcohol, views *do* shift over time. And when they do, federal power will shift with them.

We view this as a good thing. Tolerating this sort of diversity is precisely what federalism is all about. What the regulation of alcohol has taught us—and perhaps the regulation of marijuana in time might—is that seemingly universal and timeless truths can prove neither. When this is the case, allowing the federal gov-

---

[218] See *United States v Robinson*, 137 F3d 652, 656 (1st Cir 1998) (discussing Congressional purposes). See also Amy Adler, *The Perverse Law of Child Pornography*, 101 Colum L Rev 209, 236–37 (2001) (discussing the history of child pornography laws).

[219] Eva J. Klain, Heather J. Davies, and Molly A. Hicks, *Child Pornography: The Criminal-Justice-System Response* *26–34 (report, ABA Center on Children and the Law, Mar 2001), online at http://www.popcenter.org/problems/child_pornography/PDFs/Klain_etal_2001.pdf (discussing the various state child pornography laws and their differences and similarities).

ernment to supplant state action cheats the sort of checkerboard regulation that enables the values of federalism to find full expression.

IV. Conclusion

Our argument is straightforward: Congress's power "to regulate" interstate commerce does not include the power to prohibit commerce in products or services that the states themselves, or some of them, do not want to prohibit. This interpretation of the Commerce Clause is supported by history, and by the structure and theory of the Constitution. Returning to this original understanding would do little to displace federal power in many areas in which central decision making is essential. But it would deprive Congress of a police power that an accident of history bestowed upon it.

BARRY CUSHMAN

CAROLENE PRODUCTS AND
CONSTITUTIONAL STRUCTURE

Justice Harlan Fiske Stone's opinion for the majority in the U.S.
Supreme Court's 1938 decision in *United States v Carolene Products*[1]
is well known for its statement of two principles. The first concerns
the presumption of constitutionality to be accorded to legislation
regulating economic activity when challenged under the Due Process Clauses. "[R]egulatory legislation affecting ordinary commercial transactions is not to be pronounced unconstitutional," Stone
maintained, "unless in the light of the facts made known or generally
assumed it is of such a character as to preclude the assumption that
it rests upon some rational basis within the knowledge and experience of the legislators."[2] The second principle emerges from
Stone's immediate qualification of the first principle in the famous
Footnote Four, where he suggested that such deferential review
would not be appropriate "when legislation appears on its face to
be within a specific prohibition of the Constitution, such as those
of the first ten Amendments, which are deemed equally specific

Barry Cushman is John P. Murphy Foundation Professor of Law, Notre Dame Law
School.

AUTHOR'S NOTE: Thanks to A. J. Bellia, Michael Collins, Patty Cushman, John Finnis,
Rick Garnett, Joel Goldstein, John Harrison, Fred Konefsky, Daryl Levinson, Caleb Nel-
son, and James Stern for helpful comments and conversation, and to Patrick Bottini and
Ben Pulliam for splendid research assistance.

[1] 304 US 144 (1938).

[2] Id at 152.

when held to be embraced within the Fourteenth."[3] Nor would such a robust presumption of constitutionality be warranted with respect to "legislation which restricts those political processes which can ordinarily be expected to bring about repeal of undesirable legislation," nor with respect to "statutes directed at particular religious," "national," "racial," or other "discrete and insular minorities."[4]

This understanding of the meaning of *Carolene Products* is now so firmly established[5] that it is easy to overlook the fact that the decision once was regarded as marking an important step in the development of Commerce Clause jurisprudence. This was so not simply because the Court there upheld an exercise of the commerce power—the Filled Milk Act of 1923[6]—which prohibited the interstate shipment of the substance for which it was named. At a deeper level, it was true because of the vital if often implicit role that Fifth Amendment due process concepts had played in shaping and constraining federal power to prohibit transportation in interstate commerce. The understanding that lawyers once had of this relationship between structural constitutional federalism and individual rights has long been lost to us. It is the ambition of this article to reconstruct that understanding, and to show how Justice Stone's resolution of that relationship in *Carolene Products* laid the groundwork not only for modern conceptions of judicial review, but also for a conception of federal power that would predominate throughout the remainder of the twentieth century.

Part I of this article charts the development of our modern understanding of the meaning of *Carolene Products*. For the first decade or so following its announcement, we find, the case was treated by the Court and by academics as a significant Commerce Clause precedent. It was only in the years following World War II, when earlier understandings of Commerce Clause jurisprudence began to fade,

---

[3] Id at 152 n 4.

[4] Id at 152–53 n 4.

[5] The literature here is vast. Among the more noteworthy contributions are John Hart Ely, *Democracy and Distrust: A Theory of Judicial Review* (Harvard, 1980); David A. Strauss, *Is Carolene Products Obsolete?* 2010 U Ill L Rev 1251 (2010); Bruce A. Ackerman, *Beyond Carolene Products*, 98 Harv L Rev 713 (1985); Robert Cover, *The Origins of Judicial Activism in the Protections of Minorities*, 91 Yale L J 1287 (1982).

[6] An Act to Prohibit the Shipment of Filled Milk in Interstate or Foreign Commerce ("Filled Milk Act"), 42 Stat 1486 (1923).

that the modern understanding began to eclipse its more inclusive predecessor.

Part II provides the doctrinal and analytic framework necessary to appreciate the significance of *Carolene Products'* contribution to Commerce Clause development. This part offers a reinterpretation of the line of cases upholding the constitutionality of federal statutes prohibiting the interstate shipment of such disfavored items as lottery tickets,[7] adulterated or mislabeled food and drugs,[8] alcoholic beverages,[9] and stolen automobiles.[10] These decisions stand in stark contrast to the case of *Hammer v Dagenhart*,[11] where the Court invalidated the Keating-Owen Child Labor Act of 1916,[12] which prohibited the interstate shipment of goods made by firms employing children. The apparent inconsistencies in this line of cases have long puzzled and frustrated students of American constitutional history. Part II aims to reconcile this seemingly contradictory body of case law. The key to doing so, I argue, lies in seeing that what we have regarded as "Commerce Clause cases" are in fact best understood as turning on issues of vested rights and substantive due process. More particularly, I maintain that these cases are best understood, as a number of sophisticated contemporary legal observers understood them, as standing for the following proposition: that once a property right in an item had vested under the applicable state law, the Due Process Clauses prohibited either Congress or sister state legislatures from disadvantageously regulating the disposition of that item unless such a disposition threatened the infliction of a cognizable harm within the legislative jurisdiction of the regulating sovereign. In the absence of a threat that such a

---

[7] An Act for the Suppression of Lottery Traffic Through National and Interstate Commerce and the Postal Service Subject to the Jurisdiction and Laws of the United States, 28 Stat 963 (1895), upheld in *Champion v Ames (The Lottery Case)*, 188 US 321 (1903).

[8] An Act for Preventing the Manufacture, Sale, or Transportation of Adulterated or Misbranded or Poisonous or Deleterious Foods, Drugs, Medicines, and Liquors, and for Regulating Traffic Therein, and for Other Purposes ("Pure Food Act"), 34 Stat 768 (1906), upheld in *Hipolite Egg Co. v United States*, 220 US 45 (1910).

[9] An Act Divesting Intoxicating Liquors of Their Interstate Character in Certain Cases ("Webb-Kenyon Act"), 37 Stat 699 (1913), upheld in *Clark Distilling Co. v Western Maryland Railway Co.*, 242 US 311 (1917).

[10] An Act to Punish the Transportation of Stolen Motor Vehicles in Interstate or Foreign Commerce ("National Motor Vehicle Theft Act"), 41 Stat 324 (1919), upheld in *Brooks v United States*, 267 US 432 (1925).

[11] 247 US 251 (1918).

[12] An Act to Prevent Interstate Commerce in the Products of Child Labor, and for Other Purposes ("Keating-Owen Child Labor Act"), 39 Stat 675 (1916).

cognizable harm might be inflicted within Congress's legislative
jurisdiction, therefore, a federal prohibition on the interstate shipment of an item deprived its owner of property without due process
of law. Equipped with this understanding of the doctrine, we can
then see that the decision in *Hammer* is best understood as turning
on a distinction between the types of extraterritorial harm that the
Court regarded as legally privileged,[13] and those that the Justices
were prepared to recognize as falling outside the protection of the
Due Process Clause.

Part III begins the effort to specify the role of *Carolene Products*
in transforming this body of doctrine. Here I reconstruct the legislative history of the Filled Milk Act of 1923, demonstrating that
the debates over its constitutionality turned on conceptions of harm
derived from the Court's due process jurisprudence. Part IV follows
the litigation over that act to the Supreme Court. Here we see that
Justice Stone accomplished two important tasks. First, he clarified
the doctrine by recognizing that in cases involving federal prohibitions on interstate shipment, the due process issue was analytically
distinct from the Commerce Clause issue, and was in fact the issue
on which the question of constitutionality hinged. Second, and more
famously, Justice Stone announced that henceforth, in these and
other cases involving challenges to economic regulation under the
Due Process Clauses, the Court would accord a broad measure of
deference to legislative judgments concerning harm. Part V then
examines the contemporary significance of this liberation of the
commerce power from its former due process restraints, documenting the important role that it played in the legislative history
of the Fair Labor Standards Act of 1938, and in the Court's decision
upholding that act and overruling *Hammer* in *United States v Darby
Lumber Co.*[14] Part VI reviews the underappreciated role of individual
rights in shaping the history and functioning of American constitutional federalism.

I. CAROLENE PRODUCTS IN HISTORICAL MEMORY

It is not surprising that *Carolene Products* is today remembered for the principles of deferential review of economic regulation

---

[13] See, for example, Oliver Wendell Holmes, Jr., *Privilege, Malice, and Intent*, 8 Harv L
Rev 1 (1894); Wesley N. Hohfeld, *Some Fundamental Legal Conceptions as Applied in Judicial
Reasoning*, 23 Yale L J 16 (1913).

[14] 312 US 100 (1941).

and heightened review under Footnote Four, because those are the principles for which it is cited in our casebooks on Constitutional Law.[15] This has now been the case for more than half a century. When Professor John Frank of Yale Law School published his casebook in 1950, he included *Carolene Products* as a principal case in the section on due process and economic regulation,[16] and placed a discussion of Footnote Four in the section on speech and reli-

---

[15] See Jesse H. Choper et al, *Constitutional Law: Cases—Comments—Questions* (West, 11th ed 2011) (due process holding briefly summarized at p 368; every other mention is of Footnote Four, see pp 295, 368, 376, 377, 378, 379, 380, 449, 577, 578, 1361, 1374, 1375, 1425, 1472, 1489, 1490, 1498, 1662); Erwin Chemerinsky, *Constitutional Law* (Aspen, 3d ed 2009) (all references are to Footnote Four, either together with the due process holding, see pp 626–28, 724, or alone, see pp 755, 946); Gregory E. Maggs and Peter J. Smith, *Constitutional Law: A Contemporary Approach* (West, 2d ed 2011) (due process holding briefly summarized at p 526; remaining references are to Footnote Four, see pp 526–27, 634, 811); Kathleen M. Sullivan and Gerald Gunther, *Constitutional Law* (Foundation, 17th ed 2010) (every mention is either to due process and Footnote Four together, see pp 391–92, or to Footnote Four alone, see p 768); Michael Stokes Paulsen et al, *The Constitution of the United States* (Foundation, 2010) (every mention is either to due process, see p 1522, or to due process together with Footnote Four, see p 1527); Calvin Massey, *American Constitutional Law: Powers and Liberties* (Aspen, 2d ed 2005) (every mention is to due process, see p 473, or to Footnote Four, see pp 48, 613, 645, 665, 717, 723); Jerome A. Barron et al, *Constitutional Law: Principles and Policies* (LexisNexis, 7th ed 2006) (every mention is to due process together with Footnote Four, see pp 474–75, or to Footnote Four alone, see pp 663, 910–11); William C. Banks and Rodney A. Smolla, *Constitutional Law: Structure and Rights in Our Federal System* (LexisNexis, 6th ed 2010) (every mention is to Footnote Four, see pp 525–26, 598); William D. Araiza and M. Isabel Medina, *Constitutional Law: Cases, History, and Practice* (LexisNexis, 4th ed 2011) (every mention is either to due process together with Footnote Four, see pp 725–27, or to Footnote Four alone, see pp 754, 755, 970, 1211, 1214, 1245); Daniel A. Farber, William N. Eskridge, Jr., and Phillip P. Frickey, *Cases and Materials on Constitutional Law: Themes for the Constitution's Third Century* (West, 4th ed 2009) (every mention is to due process, see p 497, Footnote Four, see pp 36–38, or the two of them together, see p 35); John E. Nowak and Ronald D. Rotunda, *Constitutional Law* (West, 8th ed 2010) (every mention is to due process together with Footnote Four, see pp 482, 486, 1271–72, or to Footnote Four alone, see pp 392, 494, 499, 750); Geoffrey R. Stone et al, *Constitutional Law* (Aspen, 6th ed 2009) (every mention is to due process, see pp 501, 755, 756, 758, Footnote Four, see pp 147, 523, 524, 684, 687, 688, 692, 764, 766, 852, or the two together, see pp 693, 760, 761); Charles A. Shanor, *American Constitutional Law: Structure and Reconstruction* (West, 3d ed 2006) (every mention is to Footnote Four, see pp 8, 680, 712); Laurence H. Tribe, *American Constitutional Law* (Foundation, 2d ed 1988) (every mention is to Footnote Four, see pp 129, 607, 644, 772, 778, 780, 845, 1320, 1452, 1465, 1515, 1523, 1544, 1588, 1614, 1686, or to Footnote Four together with due process, see p 582). See also Norman Redlich, John Attanasio, and Joel K. Goldstein, *Constitutional Law* (LexisNexis, 5th ed 2008) (citations to Footnote Four at pp 393, 586, 650, 686); Jonathan D. Varat, William Cohen, and Vikram D. Amar, *Constitutional Law: Cases and Materials* (Foundation, 13th ed 2009) (citations to due process and Footnote Four at pp 564–66); Paul Brest et al, *Processes of Constitutional Decisionmaking: Cases and Materials* (Aspen, 4th ed 2000) (citations to due process at p 523, to Footnote Four at pp 99, 618, 897, 948, 1040, 1126, 1280, 1291, 1493, 1500, and to both at pp 428–33, 869); David Crump et al, *Cases and Materials on Constitutional Law* (LexisNexis, 5th ed 2009) (citations to due process and Footnote Four at pp 38, 349, and to Footnote Four alone at p 626).

[16] John P. Frank, *Cases and Materials on Constitutional Law* 671–74 (Callaghan, 1950).

gion.[17] That same year Columbia Professor Noel Dowling published the fourth edition of his casebook, where he featured Footnote Four in the introduction to the section on free speech and
press.[18] The presence of Footnote Four in the Dowling text would
expand in subsequent editions, after Gerald Gunther joined the
casebook.[19] When Harvard's Paul Freund, Arthur Sutherland, Mark
De Wolfe Howe, and Ernest Brown published the first edition of
their casebook in 1954, every mention of *Carolene Products* was of
Footnote Four.[20] University of Michigan Professor Paul Kauper's
first edition, published the same year, also emphasized Footnote
Four,[21] along with a brief mention in a string cite of economic
regulations upheld against due process challenges in the Progressive
and New Deal periods.[22] By 1959, the lone citation to *Carolene
Products* in Tulane Dean Ray Forrester's casebook would be as the
origin of the notion that the First Amendment occupied a "preferred
status."[23] By the 1960s and 1970s, the understanding of *Carolene
Products* that emerges from a review of today's teaching materials
had begun to take firm shape.

This presentation of *Carolene Products* in our casebooks mirrors
the Supreme Court's treatment of the precedent in the years following World War II. In the 1950s the Justices cited the decision
in only four cases, each time for one of the two principles identified
above.[24] In the 1960s the Court cited the case only a half-dozen
times, in equal proportions for deferential review and Footnote

---

[17] Id at 838.

[18] Noel Dowling, *Cases on Constitutional Law* 925–26 (Foundation, 4th ed 1950).

[19] See Gerald Gunther and Noel Dowling, *Cases and Materials on Constitutional Law*
(Foundation, 8th ed 1970) at 755, 838, 1031, 1051, 1102, 1385; Gerald Gunther, *Cases
and Materials on Constitutional Law* (Foundation, 9th ed 1975) at 24, 309, 377, 584, 593,
637, 653, 681, 684, 754, 755, 1028, 1041, 1047. Citations to Footnote Four would taper
off dramatically in later editions. See, for example, Gerald Gunther, *Cases and Materials
on Constitutional Law* (Foundation, 10th ed 1980) at 284, 534, 541, 1106; Gerald Gunther,
Constitutional Law (Foundation, 12th ed 1991) at 458, 463, 996.

[20] Paul A. Freund et al, *Constitutional Law: Cases and Materials* 1350, 1433, 1482 (Little,
Brown, 1954).

[21] Paul Kauper, *Constitutional Law: Cases and Materials* 71, 890 (Prentice-Hall, 1954).

[22] Id at 779.

[23] Ray Forrester, *Constitutional Law: Cases and Materials* 717 (West, 1959).

[24] *Breard v City of Alexandria*, 341 US 622, 640 n 29 (1951); *Dennis v United States*, 341
US 494, 525–27, 559 (1951); *American Communications Association, CIO v Douds*, 339 US
382, 423 n 1 (1950) (Jackson, J, concurring and dissenting); *Secretary of Agriculture v
Central Roig Refining Co.*, 338 US 604, 616 (1950).

Four.[25] Citations more than doubled in the 1970s, and here references to Footnote Four began to predominate.[26] In the 1980s, following John Hart Ely's elegant elaboration of Footnote Four into a general representation-reinforcement theory of judicial review,[27] citations nearly doubled again, with Footnote Four retaining its preeminence.[28] In the past two decades the frequency of citation has declined, but Footnote Four remains the principal reason for judicial mention of the decision.[29] In our modern constitutional

---

[25] *Katzenbach v Morgan*, 384 US 641, 655 n 15 (1966); *Katzenbach v McClung*, 379 US 294, 304 (1964); *Florida Lime & Avocado Growers, Inc. v Paul*, 373 US 132, 175 (1963) (White, J, dissenting); *Goldblatt v Town of Hempstead*, 369 US 590, 596 (1962); *Braunfeld v Brown*, 366 US 599, 613 (1961) (Brennan, J, dissenting); *Poe v Ullman*, 367 US 497, 544 (1961).

[26] *Cannon v University of Chicago*, 441 US 677, 737–38 n 8 (1979) (Powell, J, dissenting); *Vance v Bradley*, 440 US 93, 113, 120 n 6 (1979) (Marshall, J, dissenting); *New Motor Vehicle Board of California v Orrin W. Fox Co.*, 439 US 96, 125 n 28 (1978) (Stevens, J, dissenting); *Regents of University of California v Bakke*, 438 US 265, 288–92, 357 (1978); *Foley v Connelie*, 435 US 291, 294 (1978); *Nyquist v Mauclet*, 432 US 1, 17 (1977) (Rehnquist, J, dissenting); *Usery v Turner Elkhorn Mining Co.*, 428 US 1, 24, 44 (1976); *Massachusetts Board of Retirement v Murgia*, 427 US 307, 313 (1976); *Application of Griffiths*, 413 US 717, 721 (1973); *Sugarman v Dougall*, 413 US 634, 642 (1973) (Rehnquist, J, dissenting); *San Antonio Independent School District v Rodriguez*, 411 US 1, 105 (1973) (Marshall, J, dissenting); *United States v Caldwell*, 408 US 665, 719 n 8 (1972); *Graham v Richardson*, 403 US 365, 372 (1971); *Oregon v Mitchell*, 400 US 112, 248, 295 n 14 (1970) (Harlan, J, dissenting).

[27] John Hart Ely, *Democracy and Distrust: A Theory of Judicial Review* (Harvard, 1980).

[28] *City of Richmond v J. A. Croson Co.*, 488 US 469, 495 (1989); *New York State Club Association, Inc. v City of New York*, 487 US 1, 17 (1988); *South Carolina v Baker*, 485 US 505, 513 (1988); *Nollan v California Coastal Commission*, 483 US 825, 844 n 1 (1987) (Brennan, J, dissenting); *Bowen v American Hospital Association*, 476 US 610, 627 (1986); *Wygant v Jackson Bd. of Education*, 476 US 267, 317 n 10 (1986) (Stevens, J, dissenting); *City of Cleburne, Texas v Cleburne Living Center*, 473 US 432, 471–72 (1985) (Marshall, J, concurring and dissenting); *Metropolitan Life Insurance Co. v Ward*, 470 US 869, 881, 887, 893 (1985); *Selective Service System v Minnesota Public Interest Research Group*, 468 US 841, 878 n 21 (1984) (Marshall, J, dissenting); *Hudson v Palmer*, 468 US 517, 557 n 36 (1984) (Stevens, J, concurring and dissenting); *Anderson v Celebrezze*, 460 US 780, 793 n 16 (1983); *Crawford v Board of Education of Los Angeles*, 458 US 527, 547 (1982) (Blackmun, J, concurring); *Washington v Seattle School District No. 1*, 458 US 457, 458, 486 (1982); *Toll v Moreno*, 458 US 1, 23 (1982) (Blackmun, J, concurring); *Plyler v Doe*, 457 US 202, 217 n 14 (1982); *Hodel v Virginia Surface Mining and Reclamation Association, Inc.*, 452 US 264, 280 n 20, 291 (1981); *Western & Southern Life Insurance Co. v State Board of Equalization of California*, 451 US 648, 672–74 (1981); *Pennhurst State School and Hospital v Halderman*, 451 US 1, 19 (1981); *Minnesota v Clover Leaf Creamery Co.*, 449 US 456, 464, 469, 478 n 2 (1981); *Industrial Union Department, AFL-CIO v American Petroleum Institute*, 448 US 607, 695 n 9 (1980) (Marshall, J, dissenting); *Richmond Newspapers, Inc. v Virginia*, 448 US 555, 587 (1980) (Brennan, J, concurring); *Fullilove v Klutznick*, 448 US 448, 518–19 (1980) (Marshall, J, concurring); *Harris v McRae*, 448 US 297, 344 (1980) (Marshall, J, dissenting); *O'Bannon v Town Court Nursing Center*, 447 US 773, 800 n 8 (1980) (Blackmun, J, concurring).

[29] *Sorrell v IMS Health Inc.*, 131 S Ct 2653, 2675 (2011) (Breyer, J, dissenting); *McDonald v City of Chicago*, 130 S Ct 3020, 3101, 3116, 3124–25 (2010) (Stevens, J, dissenting) (Breyer, J, dissenting); *District of Columbia v Heller*, 554 US 570, 628 n 27 (2008); *Kelo v*

order, *Carolene Products* has come to stand for differential standards of review applied in cases involving economic regulation, on the one hand, and civil rights and civil liberties on the other.

This was not always the case. For *Carolene Products* involved the question, at the time a subject of considerable vexation, of the power of Congress to prohibit the interstate shipment of disfavored articles under its commerce power. In the first decade or so following its announcement, *Carolene Products* was cited by the Court as a precedent concerning the scope of the commerce power[30] as frequently as it was invoked either for its position on the standard of review in cases involving ordinary commercial transactions[31] or for the heightened scrutiny for civil liberties and minority rights suggested

---

City of New London, 545 US 469, 521–22 (2005) (Thomas, J, concurring); *Vieth v Jubelirer*, 541 US 267, 312 (2004) (Kennedy, J, concurring); *Washington v Glucksberg*, 521 US 702, 766 (1997) (Souter, J, concurring); *United States v Virginia*, 518 US 515, 575 (1996) (Scalia, J, dissenting); *Miller v Johnson*, 515 US 900, 948 (1995) (Ginsburg, J, dissenting); *Adarand Constructors, Inc. v Pena*, 515 US 200, 218 (1995); *United States v Lopez*, 514 US 549, 604, 606–07, 610 (1995) (Souter, J, dissenting); *Heller v Doe*, 509 US 312, 326 (1993); *Lucas v South Carolina Coastal Council*, 505 US 1003, 1045 (1992) (Blackmun, J, dissenting); *Gregory v Ashcroft*, 501 US 452, 468 (1991); *Air Line Pilots Association, International v O'Neill*, 499 US 65, 75, 78 (1991); *United States v Munoz-Flores*, 495 US 385, 406 (1990) (Stevens, J, concurring).

[30] See *Joseph v Carter & Weekes Stevedoring Co.*, 330 US 422, 426 (1947) ("The Commerce Clause bears no limitation of power upon its face and, when the Congress acts under it, interpretation has suggested none, except such as may be prescribed by the Constitution."); *Morgan v Virginia*, 328 US 373, 380 (1946) ("Congress, within the limits of the Fifth Amendment, has authority to burden commerce if that seems to it a desirable means of accomplishing a permitted end."); *Roland Electrical Co. v Walling*, 326 US 657, 669 (1946) ("The primary purpose of the [Fair Labor Standards] Act is . . . to prohibit the shipment of goods in interstate commerce if they are produced under substandard labor conditions. Such a prohibition is an appropriate exercise of the power of Congress over interstate commerce."); *Federal Power Commission v Natural Gas Pipeline of America*, 315 US 575, 582 (1942) ("The sale of natural gas originating in one State and its transportation and delivery to distributors in any other State constitutes interstate commerce, which is subject to regulation by Congress. . . . It is no objection to the exercise of the power of Congress that it is attended by the same incidents which attend the exercise of the police power of a State."); *United States v Darby*, 312 US 100, 114 (1941) ("It is no objection to the assertion of the power to regulate interstate commerce that its exercise is attended by the same incidents which attend the exercise of the police power of the states."); *United States v Appalachian Electric Power Co.*, 311 US 377, 427 (1940) ("It is no objection to the terms and to the exertion of the [commerce] power that 'its exercise is attended by the same incidents which attend the exercise of the police power of the states.'"). See also *Apex Hosiery Co. v Leader*, 310 US 469, 484 n 2 (1940); *Carolene Products Co. v United States*, 323 US 18, 23, 31–32 (1944).

[31] *Alabama State Federation of Labor v McAdory*, 325 US 450, 466 (1945); *Sage Stores Co. v Kansas*, 323 US 32, 35 (1944); *Carolene Products Co*, 323 US at 18; *Yakus v United States*, 321 US 414, 466, 484 (1944) (Rutledge, J, dissenting); *West Virginia Board of Education v Barnette*, 319 US 624, 648 (1943) (Frankfurter, J, dissenting); *Federal Security Administrator v Quaker Oats*, 318 US 218, 229 (1943); *United States v Lowden*, 308 US 225, 240 (1939); *Clark v Paul Gray, Inc.*, 306 US 583, 594 (1939).

by Footnote Four.[32] This earlier understanding of the case was similarly reflected in the teaching materials of the day. The 1941 edition of University of Chicago political science professor Walter Dodd's casebook treated *Carolene Products* as an important precedent concerning not only due process[33] but also the commerce power,[34] and that treatment would persist through his remaining editions up to 1954.[35] Professor John Sholley's 1951 casebook similarly recognized *Carolene Products* not only for Footnote Four,[36] but also as a significant Commerce Clause precedent.[37]

Today it is the exceptional casebook that includes *Carolene Products* in its treatment of the commerce power.[38] Indeed, a recently published casebook with the title *American Constitutional Structure* does not even mention the decision.[39] Again, given the Supreme Court's recent treatment of the precedent, this is not surprising.

---

[32] *Kovacs v Cooper*, 336 US 77, 90–91 (1949) (Frankfurter, J, concurring); *United States v Congress of Industrial Organizations*, 335 US 106, 140 (1948) (Rutledge, J, concurring); *Everson v Board of Education of Ewing*, 330 US 1, 62 n 61 (1947) (Rutledge, J, dissenting); *Thomas v Collins*, 323 US 516, 530 (1945); *Prince v Massachusetts*, 321 US 158, 173 (1944) (Murphy, J, dissenting); *Skinner v Oklahoma*, 316 US 535, 544 (1942) (Stone, CJ, concurring); *American Federation of Liberty v Swing*, 312 US 321, 325 (1941); *Minersville School District v Gobitis*, 310 US 586, 606 (1940) (Stone, J, dissenting); *Thornhill v Alabama*, 310 US 88, 95 (1940).

[33] Walter F. Dodd, *Cases on Constitutional Law* 84 (West, 3d ed 1941).

[34] Id at 613.

[35] Walter F. Dodd, *Cases and Materials on Constitutional Law* 87, 619 (West, 4th ed 1949); Walter F. Dodd, *Cases on Constitutional Law* 81, 595 (5th ed 1954).

[36] John B. Sholley, *Cases on Constitutional Law* 1035–36 (Bobbs-Merrill, 1951).

[37] Id at 514.

[38] The following casebooks make no mention of the case in their sections on the commerce power: Choper et al, *Constitutional Law*; Chemerinsky, *Constitutional Law*; Maggs and Smith, *Constitutional Law*; Sullivan and Gunther, *Constitutional Law*; Paulsen et al, *The Constitution of the United States*; Massey, *American Constitutional Law*; Barron et al, *Constitutional Law*; Banks and Smolla, *Constitutional Law*; Araiza and Medina, *Constitutional Law*; Varat, Cohen, and Amar, *Constitutional Law*; Farber, Eskridge, Jr., and Frickey, *Cases and Materials on Constitutional Law*; Nowak and Rotunda, *Constitutional Law*; Stone et al, *Constitutional Law*; Shanor, *American Constitutional Law: Structure and Reconstruction*; and Tribe, *American Constitutional Law* (all cited in note 15). The casebook that best recognizes *Carolene Products* as an important Commerce Clause decision is Redlich, Attansaio, and Goldstein, *Constitutional Law* at 81 (cited in note 15), which includes the case in its discussion of Commerce Clause development. See also Ronald D. Rotunda, *Modern Constitutional Law* 234–35 (West, 9th ed 2009) (*Carolene Products* included in Commerce Clause section, though focusing on due process and Footnote Four); Crump et al, *Materials on Constitutional Law* at 128 (cited in note 15) (*Carolene Products* cited in edited version of *Katzenbach v McClung*); Brest et al, *Processes of Constitutional Decisionmaking* at 523, 618 (cited in note 15) (*Carolene Products* cited in edited version of Justice Souter's dissent in *United States v Lopez*, and in connection with Justice Stone's dormant Commerce Clause opinion in *South Carolina Highway Dept. v Barnwell Bros.*).

[39] William Funk, *Introduction to American Constitutional Structure* (West, 2008).

Since 1947, the Court has cited *Carolene Products* only once for a principle of Commerce Clause jurisprudence, and that lone event is now more than three decades past.[40] But at the time of its decision, *Carolene Products* was regarded as establishing an important principle of constitutional federalism.

II. HAMMER V DAGENHART REVISITED

A. VESTED RIGHTS AND DUE PROCESS

To understand why this was so, we need to recall that *Carolene Products* concerned the constitutionality of a federal statute prohibiting the interstate shipment of filled milk.[41] Prohibition of interstate shipment of disfavored articles had become a common technique of congressional regulation since the 1890s. In 1903, the Court had upheld a federal statute prohibiting interstate shipment of lottery tickets.[42] On the basis of this precedent, Congress enacted the Pure Food and Drugs Act of 1906,[43] which forbade interstate transportation of adulterated or inadequately labeled food and drugs. The Court sustained the statute by a unanimous vote in 1910.[44] Encouraged by these decisions, Congress in 1916 passed the Keating-Owen Child Labor Act,[45] which prohibited interstate shipment of goods made by enterprises employing child labor. But in 1918 the Court broke the string of congressional victories, invalidating the statute by a vote of 5–4 in the case of *Hammer v Dagenhart*.[46]

In keeping with long-standing principles of constitutional adjudication, Justice William Day's majority opinion disclaimed any inquiry into the purpose or intent of Congress in enacting the

---

[40] *Hodel v Virginia Surface Mining and Reclamation Association, Inc.*, 452 US 264, 291 (1981) ("The Court long ago rejected the suggestion that Congress invades areas reserved to the States by the Tenth Amendment simply because it exercises its authority under the Commerce Clause in a manner that displaces the States' exercise of their police powers. . . . 'it is no objection to the exertion of the power to regulate interstate commerce that its exercise is attended by the same incidents which attend the exercise of the police power of the states.'").

[41] Filled Milk Act, 42 Stat at 1486.

[42] *Champion v Ames (The Lottery Case)*, 188 US 321 (1903).

[43] Pure Food Act, 34 Stat at 768.

[44] *Hipolite Egg Co. v United States*, 220 US 45 (1910).

[45] Keating-Owen Child Labor Act, 39 Stat at 675.

[46] 247 US 251 (1918).

statute.[47] Nevertheless, Day maintained that "[a] statute must be judged by its natural and reasonable effect,"[48] and concluded, "In our view the necessary effect of this act is, by means of a prohibition against the movement in interstate commerce of ordinary commercial commodities to regulate the hours of labor of children in factories and mines within the states, a purely state authority."[49] Congress could not regulate employment relations in manufacturing directly, and therefore could not do so through the indirection of penalizing the employer by denying him access to interstate markets.

But as Justice Oliver Wendell Holmes pointed out in his dissent, Congress had been granted expressly the power to regulate interstate commerce, and "the exercise of its otherwise constitutional power by Congress" could not "be pronounced unconstitutional because of its possible reaction upon the conduct of the States in a matter upon which . . . they are free from direct control."[50] In Holmes's view, "that matter had been disposed of so fully as to leave no room for doubt."[51] The Court's "most conspicuous decisions" had "made it clear that the power to regulate commerce and other constitutional powers could not be cut down or qualified by the fact that it might interfere with the carrying out of the domestic policy of any State."[52] For example, the Court had sustained a 10 cent per pound excise tax on the production of colored oleomargarine notwithstanding its probable effect on the manufacture of the product.[53] Holmes might also have observed that the necessary effect of a prohibition on interstate shipment of lottery tickets was to reduce the level of production of those items within any given state; and that the necessary effect of a prohibition on the interstate shipment of impure foods and adulterated or mislabeled drugs was to regulate the conditions of their manufacture and production within the states in which they were pro-

---

[47] Id at 276 ("We have neither authority nor disposition to question the motives of Congress in enacting this legislation."); see Caleb Nelson, *Judicial Review of Legislative Purpose*, 83 NYU L Rev 1784 (2008).

[48] *Hammer*, 247 US at 275.

[49] Id at 276.

[50] Id.

[51] Id.

[52] Id at 278.

[53] Id.

duced. Even though direct regulation of manufacturing and production was a power reserved to the states and thus beyond congressional authority, indirect federal regulations of production through the exercise of enumerated powers had been upheld repeatedly.[54]

Justice Day therefore was obliged to draw a distinction between the statutes upheld in the Lottery Act and Pure Food and Drugs Law cases, on the one hand, and the Keating-Owen Child Labor Act on the other. Day's answer was that "[i]n each of these [former] instances the use of interstate transportation was necessary to the accomplishment of harmful results."[55] Each of these items inflicted a harm outside the state of origin. Lottery tickets corrupted morals and contributed to penury by promoting gambling; impure food and adulterated or mislabeled drugs posed risks to public health and safety. By contrast, goods manufactured by companies employing child labor, Day argued, were "of themselves harmless."[56] They posed no risk to the health or safety of the consumer of the product.

The principle that emerged from *Hammer v Dagenhart*, then, was that Congress could prohibit the interstate transportation of an item, notwithstanding the significant effects that such a prohibition might have on the levels or conditions of its production in a state, if such a prohibition was necessary to prevent a cognizable harm outside the state of origin. Interstate shipment of harmful items could be forbidden, but such shipment of harmless items could not. Such regulation of interstate shipment might have the collateral effect of reducing harms in the state of manufacture, but the redress of such harms alone was beyond federal authority, and such harms therefore could not provide a warrant for such exercises of the commerce power.

---

[54] See Thomas Reed Powell, *Vagaries and Varieties in Constitutional Interpretation* 64 (Columbia, 1956) ("The lottery enterprise then conducted in Louisiana was curtailed by the Anti-Lottery Act sustained by the *Lottery* case. The production of impure foods was curbed when the national Pure Food and Drug Act punished their shipment to sister states."); Thurlow M. Gordon, *The Child Labor Law Case*, 32 Harv L Rev 45, 58 (1918); Thomas Reed Powell, *The Child Labor Law, the Tenth Amendment, and the Commerce Clause*, 3 Southern L Q 175, 182–83, 197 (1918); Thomas Reed Powell, *The Child-Labor Decision*, 106 The Nation 730 (June 22, 1918); Thomas I. Parkinson, *Congressional Prohibitions of Interstate Commerce*, 16 Colum L Rev 367, 377–80 (1916); Thomas I. Parkinson, *The Federal Child-Labor Law: Another View of Its Constitutionality*, 31 Pol Sci Q 531, 531–32 (1916).

[55] *Hammer*, 247 US at 271.

[56] Id at 272.

This principle was at the time and ever since has been subjected to derisive criticism.[57] Understandably, commentators often have depicted *Hammer* as inconsistent with the Court's earlier decisions upholding prohibitions on interstate shipment of lottery tickets and adulterated or misbranded food and drugs, and some writers have accused the *Hammer* majority of harboring ulterior motivations. Professor Erwin Chemerinsky, after contrasting the *Lottery Case* with *Hammer*, mildly maintains that "the Court did not consistently define the zone of activities reserved to the states,"[58] and notes that "[s]ome commentators argue that there is no principled distinction between the cases; that the only distinction is that a conservative court approved regulation of gambling, but not regulation of businesses' employment practices."[59] Professor Laurence Tribe argues that in *Hammer*, "the Court departed in an unprincipled way from its precedents and confused Commerce Clause jurisprudence by dramatically narrowing its application."[60] The majority's attempt to distinguish the earlier decisions on the ground that "those cases had involved federal regulation of items whose very shipment could be harmful," Professor Tribe charges, was "transparently unconvincing."[61] Another leading text characterized *Hammer*'s distinction between harmful and harmless goods as "an unconvincing exercise in judicial ingenuity,"[62] while Professor David Currie concluded that "[i]t is hard to believe that

---

[57] See William Carey Jones, *The Child Labor Decision*, 6 Cal L Rev 395, 408–11 (1918); Gordon, 32 Harv L Rev at 48–56 (cited in note 54); Powell, 3 Southern L Q at 189–97 (cited in note 54); Comment, *Constitutional Law—Federal Child Labor Law Invalid*, 27 Yale L J 1092, 1093 (1918); Comment, *Child Labor Law Case—Commerce Power of Congress and Reserved Powers of the States*, 17 Mich L Rev 83, 86–87 (1918); Henry Wolf Bikle, *The Commerce Power and Hammer v. Dagenhart*, 67 U Pa L Rev 21, 29–31 (1919). The criticism continued in the 1920s, see William A. Sutherland, *The Child Labor Cases and the Constitution*, 8 Cornell L Q 338, 341, 343–48 (1923); and the 1930s, see Edward S. Corwin, *Congress's Power to Prohibit Commerce: A Crucial Constitutional Issue*, 18 Cornell L Q 477, 494–96 (1933); John Dickinson, *"Defect of Power" in Constitutional Law*, 9 Temple L Q 388, 395 (1934).

[58] Erwin Chemerinsky, *Constitutional Law: Principles and Policies* 249–50 (Aspen, 2d ed 2002).

[59] Erwin Chemerinsky, *Constitutional Law* 117 (Aspen, 2001). Another scholar archly surmised that "[i]t turned out that the Court was more interested in suppressing moral deviants than economic malefactors." Lucas Scot Powe, *The Supreme Court and the American Elite 1789–2008* 183 (Harvard, 2009).

[60] Laurence H. Tribe, 1 *American Constitutional Law* 828 n 10 (Foundation, 3d ed 2000).

[61] Id.

[62] Alfred Kelly, Winfred A. Harbison, and Herman Belz, 2 *The American Constitution: Its Origins and Development* 447 (W. W. Norton, 7th ed 1991).

the majority found its own distinctions persuasive."[63]

Such scholarly disenchantment with this principle proceeds in no small measure, I suggest, from the fact that Justice Day presented it as a principle of federalism that could be derived from the Commerce Clause alone. As Justice Holmes argued persuasively in dissent, it could not. But we should not conclude from this that contemporary lawyers would have agreed that the principle could not be derived from the Constitution. For Justice Day was characterizing as a principle of federalism what was in fact a principle of substantive due process.[64]

I will refine this idea as the discussion progresses, but here is the basic structure of the underlying thought: Proper exercises of a state's police power that protected public health, safety, or morals did not deprive anyone of a constitutionally protected liberty or property right without due process, because no one had a constitutionally protected right to harm the health, safety, or morals of the public. The same was true of exercises of congressional power prohibiting uses of the channels of interstate commerce that inflicted harm on public health, safety, or morals. But legislation that restricted the use of lawfully acquired property without such an adequate justification grounded in the protection of the public deprived its owner of his property without due process of law. To be sure, an employer in North Carolina, for example, had no constitutionally protected right to employ children—the state legislature could prohibit child labor without violating the Fourteenth Amendment.[65] But if North Carolina elected to permit the employment of children in its factories, the employer of child labor in that state acquired vested property rights in the product of that labor under the law of his state. And Congress had no power to displace that local law of property with its own law of property. Congress could exercise its commerce power to prevent the interstate shipment of that product if such a prohibition were necessary to prevent harms to interstate commerce itself, or to the inhabitants of other states, because the owner had no constitu-

---

[63] David P. Currie, *The Constitution in the Supreme Court: The Second Century 1888–1986* 98 (Chicago, 1990).

[64] See Thomas Reed Powell, *Constitutional Law in 1917–1918, I*, 13 Am Pol Sci Rev 47, 48 (1919) ("No fault was found with the statute under the due-process clause of the Fifth Amendment.").

[65] *Sturges and Burn Manufacturing Co. v Beauchamp*, 231 US 320 (1913).

tionally protected right to use his lawfully acquired property so
as to inflict such harms. As the Lottery and Pure Food and Drugs
Cases demonstrated, the fact that such a prohibition had a collateral effect on levels or conditions of production in the sending
state did not vitiate the constitutionality of the federal regulation.
But Congress could not prohibit such interstate shipment if it
were not necessary to prevent such a harm, because to do so would
be to deprive the owner of his lawfully acquired property without
due process of law. Only if the Due Process Clause were violated
would the collateral effect on production be considered problematic; and, indeed, that collateral effect was superfluous so far as
constitutional analysis was concerned, because the due process
violation alone condemned the statute. In truth, then, the restriction on congressional power to prohibit interstate shipment of
products was derived neither from the internal limitations of the
Commerce Clause, nor from whatever affirmative limitations the
Tenth Amendment might impose, but instead from the limitations
of the Due Process Clause of the Fifth Amendment.[66]

This view was articulated with varying degrees of clarity, awareness, and sophistication in a variety of settings well before *Hammer*
was decided. Examination of a controversy in the state courts may
help us to see the due process issue more clearly. In 1894, in an
effort to reduce the competition of goods made by convict labor
with those made by free laborers, the voters of New York adopted
an amendment to the state constitution adopting the "state-use"
system of convict labor. Under the terms of the amendment, the
state was forbidden to hire out the labor of its convicts to private
parties, and goods made by convicts in state institutions could be
disposed of only to the state and its political subdivisions, and not
placed on the private market. Goods produced by convicts incarcerated in the prisons of sister states continued to enter New York
markets, however, and to compete with goods made by free labor
in New York and elsewhere. In 1896 the New York legislature
responded by enacting a statute making it a misdemeanor to sell
or expose for sale goods made in any prison without attaching to
them a label disclosing them to be "convict-made," and revealing

[66] Thomas Reed Powell did not see the complete structure of the argument clearly, but
he did recognize that the majority's position was "built upon a due-process distinction,
and then unwarrantably transferred to the commerce clause." Powell, 3 Southern L Q at
194 (cited in note 54).

the name of the prison in which they had been produced. The state regime thus prohibited the sale on the private market of convict-made goods produced in New York, and required the labeling of convict-made goods produced outside the state. A man named Hawkins was charged with violating the statute by offering for sale a scrub brush produced in an Ohio prison without the label required by statute. Hawkins maintained that the statute violated the dormant Commerce Clause and deprived him of property without due process of law. With respect to each issue, the question was whether the New York statute constituted a legitimate exercise of the state's police power to protect public health, safety, morals, and welfare.[67]

Both the Appellate Division and the Court of Appeals held that the statute was not such a legitimate exercise of the state's police power. For the Appellate Division, Judge Putnam observed that it had not been alleged in the indictment "that the brush was not a good one; was not the same, in all regards, as that made by other than convict labor."[68] Nor was it "claimed to have been an inferior or deceptive article." It was "an ordinary merchantable scrub brush," and not an article "clearly injurious to the lives, health, or welfare of the people."[69] Judge Dennis O'Brien's opinion for the Court of Appeals agreed that the brush was not of inferior quality, and observed that there was no "pretense that the act was passed to suppress any fraudulent practice, or that any such practice existed with respect to such goods."[70] O'Brien therefore maintained that the statute violated both the dormant Commerce Clause and the Due Process Clause of the Fourteenth Amendment. "The scrubbing brush in question was beyond all doubt an article of property in which the defendant could lawfully deal," O'Brien insisted. Yet the statute forbade him to sell it "except upon the condition that he shall attach to it a badge of inferiority which

---

[67] People v Hawkins, 51 NE 257 (NY 1898).

[68] People v Hawkins, 47 NY Supp 56, 57 (NY App Div 1897).

[69] Id at 60. An advisory opinion issued by the Supreme Judicial Court of Massachusetts on a proposed labeling statute reached the same conclusion. The bill went "beyond a lawful exercise of the police power," the Justices agreed, because there was "nothing wrong in the nature of things in prison-made goods." Such goods were "not unsanitary or so inferior in quality that their sale would constitute a fraud on the public." Were there any differences in the "grade of workmanship," they "would be as apparent without branding as in like products made in private shops." In re Opinion of the Justices, 98 NE 334, 335–36 (1912).

[70] Hawkins, 51 NE at 258.

diminishes the value and impairs its selling qualities."[71] The statute thus interfered with "the right to acquire, possess, and dispose of property," and the state could not impair the value of such lawfully acquired property "by hostile legislation without a violation of the constitutional guaranties for the protection of property."[72]

Thus, the state's police power was restricted to preventing harms occurring within its own territorial, legislative jurisdiction.[73] A state like New York might disagree with the policy of employing prisoners in the production of goods, or of employing children under the age of 16, and it was free to prohibit these activities within its own borders. New York might also believe that the terms and conditions of such employment in sister states inflicted upon those so employed objectionable harms that could be and ought to be stopped. But the Fourteenth Amendment's Due Process Clause restrained New York from seeking to prevent those harms or to influence the prison and child-labor policies pursued in sister states by forbidding or adversely regulating the sale of the products of that labor, unless those products harmed the health, safety, morals, or welfare of New York's inhabitants. And as Congressman Steven V. White of New York maintained in reluctantly opposing a federal bill prohibiting the interstate shipment of convict-made goods in 1888, Congress was similarly constrained by the Fifth Amendment from using its commerce power to prevent such employment harms inflicted outside its legislative jurisdiction, and thereby to shape the employment policies pursued in the several states. "The State which properly punishes its criminals can properly employ them at labor, and the product of that labor is property of equal dignity and consideration under the Constitution with any other product of man's labor," White argued. The bill was

---

[71] Id.

[72] Id at 259–60.

[73] *Bonaparte v Tax Court*, 104 US 592, 594 (1881); *Allgeyer v Louisiana*, 165 US 578 (1897); *Nielsen v Oregon*, 212 US 315 (1909); *Cohens v Virginia*, 19 US 267, 427–28 (1821); *New York Life Insurance Co. v Head*, 234 US 149, 161 (1914); Westel Woodbury Willoughby, *Constitutional Law of the United States* 254 (Baker Voorhis, 2d ed 1929); Donald H. Regan, *Siamese Essays: (I) CTS Corp. v. Dynamics Corp. of America and Dormant Commerce Clause Doctrine; (II) Extraterritorial State Legislation*, 85 Mich L Rev 1865, 1884–91, 1894–95, 1899–1900 (1987); Douglas Laycock, *Equal Citizens of Equal and Territorial States: The Constitutional Foundations of Choice of Law*, 92 Colum L Rev 249, 251, 316–22, 331, 336 (1992); Willis L. M. Reese, *Legislative Jurisdiction*, 78 Colum L Rev 1587, 1587–94 (1978); Michael G. Collins, *October Term, 1896—Embracing Due Process*, 45 Am J Legal Hist 71, 87 (2001); James Y. Stern, *Choice of Law, the Constitution, and Lochner*, 94 Va L Rev 1509, 1514–17 (2008).

therefore unconstitutional "because it takes lawful property from its owner without due process of law."[74]

Many Progressive Era commentators arrived at the same assessment of congressional bills proposing to prohibit the interstate shipment of goods made by firms employing child labor. Even Thomas Parkinson, a professor of law at Columbia, counsel to the National Child Labor Committee (NCLC), and an energetic defender of the Keating-Owen law, recognized that "[t]he individual has . . . a right to seek an interstate market, and this right Congress cannot take from him, except by due process."[75] In 1907, when Senator Albert J. Beveridge of Indiana first introduced a bill to prohibit the interstate shipment of child-made goods, Professor Andrew Alexander Bruce wrote in the *Michigan Law Review* that under the Due Process Clause "[t]he right to liberty and property would certainly include the continuance of the right of interstate traffic in goods which were in themselves harmless and innocent."[76] That same year George Talley wrote of the Beveridge bill in the *Chicago Legal News*, "Since the fifth amendment was passed, there is no question but what the commerce clause was limited to the full extent of the amendment."[77] "To restrict one man's goods and allow the sale of others, where they are all equally innocuous, is the deprivation of 'liberty and property.'"[78] In 1917 Professor Frederick Green wrote in the *Illinois Law Bulletin* that the Keating-Owen Law "should be held invalid as denying due process of

---

[74] 19 Cong Rec 4528 (May 22, 1888).

[75] Parkinson, 31 Pol Sci Q at 534 (cited in note 54). See also 41 Cong Rec 1870 (January 28, 1907) (remarks of Sen. McCumber). For general recognition that the commerce power was limited by the Fifth Amendment and could not be exercised arbitrarily, see Parkinson, 31 Pol Sci Q at 532, 534, 539–40 (cited in note 54); Powell, 3 Southern L Q at 192–94, 200 (cited in note 54); Gordon, 32 Harv L Rev at 54 (cited in note 54); Bikle, 67 U Pa L Rev at 31, 35 (cited in note 57); Jones, 6 Cal L Rev at 408 (cited in note 57); B. L., Comment, *The Child Labor Law*, 26 Yale L J 242, 244 (1916); Edgar Watkins, *Is the Federal Child Labor Statute Constitutional?* 23 Case & Comm 906, 910 (1917); Jasper Yeates Brinton, *The Constitutionality of a Federal Child Labor Law*, 62 U Pa L Rev 487, 499–502 (1914); Robert B. Troutman, *Constitutionality of a Federal Child Labor Law*, 26 Green Bag 154, 154, 158–59 (1914). See also Parkinson, 16 Colum L Rev at 380–85 (cited in note 54); Philander C. Knox, *The Development of the Federal Power to Regulate Commerce*, 17 Yale L J 139, 146–47 (1908).

[76] Andrew Alexander Bruce, *The Beveridge Child Labor Bill and the United States as Parens Patriae*, 5 Mich L Rev 627, 636 (1907).

[77] George A. Talley, *Interstate Commerce and the Police Power*, 40 Chi Legal News 12, 13 (1907).

[78] Id at 12.

law."[79] "To prohibit an employer to ship articles into another state because they were made by children, is to deprive a man, who has done nothing but what he was entitled to do, of liberty to do a harmless, and presumably a beneficial act essential to the ordinary use of his property and the ordinary prosecution of his business."[80] That same year Professor D. O. McGovney maintained in the *Iowa Law Bulletin* that "Congress may not absolutely prohibit the carriage in interstate commerce of innocuous commodities, being restrained therefrom by the Fifth Amendment."[81]

Such criticisms also were voiced during the congressional floor debates over the Keating-Owen Act. Representative Samuel J. Nicholls of South Carolina charged that the bill was "unquestionably a violation of that clause of the Constitution which guarantees that no citizen can be deprived of his property without due process of law," "because of what value would cotton goods be to the manufacturer or to the purchaser who had purchased them for the purpose of selling them if he had absolutely no way to dispose of them?"[82] Nicholls reminded his colleagues of the principle that Judge O'Brien had articulated in *Hawkins*: "'The citizen can not be deprived of his property without due process of law. Any law which annihilates its value, restricts its use, or takes away any of its essential attributes comes within the purview of this limitation.'"[83] The Keating-Owen bill proposed to deprive the citizen of his property without due process by putting him "in such a position that his property is absolutely worthless to him because he has no way of selling and delivering same."[84] Cases upholding the exclusion of articles from interstate commerce all "rested upon the principle that the articles upon which an embargo was laid never had the right to enter commerce or to use its instrumentalities," explained Representative Walter Allen Watson of Virginia.[85] Such a principle would not permit Congress to "arbitrarily deny admission to interstate commerce of a bolt of cloth,"

[79] Frederick Green, *The Child Labor Law and the Constitution*, 1 Ill L Bulletin 3, 7 (1917).

[80] Id at 6. See also id at 12, 23.

[81] D. O. McGovney, *The Webb-Kenyon Law and Beyond*, 33 Iowa L Bulletin 145, 149 (1917). See also id at 149.

[82] 53 Cong Rec 1583 (January 26, 1916).

[83] Id.

[84] Id.

[85] Id at 1589.

"sound in itself, not misbranded, of use and value, and incapable of affecting the peace and morals of those to whom it is consigned," simply because it had been made by a child in North Carolina.[86] Asked by Senator William Borah of Idaho whether an employer prohibited from shipping his child-made goods in interstate commerce would have a claim under the Fifth Amendment, Senator Frank B. Brandegee of Connecticut responded, "I claim that absolutely. . . . I think the fifth amendment would protect the property, innocent in itself, in interstate transportation against the prohibitions of this bill."[87] To deny such products admission to interstate commerce, Brandegee insisted, "would be the taking of property without compensation."[88]

Years after the Court decided *Hammer*, scholars and lawyers would continue to translate Justice Day's confused majority opinion into the appropriate analytic idiom. As Professor William A. Sutherland wrote in the *Cornell Law Quarterly* in 1923, "the real trouble which the court had in mind" in *Hammer*, "which it did not express and which has not been clearly expressed in any of the criticisms of the decision which we have seen, was substantially this: The statute is a regulation of interstate commerce. But the commodity which it seeks to deny the privilege of carriage in interstate commerce is an absolutely harmless commodity. The statute, therefore, arbitrarily deprives the defendant of liberty and property and is in violation of the fifth amendment."[89] Sutherland's analysis was echoed by New York attorney Milward Martin in 1935: "instead of reasoning, as the Court did in the *Child Labor Case*, that the power to regulate interstate commerce does not include power to exclude harmless matter from such commerce, it would seem more accurate to say that the delegated power to regulate interstate commerce gives the Congress sovereign power over such commerce, but that that power is limited by the Bill of Rights; that the Congress may not close the channels of interstate commerce to inherently harmless matter, because to do so would

[86] Id.

[87] Id at 12283 (August 8, 1916).

[88] Id.

[89] Sutherland, 8 Cornell L Q at 343 (cited in note 57).

be confiscatory hence violative of the due process requirements of the Fifth Amendment."[90]

Just four years before *Hammer* was decided, Princeton University political science professor Edward S. Corwin published a famous article in the *Michigan Law Review* in which he proclaimed that the "Doctrine of Vested Rights" was "The Basic Doctrine of American Constitutional Law."[91] That "fundamental" doctrine treated "any law impairing *vested rights*, whatever its intention," as "void."[92] It was that "basic doctrine," only tacit in the opinion but ubiquitous in the contemporary legal culture, that guided the Justices in the *Hammer* majority.

B. RECONCILING THE PRECEDENTS

Before proceeding further, it is worth pausing to clarify two points. First, the contention here is not that the Justices in the *Hammer* majority and others articulating the "harmful goods" rationale were necessarily thinking explicitly in the vested rights/ due process terms that I have outlined. Had they actually expressed themselves more clearly in those terms, there would be little need to offer such an interpretation of their views. I contend only that the terms that I have sketched are those in which the Justices would best have explained what they intuited, had they thought more clearly. That they did not so express themselves may be attributable in part to the fact that the party challenging the Keating-Owen Act's constitutionality did not brief the case in these terms. But as the sources that I have canvassed demonstrate, there were several sophisticated contemporary legal thinkers who did engage in clear and serious reflection about the doctrine, and expressed the ideas in precisely the terms that I have identified.

The second point, which I will elaborate in future work, is that the vested rights/due process reading of *Hammer* enables us to reconcile the otherwise puzzling line of cases involving federal prohibitions on the interstate transportation of disfavored items. Consider first the case of alcoholic beverages. There was no doubt that, because of the threat that their use posed to public health,

---

[90] Milward W. Martin, *Constitutionality of the Securities Exchange Act of 1934*, 21 ABA J 811, 813 (1935).

[91] Edward S. Corwin, *The Basic Doctrine of American Constitutional Law*, 12 Mich L Rev 247 (1914).

[92] Id at 247, 255.

safety, and morals, the sale of intoxicants could be prohibited without depriving their owners of any vested right protected by the Due Process Clause.[93] Not all states prohibited their production and sale, however, and in 1890 the Supreme Court held that the dry state of Iowa could not prohibit the sale of beer shipped in from the wet state of Illinois so long as the product remained in its "original package." While the product was still in transit, or remained in its original package, the Court held, it remained within the exclusive legislative jurisdiction of Congress, and beyond the reach of the destination state's police power.[94] This ruling resulted in the opening of a series of "original package saloons" along the Illinois-Iowa and Missouri-Kansas borders, where thirsty Hawkeyes and Jayhawks could purchase their beverages of choice unperturbed by the meddling police powers of their native states.[95] One reaction of Congress was to enact the Webb-Kenyon Act of 1913, which prohibited the interstate shipment of liquor into a state where it was intended to be received, possessed, or sold in violation of state law.[96] The Supreme Court upheld the statute against constitutional challenge in 1917, holding that, because of its "exceptional nature," Congress could absolutely prohibit the interstate shipment of intoxicating liquor.[97] The owner of liquor acquired in a wet state had no vested right to inflict the harm of its sale in another state.

Similarly, there was no doubt that the sale of lottery tickets could be prohibited by a competent legislature without impairing any vested rights of their owners.[98] By the time that Congress enacted the Lottery Act in 1895, in fact, lotteries had been outlawed in every state of the Union except for Delaware, which followed suit in 1897.[99] When the Court decided the *Lottery Case*

---

[93] *Mugler v Kansas*, 123 US 623 (1887); *Boston Beer Co. v Massachusetts*, 97 US 25 (1877).

[94] *Leisy v Hardin*, 135 US 100 (1890).

[95] Richard F. Hamm, *Shaping the Eighteenth Amendment: Temperance Reform, Legal Culture, and the Polity, 1880–1920* 70–73 (North Carolina, 1995).

[96] Webb-Kenyon Act, 37 Stat 699.

[97] *Clark Distilling Co. v Western Maryland Railway Co.*, 242 US 311, 325–26, 331–32 (1917).

[98] *Stone v Mississippi*, 101 US 814 (1879).

[99] See United States Department of Justice, *The Development of the Law of Gambling: 1776–1976* 87, 272–73, 311–14, 337, 396–98 (1977); John Samuel Ezell, *Fortune's Merry Wheel: The Lottery in America* 241–70 (Harvard, 1960); 26 Cong Rec 4313 (May 2, 1894) (remarks of Sen. Gorman); id at 4314 (remarks of Sen. Hoar); 27 Cong Rec 3013 (March 1, 1895) (remarks of Mr. Broderick).

in 1903, therefore, there was no state in the Union in which one could acquire a vested right in a lottery ticket.[100] But even were one or more states to defect from this policy consensus, the interstate shipment of a lottery ticket acquired in such a state could inflict a harm to morals outside that state's legislative jurisdiction. Indeed, it might inflict that harm if purchased by a person while the ticket remained in actual interstate transit, or it might inflict that harm while it remained in its original package and thus within Congress's legislative jurisdiction.[101] As Justice Harlan wrote for the majority, Congress was "the only power competent" to meet and crush "an evil of such an appalling character, carried on through interstate commerce."[102] If a state could exercise its police power so as to suppress lotteries within its own limits, asked Justice Harlan, then "why may not Congress, invested with the power to regulate commerce among the several States, provide that such commerce shall not be polluted by the carrying of lottery tickets from one state to another?"[103] "As a State may, for the purpose of guarding the morals of its own people, forbid all sales of lottery tickets within its own limits, so Congress, for the purpose of guarding the people of the United States against the 'widespread pestilence of lotteries' and to protect the commerce which concerns all the States, may prohibit the carrying of lottery tickets from one State to another."[104]

Harlan recognized that the power to prohibit interstate transportation "cannot be deemed arbitrary, since it is subject to such limitations or restrictions as are prescribed by the Constitution. This power, therefore, may not be exercised so as to infringe any rights secured or protected by that instrument."[105] But the Lottery Act did not present such a case. For as Harlan observed, "surely it will not be said to be a part of anyone's liberty, as recognized by the supreme law of the land, that he shall be allowed to introduce into commerce among the States an element that will be confessedly injurious to the public morals."[106] "It is a kind of traffic

---

[100] See *Champion v Ames*, 188 US at 357.
[101] *Leisy*, 135 US at 100; *Schollenberger v Pennsylvania*, 171 US 1 (1898).
[102] *Champion*, 188 US at 357–58.
[103] Id at 356.
[104] Id at 357.
[105] Id at 362–63.
[106] Id at 357.

which no one can be entitled to pursue as of right."[107] Because no one had a right to inflict such a harm, the interstate transportation of lottery tickets could be forbidden by Congress without depriving anyone of vested rights protected by the Due Process Clause.

A similar analysis applies to the Pure Food and Drugs Act. As one of the measure's principal supporters observed on the floor of the Senate in 1906, "[n]early every State in the Union already has a pure-food law or a code pertaining to the introduction of pure food."[108] But even if an outlier state permitted one to acquire a vested right in adulterated or misbranded food or drugs, that vested right did not entail the privilege of inflicting harm to the health of persons outside that state's jurisdiction, nor of defrauding such persons through deceptive labeling. Congressmen feared that the protection of the original package doctrine would permit purveyors of such items to inflict such harms while the items remained in the federal legislative jurisdiction and thus beyond the regulatory authority of the destination state. "[I]n the construction of the interstate-commerce law," explained Senator Porter J. McCumber of North Dakota, "it has been declared that the term 'commerce' not only covers an article in its transit from one State to another, but it protects and shields that article until it is sold in original packages in the State of its consumption . . . the root of the evil is planted in that territory over which the State has no control and over which Congress has complete control—that is, the jurisdiction over interstate commerce."[109] Under the original package doctrine, adulterated or mislabeled food and drugs "may be shipped into a State contrary to the laws of the State and may be sold in the original unbroken packages in that State."[110] Accordingly, McCumber concluded, Congress alone could protect the people of destination states from the sale of such goods within the exclusive federal jurisdiction. "The States are helpless under the law. Under the Constitution, as it has been construed by the Supreme Court of the United States, these goods may go from one State to another in unbroken packages, and it is not until the

[107] Id at 358.

[108] 40 Cong Rec 1216 (January 19, 1906) (remarks of Sen. McCumber). See also id at 1415 (January 23, 1906); id at 2655 (February 19, 1906); id at 2761 (February 21, 1906); id at 895 (January 10, 1906) (remarks of Sen. Heyburn).

[109] 40 Cong Rec 1416 (January 23, 1906) (remarks of Sen. McCumber).

[110] Id at 1217 (January 19, 1906).

package is broken that the jurisdiction of the State attaches." It was therefore imperative that Congress "afford relief against the impositions that come from one State to another."[111] The owners of such goods had no vested rights to inflict such impositions, and only Congress could prevent such harms within its own exclusive legislative jurisdiction.

The vested rights/due process account of the doctrine also explains decisions upholding federal statutes prohibiting the interstate transportation of goods acquired in violation of the law of the state of origin. For example, the Lacey Act,[112] which was upheld by the Eighth Circuit in *Rupert v United States*,[113] prohibited the interstate shipment of game taken in violation of the law of the state in which the poaching took place. Congressional prohibition of such interstate shipment did not deprive the possessor of the game of any vested right protected by the Due Process Clause, because the manner in which he had taken the game prevented him from acquiring any property in it. As the court put it, "[t]he individual having no ownership in the game . . . it does not become the general subject of commerce free from all inhibitions."[114] Similarly, the Connally Act,[115] which was repeatedly upheld by the Fifth Circuit[116] and assumed to be valid by the Supreme Court of the United States,[117] prohibited the interstate transportation of "hot oil," that is, petroleum "produced or withdrawn

---

[111] Id at 1417 (January 23, 1906). See also id at 1216 (January 19, 1906); id at 895 (January 10, 1906) (remarks of Sen. Heyburn); id at 2656, 2657 (February 19, 1906) (remarks of Sen. Money); C. C. Regier, *The Struggle for Federal Food and Drugs Legislation*, 1 L & Contemp Probs 3, 5 (1933). Whether the principle of *Leisy* in fact extended to the articles regulated by the bill was a matter of debate in the House, see 40 Cong Rec 9049–51 (June 23, 1906) (remarks of Mr. Bartlett), and the Senate, see id at 2758–67 (February 21, 1906) (remarks of Sen. Bailey); but the bill ultimately passed the House by a vote of 241–17, id at 9075–76 (June 23, 1906), and the Senate by a similarly lopsided vote of 63–4, id at 2773 (February 21, 1906).

[112] An Act to Enlarge the Powers of the Department of Agriculture, Prohibit the Transportation by Interstate Commerce of Game Killed in Violation of Local Laws, and for Other Purposes ("Lacey Act"), 31 Stat 187 (1900).

[113] 181 F 87 (8th Cir 1910).

[114] Id at 90.

[115] An Act to Regulate Interstate and Foreign Commerce in Petroleum and Its Products by Prohibiting the Shipment in Such Commerce of Petroleum and Its Products Produced in Violation of State Law, and for Other Purposes ("Connally Act"), 49 Stat 30 (1935).

[116] *The President of the United States v Skeen*, 118 F2d 58 (5th Cir 1941); *Hurley v Federal Tender Board No. 1*, 108 F2d 574 (5th Cir 1939); *Griswold v The President of the United States*, 82 F2d 922 (5th Cir 1936).

[117] *United States v Powers*, 307 US 214 (1939).

from storage in excess of the amount permitted . . . by any State law." The law of the state of Texas, the primary site of the wildcat drilling at which the law was aimed, made such oil contraband, prohibited its acquisition, purchase, sale, or transportation, and made all such unlawful oil forfeit to the state.[118] Because the producer of such petroleum had taken possession of the oil in violation of state law and had acquired no right to alienate the product under applicable state law, the prohibition on interstate shipment did not deprive him of any vested right protected by the Due Process Clause.

Finally, the vested rights/due process account also reconciles the Court's decision in *Brooks v United States*,[119] which upheld the Dyer Act of 1919.[120] That statute made it a federal crime to transport or cause to be transported in interstate commerce "a motor vehicle, knowing the same to be stolen." Chief Justice Taft's opinion for a unanimous bench brusquely rejected the constitutional challenge to the act, characterizing the interstate transportation of stolen cars as "a gross misuse of interstate commerce."[121] "Congress can certainly regulate interstate commerce," Taft insisted, "to the extent of forbidding and punishing the use of such commerce as an agency to promote immorality, dishonesty or the spread of any evil or harm to the people of other States from the State of origin."[122]

The contrast between *Brooks* and *Hammer* has long perplexed legal commentators. Professor Robert Post, for example, finds inadequate Taft's effort to distinguish the Dyer Act from the Child Labor Law on the ground that the latter was "really not a regulation of interstate commerce"[123] but instead was "'a congressional attempt to regulate labor in the State of origin, by an embargo on its external trade,' banning from interstate commerce goods that 'were harmless, and could be properly transported without injuring any person who either bought or used them.'"[124] As Pro-

---

[118] See *Griswold*, 82 F2d at 923–24.

[119] 267 US 432 (1925).

[120] National Motor Vehicle Theft Act, 41 Stat 324.

[121] *Brooks*, 267 US at 439.

[122] Id at 436.

[123] Id at 438.

[124] Robert C. Post, *Federalism in the Taft Court Era: Can It Be Revived?* 51 Duke L J 1513, 1575 (2002), quoting *Brooks*, 267 US at 438.

fessor Post observes, "a similar characterization could be applied to the [Dyer Act], which was a congressional effort to regulate theft in the state of origin by banning from interstate commerce vehicles that were harmless in themselves."[125] The Dyer Act "was not," as Taft suggested, "meant to prevent 'the spread of any evil or harm to the people of other States from the State of origin,'" Professor Post maintains, but instead, like the Child Labor Law, was designed "to prevent harms within the state of origin."[126] Similarly, Professor David Currie noted that Chief Justice Taft "made no effort to show that stolen cars were harmful to anyone in the state to which they were transported. He thus left *Hammer* dangling without visible support and exposed the Court to a serious charge of inconsistency."[127] Professor Paul Murphy scored *Brooks* as another example of "constitutional inconsistency," and criticized the Court for "ignoring the obvious similarity between the measure and the first Child Labor Law," both of which prohibited interstate transportation of "things not in themselves harmful."[128] Professors Melvin Urofsky and Paul Finkelman likewise observe that the Dyer Act "bore a striking resemblance to the Child Labor Law, which had also prohibited the movement of things that were not in themselves harmful." The contrast between the outcomes in the two cases suggests to these scholars that "[f]ederal authority could thus be extended without regard to legal fine points to achieve a socially desirable end, provided the courts approved of the goal; if they did not, then legal fine points could become significant limits on state and federal power."[129]

These scholars understandably express frustration with the failure of the Court's opinion to do a satisfactory job both of distinguishing *Hammer* and of identifying an extraterritorial harm inflicted by interstate auto theft. A private memorandum located in

[125] Post, 51 Duke L J at 1575 (cited in note 124).

[126] Id n 222, quoting *Brooks*, 267 US at 436.

[127] Currie, *The Constitution in the Supreme Court* at 176 (cited in note 63). Professor Currie nevertheless recognized that "there may be more to *Brooks* than a mere judicial conviction that car theft is worse than child labor," noting that the Dyer Act reinforced state policy rather than undermining state autonomy. Id. Professor Currie also suggested that Taft might have argued "that buyers in the receiving state would be injured by the possibility of having to return the vehicles to their rightful owners without compensation, but he did not." Id n 34.

[128] Paul L. Murphy, *The Constitution in Crisis Times 1918–1969* 61–62 (Harper, 1972).

[129] Melvin I. Urofsky and Paul Finkelman, 2 *A March of Liberty: A Constitutional History of the United States* 705 (Oxford, 3d ed 2011).

Taft's papers at the Library of Congress shows him grappling with the issue more frankly than he did in the published opinion. "If the result of interstate transportation will be to spread some harmful matter or product," Taft wrote, "Congress may interfere without violating the Tenth Amendment. The facilities of interstate commerce may be withdrawn from those who are using it to corrupt others physically or morally. But if the transportation is being used to transport something harmless in itself and not calculated to spread evil, like cotton cloth, Congress may not prohibit its interstate transportation, although its inception may have been in some evil which is the legitimate object of the police power, such as child labor." Taft next proceeded to distinguish earlier precedents from *Hammer* on this basis. "[T]he interstate carriage of lottery tickets will communicate the gambling fever, of obscene literature will communicate moral degeneracy, of impure food will endanger health, [and] of diseased cattle will infect local cattle. . . ." In each of these instances, interstate transportation of the item inflicted a harm outside the state of origin. The "justification" for the doctrine, Taft concluded, "must be that Congress can prohibit the interstate spread of an evil thing, although it cannot prohibit the spread of something harmless in itself in order to suppress an evil which is properly the object of state police regulation."[130]

Taft then confronted the question of the doctrine's application to the Dyer Act. "At first I had a little difficulty with stolen automobiles," he confessed, "as the chief evil in connection therewith is the stealing and that of course is over before the machine takes on its character as a stolen automobile. This makes it look something like Hammer v. Dagenhart." But the Chief Justice had gotten over that concern, he explained, for "a stolen automobile is a canker. It attracts shady and disreputable individuals and leads to secret and underhanded dealings. Certainly it is not ultra vires for Congress to prohibit the interstate communication of this canker."[131]

For whatever reasons, these colorful meditations on the similarities between a stolen car and an open sore did not find their way into the Court's published opinion. But a moment's reflection

---

[130] Brooks v. United States, in Reel 614 *William Howard Taft Papers* 6–7 (Library of Congress).

[131] Id at 7.

on the analogy to the Lacey Act might have enabled Taft to see that the distinction he was groping for was grounded in due process. Just as the poacher acquired no "ownership" in game taken in violation of state law, so neither did one who stole a motor vehicle or knowingly took from the thief acquire any vested right in the pilfered automobile.[132] Congressional prohibition of interstate transportation of a stolen vehicle therefore did not deprive anyone of a property right protected by the Due Process Clause. Indeed, as Taft pointed out in his opinion, the Dyer Act properly punished the interstate transportation of stolen cars "because of its harmful result and its defeat of the property rights of those whose machines against their will are taken into other jurisdictions."[133] Rather than impairing vested rights, the Dyer Act protected them.

Each of these cases, therefore, presented two analytic questions. First, did the party prohibited from transporting the item have a vested property right in the thing to be transported? and, second, would that transportation inflict a cognizable harm outside the state of origin? If the answer to the first question were negative, prohibition of the item's interstate shipment would be constitutionally unproblematic, for it would not deprive anyone of property without due process. And the same would be true if the answer to the second question were affirmative, for no one had a due process right to use his property in a manner that would be harmful to others. The inquiry into whether a particular good was harmful or harmless was merely a way of formulating the second question. But a fixation on that inquiry could obscure the fact that the first question was analytically anterior.

C. DUE PROCESS AND COMPETITIVE INJURY

The critical question in *Hammer*, then, was whether the interstate shipment of a child-made good in which an owner had acquired a vested right under the law of his state inflicted a cognizable harm outside the legislative jurisdiction of that state. Here again, the convict-made goods analogy is illuminating. In his dissenting opinion in *Hawkins*, Judge Edward T. Bartlett insisted for himself and Judges Albert Haight and Alton B. Parker that convict-

---

[132] See Jesse Dukeminier et al, *Property* 162 (Aspen, 7th ed 2010).

[133] *Brooks*, 267 US at 439.

made goods were not harmless or innocuous, and that their un-
restricted sale in New York did in fact inflict a harm on its inhabitants. The labeling requirement, he maintained, constituted
a legitimate exercise of the police power "to promote the public
welfare and prosperity" by implementing "the deliberate policy of
this state that free labor shall be protected from disastrous competition with the convict system, which pays to the workman no
wages, and therefore finds little difficulty in supplanting the wage
earner in the public markets."[134] Similarly, in *Hammer*, government
attorneys insisted that interstate shipment of goods made by employers of child labor, like the interstate shipment of lottery tickets,
impure food, and misbranded drugs, was in fact harmful to the
inhabitants of destination states.[135] They argued that interstate
shipment of goods made by cheap child labor created "unfair competition"[136] with competing manufacturers in states where child
labor had been "more rigorously restrained."[137] Part of the underlying concern was that this competition would create pressure
for the more child-protective states to lower their standards, resulting in harm to their juvenile populations.[138] As the appellant
argued, "[t]here is no right to use the channels of interstate commerce to affect injuriously the health of the people in competing
states . . . nor in unfair competition."[139] And because such a competitive harm might result from the sale of the good in its original
package, the harm was inflicted in the federal legislative jurisdiction. Indeed, the dormant Commerce Clause prevented a destination state from regulating the sale of out-of-state child-made
goods still in their original packages,[140] and destination states typically would have no reliable way of determining which goods
within their borders had been produced elsewhere by children.[141]

---

[134] *Hawkins*, 51 NE at 263.

[135] Brief for Appellant, *Hammer v Dagenhart*, No 704, *41–42, 44 (US filed Sept 26, 1917) ("Hammer Brief").

[136] *Hammer*, 247 US at 254, 258, 273; Hammer Brief at *16–21, 45–48.

[137] *Hammer*, 247 US at 273.

[138] Id at 254; Hammer Brief at *23–36, 40; Gordon, 32 Harv L Rev at 55 (cited in note 54).

[139] Hammer Brief at *38. See also 53 Cong Rec 1585 (January 26, 1916) (remarks of Mr. Lenroot); id at 2011 (February 2, 1916) (remarks of Mr. Reavis).

[140] See *Leisy*, 135 US at 100; *Schollenberger*, 171 US 1; 53 Cong Rec App 227 (January 26, 1916) (extension of remarks of Mr. Keating).

[141] 53 Cong Rec App 227 (January 26, 1916) (extension of remarks of Mr. Keating).

The federal government was therefore the only sovereign with
effective legislative jurisdiction to prevent the child labor policies
of one state from inflicting competitive harm in a neighboring
state through the medium of interstate shipment.[142]

Judge O'Brien rejected this argument from competitive harm
in *Hawkins*, insisting that the state could not exercise its police
power "to enhance the price of labor by suppressing, through the
instrumentality of the criminal law, the sale of the products of
prison labor."[143] And that principle, as the court would reaffirm a
dozen years later, applied equally where the goods in question had
lost their character as interstate commerce and become part of
the general merchandise of the state, so that the dormant Commerce Clause was no longer implicated. *Phillips v Raynes*[144] involved
a subsequently enacted New York statute requiring anyone dis-
playing convict-made goods for sale to pay an annual license fee
of 500 dollars. The *Raynes* court observed that the "obvious purpose" of the statute, "writ so plain that all may read," was "to
prohibit by onerous and exasperating restrictions . . . the buying
and selling within this state of convict-made goods." But setting
this aside and treating the statute "purely as a revenue or tax law,"
the court found that its classification was "unreasonable and ca-
pricious." "That classification is based upon the origin of the goods
dealt in, without regard to the quality or character or nature of
the goods themselves." "If such classification be valid," the judges
reasoned, "and if the purpose of the act, as is claimed, is to protect
free labor from prison labor, why in these days of contest between
organized and unorganized labor should not an act be passed which
provided for such a license for selling all goods made in a shop
which did not employ union labor, and then, if the advocates of
a free shop were in power, repeal it, and provide for such license
for all goods made in shops which employed union labor."[145] As

---

[142] Id.

[143] *Hawkins*, 51 NE at 258.

[144] 120 NY Supp 1053, 1056–57 (NY App Div 1910), aff'd per curiam 92 NE 1097
(NY 1910).

[145] Id at 1057–58. Justice Harlan had made clear only two years earlier that such a
discrimination between union and nonunion labor violated the Fifth Amendment's Due
Process Clause. *Adair v United States*, 208 US 161, 169, 179–80 (1908). See also Ernst
Freund, *The Police Power: Public Policy and Constitutional Rights* 752–53 (Callaghan, 1904);
Barry Cushman, *Some Varieties and Vicissitudes of Lochnerism*, 85 BU L Rev 881, 926–28
(2005).

Judge O'Brien concluded in *Hawkins*, "One state may have natural advantages for the production of certain goods by reason of location, climate, or the rate of wages over another state where it costs more to produce them, but the latter cannot by hostile legislation drive the cheaper-made goods out of its markets, even though such legislation would increase the wages of its own workmen."[146]

Justice Day similarly rejected the notion that such "possible unfair competition" was a harm that Congress was empowered to prevent.[147] Echoing O'Brien's opinion in *Hawkins*, Day observed that "[m]any causes may co-operate to give one state, by reason of local laws or conditions, an economic advantage over others."[148] But "[t]he commerce clause was not intended to give to Congress a general authority to equalize such conditions."[149] For example, "[i]n some of the states laws have been passed fixing minimum wages for women, in others the local law regulates the hours of labor of women in various employments. Business done in such states may be at an economic disadvantage when compared with states which have no such regulations; surely, this fact does not give Congress the power to deny transportation in interstate commerce to those who carry on business where the hours of labor and the rate of compensation for women have not been fixed by a standard in use in other states and approved by Congress."[150]

The difficulty in *Hammer*, therefore, was in the Court's broad construction of the Fifth Amendment limitation on the exercise of the commerce power. Such unfair competition resulting from different labor standards was not a cognizable harm authorizing federal restriction of lawfully acquired property rights. The story of the demise of *Hammer* is thus the story of the relaxation of this

---

[146] *Hawkins*, 51 NE at 261–62.

[147] *Hammer*, 247 US at 273.

[148] Id.

[149] Id.

[150] Id. This view was anticipated by Professor Bruce in 1907: "[I]f we once establish the precedent and grant to Congress the unlimited right to destroy commerce, not as a punishment for crime, or because the thing transported is injurious, but because it enters into competition with other articles, or its method of manufacture, is not approved by the majority in Congress, we place in the hands of the national legislature a power which may prove absolutely subversive of individual liberty and of that freedom of commerce which the Constitution was, above all other things, created to preserve." Bruce, 5 Mich L Rev at 638 (cited in note 76).

Fifth Amendment limitation. And it is to that story that the *Car-olene Products* case made a signal contribution.

III. CAROLENE PRODUCTS IN CONGRESS

Filled milk, or compound milk, as its producers preferred to call it,[151] was a form of condensed or evaporated skimmed milk, with the removed butterfat replaced by vegetable or coconut oil.[152] The resulting product was indistinguishable in taste, odor, color, and consistency from condensed whole milk, and the difference could be detected only by expert chemical analysis.[153] The extracted butterfat could be sold for approximately 36 cents per pound, while coconut oil cost only about 12 cents per pound.[154] As a result, filled milk could be sold at a unit price considerably below that of name-brand condensed or evaporated milk such as Borden's Eagle brand.[155] Dairy farmers resented this competition from what they denounced as "the Coconut Cow of the South Seas Islands,"[156] and sought relief from state legislators. By 1921, eleven states, mostly in the north and west, had enacted legislation prohibiting or regulating the production and sale of filled milk,[157]

---

[151] Geoffrey P. Miller, *The True Story of Carolene Products*, 1987 Supreme Court Review 397, 398 n 10 (1987).

[152] Filled-Milk Legislation, HR Rep No 67-355, 67th Cong, 1st Sess 1–2 (1921); Filled Milk, Hearings on H.R. 6215 Before the House Committee on Agriculture, 67th Cong, 1st Sess 112 (1921) ("House Hearings"); Filled Milk, Hearings on H.R. 8086 Before a Subcommittee of the Senate Committee on Agriculture and Forestry, 67th Cong, 2d Sess 2 (1922) ("Senate Hearings"); Brief for the Carolene Products Co., *United States v Carolene Products*, No 604, *68 (US filed Feb 28, 1938) ("Carolene Brief").

[153] HR Rep No 67-355 at 2 (cited in note 152); Carolene Brief at *7; see also House Hearings, 67th Cong, 1st Sess at 40–41 (cited in note 152); Senate Hearings, 67th Cong, 1st Sess at 2 (cited in note 152).

[154] 62 Cong Rec 7608 (May 24, 1922) (remarks of Mr. Gernerd); see also House Hearings, 67th Cong, 1st Sess at 87–88 (cited in note 152); Senate Hearings, 67th Cong, 1st Sess at 5 (cited in note 152).

[155] HR Rep No 67-355 at 2 (cited in note 152); Filled Milk Legislation, S Rep No 67-987, 67th Cong, 4th Sess 3 (1923); Carolene Brief at *7. See also House Hearings, 67th Cong, 1st Sess at 12, 87–88, 121 (cited in note 152); Senate Hearings, 67th Cong, 1st Sess at 2 (cited in note 152).

[156] Letter from Paul McKee of the Carnation Milk Products Company to Rep. James B. Aswell, dated April 22, 1922, reprinted at 62 Cong Rec 7584 (May 24, 1922). See also HR Rep No 67-355 at 4 (cited in note 152); House Hearings, 67th Cong, 1st Sess at 37–39 (cited in note 152); Senate Hearings, 67th Cong, 1st Sess at 3–5, 241–49 (cited in note 152).

[157] HR Rep No 67-355 at 6 (cited in note 152); S Rep No 67-987 at 6 (cited in note 155) ("Eleven States now have laws either prohibiting entirely the manufacture and sale of filled milk or restricting the business in such a way as to make the commercial ex-

but competition persisted in unregulated markets. So in 1921 a bill to prohibit the interstate shipment of filled milk was introduced in the House of Representatives by Republican Edward Voigt, who perhaps coincidentally represented the good people in and around Sheboygan, Wisconsin.[158]

In the committee hearings and floor debates over the bill, discussion focused on precisely the considerations that would inform an adjudication of whether comparable state legislation was a proper exercise of the police power and therefore consistent with the Due Process Clause of the Fourteenth Amendment. Proponents of the bill argued that filled milk was a fraudulent, counterfeit substance palmed off on an unsuspecting public as the genuine article.[159] And though the bill's backers conceded that filled milk was in itself neither unwholesome nor poisonous,[160] they contended that it was nevertheless deleterious to health.[161] The vitamin A in butterfat, which was entirely absent from coconut oil, was vital to proper physical development in infants, and its insufficiency in their diet exposed them to a significant risk of rickets, scurvy, beriberi, and diseases of the eye.[162] Opponents of the bill denounced it as "flagrant," "vicious" special interest legislation, designed to destroy a legitimate business for the benefit

---

ploitation impossible. These States are: Utah, Maryland, Florida, California, Colorado, Connecticut, Oregon, Ohio, New York, New Jersey, Wisconsin."); 62 Cong Rec 7583 (May 24, 1922).

[158] 61 Cong Rec 4691 (August 4, 1921). The bill also prohibited manufacture of filled milk in the District of Columbia, the Territories, and the insular possessions, and forbade its shipment in foreign commerce. HR Rep No 67-355 at 1 (cited in note 152). The Pure Food and Drugs Act of 1906 did not apply to the interstate shipment of filled milk because of a proviso stating that an article would not be considered adulterated or misbranded if it was a compound of ingredients offered for sale under its own name and not a imitation of another article. Pure Food Act, 34 Stat at 771; Miller, 1987 Supreme Court Review at 406 (cited in note 151). The bill was originally introduced as an amendment to the Pure Food and Drugs Act, see 62 Cong Rec 7581 (May 24, 1922) (remarks of Mr. Voigt), but was reported out of committee as free-standing legislation.

[159] See HR Rep No 67-355 at 2 (cited in note 152); S Rep No 67-987 at 4 (cited in note 155); House Hearings, 67th Cong, 1st Sess at 11–13, 15, 40 (cited in note 152); Senate Hearings, 67th Cong, 1st Sess at 2 (cited in note 152).

[160] See House Hearings, 67th Cong, 1st Sess at 15 (cited in note 152) (Mr. Voigt); Senate Hearings, 67th Cong, 1st Sess at 2 (cited in note 152).

[161] S Rep No 67-987 at 5, 7 (cited in note 155); House Hearings, 67th Cong, 1st Sess at 34–35 (cited in note 152); Senate Hearings, 67th Cong, 1st Sess at 2 (cited in note 152).

[162] See HR Rep No 67-355 at 3–4 (cited in note 152); S Rep No 67-987 at 3–4 (cited in note 155); House Hearings, 67th Cong, 1st Sess at 10, 15 (cited in note 152); Senate Hearings, 67th Cong, 1st Sess at 6 (cited in note 152).

of a grasping competitor and at the expense of the consumer.[163]
They asserted that the skimmed milk in filled milk contained significant amounts of vitamin A, though not as much as in whole
milk.[164] Moreover, there were a great many foods that were lacking
in vitamin A or improper for infant consumption—turnip greens
seems to have been the favored example[165]—but that this did not
authorize Congress to prohibit *their* interstate shipment.[166] And
they observed that the labels placed on cans of filled milk by their
producers prominently revealed their contents, recommended that
the product be used for cooking and baking, and explicitly stated
that it was not to be used in place of milk for infants.[167] Proponents
responded that consumers often did not read the labels;[168] that
retailers displayed filled milk next to condensed milk and represented it as "the same as" or "as good as" condensed milk;[169] that
the less expensive product was often purchased by poor, unlettered,
or immigrant consumers;[170] and that the patrons of restaurants,
hotels, and boarding houses might unknowingly be served the

---

[163] 62 Cong Rec 7583–84 (May 24, 1922); see also HR Rep No 67-355 at 2 (cited in
note 152); House Hearings, 67th Cong, 1st Sess at 98 (cited in note 152); Senate Hearings,
67th Cong, 1st Sess at 62–65 (cited in note 152). *Accord*, Miller, 1987 Supreme Court
Review at 398–99 (cited in note 151) (denouncing the statute as "an utterly unprincipled
example of special interest legislation," and the justifications offered for its enactment as
"patently bogus." Its consequence "was to expropriate the property of a lawful and beneficial industry; to deprive working and poor people of a healthful, nutritious, and low-
cost food; and to impair the health of the nation's children by encouraging the use as
baby food of a sweetened condensed milk product that was 42 percent sugar."); id at 416.

[164] See, for example, 62 Cong Rec 7585 (May 24, 1922) (remarks of Mr. Aswell).

[165] Id at 7609 (remarks of Mr. Sisson); id at 7614 (remarks of Mr. Echols).

[166] 62 Cong Rec 7614 (May 24, 1922) (remarks of Mr. Echols). See also Senate Hearings,
67th Cong, 1st Sess at 87 (cited in note 152).

[167] HR Rep No 67-355 at 7 (cited in note 152) (Minority Views of J. B. Aswell); House
Hearings, 67th Cong, 1st Sess at 39 (cited in note 152); Senate Hearings, 67th Cong, 1st
Sess at 85 (cited in note 152). See Miller, 1987 Supreme Court Review at 406, 420–21
(cited in note 151).

[168] See House Hearings, 67th Cong, 1st Sess at 19 (cited in note 152); Senate Hearings,
67th Cong, 1st Sess at 6 (cited in note 152); 62 Cong Rec 7582 (May 24, 1922) (remarks
of Mr. Voigt); id at 7588 (remarks of Mr. Haugen); id at 7593 (remarks of Mr. Clarke of
New York).

[169] See HR Rep No 67-355 at 2 (cited in note 152); S Rep No 67-987 at 3 (cited in
note 155); House Hearings, 67th Cong, 1st Sess at 12 (cited in note 152); Senate Hearings,
67th Cong, 1st Sess at 2 (cited in note 152).

[170] See HR Rep No 67-355 at 2–3 (cited in note 152); House Hearings, 67th Cong, 1st
Sess at 10, 33–34, 41–42, 49, 50, 154 (cited in note 152); Senate Hearings, 67th Cong,
1st Sess at 2, 6, 9, 14, 16, 19, 26, 44, 46, 50 (cited in note 152); 62 Cong Rec 7582, 7588,
7590, 7590–91, 7592–92, 7596, 7609 (May 24, 1922).

product without ever seeing the label.[171] In the end the bill was passed in the House by a vote of 250–40,[172] and in the Senate by a voice vote.[173]

The hearings on the bill were dominated by farmers, manufacturers, and nutritionists, and did not elicit much in the way of constitutional discussion.[174] Nevertheless, the report of the House Committee on Agriculture included a discussion of the bill's constitutionality insisting that there was "nothing new in the proposal that milk products not containing a certain amount of butter fat shall not be transported or sold in interstate or intrastate commerce." Under the Pure Food and Drugs Act, milk and condensed milk could not be shipped in interstate commerce unless they contained a certain percentage of butterfat, and it was certainly "proper to insist upon the same standard in an imitation or substitute article." That act had barred from interstate commerce many drugs and articles of food that did not comply with certain standards, just as Congress had barred obscene literature and lottery tickets.[175] The committee relied upon the precedents upholding the Lottery Act and the Pure Food and Drugs Act for the proposition that exercises of the commerce power "may have the quality of police regulations," and that the commerce power could be used to "to protect the public morals," "the public health," and "the economic welfare of the people." Congress had "full power to bar from the channels" of interstate commerce "illicit and harmful articles," and could "itself determine means appropriate to this purpose." So long as those means did "no violence to the other provisions of the Constitution," Congress

---

[171] See S Rep No 67-987 at 3 (cited in note 155); House Hearings, 67th Cong, 1st Sess at 10, 41 (cited in note 152); Senate Hearings, 67th Cong, 1st Sess at 6, 46 (cited in note 152).

[172] 62 Cong Rec 7669–70 (May 25, 1922). One member voted "present" and 140 did not vote.

[173] 64 Cong Rec 4986 (March 1, 1923). The House agreed to the Senate amendments and the enrolled bill was signed in the House on March 2, 1923. Id at 5075, 5241 (March 2, 1923). It was presented to the president for his approval and signed by the president the following day. Id at 5554, 5556 (March 3, 1923).

[174] See S Rep No 67-987 at 6 (cited in note 155) ("The question of constitutionality was not seriously pressed before the committee."). The exception came in the testimony J. Wallace Bryan offered in support of the bill's constitutionality at the end of the Senate hearing, and in Mr. Jackman's response. See Senate Hearings, 67th Cong, 1st Sess at 277–81 (cited in note 152).

[175] HR Rep No 67-355 at 5 (cited in note 152).

was "itself the judge of the means to be employed."[176] The only other provision of the Constitution to which the bill might do violence was the Due Process Clause of the Fifth Amendment, and just a few years earlier the Supreme Court had held that prohibition of the sale of filled milk did not violate the Due Process Clause of the Fourteenth Amendment.[177]

The litigation from which this holding emerged had arisen in central Ohio. A series of statutes enacted in the late nineteenth century, well before filled milk had been invented, prohibited the manufacture and sale of condensed skimmed milk.[178] Hebe, the brand name of Carnation's filled milk, was of course a species of condensed skimmed milk, and the Ohio attorney general rendered an opinion that its sale in the state violated the Ohio General Code.[179] The Chief of the Division of Dairy and Food of the State Board of Agriculture thereupon informed the company and those selling its product that, unless further sales of Hebe in the state were discontinued, prosecutions would follow and the penalties provided for by statute would be inflicted on all who should fail to desist.[180] Hebe responded by seeking injunctive relief against enforcement of the pertinent sections of the code by the state's officers on the ground that those provisions were unconstitutional.[181] The state did not contend that the product, nor that either of its ingredients, was impure or unwholesome.[182] Instead Ohio maintained that Hebe was "regarded by a large percentage of the public as genuine condensed [whole] milk, whereby the public is misled and deceived into its purchase and use."[183] Hebe countered that its product was "pure, wholesome, and nutritious," and "plainly and fairly labeled in a conspicuous manner."[184] The

---

[176] Id at 5–6. The report of the Senate Committee on Agriculture and Forestry similarly relied on the Lottery Act and Pure Food and Drugs Act precedents in concluding, "[w]e are thoroughly satisfied that Congress has the power to exclude from interstate and foreign commerce any article which is in the exercise of fair judgment injurious to the public health." S Rep 67-987 at 6 (cited in note 155).

[177] HR Rep No 67-355 at 5–6 (cited in note 152).

[178] *Hebe Co. v Calvert*, 246 F 711, 715–16 (SD Ohio, 1917).

[179] Id at 713.

[180] Id at 712, 714.

[181] Id at 714.

[182] Id.

[183] Id at 713–14. See also Brief and Argument for Appellees, *Hebe Co. v Shaw*, No 664, *24–39 (US filed Dec 6, 1919) ("Shaw Brief").

[184] *Hebe Co.*, 246 F at 714–15.

prohibition of its sale therefore deprived the company of liberty and property without due process of law and denied it equal protection of the laws by "arbitrarily, unjustly, unduly, and in a confiscatory manner" discriminating against it.[185]

The case was argued on behalf of Hebe before a three-judge panel of the United States District Court for the Southern District of Ohio by Augustus T. Seymour of the Columbus firm of Vorys, Sater, Seymour and Pease.[186] The opinion ruling against Hebe was written by Seymour's former law partner, Judge John Elbert Sater,[187] and delivered in November of 1917, just months after the United States had declared war on Germany. Judge Sater observed that there was "a conflict in the evidence" as to whether Hebe was "as nutritious and as effective as a growth producer, and therefore as a health promoter and maintainer, as the legally recognized condensed [whole] milk." As long as that question was "debatable," the legislature was "entitled to its own judgment," which could not be "superseded by the court." "With the wisdom of the exercise of that judgment," Sater maintained, "the court has no concern; and, unless it clearly appears that the enactments have no substantial relation to a proper purpose, it cannot be said that the limit of legislative power has been transcended."[188]

By contrast, there was "substantial and uncontradicted evidence" of deception of consumers in the sale of Hebe.[189] The difference between the prices at which condensed milk and filled milk could be manufactured and sold was such "that the temptation to impose upon the public" had been "too great to be resisted."[190] It mattered not whether the company intended to deceive the public, nor that it had instructed its representatives to sell the product "for what it really is," nor that the label informed the consumer of its con-

---

[185] Id at 715. See also Brief and Argument for Appellants, *Hebe Co. v Shaw*, No 664, *56–71 (US filed Nov 23, 1918) ("Hebe Brief").

[186] *Hebe Co.*, 246 F at 712.

[187] Id at 713; J. F. Laning, ed, *The New Federal Judge: Hon. John E. Sater*, 52 Ohio L Bulletin 197 (1907).

[188] *Hebe Co.*, 246 F at 717. An earlier decision by the Court of Appeals of Maryland had assumed that a prohibition on the sale of condensed skimmed milk unless packaged and labeled as required by statute was a legitimate health measure. See *Reiter v State*, 71 A 975, 977 (Md Ct App 1909).

[189] *Hebe Co.*, 246 F at 717.

[190] Id.

tents.[191] Filled milk did not differ in appearance or taste from condensed whole milk, and the "unwary consumer" could not be blamed for failing to scrutinize the label closely, particularly when an unscrupulous retailer presented it as condensed whole milk.[192] The company manufactured a product that was capable of and was in fact being "used as an instrument of fraud."[193] The Constitution of the United States did not "secure to anyone the privilege of manufacturing and selling an article offered in such a manner as to induce purchasers to believe they are buying something which is in fact different from that which is offered for sale."[194] The statute's effort "to promote fair dealing" and to "prevent the sale of an adulterated or deceptive article" therefore did not "contravene any provision of the federal Constitution."[195]

The company soon brought a bill in equity, again in the United States District Court for the Southern District of Ohio, to restrain threatened prosecutions for violation of the Ohio statutes.[196] The district judge adopted Judge Sater's opinion as his own and dismissed the bill.[197] Hebe appealed that ruling to the Supreme Court of the United States, where the company was represented by former Associate Justice Charles Evans Hughes.[198] Justice Holmes wrote the opinion for a 6–3 majority affirming the judgment of the District Court.[199] The addition of coconut oil to condensed skimmed milk, Holmes observed, made "the cheaper and forbidden substance more like the dearer and better one and thus at the same time more available for a fraudulent substitute."[200] It was true that the label on the company's product was truthful, "but the consumer in many cases never sees it."[201] Applying a very deferential standard of review, Holmes concluded that the Ohio statute did not violate the Fourteenth Amendment. "The purposes

---

[191] Id at 717–18.
[192] Id.
[193] Id.
[194] Id at 718.
[195] Id.
[196] See *Hebe Co. v Shaw*, 248 US 297, 301 (1919).
[197] Id.
[198] Id at 298.
[199] Id at 301.
[200] Id at 303.
[201] Id.

to secure a certain minimum of nutritive elements and to prevent fraud may be carried out in this way even though condensed skimmed milk and Hebe both should be admitted to be wholesome."[202]

Justice Day, the author of *Hammer*, subjected the statute to more searching scrutiny in a dissenting opinion written on behalf of himself, Justice Willis Van Devanter, and Justice Louis D. Brandeis. Day asserted that Hebe made "no pretense" to being condensed whole milk. Its label disclosed "in unmistakable words in large print" that it was "a food compound consisting in part of condensed skimmed milk." "The label states with all the emphasis which large type can give that it is a compound made of 'evaporated skimmed milk and vegetable fat,'" Day observed. "The proportions of the ingredients" were "stated" on the "striking label," which did not "describe condensed milk, and he who reads it cannot be misled to the belief that he is buying that article." Moreover, Hebe was "shown to be wholesome and free from impurities."[203] Day conceded that the public was "entitled to protection from deception as well as from impurity," and noted that the record disclosed "that in one or more instances" dealers had represented Hebe to be condensed whole milk. "But an act or two of this sort by fraudulent dealers," Day insisted, "ought not to be the test of the plaintiffs' right." "If such were the case, very few food compounds would escape condemnation." Moreover, "[t]he few instances of deception shown had not the sanction" of the company's authority. Such acts of deception "did violence to the plain terms" of the printed label. That label "so truly expresses just what the substance is," Day concluded, that it was "difficult to believe that any purchaser could be deceived into buying the article for something other than it is."[204]

In the floor debates on the filled milk bill, opponents predictably invoked the authority of *Hammer*. They argued that filled milk was neither injurious, deleterious, unwholesome, nor harmful to health, nor was it sold fraudulently, and therefore Congress lacked the power to prohibit its interstate shipment.[205] To this proponents

[202] Id.

[203] Id at 306.

[204] Id at 307 (Day and Brandeis, JJ, dissenting).

[205] 62 Cong Rec 7581, 7584, 7588, 7593–94, 7614 (May 24, 1922). See also Senate Hearings, 67th Cong, 1st Sess at 280–81 (cited in note 152).

responded with citations to *Hebe*.[206] Because filled milk was, on their view, "deleterious to health"[207] and "a fraudulent article,"[208] Congress could prohibit its interstate shipment.[209] *Hammer* therefore had "nothing to do" with the question of the bill's constitutionality.[210] The bill was instead governed by the precedents upholding the Lottery Act and the Pure Food and Drugs Act.[211]

The legislators engaged in this debate did not expressly frame the issue of constitutionality in terms of the Due Process Clause of the Fifth Amendment.[212] But they shared a tacit premise: if an item was sufficiently deleterious that its sale could be prohibited under the state's police power consistent with the requirements of the Fourteenth Amendment's Due Process Clause, then Congress had the power to exclude the article from interstate commerce. The central issue upon which the disputants differed, therefore, was whether the Court had correctly resolved the due process issue in *Hebe*. That was an issue that would soon divide the state courts as well.

IV. CAROLENE PRODUCTS IN COURT

As the agricultural depression of the 1920s deepened, most of the states in the Union passed laws prohibiting the manufacture and/or sale of filled milk. By 1938, thirty-four of the forty-eight states had enacted such statutes, while an additional three subjected the sale to strict regulations.[213] Not surprisingly, the Supreme Court of Wisconsin followed *Hebe* in sustaining the state's filled milk statute as a health and fraud prevention measure in

---

[206] 62 Cong Rec 7581, 7612 (May 24, 1922). See also Senate Hearings, 67th Cong, 1st Sess at 277–78, 281 (cited in note 152).

[207] 62 Cong Rec 7588, 7613, 7617 (May 24, 1922); Senate Hearings, 67th Cong, 1st Sess at 278 (cited in note 152).

[208] 62 Cong Rec 7590, 7588, 7593, 7596, 7613, 7617 (May 24, 1922); Senate Hearings, 67th Cong, 1st Sess at 278 (cited in note 152).

[209] 62 Cong Rec 7590, 7592–93, 7596, 7613, 7617 (May 24, 1922); 64 Cong Rec 3949 (February 19, 1923). See also Senate Hearings, 67th Cong, 1st Sess at 277–78 (cited in note 152).

[210] 62 Cong Rec 7596 (May 24, 1922) (remarks of Mr. Hersey). See also Senate Hearings, 67th Cong, 1st Sess at 278–79 (cited in note 152).

[211] 62 Cong Rec 7583, 7593 (May 24, 1922).

[212] By contrast, J. Wallace Bryan did so at the Senate hearings. See Senate Hearings, 67th Cong, 1st Sess at 277–78 (cited in note 152).

[213] *Carolene Products*, 304 US at 150–51 n 3.

1922.[214] In the 1930s, however, the Carolene Products Company began a litigation campaign with the objective of persuading various state courts to hold that their filled milk statutes violated provisions of their own state constitutions. The highest courts of Illinois,[215] Michigan,[216] and Nebraska[217] agreed that there was no significant evidence of fraud in the sale of filled milk, and that the product and its ingredients were wholesome and healthful. Prohibitions on its manufacture and sale therefore exceeded the state's police power. The company also secured injunctions against enforcement of the statutes of Alabama, Iowa, Missouri, Virginia, and West Virginia.[218] The Illinois Supreme Court's decision established that state as a safe haven for the production of filled milk in 1931,[219] and the Carolene Products Company continued manufacture of its product there at the Litchfield Creamery south of Springfield.[220]

The company's successful campaign in the state courts spurred federal officials to action. In June of 1935, the company was indicted in the United States District Court for the Southern District of Illinois under the federal statute for unlawfully shipping filled milk from Litchfield, Illinois, to the General Grocer Company in St. Louis, Missouri.[221] The company immediately filed a motion to quash the indictment,[222] on which the trial court inexplicably sat for over two years before overruling it in July of

[214] *Carnation Milk Products Co. v Emery*, 189 NW 564 (Wis 1922).

[215] *People v Carolene Products Co.*, 345 Ill 166, 170 (1931) (distinguishing *Hebe* on the ground that "[i]n the case before us the wholesomeness of the product is admitted, with no question of imitation or deceit involved, so there is no debatable question of fact before the court, as there was in the Ohio case."); *Carolene Products Co. v McLaughlin*, 365 Ill 62 (1936) (following its earlier decision in invalidating revised statute).

[216] *Carolene Products Co. v Thomson*, 267 NW 608, 612 (Mich 1936) (doubting *Hebe*'s continuing authority, distinguishing details of the Michigan and Ohio statutes, and holding that the Michigan statute violated both the Fourteenth Amendment and the Due Process Clause of the state constitution).

[217] *Carolene Products Co. v Banning*, 268 NW 313 (Neb 1936) (following the reasoning of *Thomson* in holding that the statute violated both the Fourteenth Amendment and the Due Process Clause of the Nebraska constitution).

[218] Carolene Brief at *68.

[219] *Carolene Products Co.*, 345 Ill 166; Miller, 1987 Supreme Court Review at 411 (cited in note 151).

[220] Carolene Brief at *7.

[221] Brief for the United States, *United States v Carolene Products*, No 604, *4–5 (US filed Feb 28, 1938) ("United States Brief I").

[222] Id at 5.

1937.[223] The company then filed a demurrer to the indictment, alleging that the federal Filled Milk Act was unconstitutional.[224] That October, some six months after the Supreme Court had upheld the National Labor Relations Act the preceding April,[225] the trial court sustained the company's demurrer on the authority of *Hammer*, following the reasoning of a 1934 opinion by Judge FitzHenry of the United States District Court for the Southern District of Illinois.[226] Judge FitzHenry had reasoned that Carolene's product was "wholesome and plainly labeled," and therefore beyond congressional power to exclude from interstate commerce.[227] Seeking to distinguish *Hebe*, FitzHenry concluded that *Hammer* made it "clear that the Supreme Court recognized a broad discretion in the states in the exercise of their legislative police powers, but denies the exercise of the same power to Congress, under the guise of regulating interstate commerce."[228] The United States then filed an appeal,[229] and the Supreme Court noted probable jurisdiction under the Criminal Appeals Act.[230] On April 25, 1938, the Court announced its decision reversing the trial court and upholding the constitutionality of the Filled Milk Act.[231]

The first key move in Justice Stone's opinion for the majority was to disentangle the Commerce Clause issue from the due process issue. The power to regulate interstate commerce, which in-

---

[223] Id.

[224] Id.

[225] *Labor Board Cases*, 301 US 1 (1937).

[226] United States Brief I at *5. The trial court sustained the demurrer "for the reasons assigned in the opinion of Judge FitzHenry, reported in 7 Fed Supp 500." Id.

[227] *United States v Carolene Products*, 7 F Supp at 500, 508 (SD Ill 1934). The government's brief before the Supreme Court explained that Judge FitzHenry's decision "was not appealed by the United States because the case arose on an information, and the sustaining of a demurrer thereto is not appealable under the Criminal Appeals Act." United States Brief I at *9 n 1.

[228] *Carolene Products*, 7 F Supp at 508. FitzHenry appeared to believe that the statute was "a plain attempt on the part of Congress" to "prohibit the manufacture" of filled milk in the several states, id at 504, and that this "strik[ing] down [of] a well-known lawful industry" deprived the company of property without due process. Id at 507.

[229] United States Brief I at *5.

[230] Id; *Carolene Products*, 304 US at 146.

[231] *Carolene Products*, 304 US at 144–45. On January 7, 1938, the Seventh Circuit had upheld the act in a deferential opinion ruling against the Carolene Products Company in an antitrust action the company brought against the Evaporated Milk Association. *Carolene Products Co. v Evaporated Milk Assn.*, 93 F2d 202 (7th Cir 1938). The Supreme Court of Pennsylvania had upheld that state's filled milk act on the authority of *Hebe* on March 2, 1938. *Carolene Products Co. v Harter*, 329 Pa 49 (1938).

cluded the power to prohibit interstate shipment, Stone reminded
his readers, was "'complete in itself, may be exercised to its utmost
extent, and acknowledges no limitations other than are prescribed
by the Constitution.'"[232] Decisions such as those upholding the
Lottery Act and the Pure Food and Drugs Act established that
Congress was "free to exclude from interstate commerce articles
whose use in the states for which they are destined it may reasonably conceive to be injurious to the public health, morals, *or
welfare.*"[233] Such regulations were "not prohibited unless by the
due process clause of the Fifth Amendment."[234] "The prohibition
of the shipment of filled milk in interstate commerce" was therefore "a permissible regulation of commerce, subject only to the
restrictions of the Fifth Amendment."[235] Stone's opinion thus established that the power to prohibit interstate shipment was not
constrained by any internal limitation on the commerce power,
but was instead plenary, and was qualified only by affirmative limitations derived from other applicable provisions of the Constitution—namely, the Due Process Clause.

Having disposed of the commerce power issue, Stone turned to
the due process issue, which it was now clear would be dispositive.
That issue was properly analyzed separately, employing the categories developed in cases adjudicating Fifth and Fourteenth
Amendment challenges to regulatory legislation. Stone remarked
that the committee hearings had demonstrated "that the use of
filled milk as a substitute for pure milk" was "generally injurious
to health and facilitates fraud on the public."[236] In other words,
it fell into two categories under which the Court had sustained
state exercises of the police power. Indeed, it was on the basis of
such evidence that the Court had upheld the Ohio statute challenged in *Hebe* against a Fourteenth Amendment due process challenge twenty years earlier.[237] That alone would seem to have been
sufficient to decide the case.

But here Stone went further. Even without the evidence to
which he had referred, "the existence of facts supporting the leg-

---

[232] *Carolene Products*, 304 US at 147, quoting *Gibbons v Ogden*, 9 Wheat 1, 196 (1824).

[233] *Carolene Products*, 304 US at 147 (emphasis added).

[234] Id.

[235] Id at 148.

[236] Id at 148–49.

[237] *Carolene Products*, 304 US at 148, citing *Hebe Co. v Shaw*, 248 US 297 (1918).

islative judgment" was "to be presumed," he wrote, "for regulatory legislation affecting ordinary commercial transactions is not to be pronounced unconstitutional unless in the light of the facts made known or generally assumed it is of such a character as to preclude the assumption that it rests upon some rational basis within the knowledge and experience of the legislators."[238] Had the statute contained no findings concerning the dangers filled milk posed to the public, Stone observed, some such findings "would be presumed."[239] Inquiries into a statute's compliance with the Due Process Clause, "where the legislative judgment is drawn in question, must be restricted to the issue whether any state of facts either known or which could reasonably be assumed affords support for it."[240] That is, as Stone put it, the Court might have decided the due process issue "wholly on the presumption of constitutionality."[241] But it was "evident from all the considerations presented to Congress," Stone continued, "that the question is at least debatable whether commerce in filled milk should be left unregulated, or in some measure restricted, or wholly prohibited."[242] Whether to protect the public through the imposition of a labeling requirement or through a prohibition on shipment "was a matter for the legislative judgment and not that of courts."[243] "[T]hat decision was for Congress."[244] The prohibition of the interstate shipment of filled milk thus did "not infringe the Fifth Amendment";[245] and therefore, Stone concluded, that prohibition was "a

---

[238] Id at 152.

[239] Id at 153.

[240] Id at 154. Just two months earlier, Stone had anticipated this formulation in announcing that nondiscriminatory state legislation would be subjected to the same standard of review under the dormant Commerce Clause and the Fourteenth Amendment. See *South Carolina Highway Dept. v Barnwell Bros.*, 303 US 177, 190–91 (1938) ("In the absence of [congressional] legislation the judicial function, under the commerce clause, . . . as well as the Fourteenth Amendment, stops with the inquiry whether the state Legislature in adopting regulations such as the present has acted within its province, and whether the means of regulation chosen are reasonably adapted to the end sought. . . . Being a legislative judgment it is presumed to be supported by facts known to the Legislature unless facts judicially known or proved preclude that possibility.").

[241] *Carolene Products*, 304 US at 148.

[242] Id at 154.

[243] Id at 151.

[244] Id at 154.

[245] Id at 148.

constitutional exercise of the power to regulate interstate commerce."[246]

Two years earlier, in *Whitfield v Ohio*, the Court unanimously had upheld an Ohio statute prohibiting the sale of convict-made goods within the state against a Fourteenth Amendment challenge. Congress had enacted a statute divesting convict-made goods of their interstate character upon their arrival in a destination state, thereby removing the dormant Commerce Clause disability under which the state otherwise would labor by virtue of the original package doctrine. The sole question concerning the state law's constitutionality thus was whether the Ohio statute deprived the owner of the goods of his property without due process. The Justices agreed that Ohio had "the right and power" to base its legislation upon the "conception" that "the sale of convict-made goods in competition with free labor is an evil."[247] The Court thus rejected Judge O'Brien's insistence in *Hawkins* that the prevention of such "unfair competition" was not a legitimate police power justification for the regulation of such sales, and some contemporary commentators maintained that this development cast significant doubt on the continuing vitality of *Hammer*.[248] Others were more circumspect, suggesting only that Congress could enact a similar divesting statute for child-made goods without calling into question *Hammer*'s continuing authority.[249]

In January of 1937, the Court unanimously upheld the federal Ashurst-Sumners Act, which prohibited the interstate shipment of convict-made goods into states where their sale was prohibited by

---

[246] Id at 154. Justice Butler concurred in the result. His opinion indicated that he agreed with the majority's mode of Commerce Clause analysis, but that he differed with its due process views. Butler maintained that at the ensuing trial the Carolene Products Company "may introduce evidence to show that the declaration of the act that the described product is injurious to public health and that the sale of it is a fraud upon the public are without any substantial foundation. . . . If construed to exclude from interstate commerce wholesome food products that demonstrably are neither injurious to health nor calculated to deceive, they are repugnant to the Fifth Amendment." Id at 155 (Butler, J, concurring).

[247] *Whitfield v Ohio*, 297 US 431, 439–40 (1936).

[248] See J. A. C. Grant, *State Power to Prohibit Interstate Commerce*, 26 Cal L Rev 34, 67 (1937); Hugh Evander Willis, *Constitution Making in 1935–36*, 22 Wash U L Q 206, 214 (1936); Comment, *Interstate Commerce—Power of Congress—Validity of Hawes-Cooper Act and State Statute Prohibiting Sale of Convict-Made Goods*, 49 Harv L Rev 1007, 1008 (1936).

[249] Marvin M. Finder, *Constitutional Law—Divesting Prison-Made Goods of Their Interstate Character—Original Package Doctrine*, 27 J Am Inst Crim L & Criminol 283, 284–85 (1936); Note, *The Power of Congress to Subject Interstate Commerce to State Regulation*, 3 U Chi L Rev 636, 639–40 (1936).

local law.[250] Again, a number of sanguine commentators proclaimed the demise of *Hammer*.[251] Yet the act's cooperative formula differed from the absolute prohibition on interstate shipment imposed by the Keating-Owen Child Labor Act, and Chief Justice Hughes accordingly declined the opportunity to overrule *Hammer*. Instead, he tersely distinguished the precedent, maintaining that the act under review could be sustained without impairing *Hammer*'s vitality.[252] Even after that decision, therefore, numerous commentators continued to believe that *Hammer* remained good law.[253] After *Carolene Products* had made clear that the commerce power was subject only to a due process limitation and that that limitation would be interpreted very narrowly, however, such views would dissipate. For if Justice Stone's proclamation of deferential review under the Due Process Clause clarified anything, it was that the traditional understanding of the Doctrine of Vested Rights was no longer the basic doctrine of American constitutional law.

---

[250] *Kentucky Whip & Collar Co. v Illinois Central Railroad Co.*, 299 US 334 (1937).

[251] Edward S. Corwin, *National-State Cooperation—Its Present Possibilities*, 46 Yale L J 599, 613–15, 623 (1937); Grant, 26 Cal L Rev at 34, 69–70 (cited in note 248); Anthony Yturri, Note, *Constitutional Law—Interstate Commerce—Convict-Labor Goods—Ashurst-Sumners Act*, 16 Or L Rev 374, 380–82, 384 (1937); Comment, *Constitutional Law—Exclusion of Prison-Made Goods from Interstate Commerce*, 14 Tenn L Rev 538, 539–41 (1937); Comment, *Constitutional Law—Commerce Clause—Validity of Statute Regulating Interstate Transportation of Convict-Made Goods*, 85 U Pa L Rev 529, 530 (1937); E. A. M., Comment, *Constitutional Law—Convict-Made Goods—Interstate Commerce*, 12 Ind L J 430, 431–32 (1937); L. E., Comment, *Constitutional Law—Interstate Commerce—Prison-Made Goods—Power of Federal Government to Prohibit Shipment of Prison-Made Goods Into Any State in Violation of Its Laws*, 6 Brooklyn L Rev 385, 386 (1937).

[252] *Kentucky Whip*, 299 US at 350.

[253] See, for example, Joseph H. Mueller, Comment, *Constitutional Law—Interstate Commerce—Validity of Federal Statute Prohibiting Interstate Shipment of Prison-Made Goods*, 35 Mich L Rev 615, 617–20 (1937); John H. Foard, Comment, *Constitutional Law—Interstate Commerce—Federal Control of Child Labor as Suggested by the Recent Convict Labor Cases*, 2 Mo L Rev 341, 342–46 (1937); Marjorie Hanson, Comment, *Constitutional Law—Interstate Commerce—Power of Congress to Protect State Laws*, 3 U Pitt L Rev 233, 235–36 (1937); Milton J. Schloss, Comment, *Child Labor Regulation Under the Kentucky Whip and Collar Co. v. Illinois Central Railroad Case*, 11 U Cin L Rev 357, 358–59 (1937); Comment, *Constitutional Law—Interstate Commerce—Power of Congress to Regulate Interstate Transportation of Prison-Made Goods*, 6 Fordham L Rev 299, 302–03 (1937); J. T. N., Comment, *Constitutional Law—Commerce—Power of Congress to Give Effect to State Law*, 15 Tex L Rev 371, 372 (1937); E. J. H., Jr., Note, *Federal Legislation—Regulation of Child Labor Resurrected*, 25 Geo L J 671, 678, 682, 687 (1937). Still others expressed uncertainty about *Hammer*'s status. See, for example, Osmond K. Fraenkel, *What Can Be Done About the Constitution and the Supreme Court?* 37 Colum L Rev 212, 213, 215 (1937); S. R., Comment, *Constitutional Law—Interstate Commerce—Prohibiting Interstate Shipment of Prison-Made Goods*, 11 Temple L Q 427, 429–30 (1937).

V. The Contemporary Significance of Carolene Products

To appreciate the impact of *Carolene Products* on Commerce Clause jurisprudence, consider the legislative history of the Fair Labor Standards Act of 1938. In May of 1937, nearly a year before the Court would decide *Carolene Products*, the Senate Committee on Interstate Commerce conducted a series of hearings on five bills concerning child labor.[254] Some of the bills, like the statute invalidated in *Hammer*, would have prohibited interstate shipment of goods made by firms employing child labor.[255] Others took different approaches that would not directly have called into question *Hammer*'s continuing authority, either divesting child-made goods of their interstate character upon arrival in a destination state, or prohibiting interstate shipment of child-made goods into states prohibiting their sale.[256] Even after the Court's dramatic decisions upholding the National Labor Relations Act as an exercise of the commerce power the previous month,[257] two liberal New Dealers on the committee expressed doubt that the Court was prepared to overrule *Hammer*. Burton Wheeler of Montana believed that the Court "would probably not" overrule *Hammer*. There was "not very much hope," he opined, "of the Supreme Court reversing itself in this matter."[258] Sherman Minton of Indiana agreed: "I do not think we need place much hope on a reversal of the child labor opinion." "I do not think that there is much use of our looking for a reversal of form on the part of the Court."[259] Some of the witnesses expressed similar reservations,[260]

---

[254] To Regulate the Products of Child Labor, Hearings on S 592, S 1976, S 2068, and S 2345 before Senate Committee on Interstate Commerce, 75th Cong, 1st Sess (1937) ("Senate Interstate Commerce Hearings").

[255] S 2068, 75th Cong, 1st Sess and S 2345, 75th Cong, 1st Sess, in Senate Interstate Commerce Hearings, 75th Cong, 1st Sess (cited in note 254).

[256] S 592, 75th Cong, 1st Sess and S 1976, 75th Cong, 1st Sess, in Senate Interstate Commerce Hearings, 75th Cong, 1st Sess (cited in note 254). S 2226, 75th Cong, 1st Sess, in Senate Interstate Commerce Hearings, 75th Cong, 1st Sess (cited in note 254) combined each of the approaches.

[257] See *Labor Board Cases*, 301 US 1 (1937).

[258] Senate Interstate Commerce Hearings, 75th Cong, 1st Sess at 12, 13 (cited in note 254).

[259] Senate Interstate Commerce Hearings, 75th Cong, 1st Sess at 13 (cited in note 254).

[260] Senate Interstate Commerce Hearings, 75th Cong, 1st Sess at 152–58 (cited in note 254) (James A. Emery, National Association of Manufacturers, maintaining that *Hammer* was still good law); id at 133 (Henry Root Stern, of Mudge, Stern, Williams, & Tucker, suggesting that there was an even chance that the Court would overrule *Hammer*).

and on June 14 the committee favorably reported the Wheeler-Johnson bill that combined the Keating-Owen approach with the other methods in the event that the Court reaffirmed *Hammer*.[261] It was the committee's judgment that "much hope could not be practically entertained that the Supreme Court would overrule the *Hammer v Dagenhart* case at this time."[262]

Meanwhile, on May 24 the Administration sent to Congress what would become known as the Black-Connery bill, which ultimately would form the basis for the Fair Labor Standards Act of 1938.[263] At joint hearings held by the Senate Committee on Education and Labor and the House Committee on Labor, several witnesses continued to opine that *Hammer* was still good law,[264] but on July 8 the Senate Committee on Education and Labor reported favorably a version of the bill relying entirely on a provision modeled on the Keating-Owen Child Labor Act.[265] When the bill reached the floor of the Senate, however, Wheeler argued that it was imprudent to enact a measure "flying directly in the face of the Supreme Court decision in *Hammer v Dagenhart*," and urged his colleagues to substitute the Wheeler-Johnson bill for the child labor provisions of the Black-Connery bill.[266] His colleagues apparently agreed with Wheeler's assessment, for they approved the amendment by a vote of 57–28,[267] and the bill as amended was passed by a vote of 56–28.[268] The House Labor Committee did not agree, however—its reported bill stripped out the Wheeler-Johnson provisions and reinserted the child labor provisions that Wheeler had considered so objectionable.[269] The

[261] Regulating the Products of Child Labor, S Rep No 75-726, 75th Cong, 1st Sess (1937); 81 Cong Rec 5639 (June 14, 1937).

[262] S Rep No 75-726 at 2–3 (cited in note 261).

[263] Message from the President of the United States, H Doc 225, 75th Cong, 1st Sess (May 24, 1937); 81 Cong Rec 4954 (May 24, 1937) (referencing S 2475, 75th Cong, 1st Sess introduced by Mr. Black); id at 4998 (referencing HR 7200, 75th Cong, 1st Sess introduced by Mr. Connery).

[264] Fair Labor Standards Act of 1937, Hearings on S. 2475 and H.R. 7200 before the Senate Committee on Education and Labor, and House Committee on Labor, 75th Cong, 1st Sess 626–27 (1937) ("Joint Hearings"); id at 681–82, 855–59.

[265] Fair Labor Standards Act, S Rep No 75-884, 75th Cong, 1st Sess (1937); 81 Cong Rec 6894 (July 8, 1937).

[266] 81 Cong Rec 7667 (July 27, 1937); id at 7666; id at 7930–32 (July 31, 1937); id at 7949.

[267] 81 Cong Rec 7949–51 (July 31, 1937).

[268] Id at 7957.

[269] Fair Labor Standards Act, HR Rep No 1452, 75th Cong, 1st Sess 20 (1937).

House Rules Committee refused to allow the Labor Committee's bill to come to the floor,[270] so on August 19 Wheeler urged his Senate colleagues to pass the Wheeler-Johnson bill as a separate piece of legislation,[271] which they did without a record vote.[272]

When the Black-Connery bill was finally brought to the House floor in November through the use of a discharge petition,[273] Representative John Martin of Colorado followed Wheeler in cautioning his colleagues not to rely on the hope that the Court would overrule *Hammer*. Instead, he urged his fellow Democrats to replace the bill's child labor provisions with those of the Wheeler-Johnson bill.[274] The bill was recommitted to the House Labor Committee on December 17,[275] and the committee did not report it back until April 21.[276] When the bill was debated on the floor of the House in May of 1938, however, Martin's lengthy speech opposing the measure no longer expressed concerns about the constitutionality of a prohibition on interstate shipment of goods made by firms employing children.[277] Now no one in the House debate objected to the bill on the ground that *Hammer* was still good law. The House passed the bill relying on the assumption that *Hammer* would be overruled,[278] and the conference committee accepted the House bill's child labor provisions.[279] Senator Elbert Duncan Thomas of Utah explained to his colleagues that "[t]he conference committee felt that in view of the trend of decisions in the Supreme Court this was safe procedure," and no one con-

[270] See William Lasser, *Benjamin V. Cohen: Architect of the New Deal* 180 (Yale, 2002); John S. Forsythe, *Legislative History of the Fair Labor Standards Act*, 6 Law & Contemp Probs 464, 470 (1939); Paul H. Douglas and Joseph Hackman, *The Fair Labor Standards Act of 1938, Part I*, 53 Pol Sci Q 491, 507–08 (1938).

[271] 81 Cong Rec 9318 (August 19, 1937).

[272] Id at 9318–20.

[273] 82 Cong Rec 1386, 1389–90 (December 13, 1937); Forsythe, *Legislative History* at 471 (cited in note 270); Douglas and Hackman, 53 Pol Sci Q at 509 (cited in note 270); Frances Perkins, *The Roosevelt I Knew* 260 (Viking, 1946); *Rally Democrats Behind Wage Bill*, New York Times 9 (Nov 30, 1937); *218 Sign Petition*, New York Times 1 (Dec 3, 1937).

[274] 82 Cong Rec 1412–23 (December 13, 1937); id at 1579–99 (December 15, 1937); id at 1780–83 (December 17, 1937); id at 1829–30.

[275] Id at 1834–35 (December 17, 1937).

[276] Fair Labor Standards Act of 1938, HR Rep No 2182, 75th Cong, 3d Sess (1938); 83 Cong Rec 5680 (April 21, 1938).

[277] See 83 Cong Rec 7398–7400 (May 24, 1938).

[278] Id at 7449–50.

[279] Id at 9161, 9164 (June 14, 1938) (remarks of Sen. Thomas).

tradicted him.[280] Senator Thomas did not cite the decisions upon which he was relying, but the Court had decided only two pertinent cases since Wheeler, Minton, Martin, and others had evinced their concerns that *Hammer* was still good law. One was a decision upholding portions of the New Deal securities law program;[281] the other was *Carolene Products*.

Two commentators anticipating a favorable Court ruling on the constitutionality of the Fair Labor Standards Act noted in 1938 that *Carolene Products* had recognized "the power of Congress to prohibit interstate shipments of products harmful to the health, morals, or welfare of the public," and insisted that "[e]conomic evil or harm as well as harm to the human body is within the police power of Congress to control by prohibitory regulation of interstate commerce."[282] Another observer cautioned that, after *Carolene Products*, "serious thought must be given to the possibility of revolutionary expansion in Congress' exercise of the commerce power." It was now conceivable, he argued, that the Court would soon adopt the view expressed by Justice Holmes in his dissent in *Hammer*: that Congress may by the regulation of interstate commerce "'prohibit any part of such commerce that Congress sees fit to forbid.'"[283]

When the Fair Labor Standards Act was challenged before the Supreme Court in *United States v Darby Lumber*, the brief for the United States repeatedly cited *Carolene Products* in support of the central claims of its argument.[284] The act's prohibition on interstate shipment was a regulation of interstate commerce,[285] and the Court had often "proclaimed that the power of Congress to regulate commerce 'is complete in itself, may be exercised to its utmost extent, and acknowledges no limitations, other than are pre-

[280] Id at 9164 (1938). The House approved the conference report by a vote of 291–89, and the Senate followed suit without a record vote. 83 Cong Rec 9178, 9266–67 (June 14, 1938).

[281] *Electric Bond & Share Co. v SEC*, 303 US 419 (1938).

[282] Alexander Feller and Jacob Hurwitz, *How to Operate Under the Wage-Hour Law* 142–43 (Alexander, 1938).

[283] Recent Decision, *Constitutional Law—Power to Prohibit Wholesome Synthetic Food from Interstate Commerce*, 17 NYU L Q Rev 118, 121 (1939).

[284] See Brief for the United States, *United States v Darby*, No 82, *41, 63, 65, 101 (US filed Sep 23, 1940) ("United States Brief II").

[285] Id at 61.

scribed in the constitution,'"[286] the government argued. "Congress possesses, therefore, the same unlimited authority as do the states within their field to exercise 'the police power, for the benefit of the public, within the field of interstate commerce.'"[287] The public benefit to be secured here, as the United States contended at length, was the prevention of the spread of substandard labor conditions through unfair competition carried on through the channels of interstate commerce.[288] "The determination of what practices are against public policy" was "obviously a legislative matter," the government asserted.[289] It was "for Congress to decide whether low labor standards" were "as harmful" as the acts prohibited by the antitrust laws and the Federal Trade Commission Act.[290] The employer could "rely upon no fact in the record," and had "as yet presented none which is subject to judicial notice, to show that the legislation" was "arbitrary."[291] As *Carolene Products* had established, "[t]he burden of supporting the charge of unconstitutionality" was "on the assailant of the statute. In the absence of facts demonstrating its invalidity the constitutionality of the law must be presumed."[292]

When Chief Justice Hughes brought the case before the conference, his doctrinal analysis was a virtual facsimile of Stone's in *Carolene Products*. Hughes regarded the branch of the case concerning the prohibition of interstate shipment as utterly unproblematic. "Congress's interstate commerce power knows no limitation except as in the Constitution itself," Hughes argued.[293] The

---

[286] Id at 63.

[287] Id at 64–65. Similarly, in a proposed model opinion upholding the Fair Labor Standards Act, Robert Stern relied upon *Carolene Products* for the proposition that "an exercise of federal power is not invalid because of its effect upon transactions which might lie outside the sphere of federal regulation." Robert L. Stern, *An Opinion Holding the Act Constitutional*, in *How the Supreme Court May View the Fair Labor Standards Act*, 6 Law & Contemp Probs 431, 434 (1939).

[288] United States Brief II at *9, 20–43, 59–60.

[289] United States Brief II at *77.

[290] Id.

[291] Id at 101.

[292] Id. The appellee by contrast maintained that under *Carolene Products* the presumption of constitutionality attached only to the means selected for exercising an enumerated power. Whether Congress was in fact exercising an enumerated power, that is, whether a statute was within the commerce power, remained a question for judicial determination. Brief for the Appellee, *United States v Darby*, No 82, *23–25 (US filed Dec 12, 1940) ("Darby Brief").

[293] Del Dickson, ed, *The Supreme Court in Conference (1940–1985)* 217 (Oxford, 2001).

Chief therefore rejected the authority of *Hammer v Dagenhart*. "Transportation is an act in commerce, and unless due process is involved, Congress can do as it wants. Congress must not impinge on the constitutional qualifications of its power, and this qualification is in the due process provision. Unless the Fifth Amendment intervenes, Congress can use its power for any purpose it sees fit."[294] But here, Hughes concluded, there was "no deprivation of property in a due process sense."[295]

Justice Stone's opinion for a unanimous Court also clearly followed the template that he had established in *Carolene Products*. While manufacture was "not of itself interstate commerce," the interstate shipment of manufactured goods was, and "the prohibition of such shipment by Congress" was "indubitably a regulation" of that commerce.[296] The power of Congress over interstate commerce was "'complete in itself, may be exercised to its utmost extent, and acknowledges no limitations, other than are prescribed by the constitution.'"[297] "Congress, following its own conception of public policy concerning the restrictions which may appropriately be imposed on interstate commerce," was "free to exclude from the commerce articles whose use in the states for which they are destined it may conceive to be injurious to the public health, morals or welfare, even though the state has not sought to regulate their use."[298] And then, with a citation to *Carolene Products*, Stone asserted, "Such regulation . . . is not prohibited unless by other Constitutional provisions. It is no objection to the assertion of the power to regulate interstate commerce that its exercise is attended by the same incidents which attend the exercise of the police power of the states."[299] "Whatever their motive and purpose, regulations of commerce which do not infringe some constitutional prohibition are within the plenary power conferred on Congress by the Commerce Clause."[300] In *Hammer*, "it was held by a bare majority of the Court over the powerful and now classic dissent of Mr. Justice Holmes," "that Congress was without power to exclude

[294] Id.
[295] Id at 218.
[296] *Darby*, 312 US at 113.
[297] Id at 114.
[298] Id.
[299] Id.
[300] Id at 115.

the products of child labor from interstate commerce. The reasoning and conclusion of the Court's opinion there cannot be reconciled with the conclusion which we have reached, that the power of Congress under the Commerce Clause is plenary to exclude any article from interstate commerce subject only to the specific prohibitions of the Constitution."[301]

The only specific prohibition to be addressed was the Due Process Clause of the Fifth Amendment. And Stone regarded it as obvious that the interstate shipment of goods made under substandard labor conditions caused a harm that it was within congressional power to prevent. A purpose of the act, Stone explained, was "to prevent the use of interstate commerce as the means of competition in the distribution of goods" produced "under conditions detrimental to the maintenance of the minimum standards of living necessary for health and general well-being," "and as the means of spreading and perpetuating such substandard labor conditions among the workers of the several states."[302] The motive and purpose of the act were "plainly to make effective the Congressional conception of public policy that interstate commerce should not be made the instrument of competition in the distribution of goods produced under substandard labor conditions, which competition" was "injurious" to the states "to which the commerce flows."[303] "[T]he evils aimed at by the Act" were "the spread of substandard labor conditions through the use of the facilities of interstate commerce" through the competition of goods produced under substandard labor conditions with goods produced under fair labor standards, and the "impairment or destruction of local businesses by competition made effective through interstate commerce."[304] The act was thus, like the Ohio convict-made goods statute upheld in *Whitfield*, "directed at the suppression of a method or kind of competition in interstate commerce which it has in effect condemned as 'unfair.'"[305] In short, the Court was now explicitly broadening the category of harms that could be redressed by the commerce power without violating the Due Process Clause, recognizing as a federally remediable

---

[301] Id at 115–16.

[302] Id at 109–10.

[303] Id at 115.

[304] Id at 122.

[305] Id.

harm in destination states the very sort of unfair competition resulting from differential labor standards that the Court had refused
to countenance in *Hammer*. Thus, it did not matter whether the
goods to be shipped in interstate commerce had been made under
conditions permitted by the law of the state of production. The
producer might have acquired a vested property interest in the
goods under that state's law, but he had not thereby acquired any
right to inflict the harm of unfair competition outside the legislative jurisdiction of that state. Because the statute did not violate
the Due Process Clause, the Court concluded "that the prohibition
of the shipment interstate of goods produced under the forbidden
substandard labor conditions" was "within the constitutional authority of Congress."[306]

Legal commentators remarking upon the *Darby* decision clearly
saw its roots in Stone's 1938 opinion. With a citation to *Carolene
Products*, an observer writing in the *University of Pennsylvania Law
Review* opined now that "[t]he weight of authority is that Congress
can prohibit goods from interstate commerce regardless of their
nature, or regardless of the motive of Congress in so enacting."[307]
With another citation to *Carolene Products*, an editor of the *Tennessee Law Review* astutely noted, "Thus the separate regulatory
power of the states, once so jealously guarded, is made to rest
squarely on whatever due process restrictions the fifth amendment
imposes on Congress."[308] That, of course, is precisely what *Carolene Products* had clarified; and it had further made clear that those
restrictions were few indeed.

---

[306] Id at 115. For a discussion of developments in the constitutional law of competitive
injury that anticipated *Darby*, see Barry Cushman, *Ambiguities of Free Labor Revisited: The
Convict-Labor Question in Progressive-Era New York*, in R. B. Bernstein and Daniel J. Hul-
sebosch, eds, *Making Legal History: Essays on the Interpretation of Legal History in Honor of
William E. Nelson* (NYU Press, forthcoming 2013) (on file with author).

[307] Recent Case, *Constitutional Law—Power of Congress to Regulate Wages and Hours in
Industries Producing for and Shipping in Interstate Commerce*, 89 U Pa L Rev 819, 820 n 4
(1941). Other commentators on *Darby* also saw *Carolene Products* as a supportive Commerce
Clause precedent. See John A. Wright, Case Note, *Fair Labor Standards Act: Regulation of
Wages and Hours in Production of Goods for Interstate Commerce Held Constitutional—Re-
quirement of Keeping Records Upheld—Validity of Minimum Wage Order Sustained*, 6 John
Marshall L Q 451, 452 (1941); M. W. M., Note, *Constitutional Law—Power of Congress to
Prohibit Interstate Transportation of Products Made Under Substandard Conditions—Fair Labor
Standards Act of 1938*, 15 Tulane L Rev 609, 611 (1941).

[308] A. D. B., Jr., Recent Case, *Commerce—Regulation Under Fair Labor Standards Act*, 16
Tenn L Rev 987, 988 (1941).

VI. Conclusion: Carolene Products and Constitutional Structure

Darby would become the canonical case standing for the proposition that congressional power to prohibit interstate shipment is virtually plenary. It was the seminal case upholding the Fair Labor Standards Act—a much more important statute than the Filled Milk Act of 1923—and it was the case that overruled *Hammer v Dagenhart*. But the doctrinal analysis on which the Court relied in *Darby* was already fully developed by Stone's opinion in *Carolene Products*. *Carolene Products* untangled the confusions created by *Hammer's* conflation of Fifth and Tenth Amendment limitations, making it clear that the restraint on Congress's power to prohibit interstate shipment had always been the Due Process Clause rather than a principle of constitutional federalism. Through the limits that it had placed on federal regulatory authority and the protection it had afforded to vested property rights, the Due Process Clause had licensed interjurisdictional regulatory competition and underwritten policy heterogeneity among the states.[309] It was the relaxation of that due process limitation by an announced standard of deferential review that cleared the way for national policies implemented through prohibitions on interstate shipment.

We have grown understandably accustomed to dividing our courses in and our conversations about Constitutional Law into the categories of Constitutional Structure and Constitutional Rights. But we shouldn't allow that often convenient conceptual division to obscure the deep and important relationships that often have obtained between these two domains of constitutional doctrine. The idea that constitutional federalism acts to preserve individual rights and liberties by diffusing government power has become familiar.[310] Less often appreciated is the fact that individual

---

[309] The role played by the Due Process Clause in this line of Commerce Clause cases also serves further to underscore the centrality of vested rights concepts to substantive due process jurisprudence in the early twentieth century. Substantive due process often is associated with the sorts of liberty claims implicated in decisions such as *Lochner v New York*, 198 US 45 (1905), and *Meyer v Nebraska*, 262 US 390 (1923). Yet a review of all of the cases in which the *Lochner*-era Court invalidated a law on the ground that it violated one of the Due Process Clauses reveals that decisions safeguarding vested property rights far outnumbered those vindicating such unenumerated liberty rights. See Cushman, 85 BU L Rev at 883–924, 941–44, 958–80, 998–99 (cited in note 145).

[310] See, for example, *New York v United States*, 505 US 144, 181 (1992) ("'[F]ederalism secures to citizens the liberties that derive from the diffusion of sovereign power.'"),

rights, particularly economic rights protected by the Due Process
Clause, themselves operated as structural mechanisms. Such rights
did not merely mark the boundaries between individual liberty
and sovereign authority. They also functioned to allocate power
among the state and federal governments. Just as structural mechanisms could have consequences for rights, so rights could have
significant consequences for constitutional structure.[311] Because of
its role in illuminating such an important dimension of this phenomenon, Justice Stone's opinion in *Carolene Products* is, if anything, even richer and more rewarding than we have recognized.

---

quoting *Coleman v Thompson*, 501 US 722, 759 (1991) (Blackmun, J, dissenting); Harry
N. Scheiber, *American Federalism and the Diffusion of Power: Historical and Contemporary
Perspectives*, 9 U Toledo L Rev 619 (1978); Andrzej Rapaczynski, *From Sovereignty to Process:
The Jurisprudence of Federalism After Garcia*, 1985 Supreme Court Review 341, 385–86,
388–89 (1986).

[311] For discussions of other contexts in which the Fifth Amendment's Due Process Clause
played an important role in the allocation of regulatory authority among the state and
federal governments, see Barry Cushman, *Rethinking the New Deal Court: The Structure of
a Constitutional Revolution* 139–225 (Oxford, 1998); Barry Cushman, *Formalism and Realism
in Commerce Clause Jurisprudence*, 67 U Chi L Rev 1089, 1126–37 (2000); Barry Cushman,
The Structure of Classical Public Law, 75 U Chi L Rev 1917, 1936–47 (2008).